The Right Side of the Dyke

Cover design by Clare Brayshaw

Set in Georgia 11pt

Prepared by:

York Publishing Services Ltd
64 Hallfield Road
Layerthorpe
York YO31 7ZQ
Tel: 01904 431213
Website: www.yps-publishing.co.uk

The Right Side of the Dyke

Margaret Smith and Rita Sellars

Preface

When Margaret Smith and Rita Sellars brought their collection of conversations with old Flamborians for me to read the three of us thought that it might be a good idea to 'edit' them. As I began to read through this amazing story of Flamborough's history; not a word should be lost. It is my hope that a local historical society will publish this wonderful collection in its entirety. We are able to glimpse into a world, which has all but vanished – and yet we are looking back over some sixty or seventy years, not hundreds of years!

What is most striking is the close community spirit. For most folk, life was hard but there was plenty of fun and laughter, fresh vegetables from the garden and the disputes and intrigues, which were the very stuff of village life until the final decades of the twentieth century.

One of our characters remarks that in "not all change is good". When one discovers how many shops and trades flourished in the village, these good souls have witnessed the slow demise of a community which was totally self sufficient. In my experience, real Flamborians are justly proud of their heritage – long may the sword dance continue to flourish and all the old traditions be kept alive.

I heard of one old lady who walked every Saturday night from Ocean View Farm to the village so that she could buy her fish and chip supper. Fish and Flamborough go together like salt and pepper. There are few fishermen now but if you read the memories of these old folk, you will realise that this community has its roots as much in the sea as on the land. In recent years we have revived the Harvest of the Sea Service at the parish church. You only have to hear the singing of "Pull for the Shore" and "Eternal Father, Strong to Save" to know that salt water still runs in the veins.

Like most coastal communities, the old ways and old sayings are diluted by changing life styles and new developments. For this reason this book deserves to be preserved and to be read in Flamborough and beyond.

Michael Cartwright
(Vicar of Flamborough, 2003)

Revised by Peter Pike
(Vicar of Flamborough, 2007)

Introduction and Acknowledgements

This book was born out of a conversation I had with visitors at an event at the Victoria Institute in Flamborough during the summer of 1994. They said they enjoyed talking to my husband, Laurie Smith, and when I asked why, they said it was because when they got him to talk about the past in Flamborough, telling them of the ways and tricks of the locals; it was both entertaining and interesting.

I had retired from my part-time job and I said I thought I'd have a go and Laurie said, "How?" I said people needed to be taped talking and his reply was, "They won't talk on tape and you can't do it cos you're not Flamborough". I replied, "No, but Rita was retired and another friend, Joyce Woodcock, would probably help and they were both born and brought up in Flamborough".

We started with Laurie and his good friend George Nordass talking on tape and ater that we contacted other older Flamborians who were all willing to talk on tape when we said that if it got into print any profits would be divided between the Church and Chapel.

Unfortunately Joyce had to drop out of the project, but over the years, Rita and I have plodded on and we wish to thank everyone who has helped us; especially the people who kindly invited us into their homes and shared their memories of Flamborough.

On advice from Caroline Coath, leader and Community Development Worker for Humber and the Wolds, we founded the Flamborough Oral History Project with the Reverend Dr. Peter Pike, vicar of Flamborough.

Particular thanks go to:

- The late Mrs Lilian Bond for letting us use the history of her family, which she had already recorded for her grandchildren.
- The Reverend Michael Cartwright and the Reverend Dr. Peter Pike (former and present vicars of Flamborough) for their help anf encouragement.
- Dr Walker of Hull University
- Mrs Caroline Coath, leader and Community Development Worker for Humber and the Wolds.
- All the people who lent us photographs.

Margaret Smith

The authors would like to express their thanks to their daughters Catherine and Louise for their help in preparing the manuscript electronically, to Margaret's daughter-in-law for proofreading the book and to Bob Todd for his invaluable assistance with the map and photographs.

Funding for this project has been provided by the Flamborough Parish Council, Thornwick Holidays, and many anonymous donors. Their generosity has made publishing this book possible.

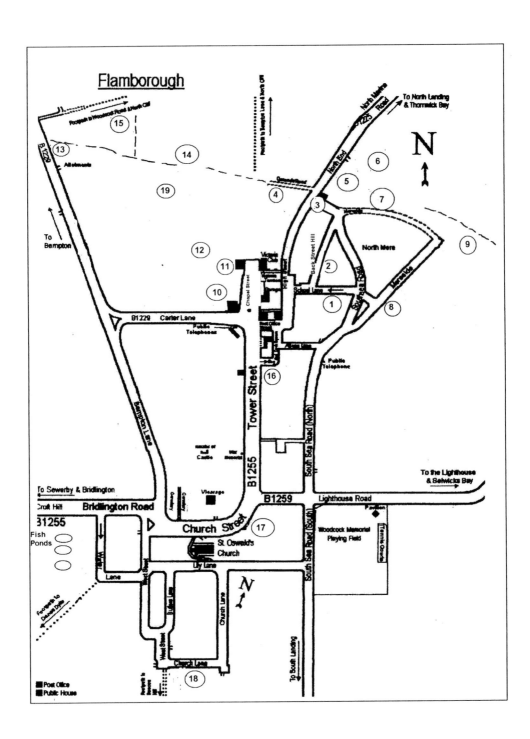

Key to Map of Flamborough

1.   The Old School
2.   Back Street Hill
3.   Donkey Lane
4.   Burstall Row Cottages
5.   Lartle Highland
6.   Big Highland
7.   Row of Cottages on Mereside
8.   Footpath to Michelmires ("Micky Mires")
9.   Primitive Methodist Chapel
10. Wesleyan Methodist Chapel
11. Waines Farm Buildings
12. Grange Farm
13. Rotherhams Footpath
14. Footpath to the Cliffs
15. Taylor's Farm
16. Church Farm
17. Beacon Farm
18. Crow Field (a paddock where donkeys were kept)

Laurie Smith & George Nordass

The only child of the local coal merchant and carrier for the railway, Laurie went into the business with his father. He was involved all his life with the Victoria Institute.

George took part in all activities associated with fishing but was apprenticed as a motor mechanic. He served in the Royal Navy during the war.

Talking about old church magazines.

Laurie	Rita has some from her Grandmother Cross and some from Billy Gibbon's. There was summat to do wi' drill shed.
George	There was births, deaths and marriages of everybody in Flamborough in them. There used to be pictures of missionaries in Africa; you know all these black men wi' spears. Now, they got this photograph of North Landing blown up, and that's way back 'cos there's as many cobles at top as there is on slipway. I think there's seventeen that I could count down below, and there were three or four oot at sea.
Laurie	That's trouble now, 'everything out'! Some of 'em chuck 'em away on purpose. Connie Cross med 'em burn all hers, which was a disgrace. Aye, Walter Shipley went roond when Norths were having a fire. He says "What are you deeing?" "Well I'm burning this. It was in her Will". Tant wouldn't have done it, they would have kept it. She had some stuff.
George	Aye, she had. Tace Robson had an' all. Did you see that great book he had of all them cuttings? Fred was always at him to let

	me have it? "No, lad", he says, "I'm going to keep this." I reckon he would tek it away with him when he went away. You lose a lot of history like that.
Margaret	Laurie says you were in the band before the war.
George	I was in when war came and after for a short time. It didn't last long, it soon fizzled out. Tommy Walls wanted it setting going again. It went right back to Royal Artillery. It went back to the 1800's. There's still a platform up yonder, on golf-course cliff. It's still there; a concrete ring with all iron staples for gun mounting. They had a band you see; they were like volunteers.
Laurie	It was start of Territorials. This bit that Rita had out of Church magazine was that this fella had been in 25 years in 1895.
George	Aye, that's right. Warn't it them that were in band when they had that procession for Crosses coble disaster, in 1909?
Joyce	Was that when Jack Cowling's dad was drowned?
George	Oh no, that was Gibbon and Major, two lads of Crosses and Bucky their father, what his fost name was I deean't know. I've seen a photo, and he was ginger haired, Laur, only a little slim fella. And these two lads he had wi' him, they warn't very old. They were none of 'em very big were they?
Margaret	What did the band do then? I know they practiced above the Drill Shed there. Where did you play?
George	Up at North Landing. August Bank Holiday and them sort of things like that; and Danes Dyke House at Christmas. And we did Lifeboat christening and owt like that; Galas, and at Jubilee and Coronation. What I'm thinking aboot, is when her up at North Landing way, Mrs Knighton's niece, was 'Britannia', and Dorothy Kingston was the 'May Queen'.
Laurie	Aye, why that would be 1935 then?
George	Aye, I know we played for that and it was a horrible day. It had been blowing a gale, and raining in night time. Right opposite you, Jo Billy lived and he says to me, "Look you", he says, "Them's my taties on road". And they were, because what had happened was gutter at back goes under road – no grate ower it – and it just bunged up. I can see it now: Clarke Sunley, (you know where Dinah Gibbon lived, that row he had – them gardens right away down), and he dug it all up 'cos that's were pot went. He come across road and down there, there was a five gallon drum like

	that partly in it. There was all sorts had getten in it, all way down her garden.
Laurie	It used to cum up a sheet of watter across there when it rained hard 'cos there was a great pond formed, and it used to cum ower that deep gutter.
Joyce	It used to come like a river down Marguerite's drive *[next door to Rose & Crown]*, and the band were marching along, and they had to march straight through it!! They got their feet wet, didn't they?
George	And another thing; there, just below footpath, it had broken through road and there was round hole aboot like that, and it was shooting up in air – 'cos it crosses road and inti gutter aback of you.
Margaret	Who was in the band then?
George	When I fost started, there was Major Mitt and there was awd Mark and Ted Marshall, Harold Stork, Tom Stork, George Leng Major, Dick *[Major]* in for a bit and Billy Chadwick, Billy Collins. Billy Collins was only a little man but he had a big drum. Tant Fell, he was a fisherman, lived just below us up yonder *[North Landing Lane]*, and it was his brother and sister lived with his mother at next house.
	Smeddy had a wife and son and Jack. He was born January 12th and I was born August before it. Tant didn't play an instrument; he used to look after fires and open up on a night and general handyman. He used ti hod lights on a night, when we used to go out at Christmas. He had a long piece of wood with lanterns hung round. And we all shouted at him 'cos it used to be swinging round and we couldn't see what you were looking at. Bah, we had some do's.
Laurie	He used to take collection round and big cymbals – he had cymbals for a bit.
George	Aye, Mat Major had it, after Mr Bee, he took it on. He was in a few years. He'd just finished when I started;Tom Cowling took it on. Tant used to do bits of poetry. One of 'em used to be Mennick's "The Last Five Minutes before Going over the Top". He could say it off, an' all, could Tant. He had a good memory and he did actions as well. One night when he was at our house, you know these Brentwood chairs, we had one and it collapsed if you warn't careful. So mi dad got a piece of steel about like that

and he fastened it 'cos Tant was a big heavy bloke. He screwed it on side. Tant was allus up to summat. How he did it beats me, 'cos he was fat you know, but he used to get both feet at back of his neck like that. He did it in this chair and all lot collapsed and he rolled right across the kitchen.

Joyce   Of course he was a lot older when I remember him, but he used to have a collection of beautiful ships and sailing ships. He had all these ships in his shed on the shelves – whether he had made them himself or what I don't know. I used to be so envious and I used to be hanging my heart out for one, you see. He used to say, "Why, aye, thu can have yan when coos cum up". I used to be sat outside squat by little wall in front of their house, waiting for cows coming up. Because they used to come up in those days, up North Marine Road, didn't they?

George   Aye, Lennie's coos. Tant had an awd shed doon at bottom o'garden, you know, and it was covered wi' cuttings of wrecks that had happened round here frae years back. I don't know what happened ti them. I remember our Elsie talking about when Tom Cowling and him were all about the same age, and he used to stand young kids up side wall. Tant used ti tie a piece of band round top and he reckoned he were playing cowboys. And he jumped ower there and it went round one hand and very near brok his thumb off, and he always had a twisted thumb after that. He used to mek kites as well; he was a good hand at it as long as you took stuff.

Laurie-   What he did in winter was, he used to go up to North Landing and they used to tent twenty or thirty donkeys up David Lane. Nearly everybody had yan.

George   I yance let Sukey Emmerson's oot. He was gaen ti kill me. Why, everyone had a nickname you know; them Crosses – there was that many Jack Crosses – it was useless if they didn't have another name for 'em.

Laurie   And Jack Majors and Dick Majors. Jackie Oss was a Cross and there was another Jack Cross – Iris's father. He always got 'Jack'.

George   There was Codner – Codner and Slink; Sneb – that was another.

Laurie   That was another Cross;, nickname was only name you knew. You had to say Mr Major or you were up the creek.

George	Majors was same on Mar front. They called him Aaron but his name was George; then young Nicky, just up Highland; and there was Morning and Evening higher up – they were Majors. Then there was 'Dick the Green' they always called him, up here.
Laurie	Edie's father and they, cum back frae Spurn, ti cum up there – middle un, up Back Street Hill. The old lady went blind; she used to wear a man's cap back to front always. I don't know whether it was for when they were skeining, but I never remember her without one.
George	Remember Dassie Kingston? I've heard Mrs Duke say he once chucked a rabbit over when they were baiting. That caused some trouble. Rabbits and pigs – owt like that.
Laurie	Aye, Dassie Kingston! In fact Fatty Stephenson nivver went into Dog and Duck after Mitchell, the landlord, chucked a black rabbit in. If they met a woman going to sea, they would turn back. You would have thought they would have seen rabbits when they were going up to North Landing, they would eat 'em, and some had special names for them.
George	Oh yes, but you had to be careful what you said if they were baiting. They had special names for pigs didn't they and they did for rats?
Laurie	That was later on, but when we were kids you didn't mention them – not at all. Nuns was another taboo, it'll be bad weather.
Margaret	I remember Laurie saying something about uptowners and downtowners. What was that then?
George	Oh aye. Mi Grandad Hunter – you know Cotham House, they lived there and mi Aunt Kitty. He used to say "Its Christian end down here" nearest to church. He was an ex-policeman. It was his last job was Flamborough. He had to walk to meet his sergeant at Dotterel. The sergeant used to come from Filey on horseback. He got there and there was no sign of the sergeant, so he came back home and sergeant got there afterwards. I remember mi grandma saying that he sent word, he wanted to see him. So he had to turn round and walk back to Dotterel again!! Sergeant would be in Dotterel pub, I should think. Even when they had bikes, they had to go to the Dotterel. Do you remember Bryan? I was going to school and they were in that last cottage going round corner, in North Marine Road. There was Eric Bryan, I went to school with him, then there was Sybil and I think another called

	Doreen. They had another when they were first into the new police house in Tower Street. Before that there was somebody called Parker at Flamborough and his son was a policeman.
Margaret	Which policeman would it be that father used to say about setting him up and down street on Bonfire night with pots of lard?
Laurie	I forget what they called him. He telled them they couldn't have a bonfire so everything that would burn, they fetched it out. He was up and down High Street, trying to stop 'em and as he got to one end, they lit it at the other. They ran him home at finish that night. Mi Dad said they beat him. Bonfire Night was Mischief Night in those days. They didn't bother about where they had their fire, in street or anywhere.
George	I can just remember, they had a piece of thick pot tow tarred and then a lot of it rolled up in a ball and tied and then set fire and swinging it round and round.
Laurie	You cut your fingers off with cotton sneads.
George	You know where Rose and Crown is and Jubilee House. Well, they used to say t'awd man used to sit on a chair on footpath. He used to say,"I'se thy great uncle, Tom Stork". He was always giving me great handfuls of cotton sneads, for whips and tops and kites. They were all cottered up and you had 'em all to sort out. It used to take you hours, but by gum they would make your tops jump.
Laurie	I used to be across there to Stene Knaggs, before they went up street.
George	Didn't Bebe Woodhouse, George Woodhouse's father marry one of 'em? I think he was in family somehow or other. He was a tinner; lived on front there next to Rose and Crown.
Laurie	No, he was a fisherman. Collingwood was tinner; they lived next to Walt Taylor's, before Robsons lived there; they lived on opposite side of road then
George	John Willie Bayes lived there, opposite Rose and Crown, where Dor Taylor is. That was before they come here to Swiss Cottage. John Willie Bayes' lad, Frank got frozen in with Jack Stork that used to live on corner of David Lane; it was afore my time. There was a bit of a dispute about that. Bessie, Frank's sister, used to mek a big fuss when Armistice Sunday was on. When I was in choir, long before I was in band, some of 'em used ti say he wasn't even a serviceman, he was in trawlers.

Laurie	Aye, Merchant Navy; they were Wilson Line. It was Wilson's boat and it got frozzen in – in White Sea, and they stopped with skipper and Jack Stork kem away with mate.
George	Yes, there was some mystery aboot that. I nivver got ti bottom of it. They called him Lengey – Jack's father, and they called 'em Stork. They were some relation of mi dad, a long way back, but Mousey and Bill and that party were all mi dad's cousins. There was Harold an all, used to live there again Seabirds, opposite where Mousey lived. John Waud's great grandfather kem frae Beeford or somewhere wi' my granddad and they both set up i'different businesses tigither; and they both married sisters. We've that many relations, I don't know, I'm related tiv everybody.
Laurie	It's true. I got Harold Stork going on about that and he had it all same, you see, ganning back. It goes ti same start but it branched off.
George	You know Ern Major? Well, his sister looked after Jack and Tom, doon in Dog and Duck Square, after mi grandad died. She was a relation and Ern Major- mi dad's cousin. So Kathy Chadwick and all that party, they're all my half-cousins. And Peevo Jackson, Geoff's father, married awdest – Muriel, I believe they called her. I don't know where he got that name from. He kem frae Hull. He used to tell us lads he worked at Cardington aerodrome on R100.
Laurie	He worked at Brough; Geoff was born at Goole. When bomb was dropped on t'other side of road i'council houses, it knocked all winders oot of 'ooses at their side. He says "They've dropped a bomb on houses". Tom warn't a bit bothered, "Why", he says, "I can't do owt aboot it lad". That was his house across road. Bob Pockley's, y'know; they lived wi' him and it had knocked all their winders in. They bombed end uns. Pete Jameson, Joe Ross and Janie Major's. Now Janie Major and her mother were just going into 'oose when it dropped. The wall dropped on Janie; that's why she's not quite steady on her feet, and Charlie was in 'oose and a chair tummeled ower top of him. It hit Pete's, middle un – nivver saw Pete nor his dog n'more. Council 'ooses were built in 1938 and they'd just got in nicely before the war.
George	I'd been on night shift that night wi' Ron Traves and he had a little Morris 8, and when we cum home, Tommy Tottles told us about it. Charlie was working with us at time. All he had was a

	bit of a cut here, and awd man was under stairs, I think; they were lucky to ave survived.
Margaret	Whose house was it when they used to climb on and put a blanket on top then?
George	That was Lizzie Greasey's 'oose – at stile. I dean't know what her real name was; it was her and Mary Greasey and Custard. And George Claxton, he married one of lasses and they lived there. Claxton lived there for a while. Sometimes lads used to walk straight on top the roof and put a bag ower top o'chimney and drop snowballs down.
Laurie	It wasn't Knaggs, was it? There was a row of chalk cottages opposite school; there was two, then there was a yard and then there was a brick cottage and another chalk un. It belonged to John Hall's – that yard, I think. Then as you followed Mere round there was some more.
George	I'll tell you who was in there – awd Dick Mainprize 'cos he used to have ducks and geese. Then Josh, Violet's father, next door, then there were Hunters and Jimmy Robinson.
Laurie	Then Frank Wise and Jack Cockerill. Was that Thompson's? He had the nickname, Tosh, he was a farm worker. That's all there was just about, fishing and farming here. There was only Mary Greasey's you could ger on top of.
George	Aye, 'cos you see, warn't it a bit of a shed or summat attached you could gan right up and onto next roof?
Laurie	T'other one, it warn't often they were living in that one, only in now and again. She cum running out that night we were on wi' snowballs; we'd scalded her to deead wi' snowballs. Custard kem oot – his face as black as a sweep. He'd been having a look up to see wheear it was coming frae. She was coming out shouting wi' scalding her and cat burglars and all rest of it.
George	Aye, George Headley lived there an' all. When I first started going ti school, his coble was there in front of 'oose, upside down wi' sail spread ower it. She wouldn't sell it; she wouldn't sell that boat for nowt. They had it for chickens an' all. It was upside down on there, on skids. It just about rotted away. Awd woman wouldn't sell boat, stopped there till it rotted. He died, that was it. She could have sold it and made a bit of money on it, but she wouldn't sell it. It was a good coble.
Joyce	Who made cobles in those days? I was thinking before Haag Hopwood.

George	Oh, you're going back. I should think his father would. His father made 'em before him. The only time he had anybody, a nephew kem for a while, but he didn't stop long. Aye, Haag Hopwood was a marvellous man. He built a coble on his own, because he used to have an old Blackstore diesel, single cylinder thing, and he used to have band saws and a circular saw. And then he had a great bath he used ti boil watter up and blow steam at planks. They were larch planks, and he used to pull 'em in wi' ropes till he got 'em shaped- up, before he nailed 'em on. He nivver made two boats alike even if they were same length, because it was all oot his heead.
Laurie	He couldn't keep any labourers. Jim Fell, he stopped for a bit. He'd no pattern – no pattern was there, all done by eye. They nivver sailed same, allus sailed a bit different from other cobles Haag Hopwood had made.
George	Aye, even if a bow was a bit more rake on it, he nivver bothered it was just how he made 'em. A lot on it depended on shape of piece of wood he had.
Laurie	Both sides were alike. There warn't much variance in shape, once it were a coble, but it was the difference between each coble.
George	You see ribs set your pattern. You made your ribs and if you made 'em same at each side, you should cum oot right at finish. He used ti select piece of wood that was naturally bent so the grain ran in a bent line, and that's how you got the strength.
Laurie	He would go to Driffield, into a wood yard, and it was the devil's own job going with him. You nivver knew when you were getting away 'cos he'd tonn wood ower and ower till he found piece he wanted. There was any amount of wood but he didn't want them straight bits, he wanted the bent bits. Aye, and it was all sawn larch. Where there'd been a big knot, you see, and you'd ger a curve, he wanted it naturally bent.
George	They used to be sixteen foot – small boats, and then they gor up to about eighteen or nineteen; and not till Emmerson's started having these new uns built, they went to nearly twenty five foot. They fost put engines in boats that had been built for sailing, into the sixteen and eighteen footers. George Otch was one 'cos he cut stern oot of his and he had outboard. Teddy Fells had one, I think it was an Eden Rood. I can't say really when Kelvins fost cum in. Somebody must have cum down frae Scotland and flogged 'em some. Oh aye, they were ideal engines.

Laurie	When they started wi' Kelvins, they more or less built the boat for the engine. But you see they could nivver get a boat that was built with an engine ti sail properly. They were petrol-paraffin engines, start among petrol and then go onto paraffin. They'd start 'em wi' starting handle then. They were marvellous engines; they could be buried in rust but they would still go. Mind, you had to be careful, you hadn't mich room right doon on your knees wi' your head doon. If starting handle stuck, you had to have summat handy to drop ower it or else up wi' starting handle.
George	It used to be amusing though a thick weather morning, you'd be doon there when they were all going to sea, all plugs oot, chuck 'em in a tin of petrol. You thought landing was afire. I went down there and Tich Stork said to me – I think he must have fallen oot wi' Robert – "Can't thu put a mag on for me?" Anyway, when I put it on for him, that was alright. But I thought,' Why, summat's gone wrong here' – 'cos, I mean they allus went ti Robert Atkinson.
Laurie	But he was a marvellous bloke wi' them engines, was Bob Atkinson, Cameron's father. He wasn't as good on ordinary engines. He warn't bad on ordinary engines, but on coble engines, he was a real artist. They used to tek 'em out after they'd finished fishing, and ger 'em done up ready for summer.
George	They used ti ave 'em in that awd shed, there, wheear engine was for pulling up. You could have itten off floor, it was that clean. Aye, but Cameron used ti say ti me, "I'm as sick as hell of mi dad. You just get everything laid out on bench deeing something and he's up with brush sweeping all down".
Laurie	That was awd man Ripley that started that. He was same.
George	I remember George Atkinson saying awd Ripley telling Fred ti do summat – washing some parts or summat in a tray. O'course Bernard Ripley, real gruff like, wasn't he? They used to call him Sam. "Go and sweep up over there." Bernard said, "Mr Ripley told me to do this job". "Doesn't matter", he says. And it got to falling out,like, and he gev push and poor awd Fred dropped right in among all this paraffin tray. So he had a great awd brush and he hit him right ower head, and he says, "I knocked him out". Old man Riley cums round and says, "Now what's going on?" Fred told him and he says, "It serves you right. I told him to do that job. Don't interfere again". But by God, it was a hot spot, terrible in summer; glass roof from end tiv end right inti Princess Street. I've heard Fred say, a time or two, in Rose and

Crown, "Dis tha know awd Aaron's been in ti night and he'd been gettin on to a visitor that was there". And he said he'd been away at a shipyard building ships. He says, "They used ti build 'em there, ivver si lang, as far as you like; they just cut 'em off any length anybody wanted." That was a bit of Aaron – and they just used ti stick bows and starn on! This bloke said, "What about engines?" And he said, "Oh, they had that all worked out an' all". But I was only saying, at dinnertime, there was the likes of Aaron and Tant and all them – Merry and Pete – they allus had a gang of lads round 'em. If it was now, they'd have been locking 'em up. Did you ever hear the tale of 'em taking a donkey upstairs in one of those cottages in Post Office Street? I think Joyce's dad was involved. And poor old thing got stuck, so far up. Things he used ti do – and John Hall doon at Billy Beale's – there and Dump.

Margaret   Was that the one when Dad took them visitors?

Laurie   Yis. Did you ivver hear about that? Why mi dad used to go to Seabirds a bit then when Tom Woodhouse was there. Two kem in, "Did they know anywhere where they could find lodgings?" Tom Woodhouse says, "What about Billy?" and mi dad says, "Aye, come on with you". And he took 'em to Billy's. He has one look at house and lass ran back to pub. It was a one up and one down chalk cottage and Billie says, "Come in honeys. Do you want a cup of tea?" – put cup of tea on table wi' week's rings round it. This chap stopped until he found it was a joke, and they went back and he says, "I'll tell you what; you've earned a pint. I've heard about these places but I never thought I'd see one".

George   You see these alcoves, either side of fire-side, they used to be up ti top wi' sticks at Billy Beale's, right up ti top for winter. Ferret at t'other side, in a box. John Hall and Jack Cowling went there one night – they wanted him to go threshing and they'd been on about his ferret. Oh aye, marvellous ferret had Dump, do owt wi' it, put it down his neck you know. So they thought right oh; we'll have a go at Billy next and they swapped ferrets. Dump's on about this marvellous ferret and it got 'im bi lug *by the ear]*. There was blood all ower.

Laurie   Dump was a Gilbank, but don't ask me what his fost name was – I don't know. Johnny Gilbank's father and Tomp lived next to corner where Art Graham lived, near church.

George   There was Tomp Gilbank and Wor Gilbank. But Sankey Bayes had that end one, and Tomp lived next door.

Laurie	There was a right row – down the side of Seabirds, near garages; Billy Beale was at top, where Ken Chapman lives now. Ratten Row. There was four, – three on front and four up passage.
George	When I went ti school, there was a dozen "characters" I should say. There in't any people like that ti day. There was Alf Nicholson and Aaron Bielby, yon end; used ti cut shavs when they were threshing. And then there was Dump and Billy, Ellen Chorwick *[Chadwick]*, Ellen Sugar. They were in 'oose – footpath side.
Laurie	No, Ellen was up there. Herb Chadwick was at front and Robsons – and I've forgotten who was in corner. Then Becky moved into it wi' Blewitt. By, it was a dump was that. Coal 'oose was straight across from front door, under stairs. There was a cotton *[curtain]* up. It was one of them 'ooses that you knew you were going in, and you had to tak a dive straight across, dump coal and get out sharpish. You just couldn't hold your breath long enough. It did stink.
George	Mind you, she used to be on Marside, in them white cottages. That was before she went wi' Blewitt. Aye, little Jimmy. I yance remember being with George Major and George Leng Major and Alf, I should say; and we were all up there at Saddles, between King and Queen rocks. And there's Horace, right at far end, wi' his feet dangling ower end, right at far end – next piece ti Saddle this way. He didn't seem ti ave no fear. Gilbert Screeton was same; he was crackers. He used to go down Brael, flithering wiv a lantern. All sorts of stupid tricks. He used to run up and down those cliffs like a rabbit, didn't he? Fost I ivver eard aboot Gilbert: you know that field aback of oor 'oose on North Landing Road? Bethel Waines had it for cows and Gilbert's father was carrier, and he had this little white pony for carrier cart. Gilbert used to get dressed up as a cowboy on this 'oss, lassoing Bethel's cows at back of oor 'oose. And that was Gilbert! He lassoed church gate an' all, didn't he? When he was going down wi' 'oss and cart, he lassoed church gate and pulled it all ower. He was a rum bloke until he married skater – Vida – that was what did it.
Laurie-	They had a little putting green up at North Landing, next door to Burgin's café – where the entrance to the car park is now, on the left. And she used to be hiring out golf clubs for this putting green; and she had a sister. Her and her father used to go skating – roller skating – at East Riding skating rink. They used ti 'ave a little roll up slatted mat when they went skating anywhere else.

They used to go round and round on this mat, trick skating; they were fairly good at it, like. What they saw in each other, I don't know. Last hope for either of them? When they fost kem here, her family lived near here for a bit, in that bungalow when Kilvington had it. They finished up near Hetty's 'cos that's where Gilbert Screeton lived. But nobody nivver thought he would have hung himself. He was a loner and he was mad but you would nivver 'ave thought he would a dun owt like that.

George   Aye, talking about awd Aaron: when Skegness, a Hull trawler, ran ashore, I was there at back of Robert Leng's in Cowp's shed. I was putting some links on a shock absorber on his awd van. It was as thick as hedge, had been all day and neea wind, and it was nine o'clock when I gor 'ome. And Geoff Thompson was at oor 'oose at time. I just got sat doon to mi supper when there was a clap of thunder, came frae nowhere and o'course we went up ti North Landing. And there's Aaron running pell mell doon there. And when he got to Thornwick, he tummelled inti gutter and couldn't gan ni further. Then there was Matt Duke cum after him, and there was both of 'em laid back in Lifeboat House just aboot out. Silly devils, at their age, ran all way ti North Landing. There was Jackie and Charlie Overy fighting ower a jacket to go on the lifeboat. Aye, it warn't woth more than a shilling or two. To mek a fuss like that!

Laurie   Skegness was where all crew got lost. If they'd got out when she fost kem ashore, they'd have been fine; she was at High Cliff, past Buckton Hall. She warn't right under cliff, she was stuck quite a way off. That was the trouble, rocket lines wouldn't 'a reached her. They wouldn't let Flamborough cart go through. Speeton cart went and he fired all his rockets and nivver got one aboard. Flamborough were stood here waiting and they wouldn't let 'em go 'cos it was out of their area, they reckoned. But after that it was all go.

George   Why, you see, there was a trawler in Scarborough harbour called Normandale, and he'd getten her on wireless and told them to ger out and ger ashore and walk back on bottom 'cos it's a bad spot. But he wouldn't tek ni notice. He thought he would float on high tide.

Laurie   He'd nivver 'a got off. It was a bad stormy night you see, and that was it. George Leng had said he nivver saw a light at all, all time he was off wi' lifeboat. They couldn't get back into North

Landing; they had to go back to Brid. Then they went ageean – they went twice that night – it were bad weather. If they'd ivvver fun her that neet, they'd nivver 'ave done any good; they'd 'a been good enough to 'a lost themselves, they wouldn't nivver 'a got her out.

George The wind was the trouble; if they ever got near that, they were in very great danger 'cos it's all great rocks all ower there.

Laurie Lord Earnley was bad enough, and it warn't a bad neet. She was in rather deeper waters. The Dundee was before my time, in father's time. It had bobbins of cotton, bales of cloth, general cargo of all sorts. I've heard mi dad say it was just like a spider's web all doon hedges doon North Sea Lane. I've heard 'em say Customs cum round and there was Dundee cloth knocking aboot for years after. They had ti hide it, they darn't let 'em see it.

George You're talking long way back. I've heard 'em say, lads had threaded it out all doon hedges. Aye, women used ti tek their frocks off and wrap their sens in it to ger it home. I've heard mi dad say – you know were luff is, I'm talking about wartime, 1st World War – there was boxes like that, 3 ply boxes full of butter.

Laurie It would keep, wouldn't it? But remember 1st World War, same as second, there was rationing.

Joyce What about the tales they used to tell that they always used to have fish. There was nowt else but fish; they used to have it for their meals and they used to have gravy on it.

Laurie I ain't heard that one; but I'll tell you what, mi mother would have fish in any shape or form, at any time, steamed, roasted, boiled, fried. But if there was any spared, it didn't get wasted, it was next meal, she'd eat it cold.

George Like me then, I'd sooner have fish than meat any day; I'd eat fish till it kem out of mi ears, My mother sometimes made fishcakes of it.

Laurie I nivver knew mi mother mek fishcakes, maybe mi dad didn't like 'em and so that would be that. But if she got any fish and steamed it, she would keep it and eat it till it had gone, like. I mean when I was going on pier, I'd be coming in late some nights, and if she thought there were fish, she didn't have her tea, she would wait for her tea. She would say "Do you want some?" And I'd say, "I in't gannin ti wait".

George	Well, I mean up at North Landing and that, you could get a good fish, couldn't you, for very little? Why, I mean, when we were kids that was Saturday morning routine: go down and help fishermen with skids – beg a few fish. I've come home wi' seven or eight and I've nivver bothered aboot dinner. It was maybe three o'clock afore I gor home.
Laurie	There was a lot of fishes they caught; they just used ti sling 'em owerboard. They wouldn't sell and they just used ti dump 'em, and you just helped yourselves ti 'em.
George	I've seen fish five abreast on that laur and some have been three stones. All big uns, right at top and they finished up wi' meggits at bottom. I don't know what the devil they're called really. There maybe a few billets above meggits and you can't sell them.
Laurie	Nay, they came down in quality and size and they got till they wouldn't sell 'em, so you could go and pick 'em up
George	Another thing amazed me, Laur. I could nivver understand it, but they seem to catch more haddock i'North Sea now, while in them days you nivver saw ni haddock, very rare, it was all cod.
Laurie	Aye, it was all cod and there was a nice few lings and a conger or two but you nivver see them now, wuffs an' all.
George	Aye, wuffs. I should say near every coble would have a wuff. Great ugly devils they were, 'eead like that some of 'em, and teeth like a man you know, not little needle things like ordinary fish, big round teeth. Awd Ted used to say ti me, "Lad, sometimes there's been chalk steeans laid i'bottom" ('cos they used to tek ballast when they were sailing you see, a bag full of sand and gravel and a few chalk stones) "and it'd bite one clean i'two". You wouldn't need to have your boot near 'em, and conger eels same. You know, they'd grab a rib and hang on t'iv it. They used to have a great big thick stick you know, owt like that, that kem aboard, they allus killed 'em.
George	In those days, their sea-boots were leather, they'd stiffen up well. George Cross there, when he used ti live in that little spot there along by Bolton Warcups' – a pound a pair! Thigh boots made all leather; they used dubbin on 'em.
Laurie	The tops were soft leather, greased them but tops were allus soft leather.
George	You know where Jack Leng used ti live, there at bottom of David Lane, there was a pond there, and they used ti gan straight in

	there ti wash sand off. When watter left there, it was inches deep in sand that had cum off fisherman's boots, through the years.
Laurie	They all had donkeys and later they all had a pony and cart as well. If they put three lines on a donkey, they could put six on a cart.
George	You see, they found if they had a pony and cart, they could carry more than putting it on a donkey. Each man, so many apiece. I've heard tell sometimes, four of 'em gan ti sea tigither in winter; but usually three. There used to be Teddy Fell, Bill Warcup and Bill Mainpuss used to go together. All wives used to do their skeining and baiting.
Laurie	If you'd been a fisherman's daughter going to school, you would have had seea much before you went to school and then some more to do when you came home. They had to do.
George	There was Will Cross, Jim Cross and Jack Cross. Then there was Cockshurs up there; Warcups – three of them, George Cockshur, Tommy Cockshur, Bob Cockshur. Then there was Twit Warcup – he was another George. Him and Nicky and George Otch used to gan tigither and Tommy Storks' father – they called him Titton. Titch Stork was this lot up near Rose and Crown.
Laurie	Titch and Tom – he was another George Stork. What was old lady called?
George	Aye, Nan Turkey, warn't it? She used to take in visitors, well, they all did. How that cum about, she was boasting they'd had turkey for Christmas. They reckoned that turkey was a fish bone!! They called her Nan Turkey ivver after that.
Laurie-	In winter time, the main diet was fish. It was especially the poorer end of fishermen. You see, in winter all the smaller fishermen, one of 'em would go with another to mek the three up.
George-	But back-end then, when it came to harvest time, fishermen used to help, with harvest and threshing time, didn't they? Aye, 'cos maybe crabs had gone off, there was nowt doing. It was a waste of time going to sea; waste of buying bait. So I mean, ger a few bob going harvesting, stoking. Hairy Jack used to be up at Hall's or Thompson's when they were at Hill Farm. Merry, he used to be wi' Lewis' when they had Thornwick Hotel pub. T'others could survive, they would paint up or find summat else; those without a couple of sons of their own would go with his brothers. Like there was George Otch and Jack Emmerson, they nearly always

went frae South Landing and Aaron Major. I remember the day when lartle Bill was drowned. I was in Saranne Chadwick's class. We were facing the road, in that big classroom, and she saw him walk by and she said, "George Major – I wonder what's matter with him". They reckon pot end gor in his smock and dragged him ower. Tide must have tuk him, only off South Landing there. No. I was in infants.

Laurie   It was a beautiful morning, a fine summer morning. They reckon they could have got him if he'd had any hair. Bald headed and they grabbed for him and couldn't grab him. They wouldn't be far off, only in bay like; the boots would pull im down, mind you, unless he was hung up in owt. He would have cum back up wi' air in his clothes: they allus reckon they float after nine days.

Margaret   Were there many of them drowned in those days?

Laurie   There was odd ones, now and again, as it went on. Biggest lot was when Crosses was lost; that was the biggest do there was here.

George   There was always somebody years and years back 'cos there was a lot of fishermen here at this spot. You see, then they formed the coble club. If owt went wrong like, and they were in the club, they had summat ti fall back on.

Laurie   Aye, and I was at school when that coble Arrow was lost in Brid Harbour mouth. I've forgotton whose class I was in. Now, that was a rotten old day. Maybe it was Sally Bayes' [a teacher for many years at Flamborough School].

George   It was bad weather. It was open coble, like; and they'd been out and got copped in it. I know Rear Admiral Sir Guy Gaunt was putting up for Parliament for Tories and he was there. It was him that got 'em to build loars and he paid for it – for his votes, you see. He got in hands down! Will Cross brok his ankle there. They used to launch at left hand side an' it was all clay, blue clay. He got fast shoving down, once. All fishermen did the donkey work like, for it, he paid for concrete and old railway lines right across. Even then, they found they wouldn't slip down, they had to fasten wood sleepers across.

Laurie   A boat would nivver run away on concrete. No, I know when Tom Stork's – that big un of theirs – it couldn't get down cliff, Haag Hopwood had wheels to tek it down. And they daren't run it down on the wheels 'cos it wouldn't have stopped it. So they launched it, or they were going to do, and they had to keep

	putting woods under; they couldn't shift it on concrete. Why, what they used to do, they used to have a piece of wood to shove through wheels, you see, ti act as a sort of brake, going down North Landing. Or, tie up one or two wheels and let 'em skid. Even then it was asking summat, a bit dodgy; it was a hard spot. No wonder there was a lot of fishermen wi' back-ache at North Landing. A killing spot was North Landing.
George	I remember George Pod Mainpuss there; his fether – I don't know what made me just turn back – he was on footpath opposite Bob Emmersons, and he just dropped down dead on footpath. They said he'd just rushed frae North Landing – it was a real warm day, summer time – had his dinner, and he went out, and it happened. He was only a young fella. I mean George warn't very old when his father died.
Laurie	Mind you, if they were ought like Father, they would have woollen underclothes on and thick shirts. Everything woollen; great thick woollen trousers. Yis, they were all wool and then great big wadman stockings ower top as well. Their wives knitted all that lot for them, their long underpants and then sort of red flannel undershets. Then a shet on top and then a jersey; they needed 'em at sea
George	Jersey right up to the neck, and flannel shirts, you know. The only time I ever saw 'em, if they were doing a bit of rowing down at North Landing, jersey kem off. They needed 'em all. You'd be out there, at sea, at North Landing. I've been down there some Saturday mornings and its been foggy and a white frost, and all their whiskers and their beards, all been solid wi' white frost. When they'd come in, like, just been out hauling lines.
Laurie	Why, they allus used ti say, what'll keep caud oot will keep it in or t'other way roond. They'd nivver wear gloves, but when they were hauling lines, they had cloths wrapped round their hands, or mittens wi' fingers oot, and just a thumb. They wouldn't want hooks to get caught in anything when they were hauling lines out. You would always see 'em when they went ti sea wi' mittens on. They would always dip 'em in sea and wring 'em out before they put 'em on. Kept your hands warmer wi' 'em like that than if you let 'em get wet bit by bit.
George	There was poor awd Albert Duke. I don't know whether he ivver got ower it, but they reckoned he was sick ever time he went ti sea.

Laurie	I think he must 'a gotten ower it. I'll tell you who was like that – Bill Overy. He didn't go to sea a lot but when he did go ti sea, he was same, sick every time he went. Aye. "Sit thu doon, lad" – as soon as you walked in Duke's 'oose. "Sit thu doon, lad."
George	I always remember, Laur, first time I was in Navy. I'd been at Chatham, I think, eight weeks, and 'cos you know they're always mekking you deea daft things, sweating and jumping inti pool and then cross-country run right round Chatham. And I got a hell of a cold, and I lost my voice, and I thought, 'I weean't be able to get away on leave', 'cos it was fost un. Anyway, it wore off to some extent, and I got away wi' it. When I went there ti Albert's, "Gosh", she says, "What's up with thu lad? I'll give thu summat that'll cure that". And she had a little bottle of Ipipecuarna wine, half full and lemon. And do know it went just like that. Nivver had it ni more. It's only a little bottle like that, but you know it is good stuff.
	She was a big woman was Mrs Duke. But all them Stephensons were good hearted – she was Jack's sister – Fatty Stephenson and Bill and there was another died – Arthur. I expect he liked to get drunk a lot when he kem home. He'd think nowt of bringing a whole stick of bananas home for his wife – he wasn't satisfied wi' a bunch!
	He lived on front of Mar. I've heard mi dad say years since, that pond used ti cum right up ti footpath that was raised high up. It used ti cum right up ti there, and fishermen had these 'ere two masted model boats and they used ti sail 'em ageean one another when it was bad weather, 'cos there used to be some waves on mar when it was real windy. They used ti sail 'em on footpath edge, there, 'cos pond was a deal bigger than when they dug it up.
Joyce	When my mother went to school she said the Mere came as far as the footpath when they were walking to school; she said there were geese there that used to chase you.
Laurie	I've seen lots of local lads having to walk on their boot heels to get round corner. There warn't a footpath then. Where has it all gone – that watter? It's nivver wet in't Green.
George	You know Johnny Chorrick wall end? Well, I've known it when it's been right across and I've had to go back up High Street to get to school a time or two. Oh aye, right across road. It's queer where it's gone.

Joyce	Why, you see, there was that pond at bottom of Crogg's *[Croft's]* Hill;.where's that gone?
Laurie	Why, they filled it in. Why, you see there was a spring there; they had a lot of bother there. They dug two or three different channels and gutters. Then they altered it at finish, covered it all over and grassed it. Aye. And when they drained top of Crogg's Hill – drain comes through there and it's just on top of ground; it's only just buried is drain there so it takes it away.
George	You see, I don't know whether you know, Laur, but that paddock at back of us, there's a gutter runs across bottom, it's very near six foot deep. Well, a fella called Wilkinson, I think, they bowt it for a time and he went and filled bottom in and potted it, and now there's a great pond in that field every time it rains. Gor, it was a great big gutter and it tuk watter from fields far enough back. Pot got bunged up and that's it. It floods field a few times a year. Why, they always said there was a spring there across far side of Mar. In summer time it warn't very deep, but you've seen it go completely dry. There was fairs on there. At the break up of Brid Fair, so much of it used to come through to Flamborough and so much go elsewhere. And some fairs would cum here earlier to paint up. There used to be circuses on there as well: Brian Mills; Diabilo – he was another. The fost one after First World War was Robert Pain's. They cum right opposite Jo Billy Emmerson's at yon end of Green. That was fost time we ever saw a fair.
Laurie	Steam 'osses. What do you call 'em at Filey, Corrigans, they used to cum wi' chairs, between the two World Wars. I know he kem once. It was gerring on for back end and he cleared out sharpish 'cos he thought he was going ti get snowed in. And one lot used ti cum wi' swings.
George	I always remember them swing-boats, Laur. There was an awd woman used ti stand at end, looking after them. And she wrote right across bottom: No Staning Allowed. She missed 'D' off all tigither. Norman Major tummelled oot – he went right ower top. They weren't satisfied with normal, it hit bar at top both ways, went right ower top. He was knocked out for a while.
Laurie	Wheea was with him? Lad 'at worked at Matt Major's – was it Thornton? It used to be a big fair sometimes, sideshows and that.
George	Aye, they generally had circus just at top of School Lane, you know just left. It was a nice flat bit was that. There used to be a

	bank half way across, nearest to the road, you know, of Mar and they called it Simm, and it was always piled up wi' mussel shells, and it didn't half used to stink in summertime; they just used to pile 'em up in a great bank. Usually Scavenger used to tek 'em to scatter on farms. Hall's farm up at Dykes med their stackyard bottom of 'em. Good stuff; sets like a rock.
Laurie	I made that wi' shells. When I first started taking shells up there, George, you had a job ti find a spot to tonn round and when I finished, you could gan where you liked. It was a real bad stock yard, all soft but that cured it.
George	There was a lot of shells then with all them skeining whilks and all sorts. They didn't like whilk shells 'cos they cut a bit.
Laurie	Oh aye, Mill Garth, it used to be all shells. You know where Maureen Needler lives and big house where Will Cross was, that was all puddle. Will Cross kem to me one day and he says, "Has thu any shells, lad? If thu has any spare just cum and chuck 'em down 'ere". And I put a load or two down, nice and handy like and Flor Mainpuss kem by, "Bah, what a stink, have you forgotten wheea you're working for?" And it went a bit further than that and she goes ti Will Cross. She says to Will, "What are you gannin ti do about these shells being put down here? You're on Parish Council, aren't you? Wheea's gin him permission?" He says, "I have, Flor". It dried up lovely.
George	Why, aye, with all that flattening, it wouldn't smell long. After a shower or two of rain and run ower it a time or two and smell's all gone. There used to be a little path that was coble stones before White's dug 'em up. My first recollection of that up there was Pat Mainpuss and his shop; we used to buy taws there at bottom corner.

Robert Leng and his wife Ivy

Robert was from a fishing family and was a fisherman for most of his working life. His father was a famous lifeboat coxswain.

Margaret began by asking Robert how the fishermen knew – by sound – when a ship was likely to run aground.

Robert   If you had a coaster coming from the North and you were out in High Street or North End, and you heard him – say – off Filey, somewhere off there – he'd be a bit away frae land – maybe three or four miles. As he was coming South, you knew which coast he was on – if you were listening to his siren, if he was gradually going South and going away fast South; but if you were keeping him more or less in the same direction – then he was bearing onto the land. But if he was coming and passing you, he was on his right course and alright. That's when folks used, if they heard one, to set off to run, either to South Landing or North Landing. It was what folks called a 'Run'. Maybe sometimes, when you got there, either to North or South Landing, he would all of a sudden have heard fog horn and he would alter his course, then you could come away, because he'd found where he was, y'see: otherwise he'd keep coming. Twice I've been working on one that's come ashore tekking a kedge anchor out; there's maybe two or three cobles there and we've had to leave him because there's been another run ashore not s'far away. There was one that ran ashore at Danes Dyke – south side of bay. We're working on one and another kem and ran ashore. and we got him off fost because tide was ebbing and, grounded further down, as tide flowed, we gor 'im off fost. T'other one stopped two or three tides. Anyway, that's how it used to be.

Margaret	Was that you going in the lifeboat or going in your own cobles?
Robert	No, you did more of that stuff in your own cobles. If you had to go wi' lifeboat, it wasn't often you got a great lot done because it was too bad weather ti tek kedge anchors out. You liked to be there wi' your cobles. We have done it wi' lifeboat of course, as soon as ever you got the job, got aboard, put some men aboard on it. If they found a way off it, you would tek lifeboat home and bring cobles, you see.
Margaret	Do you remember ought about the Skegness coming ashore?
Robert	Oh aye, I was out at Skegness, in a boat. Now that was a bad night. Them ashore didn't know whether you were coming home or not. He kem ashore at twenty five past seven, I think it was. He was talking to a trawler in Scarborough harbour over his radio. The trawler told him to stick to his ship and he would come down to him in daylight. But the weather was worsening. It was southerly, backing out easterly and then backed to northerly. By time we got ti know, it was a raging hurricane and that was half past ten at night. By the time we got there, she was swamped and all had gone. There was no lights so we hadn't a chance. When they tried to fire a rocket-line ower her, that was Speeton Rocket Cart, it simply blew back at 'em. As soon as cable got out and wind took it, it blew back into cliff.
	I was at Lord Earnley an' all: crew out of Lord Earnley – thirteen of 'em were all saved. The lifeboat washed aboard her – it was halfway aboard her, not quite half way or he would have cockled into boat – but as sea went out we backed off her inti sea. It took half of rudder but we had anchor out.
Margaret	How many boats were there at North Landing then, fishing boats?
Robert	Well, I think when I fost went, there was about sixteen in summer time – cobles – and about twelve in winter. Then, do you see, there was all fish buyers and ya lad. Dick Bailey and Jim Smith used to lead fish for buyers and then some of 'em got their own lorries. They used to be coming up frae Landing wi' 'osses and carts and lorries and it used to be busier then in winter than it is now in summer: all fish spread all ower beach. You were fishing all night long. You had to get in 'cos if you catch four

o'clock or half past four train, buyers gev you a good price; if you missed train, buyers wouldn't give you as much money for your fish because they didn't ger it away that day. So you always had ti try ti catch market. They used ti cum down to buy fish about one o'clock, and they gor it away by train straight to Marton Station.

Rita   How old were you when you first went to sea?

Robert   About twenty – twenty-one. I was with mi father and Bob (Otch) Emmerson – not Dennis Emmerson's – Robert Emmerson's, ower in Council Houses, his uncle, not his dad, awdest – his uncle. I went with Albert Duke seea long, about five years - 'cos I also went with George Mainprize – 'im that got killed on motorbike. Art Taylor went with me a little bit; Bill (Mitt) Major and Will Cross a bit. Johnny Chadwick went with me as well. Most of folks went with three when you were fishing in winter, and when you were crabbing as well. A few there was only two.

Margaret   Did you used to skein then or not?

Ivy   Yes, down in shed.

Robert   Mi mother used to bait for me. When mi dad finished, he used to bait for me down there in that warehouse. Elsie Cross used to skein for me, and Ester Duke, Len Duke's wife, she used to skein for me and mi sister Connie.

Ivy   Mussels used to come about two o'clockish didn't they? We used to get our oilskins on. It used be "Hurry up. Mussels are here". Then down we had to get. It was a cold job.

Robert   We always had a good fire; we always kept warm. It was best when you were catching your whilks – most of us did up to Christmas. We put whilk pots in and caught our own whilks. Then we used to bait one whilk on ti hook and a mussel on next and so on. If you were using flithers *[limpets]*, every third hook would be a flither; every third a whilk, mussel and a limpet. Once, when mi dad went with Dick Major, Herby Major's dad and Bill Mainprize, he – Dick – had been a fisherman here before but had been down at Spurn wi' lifeboat and then came back. He says to mi dad and Bill, awdest lad, "We shall be half whilks tomorrow, so bait half whilks." So they were at sea and they baited, but instead of putting a whilk on one and then a mussel on next, they baited half line with whilks and next half of line all mussels. That warn't the game, they wanted it varying you see.

Margaret	Did it affect what you caught?
Robert	Why, it did; it gives fish a choice. If it was going up and down your lines, I'se think whilk bait would maybe catch a bigger fish, while smaller fish maybe would likely go for mussels.
Margaret	There was a lot of things about not doing this and that with lines wasn't there – the old superstitions?
Robert	Oh, aye. You maun't mention owt on four legs other than a horse: not a rabbit or a hare or a pig. Oh – a pig...!!
Ivy	Once, when your mother and father were baiting down in the shed, I went down and I said, "It's just like a pig in a poke". Grandma Leng, she said, "That's it, we're finished now", and banged line down. Do you remember? Were you there? I was obviously a novice. Oh, it was terrible. They were mad.
Robert	It was a hard life and befoor I went *[to sea]* there were a certain amount of sailing cobles still going to sea. Do you know when mi grandfather was drowned, and mi uncle on mi mother's side, seven years was the longest period without a crew being lost – up to mi grandfather being lost in 1903. In 1908-1909 winter, Crosses were lost – all them were lost. And so, another six or seven years, almost.
Margaret	Could any of them swim or not?
Robert	No, mi dad couldn't. None of his brothers could – barring mi uncle Jack: he was a very good swimmer and awd Jack Stephenson was. They used to ger in at North Landing and swim round as far as Thornwick and back. Often, if they were just waiting for buyers coming, they would just have a swim to Thornwick and back. They were very good swimmers, were them two, but neean of the others.
Margaret	Of course, you all wore your heavy gear then, didn't you?
Robert	Swimming was neea good to 'em with heavy sea boots and they were made of leather as well – made 'ere at Crosses.
Rita	My grandfather?
Robert	Aye, that's right; he med sea boots. They could double 'em down and there was two tabs insides. They tied line tiv 'em and tied 'em round their waist or they couldn't walk in 'em. You wouldn't know Jack Cross and Tom Cross that lived in Hull. Why, Jim Cross was a very big fella, six foot six; their coble capsized and I'll tell you who was with 'em, Laurie Cowling's father, Tom.

Margaret	Oh, I didn't realise he'd ever gone to sea, fishing.
Robert	Oh aye, his father and Jack, his brother; he was a very good swimmer and he was lost. They said he knocked the chock out of the mast and one gor hold of one end and t'other the other end and they were picked up with another coble. It was bad weather; South Landing lifeboat was out but he was lost. He'd nowt ti hang on to; heavy sea boots would tek him down. Oh, it was very sad he was lost. That's why they didn't go to sea. They'd probably both been fishermen if it hadn't happened. George Cross and Tom Cross, neither of them went again; they went to Hull.
Margaret	How did you manage? I've heard Laurie say there was either feast or famines.
Robert	Aye, that's right. It was the same at Filey and at Whitby. You'd no means of keeping fish for a long time. Why, I'll tell you, when you used to get your lines and gear – pot-tows an' that as a rule – a rep came round, a traveller frae Bridport. There was two of 'em came – one called Gail. You used to order and next time he came, you paid. The other one, they called him Ousel. He kem inti house and mi mother went upstairs and got money and paid him. He said, "You know Mrs Leng, I know where I'm going to get mi money every time I come. It doesn't matter whether I'm at Flamborough, Brid, Filey or Scarborough, it's always the same; I know where I'm going to get my money and where I'm going to have difficulty getting mi money". That was it, you see; if anybody was thrifty, they'd used their common sense and they'd put that away and say 'That's for gear'. Mi dad used to say "Good gear is good furniture".

I went to sea with mi dad and awd Johnny Chadwick, Sammy's father. We gor up one morning, two or three o'clock; I thought Johnny would have been on the go. Mi dad says, "Gan and see if he's getting up, lad". I cum on – he lived at end house here; and all doors were locked and no lights. I knocked and they nivver heard me; I rattled at door. So I went back and I says, "He's nivver getten up", and mi dad says, "Thu owt ti gone in and shouted". I Says, "I couldn't, door was locked". He says, "Door Locked *****!!!!!" I've nivver heard owt like that in mi life, a fisherman and locking doors. Gan and get summat and knock at winder". He'd overlaid had Johnny; which folks often did.

Nowadays, crab pots are netted wi' synthetic fibre; your pot-tows – they're also synthetic and they don't rot. They don't have 'em to bark and they don't have 'em ti tar. We had all that to do and if you didn't tar twice on a crab pot, they didn't fish as good. You had to bring 'em out twice a year, and you had ti change 'em. Now, they go two or three years and same wi' pot-tows you see; they don't rot. If we were at sea, and we put crab pots in middle of March, April, May and into June; you had ti change some of them pots out 'cos crabs were mekking holes in 'em ti gan out. We used to go foying *[taking visitors out to the caves]* but anybody who weren't, they had ti change two or three times a year. You could see them at North Landing, at night, getting ready for next day. They would make a pot already for netting as they were coming in and then go back at night and net it. If they were not at sea, they would have to net three or four a day, to keep in; and if it was bad weather, of course, you made on. You were always at it; you used to go into plantations to get all your bows for crab pots and all such as that. Folks thought if you warn't at sea, you warn't deeing owt. You sometimes put in a longer day when you warn't at sea than when you were. You had all your tows – you had to dry 'em: all your warps, you used t,bark 'em when you'd finished at back end of summer, and your pots and put 'em out ti dry. Pot tows – they had to be very dry and when you gor 'em properly dry, you had 'em to tar again. Then you had ti let 'em dry outside again; then when they got summat like dry you put 'em away, 'cos if you didn't they'd burn wi' sun – tar you see. You made all your own crab pots. Now, you'd buy them already made. They buy all these steel uns. I think a crab pot ready for sea is about twenty or so quid. But in those days you would know where to go for your wood: I had permission at Burton Agnes Hall. I used to go with George *[Emmerson]*. Or, I used ti go to plantations round here. You see you had all your own "feerten trees" *[skids]* to get. You were always at it.

Although, there's more water in North Landing and into the North Sea, all over than there was. If you were to go and get an old tide book, prior to decimalisation, when it was in feet and inches, you'd find then that a very, very big tide was nineteen foot or just over. Now, you get it twenty-one foot. It's in metres now, but that disn't mek ni difference; if you reckon it up in feet, you get twenty-one foot. Whether it's because ice is melting or not, I deean't know. Now, although tides are bigger, it doesn't come as high up at North Landing. It will when it's calm but, if there's a big sea, it doesn't, and if you go ti North Landing now, it's very, very seldom they have to pull boats up onti that clay. We often used ti 'av ti pull 'em right up above that; right above the chain. But there's flowers growing there now, and grass where there nivver was before, because there isn't the spray comes up. I mean, I remember once it kem up inti lifeboat house, and awd Gilbert Screeton – you remember him? He used to be carrier with 'oss and cart. He gathered back loads of wood, up again lifeboat house doors. It had washed up there, with heavy tide. Why, you nivver see that now. If you got a big sea in awd days, you could say, "Why, we needn't ton out in morning. We needn't ton out for a few days 'cos it'll tek a bit of settling". If it did settle fast, you knew that you were going to get a gale of wind frae south west. But now, you can have it breaking across sands, breaking across Smethwick, and you can go next morning and it's very near calm.

Mi dad used to say, in summertime, when maybe you gor a gale of wind from north,"It weean't bite watter, it weean't mek a big sea, there's ower mich oil in watter". It was herring time when all herrings were about, and it didn't quite settle on watter and it didn't mek a big sea. Then all ships were coal burners and sail; now they're oil burners and then there's all them oil rigs in North Sea – all ower North Sea – and therefore there's always a film of oil on top of sea. And that's my theory why you don't get the seas that there used to be. You've heard say 'pouring oil on troubled waters', we always used to in lifeboat. I don't know what they do now, we always carried an oil bag, always. It was a two gallon round tin, and it went inside a canvas bag and it had eyelets in top, and a lanyard, and it used to be twisted up tight. It was a longish lanyard, and it was always kept aft; and if it was heavy sea, and you were running before it coming in ti North Landing or boats going inti Brid harbour, you used to have it made fast aft, tail end of rope bang it on her gunnel and the lid would fly off. Then you'd throw it overboard, and it couldn't come out quick 'cos it was inside this canvas bag, and it would gradually keep leaking out. You were towing it behind you, and it would be stopping the sea breaking at you. You see a lot of 'em don't know these things. All lifeboats carried oil bag or a tin.

We joined with Filey and Bridlington; but we've had a lot of controversy sometimes, and arguments whether it was our job or Scarborough's, do you see, 'cos you can be off here often to north of North Landing and it can be even nearer to Scarborough. So there used to be argument sometimes as to whose job it was. John Willie Bayes was secretary, and Tom Woodhouse later. Aye, he was a good secretary was awd John Willie Bayes: he knew sea like, 'cos he'd been at sea hisself, in sailing ships, and he'd been a fish buyer all rest of time, so he knew what it was like. If we were going ti cobles about, he'd never query. If it was bad weather, you'd nivver ask secretary or coastguards. They were coastguards then, there were a lot of 'em here then. In fact, they weren't really coastguards – they were naval men – wireless men before war. They were dot and dash men, morse code, regular navy men – Chief Officer. You used to wait with a steamboat – unless you saw owt aground, then you went. You used to have to report to him and to secretary: but if it was for local cobles you knew better than either of them. So coxswain, that was mi dad or Tuck [*Dick Chadwick*], he would just call up and say, "I'se tekking lifeboat, John Willie". And he would say, "Go." He would never query it because you knew it was bad weather. I went in lifeboat when awd Tuck had the sailing lifeboat.

Rita	This Dick Tuck – was it Miss Chadwick's father?
Robert	Aye, her father – George Tuck: her brother was very deaf. I think I had one or two trips when I was only eighteen year awd. You were only volunteer crew then. There was thirteen in a crew but there was only three officers. There was Bowman, 2nd Coxswain and Coxswain; but the other ten were volunteers. At one time of day, before I remember, there were picked crews at each side. A full picked thirteen went in a boat; but then, they had plenty – there were a lot of fishermen in them days. They had twenty or so for North Landing and twenty for South Landing.

Mi dad had sailing boat for, I should say, three years before motor boat cum. I was in her a few times when he had her. When we fetched those three lads frae Thornwick – that was a rotten job. We had to let her go right inti cliff ti get 'em aboard. Last trip she had, last time she was afloat at North Landing (sailing boat) – we fetched them three lads. That was the last time, barring time they tuk her away, 'cos she'd already been sold, and we'd knocked all her quarter in. Of course, we had to get her repaired ti tek her away – so it would tek a bit off her value.

Margaret	You had your own donkeys then?
Robert	Aye, do you know there's a story about that donkey and I'll tell you what it was. You know Walter Hudson? Well, he was

brought up by, I don't know what his real name was, Sparrow Checks. Now, his wife used to tek bairns of well to-do-parents and look after 'em, and nurse bairns whilst the parents were out foreign or whatever; Walter Hudson was one of them. They used to call him Walter Checks. His parents bought him that donkey for when he was here. Now, mi granddad's old donkey died, and mi granddad asked if he could borrow Walter's donkey. It won donkey race up at Thornwick Hotel, and old Pat Mainprize, that's Mary Brown's granddad, he rode it.

Margaret   When did they have donkey races then?

Robert   Why, in them days there was a fella: they called him Mr Kay or McKie, Scotsman. He had that pub and it was also a farm then. He was a real sporting man and he used to have runners, I mean champions, up there, also boxers. And he had a fella called Downer up there, a runner; he was champion of Great Britain. Mi dad used to roll track for him up at Thornwick. And he used to have 'em tossing that caber, you know, and putting the shot and pigeon shooting up there; they weren't clay pigeons they used to shoot – they were tame pigeons. Oh aye, there used to be some rare do's up there.

Margaret   Did they have these donkey races every year?

Robert   They would while he was up there 'cos there was a lot of donkeys in villages. That was before mi mother was married; it was a long while ago – before 1903. When he came home frae Thornwick, Pat rode him home wi' a great big red velvet tablecloth tied round his neck that he'd won. And that's mi other grandad, Grandad Leng. If you tonn it on its side, you'll see that he's sat on part of a coble that's stood up. You can see the planking and that photograph's tuk from here, looking up past Richard Emmerson's, where Richard lives now, up to them houses that Nicky used ti 'ave, where Janie Major used to live. That's this side door where mi grandad lived at.

Margaret   Fancy wearing all those heavy black clothes.

Robert   Let me see, she would be a Fell. That photograph there, I was going to get one tuken off it and let 'em have it in Sewerby Hall; 'cos the knife he tuk out of the sailor's hand on 10th February 1871, is there. He was only twenty-four then. He tuk it out of his hand, dropped him aboard and got him ashore. There was only two survived; they were all washed overboard and drowned. In the Great February Gale, what they did was carry coble frae South Landing on sand. Turned her wrong way up, and fishermen carried her like that, 'cos lifeboat had been lost at Brid anyway. This ship was a brig and sea was breaking at her; she was broad on at Awd Fall. So they carried coble on so they could get in shelter of her. Sea was hitting ship before it was coming ashore, and that's what they did; they rowed off to her. Grandad, Tom Woodhouse's granddad, Cockcroft Warcup and t'other, I've forgot his name, four of 'em. Mi granddad, being youngest, he jumped aboard and this fella had his knife in his hand and he was in a state, tangled up in rigging – that was why they couldn't get him from clifftop [*with the rocket apparatus*]. Mi grandad had to open his hand to get knife out; cut him loose, and pull him free. He put knife in his pocket and dropped him aboard their boat, and let it drift ashore stern first, in lee of ship, and that knife is in Sewerby Hall now. When that was tuk, the photo, it would be when cameras had three legs you know, before mi grandma received that photograph, 'cos he had it ti send to her, they were both drowned before she got it, 1903. That upset her; she nivver gor ower it. She died in 1919

Mi father and Sam Leng [*no relation*] were that su'good pals that they were more like brothers than their own brothers were. They were always tigither, in trouble or not in trouble, poaching and one thing and another. They were often at court for poaching.

Margaret   Mind you, poaching, it would be a means of getting meat, wouldn't it?

Robert   I wouldn't call it poaching. Awd gamekeeper used ti gi you one, called him Lakin, Lakins of Brid. He used to say, "They're not poachers; they're pot hunters", 'cos they were after summat for their dinners. If they hadn't a'been a rabbit or a hare, there wouldn't a'been owt in their bellies many a time.

Rita   Mi dad was out of work most winters and we lived on rabbits and fish. He put a 'trot' down at South Landing and snares up Rotherhams.

Robert   I'll tell you what. Roy, your dad, had a little terrier; by, it was a good un. He could walk up Rotherhams there, and he could just go where camp is now – there were gorse bushes there then, some in middle and some down side. He would go in there and bring a rabbit out every time. He would catch 'em in gorse bushes. He was a good un. He used to walk up on a Sunday morning.

Margaret	It used to be a regular thing, the men going for a walk. I know when we were first married, Laurie used to go pick up Alf Leng and Art Taylor. Did you used to go Robert? I know they used to go up to North Landing every Sunday morning, navy blue suit and trilby hat on.
Robert	No. It isn't oft I used to go 'cos I was foying. I was busy on a Sunday. Why, winter time I did, I had mates I used to knock around with – Laurence Saul, Ted Lunn and Lija Lynn. Every Sunday morning, we did – Albert Duke an' all, Olwyn Brown – all with fisherman's ganseys on. I'll tell you summat else an all: on a Sunday night after chapel and church, North Landing Road used to be full, didn't it. Walking up there after church and chapel on a night, both young and old, it warn't just young uns.
	Why, we used to go around walking when I was at school, but we were never here in wintertime. Mi dad never fished out of Flamborough, wintertime; he went out of Brid: so we used to go and live in Brid every winter. Not just us – Cowlings, George and Dick Cowling and Tom, they were at school in Brid. I went ti Hilderthorpe School. Glentons went and stopped there; Bride Pockleys – they went and stopped at Brid. Mi Uncle George Mainprize, he went to Brid and they stopped there. Mi mother wouldn't go to live at Brid or we should have stopped there 'cos they had herring cobles and then a keel boat. We used to go and stop in Nelson Street, and in Richmond Street – right at top of hill. We used ti go into one of them boarding houses. Them as owned would be living in and we used to be living in part of it. Us, mi Uncle Bob Otch and mi Uncle Jack and mi Uncle Major – he lived in Nelson Street, at awd Willie Fairbottom's.
Margaret	There'd be no means of getting there if you were going out of Brid to go off fishing.
Robert	No, that was it. At Spring of year when Winter fishing had finished, they used to lay herring cobles up at South Landing. We used to pull her up, both sides, and tek coble out of Flamborough ti go crabbing: they were big cobles were them herring cobles. You wouldn't think that was a Flamborough coble [showing photograph of a herring coble] – she's laid up in Spurn there. They would sail her to Spurn; tek a Flamborough coble with 'em and get them farmers at Spurn to pull them herring boats up at riverside, out of road of water. They used to live in there – live aboard of her and work their crab pots out of the smaller coble, and take their crabs up to Grimsby every day. And they used to

	put all the crabs into one coble and tek turns going ti Grimsby. That one there *[in the photograph]* had four bunks and a cabin. That's mi Uncle Jack and Norah Brown's father, mi dad aft and mi Uncle Major right aft. You can see they were stood on cuddy – what they call the cabin deck. And that's the mast; they'd tuk it down. It used to lay down in what they called the crutch but whilst they were laid up they put it like that. She was forty-two feet. The lifeboat at North Landing was thirty-five or thirty-six foot long; she was forty-two. I've heard mi father say they've had forty-two cran of herrings in her, and they would have twenty nets and floats for 'em, and floats for nets in those days were small barrels which would have held seven or eight gallons. They had all that aboard and forty-two cran of herrings – there's twenty-eight stones in a cran: forty-two cran aboard!!
Rita	She'd be deep in the water then?
Robert	She was. But they were very wide boats; they were made for carriage: they used to go to Whitby and Scarborough.
Margaret	So did they used to go herringing down to Lowestoft?
Robert	No, they used to pack up 'cos it was winter fishing time then. When boats were going to Lowestoft, that was end of September. Why, winter fishing started beginning of October. May and June was best for crabbing. If it turned fine, we used to put pots in middle of March; that was time ti put 'em in, in those days. They used ti go a long way. They used ti go summer fishing frae Whitby, before herring time started. You know herring time didn't start till end of July off Skinningrove, that's when they were still under sail.
Margaret	That's a long way up and under sail, good heavens!
Robert	Everybody didn't; there were some that nivver went. There was Dick Tuck, Glentons, awd Sharp – John Kemp's granddad, Bride Pockleys not Joe Pockleys and Sam Majors and Bill Major – he used ti go, and Edmunds: they were all herringers. Oh, and Crosses, Will Crosses, they went. And like I mean, mi grandad that's on photograph, they went herringing. Went to Scarborough, when they were young; they lived aboard boats and came home at weekends but if they were at Whitby, they couldn't get home at weekends; it was too far. But if they were at Scarborough, they used ti get in on a morning you see; they were herrining all night. They came home Saturday morning and go back Sunday night or Monday morning.

Mi uncle, him as is on that herring coble, right aft, he was working out of Scarborough or Whitby, I don't know which, and he was only twelve years old – he went as lad. They took three men and a lad. Sometimes lad would be maybe fifty or sixty years old, just somebody to fill in, that hadn't a share. And when they were o'er, there was a gale of wind, he was twelve years old, and they saw this boat wrong way up – capsized. There was a lot of wind so they sailed to her to see if there was anybody in her. There had been one capsized, and they'd been trapped in air pocket, and one or two of 'em had been saved. Underneath water there was a big spar, and they sailed into it, and spar went straight through her and sunk her: they were a long way off at Scarborough. Before she went down, they got the barrels *[that they put the herrings in]* and tied two together with the lanyards that were fixed to each barrel. They were each laid between two barrels all night – he was twelve years old. I know he would tell me, they kept saying, "Now cum on honey, keep tiv us: try ti keep working your hands, paddle towards us". So they all kept together and they were picked up by a Scotsman next morning, at daylight. You would have thought he would nivver have gone ti sea again, but he was a proper hard un, was mi Uncle Major.

Margaret	I've heard Laurie say – or his dad – that they used to come round with herrings, come round selling 'em – the women.
Ivy	Twenty a shilling at one time.
Robert	Laurie's granddad used to live next door to us up there *[at North End]*. Laurie's dad went to live with Gough.
Margaret	Yes, that's right, Uncle Bill Collins.
Robert	Because that's where Cameron and all them lot live now. *[Lighthouse Road, across from the Green]* They called it Gough Dyke because it was Gough field. He must have had summat ti do wi' fishing at one time.
Margaret	Laurie said Uncle Bill was doing the carting before Dad went with him.
Robert	Yes, he was. Jim's *[Jim Smith]* mother died very young. Annie was the eldest, and she more or less brought 'em up. But Jim – Gough took him to go wi' him i' coal business.
Margaret	He always said he was born in our house, where I'm at now. *[Greenside Cottage]* Jim was born there and then his father and mother must have moved out *[to North End]*. Then Laurie was

born there and he *[Jim]* was nivver with his mother and father; he was brought up by his grandmother and Uncle Bill. Uncle Bill had a wooden leg hadn't he or something; I'm sure I've heard Laurie say he had a gammie leg, 'cos he always used to walk with him and he used to hold on to him and go all round with him, as a kid.

Robert   I deean't know but I remember him sitting at corner of Drill Shed there, in a great awd armchair, when we were kids and going to school, and talking tiv us. I wonder if he'd gone ti sea at one time, before he had his leg happen. I've heard mi dad say they were once in Scarborough and unless it was another fella of the same name, they all started to cheer, "He's here, leeaks tha". And it was Gough coming in a herring coble, going into Scarborough. So whether it was the same Gough or not I nivver took n'notice in them days, but I should think it was and he'd maybe happened his leg, and he had to give ower. I just remember him as an awd man sat outside there.

Margaret   The little window upstairs at that end that faces the shed, that's a little bedroom and Grandad always used to say he was born in that bedroom and Laurie was born in that bedroom. And the room underneath, that again faces the shed, was Uncle Bill's bedroom, and he lived in that bedroom, and great-grandma in the room at the back downstairs.

Robert   The shed was where they used to have Royal Artillery isn't it? Guns and things?

Margaret   Yes. There's still a ring of bricks, in the end wall of the Drill Hall, that they used to fire at – with blanks – for practice. They had a big gun or something in there at one time and they used to practice, and go off to summer camp somewhere.

Robert   They used to go up to North Landing on a Sunday morning. There was a little brick hut ower towards Newgum, in cliff, you know, right across that field, and that had summat ti do wi' it. And at t'other side, as you go on to cliff top, there's a spot there they still call it Powder-Hole as knows. See that's where they used to keep some powder and they used ti fire across that field. Their Artillery used to come on, some Freemans used to come on and awd Dick Bayes and Frank Bayes and awd Aaron Major – they were big Artillerymen. I know they used to come up from Brid and compete – Flamborough Artillery and Brid Artillery. They were all volunteers. That's before I can remember: it was on time of South African Wars – before I can remember. One of 'em – I think he was a blacksmith – Charlie Traves, just this side of Wiles's – he was in the Artillery. He volunteered and went to South Africa, and he was shoeing. He was shoeing 'osses and mules in South Africa. I know in First World War, I was only six, but I remember summat about it; there was some great big lorries with soldiers, and they had these big mules pulling these. They went to get their mules shod and Wiles didn't know how to do it. They were si stubborn, were those old mules, and Wiles said, "We can't get 'em shod; we can't mek owt on 'em". Charles says, "Bring one of 'em here". And he just threw it on its side, kept its feet hobbled and shoed it on its side, and then did t'other – neea trouble at all 'cos he'd done it in South Africa. Learned trick there.

Margaret   I know David Freeman used to go fishing with you: he said he learnt a lot of his seamanship from you, and helped him get his master's ticket on oil tankers. He went with you when Albert Duke was with you, didn't he?

Robert   No, he went with Albert a bit, but he went with me when Bill Mitt was with me, and our Roy was with me. He's a handy lad is David, handy with his hands.

Margaret   When you were in boats then, I've heard Laurie say, there were so many shares for the men and so many for the boat. That was how you got your money.

Robert   No, I'll tell you how we used to do. Most people would take two shillings ti pound or taking half share, most people would share out. Now, like, we had Bill Knaggs as a crew member, but he hadn't a share, although he had a share for pots, for gear; then you each had a share and half a share for coble. If you made a decent living, half share would finance your coble; it wouldn't mek you a lot of money but it would mek you a bit. But that's how you used ti do; three and a half shares, half share for coble. Of course that was after expenses that had been taken out.

              Oh aye, we used to go to Brid, I know mi dad used to have a warehouse down on Chicken Run. It was when there was some big brick buildings there, where Kay used to have his petrol and paraffin there, and we had the end one. And prior to that we used to bait up in Nelson Street – back way we had a shed: they used to bait four lines a day.

Margaret   That would be like skeining the mussels for baiting?

Robert	No, they didn't use many mussels, not at Brid, mainly whilks and flithers like. Not whilks that were caught there, they used ti send ti Wells for 'em. What we used to call Humber whilks, they were a smaller, softer shelled whilk. You'd have ti 'ave somebody knocking 'em, you know. Mi mother and mi aunt had a handcart and had ti go up ti station to fetch whilks that had come frae there and bring 'em home ti Nelson Street. They were in hundredweight bags.
Rita	Where did you get your limpets from?
Robert	Why, they used ti come onto this side of Sewerby, on there. If it was a bad weather day fishermen would go theirselves. If it wasn't, they would have some Brid men, awder men or lads gan. I've seen sometimes on a bad weather day, when you've gone ti Stacks, nearly every fisherman in Flamborough would be down there: then young uns used to go to Newgam, and Sanwick and get 'em and pull 'em up. You liked to go on your own ti Newgam and Sanwick.
	When that steam trawler, Lord Earnley, kem we had a rum job, but we should have had a worse if it hadn't been for Rocket Cart. You know Laurie's dad, Jim, and I'se think Laurie hissen would be there, and George Waud and their search light – 'cos we hadn't got one. We got one after that. If it hadn't a'been for that search light, bye..!! We'd gotten about five aboard. Summat like that and search light shining down on us, it was grand like; you could see what you were doing. All of a sudden it went out, and chaps aboard Lord Earnley, did they scream and shout. 'Course it warn't a few second before they had it on again. Jack Waud and mi dad went down ti London. Aye, they were on 'In Town Tonight' *[a very popular radio programme in those days]*.
Rita	Yes, I remember; we all listened.
Robert	Then he went down again, him and Dick Cowling, ti Buckingham Palace; got their Silver Medal.
Rita	I always remember your dad saying, "And we saw this lartle yella leet". *[light] I*t always stuck in my mind and we went the next day to Bempton, and walked up to the cliff top to see her. She was stuck right up into the cliff, wasn't she?
Robert	Aye, she was great friends wi' mi dad was your mother; and those friends of yours, – George Edgar, and Len Stipetic.

Rita	Yes, once a year, when Len was here, your dad used to take us up to Bempton Cliffs and I can remember that dolphins used to come and play with the boat.
Robert	Oh aye, I've seen 'em playing with buoy when you were putting buoys in; you know, playing with corks that's on 'em.
Margaret	Is there any of them around here now?
Robert	Why, there's pilot whales, you know – blow fish. Our Roy, they often see 'em like. Len Stipetic, he dived over at Bear island or Iceland and saved somebody didn't he? He had a gold watch or summat for it.
Rita	Yes, that's why he never went to sea again.
Robert	Aye, he dived ower for this fella but he died when they gor him aboard and they had to tek Len inti stokehold 'cos he very near went as well.
Margaret	Did Bessie [Bayes] have a brother that went to Artic?
Robert	No, that was Bessie's brother that went to Archangel. George Mainprize – 'Rennie' – had just come off a trip and he'd just been there and he says, "Wheear have you signed on for?" And these two lads said what ship, and he said, "Why, she's going to Russia". And they said, "Yes, we know". And Rennie said, "Why, you ought not to have done that because ice is starting to form now". And they went and when they were coming away, there was ice. And what they'd done – Russia was in a bad way; thar skipper had sold a lot of food and when they froze they'd nowt left. And cook came up and said, "I've boiled all we have, pea soup, that's the lot, so we'll have ti move". The skipper was boozing, he was going to die anyway. And there was a Russian Finn on board, and he says to Frank Bayes and Jack Stork, "Now, Flamborough, I'm not going with our captain 'cos he's wrong; he's just told us where a light bears, and he's wrong 'cos we've drifted, the whole ice has drifted and I'm not going with him, I'm going this way. You do as you like, Flamborough". Frank Bayes had been told always to stick to his skipper whatever and he wouldn't leave skipper. The other boy, Jack, says, "I isn't going with him, Frank, 'cos I believe this Russian knows more an' he diz about round here". There was five or six went with this Russian. Jack went with him and then went back to Frank saying, "I can't leave him" (meaning Frank). But Frank wouldn't come; and then he says, "There was like ice sort of parted and he couldn't get across so we set off to walk". Mi mother says to Jack, after he'd got back home, "What

was it like?" Jack replied, "Why sometimes you were walking on top of snow and other times you were going down into snow. What kept me alive was tewing with other people. The Russian kept saying, "Come on, Flamborough", and I kept myself with others collapsing and trying to carry 'em, and then we had 'em to leave". And I think three of 'em got back. They kem at a fella with a sledge and reindeers or summat, and they got on there and he took 'em back to this village or whatever it was. Jack said, "We owed more on that than owt else 'cos my eyes were just slits". And when they got to this place, they radioed somehow that there was men on ice and they answered that assistance was impossible. Therefore Jack, the Russian and one more were the only ones that survived.

Margaret   Was that the Jack Stork that used to live on the corner of David Lane?

Robert   Aye, mi dad's cousin, he was mi half cousin; they called him Jack Leng Stork. I know he was two or three years when he thowt he was going to lose his toes. Doctor told him he would have to have his toes off but they got another opinion; and they said they would have a go at trying to get the frost out, and he did, and he saved 'em. And that was when Frank Bayes was lost and they nivver heard nowt neeamore of him.   John   Willy   [Bayes] blamed Jack Stork, but it weren't Jack Stork. He couldn't a'done neeamore. John Willy said Jack aught not to have left Frank, but if he hadn't left him, he would have been lost as well. You would think it was the right thing to do to stay with the captain, but not always. Jack said, "I'll nivver go where it's cold again", and he went to Australia. Then he stopped in Australia, you know, and he met his wife there, a nurse she was, and they come back here.

Ivy   Pat, they called her, she was a character.

Robert   There was, like, mi grandfather there – Mainprize – two of his lads went to Australia and one of his dowters – Ella and Rick and Herbert and Stan, he was in shipping, but he died young. There was summat up with him. They went to Australia and some of ems there yit.

Do you know the story of old Thoff Traves? There was an old parson and a farmer's daughter, and she was only in her teens and parson was an old man, with whiskers. He wanted to marry her and she didn't want to marry him but they made her 'cos this old parson was well off. People had gone by house and seen her crying and all village was up in arms and Nell Sugar (a great big strong lass) and other village lasses pulled great sods of grass up outside church, wi' plenty of muck on 'em, and they threw them at the groom as he came out. Theophilus Traves was sitting waiting wi' the carriage, when the parson came out of the vicarage with a glass of rum which he handed to Thoff, who drank it. The parson said to him, "What did you think of that?" He replied, "Why it would a'been a lot better if it hadn't had si much bloody watter in it".

Margaret	There used to be some strange goings on in the village, didn't there?
Ivy	They had no other entertainment, they didn't have telly or anything like that. You don't get that gathering of folk in houses now. They used to come ti our houses and tell you some tales.
Robert	Mi dad was away in fost World War and he nivver got a leave 'cos he was in Mediterranean. He was away three years without leave. Mi mother had mi grandmother poorly and if it hadn't been for Ethel – she used to help mi mother look after her. Ethel was the youngest of Jim Smith's sisters, wasn't she?
Margaret	No, Fanny.
Robert	Ethel died young in her teens though.
Margaret	There was a Laura who died young as well. I didn't know until after our Laura was born. We called her Laura after Laurie, but we went up to see Aunt Annie with her and she said, "I is pleased you've called her Laura after our Laura". There was Aunt Annie, I think Dad was next, and then there was George. He had a shop at Old Town. Then there was Aunty Mary, she married somebody from Scarborough, then Aunt Ada and Aunt Fanny. There's only Aunt Ada left now.
Robert	At mi grandad's, George and Jim did fall out – a lang while since – I was only about twelve years old. George was coming round wi' pots and pans and he called at oor house, and then Jim kem round wi' coal, and we were talking, and George was telling us about transports driving up ti Front and he says, "We used to sell a bit of Black Market on our way". Jim's face kept changing and all of a sudden he says, "You begger! There I was bloody hungering ti deead i'trenches and there you were selling our grub". He was crazed was Jim. Aye, he had it rough, had Jim; he was right up at Front.

Margaret	Aye, he would be. I think he was shot in the knee, now you come to mention it; he never had much time for Uncle George.
Robert	Another was awd Jack Smith, by gum, he was a clever fella wi' his hands, he could mek anything.
Margaret	That was why there wasn't a stone on one of their graves. He got a stone and carved it, and took it down to cemetery and vicar wouldn't let him put it up. And when Grandma Smith died, Gardiner, stonemason, came round and Jim wouldn't entertain him making a stone for her.
Robert	I'll tell you what, he, Jack Smith, was a very independent fella with all them bairns on a farm at Bottom End. There was an election; farmer came to him and said, "Now, John, how are you voting?" He says, "I'se voting same as I allus vote". Farmer says, "I didn't ask you that, I asked you who you are voting for. Are you voting for Tories or Liberals?" He says, "I'se voting for Liberals same as I always do". The farmer says, "Then you're finished here". John says, "Why, if that's it, I finished because", he says, "I could've told you I was voting for Tories if I'd liked, and you wouldn't a known n'difference and still have voted for Liberals as I've allus voted". Farmer says, "You've finished here, then". But he got taken on at Brick Yard. He wasn't five and twenty minutes before he was foreman, a three times better job.
Margaret	Well, now him being at the Brick Yard, they used to get hot working on the kilns and come out and drink water by the bucketful. Jim always used to say, "Water's nivver n'good for you; it kills". Laurie said that they used to drink so much water at the Brick Yard that it killed Jim's father.
Robert	Aye, you see they drank beer in pits. I always remember a relation of ours lived in Middlesborough, and he kem ower in a taxi, and ther was awd Matt Duke. There was standpipes and taps in street then, weren't there? And this'n says ti awd Matt Duke, "Tha'll rust if tha drinks all tha wants ti get in there (the pub across the road)". By gor, awd Matt was rusting a long while after he'd gone! Aye, Jack Smith was a character.
Margaret	He was Bell Man as well, wasn't he? We've still got that bell; it's a big one, takes all your time to lift it.
Robert	Aye, he had a voice like a bell an all; you could hear it all ower village.
Ivy	Is it brass? Has it got a handle on? We've got one haven't we?

Robert	It's out of a ship, a packet, it's a ship's bell. Jack Smith took me to see the fost ship I saw ashore. He took me to see her, I should only be about five; mi dad was away. I know what they called her – she was right on Thornwick Bay end – they called her Lindrop. It was a steam trawler, smashed up there you know. When Herbie came the other day he said, "I'll tell thu what I was going ti ask thee. Wheea was awd fella that used ti live across here?" (Robert) "Dis tha mean Jacknie?" (Herbie) "Aye, what was his proper name?" (Robert) "They called him Gibbon". There was Jacknie and awd Sparrow Checks lived up there, and awd Mary Mallory and Lily Hope.
Rita	The Hope's, they did sell bread up there didn't they? I know 'cos my grandma used to send me. She used to give me a teacloth and say, "Go and fetch the bread from Miss Hopes; she'll have it ready now.
Robert	Yis, they did. They had this old wooden shop here on High Street, hadn't they?
Rita	They hadn't when I went; that was the butchers when I can remember. It could have been before.
Ivy	Then Phyllis Stork got it didn't she?
Robert	I remember Jack Agar being there, but I can remember Mary Mallory having it. It had one great big window, then you went through the gate – a little hand gate, up past where Fred Kirby was and awd Mrs Atkinson had that – Bob Atkinson's mother and father had that. He was blind weren't he?
Rita	Yes.
Robert	They had that, and he had chickens, and she used ti bake, and I can remember I'd never seen one before, she had that great big copper cistern for hot water. It was just near door, and it was all polished up, and she used to mek bread, and after that Mrs Kirby used to mek it, didn't she? Awd Mrs Atkinson, she used to mek bread there and all sorts of things, and mi grandmother did down in Post Office Street. She used to mek bread and pastries, and I'll tell you which house she lived in – next ti passage, just before you get to paper shop, opposite Post Office.
Margaret	Rita was trying to reckon up how many shops there used to be in the village.
Rita	Oh yes, I have a little booklet that Uncle William Readhead brought out in 1900; there were loads and loads.

Robert	I'll tell you what there was, there was Jane Collins; there was Pat Mainprize's at end here; there was Nellie Bayes' there; then there was Tom Hindle's; awd Tant's; Jim Cross's fruit shop.
Rita	Then there was one before you got there, they sold fish and butter.
Robert	Aye, that was Mary Mallory's before that.
Ivy	Miss Stephenson's you mean, a lovely white slab.
Rita	Yes, she used to terrify me. Mi grandma used to send me for butter and she, Miss Hilda Stephenson, had very bad rheumatism, hadn't she? She did everything in slow motion and she looked at me all the time to see that I didn't do aught.
Ivy	And yet she did the most beautiful embroidery, didn't she?
Robert	And then you got down to there and there was Sam Duke and his kippers, and then you got down to Readhead's at opposite side of road, there was Matt Major's.
Ivy	Longden's.
Robert	Then you came to butcher's shop t'other side of Mrs Longden's.
Rita	Jack-a-Bailey's.
Robert	Aye, Jack-a-Bailey's, and then there was awd Will Hall's, where fish shop is that was a tailor's shop and hardware and crockery and that. Front door of that shop is on our front room wall there (in photograph). You went in one side into tailor's shop and t'other side wheea he sold pots and pans.
Ivy	And Mrs Bailey selling silks and cottons and wools.
Robert	And you kem to Jack Major's fish shop just as you went into Ship Yard, and Hannah Colley's at corner of Allison Lane and Mr Tomm's where Rock shop is, which was Jennis's later.
Rita	Yes, and there was a bakery in Chapel Street and there was somebody else in Chapel Street in 1900 and at least two in Tower Street.
Robert	I had a book, one I borrowed, and it was awd and, by gor, it was a good un. It telled of don't know how many pubs and beer off shops there were in Flamborough; about somebody wheea made hats and all sorts; and there was an awd caretaker in awd lighthouse showing folks round. Do you know this is true? I was reading it one day and John Willie kem in, he says, "You're very interested in that book". I says, "Yes, it's a very good book, Mr Bayes". He says, "Will you lend me it?" And I says, "Well,

I really can't 'cos it belongs to Russ Douglas". But in the end I did, and I never got it back again. The times I went down there; I used to go every week and say, "Have you found that book, Mr Bayes?" "No, I don't know where I've misplaced it." If it had been mine, I should have been aggravated; but I was ten times more aggravated when it wasn't mine. By gor, it was a good un. Do you remember Kirby's Bakery in Chapel Street? George – he's still living in Brid.

Rita   It was Bradey's when I remember. He came round with a tall white hat and a tray on his head.

Robert   Aye, he had it after Kirby. Aye, that was him; he was a Canadian. I'll tell you what, he was a rum lad was Kirby; he's nearly ninety now. We had a schoolmaster called Veeter: in fact he retired and lived in Woodcock Road, where our Jean used to live. This lad George Kirby, he was a bit awder than me – aboot oor Connie's age. He, George, was always on top of school. School had two gable ends and lads were always going up between 'em; and schoolmaster barred us all frae going up. I hadn't been up 'cos I was too young. George went up to retrieve balls and got two strokes with cane. He didn't take a bit of notice. Another day, schoolmaster copped George up again; so he browt him in, and I don't know how many strokes he gev him ower hand but he couldn't close his hands. There was just white marks across 'em: by, he didn't half hit him. When he caught him on the roof, George just jumped off roof onto porch roof and down into the gardens next to the school, and ran home. When he came back the next day, the master did slate him with his cane. George nivver kem back ti school for a fortnight, and Veeter daren't do aught about it. But I can tell you this, I once saw George at North Landing, a few years since, and I says tiv 'im, "It's a long time since old Veetar soled thu George". He says, "Aye, it is, but I can tell thu this, I nivver stepped out of line ageean; it cured me. I needed it because if I'd have fallen down there, maister would have got blame, and that was what he was frightened of. He ower did it I know, but I nivver stepped out of line ageean."

Margaret   Would it be Veetar that Laurie used to say, when it got dark, used to give them mental arithmetic?

Robert   No, it'd be 'Artley. I'll tell you what he used ti do, an all; he used ti ger up ti ten or it might have been twelve; he used ti write 'em on board, point, and you put your hand up and if you were right,

	you could go home. Laurie was quickest. But I used to practice it in awd toilet outside, and I used ti write 'em all up, doing like 'Artley did.
Margaret	Laurie used to say that they don't do that now but it did make your mind alert.
Robert	Oh it did, 'cos old 'Artley had all sorts he used to put on the board, and go as fast as he could reckon it. I'll tell you what, he had some good concerts. By, you remember when Saranne and Sally Bayes and school teachers were in 'em and all kids? We took one to Spa; we had it for three nights in succession here, then took it to Spa.
Margaret	And they used to read "A Christmas Carol".
Robert	Every year, and he used to act it as well – as he was reading it – Scrooge and Ghosts.
	Back end of year – October – started winter fishing. We'd be going, me, Harold Cross, George Leng Major – three or four of us, I'se think; maybe Ken as well. Before daylight, we'd set off ti go to Stacks, flithering, and it would be ten o'clock by time we got ti school or maybe later. And awd 'Artley used ti say, "Now, where have you been?" "Why, we've been flithering sir". "Alright, sit down; I suppose that'll be what you'll be doing when you leave here". Aye, by gor, we've had some cawd fingers an' all going s'early; as soon as you could see, you were there in rocks.
Ivy	I used to love winkles, but you daren't have 'em now because of pollution.
Rita	We all liked winkles and we all used to go to Hartendale on the beach because they were bigger winkles there and they tasted marvellous.
Robert	I'll tell you what – a fella who used ti come frae Hull, and take 'em back. He said, if you get winkles or mussels and the water is polluted and you don't feel like eating 'em, if you put 'em in sea water that isn't polluted and leave 'em a couple of tides, they'd be clear. But I wouldn't eat 'em from South Landing now, according to what they say. Before they put that outfall there, they went and tested Brid harbour – all that mud, biggest percentage was sewage. They built that outfall there and now there isn't any sewage in the harbour, but it all comes in at South Landing and Lighthouse. Aye, it's alright them talking, when they do owt like that they should have local knowledge to know which way tides

are setting. Now then, up Brid Bay you've flood and ebb same as everywhere else; but the flood tide only runs about a couple of hours, but there's six hours flood and six hours ebb. Now, your biggest tide is what we call ebb tide, for six hours then you get flood tide up just after low tide, and then you get what you call the outset, it's a freak ebb therefore most of your tide is coming down bay; that's what causes sandbank. One tide coming down and t'other going up, that's what causes that bank there. Now, when floods running, it's running south, more or less, and it eases away as it gets to high water. Now, when you get down to Flamborough Head, it's setting straight off frae cliff, straight off inti sea more or less. But as you travel south, behind that sandbank, it's setting straight in for Sewerby. It's setting off there and in there to Sewerby and that's why that sewage comes in. It owt ti 'ave gone off behind that if they'd wanted it to go, or else to have slighted it towards t'Head so it would go off. When you get off near that buoy, its further off now, its further east now; if you wanted to haul crab pots, you couldn't at high tide; you couldn't at flood 'cos they'd go down on flood. Now, when flood starts ti ease and your buoy comes up its setting right off, right where you want ti haul 'em, so you can't haul 'em, only if tide is very easy and you can pull 'em against; but you can haul as long as you like at ebb tide, you see. Tom Cowling once kem ti me, he was trawling for a lot of plaice there and he rang up, he says, "I can't understand it. I've trawled all ebb (he was running into Grimsby), but I can't trawl at high water". And I says, "No, you weean't Tom 'cos it'll be running right across your warps and tekking your net 'cos it's setting straight off ti sea."

Ivy	He did alright for a bit, didn't he?
Robert	Oh aye, he did; he learnt – he soon learnt like.
Margaret	The trouble with a lot of 'em now, is they don't know the tides like you did.
Robert	No, they don't.
Margaret	That's what Laurie said – with that lot that went under cliff; they should never have gone in.
Robert	If he'd been schooled by anybody here, instead of that lot at Brid, he'd never a been in there.
	There was David Freeman, only a young lad about sixteen, and our Roy was with us; and they'd just got east side of Five Arches Cave – there at North Landing; and there was somebody on cliff

top, and they were waving. They said there was somebody fast in the cave just at east side of that. So they went, and it was a lad and his father. They were fast in, outside entrance. They'd been in one of them great awd tractor inner tubes, and they'd washed in there with tide running through. It goes like a bike when it's flood tide. You can't tek a coble in when its flood tide. Tide was flowing and they didn't know what to do. They were stuck up in cliff and they had a rope fastened to this awd thing. I says, "Well, we'll have ti ger 'em somehow. It's a rum job gannin through there now". I says to our Roy, "Thu gan aft, looks tha; I'll look after engine. Thu get tiv anchor, Dave, and be ready to drop it". Our Roy says, "Isn't thu going ti drop it now?" "No", I says, "We can't get tiv 'em from here. We shall have to go where we can't see 'em; we'll have to go behind corner". So we did, and dropped anchor there, and we were going hard astern backing in, "David, thu has warp right ower her stern; thu wants it down very near inti or just ti side of her bow so flood'll catch on her bow and slew her stern that way". We did that and I had to be going full astern for flood coming thru that corner for ti get 'em in. But it wasn't engine that was keeping her in – if it hadn't 'ave been for us keeping it ower her bow so tide was pushing her in off bow – pushing her stern in. And we says, "Now, as soon as touch, jump and ger aboard". Our Roy pulled 'em aboard, and as soon as he was aboard, he let go of his tyre and David, he's a rum lad, he just took boat hook – it had a big point on it – and he just drove it down, it went right through it. It did crack and bunch. "Good lad", I says 'cos if it had gone off to sea after that, we should have had a lifeboat out after that. But you see, if anybody who had gone there hadn't understood that tide, they wouldn't have got in there.

Me and Bill Knaggs, and Bill Mitt were with us – we were tekking folks round King and Queen rocks, and it was best of flood. As we were going round corner, there was a skin diver. We didn't go right near him 'cos we didn't want to put him off but just near enough to shout at him. I says, "Hey mister, you won't be able to swim back to North Landing; its flood tide". He just put his hand up; he was going lovely – he was going the same way as the tide was going. We went to King and Queen rocks and on our way back, he was trying to swim back to North Landing. We were going by him and Bill Knaggs says, "Leeak at him". The swimmer was waving to us and we had to pick him up – the tide was taking him backwards, even though he was a strong swimmer. We pulled him in, and when we were passing North Landing he said he would like to be landed as he was cold. I says tiv him, "You'll have to wait till we've been round caves (at Thornwick) but when we landed at North Landing, he daren't get out of boat till we touched. Poor awd Bill Knaggs, he says, "Why, we telled tha".

Asked about games that were played at that time and Mr Leng told about "Nine Stone Merrill".

Robert	If you draw a square and, according to size of that square, you draw another square inside that one. And inside that second square, you put another small square inside the middle. You work from the middle and you can only work along one line. The longer you have played it, the longer you can make a game last. And Bob Otch is playing it in Brierley's book.
Margaret	Rita's been looking at old books and papers that belonged to Aunty Jinnie.
Rita	I've got some old church magazines of hers. The 1895 she must have kept because it's when my great grandmother Kingston, who was at Ocean View married James Wright from Wetwang. My great grandfather Kingston was killed. They got married in Sewerby, why I do not know.
Robert	Do you know where he was killed? I can drop a stone on spot. He was killed with one lighthouse right on top of the other lighthouse.
	Aye, I've heard mi father say, "This is where – I don't know his fost name – Kingston was killed".
Rita	Richard.
Robert	It would be your relation at North Moor.
Rita	Yes, it was my great Aunt Polly.
Robert	My aunt used to work there for her.
Robert	What was their last name?
Rita	Was it Beale?
Robert	Beale – that was it.
Rita	Aunty Kate was at Lount's farm; that one past Thornwick Farm [Hill Farm].
Robert	Then William Beale was at Lount's farm when mi aunt was there.

Rita	Then it was Aunty Kate not Aunty Polly.
Robert	Yes, mi aunt worked for Aunty Kate 'cos when mi aunt used to have a night off, mi mother used to go and sit wiv her for company.
Margaret	It's amazing, when you get talking to such people as you and Harold Stork and Phyllis, how many people have come into village through service in various houses and pubs.
Ivy	Phyllis *[Stork]* was in service, wasn't she?
Robert	Grandma Smith was; she was at the Rose and Crown. And awd Tom Stephenson's wife was, she was at a pub, not at Rose and Crown; and Bob Atkinson's wife, René, was – she was up at Thornwick pub..
Margaret	Hannah Emmerson was a maid somewhere.
Robert	Why, she was at Grange Farm, and I think awd Tom Stephenson's wife, Ken's mother, I think she came as a barmaid.
Rita	I know Hannah Emmerson could lug *[carry]* corn as well as any man; she was terrifically strong when she was younger.
Robert	Oh aye, strong. I'll tell you what, she used to bark pots same as any man. She used ti put copper on whilst he was at sea; she would have 'em all barked. Strong as a hoss was Hannah!
Rita	I found a lovely photograph of Jo-Billy (George William) Emmerson, Billy Gibbon, Coll and I've forgotten who the other one was.
Robert	Aye, why they used ti 'ave awd fish shop down there, didn't they? Can't you remember awd fish shop; I don't mean this one here.
Rita	I can remember that fish shop.
Robert	Why Coll had that 'cos we used to go in back spot and eat our fish and chips whilst some lads used ti put a bag ower chimney and smoke us out.
Margaret	We had it from Cath Chadwick and Harold Stork – one of those old cottages over there.
Robert	Dick Bayes did with our Doris and Bessie Bayes and Stella Stork and Hannah Overy. They were all in spot when John Willie *[Bayes]* lived where Dor Taylor lives now. They had an awd spot at back where lasses used ti go. Dick Bayes tied door and then put a bag ower chimney and wouldn't let 'em out till they were near suffocated.

Margaret	I know when George Nordass came to our house, and him and Laurie got on about nicknames and who was who you know. I said to Rita, "You'll have to have a list of nicknames and their real names so we don't offend anyone".
Robert	There was all sorts of nicknames. You see there'd be ever so many Knaggs – maybe with the same Christian name, and you had to distinguish you see. I know, when we fost got married awd Len Duke, he was skeining for me 'cos I was at sea. Ivy had to go and fetch mussels and she went to Duke's, knocked on door and asked, "Does Mr Hardhead live here?" And he said, "No, he doesn't, soft head".
Rita	You know when Les's wife, Jean, first came to England, we had always talked about Pish and Twit. Les took Jean to Sea Birds. He said, "Oh look, there's Pish and Twit".Jean went over and said, "Good evening, Mr Pish; good evening, Mr Twit". Our Les walked straight out!!
Robert	That's what Ivy did with Teddy Robson' fether; she called him Mr Brigham.
Ivy	Hetty Knaggs' father; they sent me to Bill Lou's and I asked for Mr Luiy. Well, I didn't know.
Robert	We nivver thought you see! You know these cottages where fishermen used to live [on Back Street Hill], was there another building next up to them?
Rita	Now, Aunty Jinnie used to say there were "Ellums" for those cottages. Fishermen used to keep their donkeys in and that; and certainly when you dig, its all bits of chalk. Aunty Jinnie always used to say that there were buildings there when she was young Mi dad was always grumbling it was hard to dig.
Robert	I think there has been some houses or "Ellums", that we called them. I saw in paper a year or two back that there was a swamp there on village green and it used to flood sometimes. It didn't used ti flood, it was a Mere. Will Cross, he used to live over far side of Green in far corner there, and one year was very hot, and Mere dried up except for a bit i'middle and mud. He had his high sea boots on and he was slapping eels out as thick as your arm with garthangle. If it had been cleaned out, there would still be eels in it. There was a culvert through there – a gutter – 'cos diving birds used ti come through there and that.

Rita	It was marvellous for playing on when it was frozen for playing "Tewy" *[a game of running around on the ice until it started moving up and down and eventually cracking]*.
Robert	Skating – very near all lads could skate in them days.
Rita	They must have skated in the old days because Aunty Jinnie and Aunty Annie had skates; we've still got them.
Robert	I've seen cars all stationed round with their lights on, trained on Mere, so folks could see to skate. It seemed to be every winter then. When I was a kid, I once knew ice in Mere for sixteen weeks. I in't going to say you could skate on it. Lads were going on ice ships, ice was si thick it would carry you even when it was breaking up. It was nearly Easter when it thawed. It was a beautiful day; I can see Ern Major and awd Bradey, him as had cake shop in Chapel Street, skating on skates that curled up in front. Bradey had been used to skating down rivers in Canada. Awd Anfield, Tatty Anfield, he used to come ti skate.
Ivy	I know I was once looking out of back bedroom window – it was Spring when we first came here – and I saw all these little black things all over Mere, and a car passed by and they all dived under. They were all frogs; it was full. I've counted as many as twenty six frogs on our path. It used to be full of frogs – the Mere.
Robert	It used to be full back end of summer; you could hear 'em croaking on a night. Fisherlads learned to sail ships in Mere. They all had great ships like that, that fishermen had made. They all had a lug sail like a coble and fishermen would be at corner there, watching you and some of 'em would come and show you how to do. There was one fella there, I don't know who he was, perhaps a visitor, and he would go and stand at t'other side. You didn't sail your boat straight before the wind, you had more a side wind, and it wasn't the boat that could get across the Mere fastest but the one that could go nearest to him. That was what he wanted and that's how lads learnt ti sail.
Rita	Mi Grandfather Cross always used to say that if only they would clear the Mere out, they could make a proper park of it, when they first started planting those trees on the green just before the war.
Robert	It was a big Mere. If you could throw straight across it you were a good thrower. We've a picture of it haven't we? If they'd just cleaned it out, they could have run a bit of concrete round it if

they'd wanted. But if they'd cleaned it out as they owt ti 'ave done, they could have had an awd fisherman in a rowing boat and skiffs or lartle rowing boats; they could a'done very well in there in Summer.

Harold Stork

Harold was born in Flamborough but lived in Spurn where his father was on the lifeboat. He came to Flamborough to live with his grandparents so that he could go to school. He worked as a driver and mechanic.

Harold   There was a dispute in the village about the road leading down to South Landing beach. Mr Burton of Cliffe House claimed the road belonged to him. He closed the gate and put a chain from the post through the gate, and padlocked it. Somebody came back to the village and fetched a hammer and smashed the lock and there was a row over that. When all came out it was his for a matter of fifty or sixty yards through the gate. The gate had been erected by the Parish Council so the gate weren't his, but to prove that land was his through the gate he had to lock it once a year. Tom Woodhouse asked me about it. Did I work on it? I did and it must have belonged ti Parish Council because when I worked for that steamroller we did it frae top to bottom, 'cos they put all grey slag down. When it cums heavy rain it washes all away. But there's a right of way for fishermen 'cos they can't get to sea without going down there.

When I was living wi' mi grandmother and grandfather they had herring cobles as well as ordinary cobles to go crabbing in. Herring cobles were bigger than cobles they used to go crabbing in. They all used to be laid up as you go down, right opposite the lifeboat house on that piece of flat ground there. All of 'em tipped upside down and then when it was drawing near herring time they all used to go down – it didn't matter whether it was

Sunday, Monday, what day it was – with a lot of tar, mek a fire, melt their tar and brush all stem of boat. And if it wanted new irons on, Wiles blacksmiths used to go doon and put new skids on, ti launch it wiv.

The herring season would start up at Berwick and they worked their way down. They didn't do anything at Bridlington. They used to go herringing as far up as Whitby from here but they didn't land at South Landing wi' their herrings, they all used ti go into Whitby with 'em. Uncle George, being the eldest of mi father's family, I can just see him now coming home wi' a big square tin box. Mi grandmother used ti bake at weekend ti fill it wi' pies and all different stuff for him ti tek away wi' him. They used ti walk ti Flamborough Station if John Hall's hadn't a trap going, humping that, ger on train there and up to Scarborough, then up ti Whitby. Sometimes it was a fortnight afore he came back. It was full of herrings when he kem back.

The Scots lasses followed the boats down. They used ti barrel the herrings, salt 'em down an' send 'em ti Germany. They eat 'em raw there. These herring cobles worked from Whitby and Scarborough but not Filey, and finished up at Lowestoft or Yarmouth somewhere. Herring season used ti fall after crabbing and before fishing started. They used to go herringing till end of October.

Jack Major used ti have little fish shop.

Phyllis   When Harold used to come off the buses, last thing, he used to get six fishes an paper full of chips for sixpence. It would last us two days.

Harold   Jack Major used to say, "Call at shop when you get bus put away". George Thompson had garage then and previous to it being a garage was Wesleyan Chapel. When we lived i'Chapel Street, Bill Mitt – Bill and Rachel Major's father – used to come for me and tek me across to hear band practice and we used ti get upstairs and inti gallery. That was before they built the new Wesleyan Chapel opposite the doctor's surgery.

Noo then, I was talking ti Cameron's wife, Betty, and she said, "You were a big Wesleyan weren't you?" and I said, "Aye, 'cos we were med ti go three times on a Sunday". That was the big Wesleyan I was! I said, "Where did organ go? A beautiful organ". Betty said it went to Bridlington Boys' Grammar School. Why, there was some brass rails and plaques as well. There was a plaque of a relation of mine, William Stork. Betty said, "Oh, I have that". William Stork used to have Thompson's farm and where them houses and library are built now and Bayes had their coal – which was a big grass field wi' cart sheds – there was a gate leading into yon side of Village Hall; they used to call it Stork's Barn. Y'know it's hard to realise, just press a button and you can see it all back again.

Talking about photographs, I have that one of lifeboat and another one I got off Pallister at Sewerby. He said he'd had it a long time and he didn't know who it was. Did I know? I said, "Aye, I know – Jack Barclay and his sister Sarah with carrier cart." It's an old two wheeled cart and a little pony in it. It was took coming frae Brid past Jack Agar's towards Dykes, there's a bit of bend in there, turn left through a gate that is there. You winded round and came out at that other gate in bottom just off main road. There was two brothers and three sisters; the eldest brother, Crofton, was blind and he used ti stand up at North Landing in summer, on one o'them fish stands reading Braille. "The Lord this and that" and he used ti have a red handkerchief with a few coppers on the ground near him and visitors used to throw coppers at him. Then one of his sisters used to walk up and tek him home. Jack Barclay, the other brother, was a bit of a mis-fit and liked a drink. Now then he was carrier on this two wheeled cart. He couldn't get much in it but he used to bring prescriptions and medicines back, and if you had any pigeons you didn't want, you used to tek 'em round ti 'im and say, "How much you gonna give us?". His head was permanently over to one shoulder and he couldn't talk properly and he used to say f-f-f-fourpence meaning fourpence. Fourpence for a pigeon! Now Sarah, I don't know what she did, but there were two other sisters at home besides her and they ran a laundry. They used to do white sheets and starched collars and sike like. They didn't do owt for poor folk – they had to do their own. They used an old flat iron on the fire.

When we used ti live next door to them, Sarah used to listen to everything we did and grumble about it next day. I had a spaniel dog and she said, "Young man I want you. Young man, your dog has ruined my Golden Rod!" (She was very abrupt always) I didn't know that Golden Rod was a flower of some sort, and dog had been putting his leg up, so I had to keep him in after that. The reason why Sarah went to Brid with Jack was because he'd get kettled at Brid. If he got hod o'threepence he'd be in pub for a pint. He used to park his pony and cart in Seabirds buildings, and lads used to gan on a neet and get cart oot, get one or two of 'em yoked inti cart. Other lads used to get in and they used to leave it in the middle of the street and somebody would have to put it back into shed again. Mind you, it was difficult in those days, and it was handy him bringing stuff back frae Brid. If you wanted any wool and they hadn't it here in Flamborough, if you wrote it on a paper they would bring it frae Brid.

The doctor used to come through from Brid in a pony and trap and it was half a crown for a home visit. There used to be two or three doctors come. There was a Dr Kirkland and a Dr Whitehead and there was another one used to ride a pony. First surgery was at Screeton's, at Vida's – can you remember her? Then, at Billy Collins' for Dr Watson.

We lived near Wesleyan Chapel. The land next to it was all allotments when I was a lad. We used to etti go there on a Saturday and dig the gardens and our Tom got a start going ti pub with Norman Major and them. Mi father used ti cum up as soon as you'd had your dinner. "You're not to go away, I want to see you. Get that spade and you can gan and droon your sorrows i'garden a'back o'Chapel". He had ti go and spade garden ower. Tom says, "What about our Harold, is he coming?" No, mi father says ah've a job here for 'im. I had a job in back spot mekking crab pots and tarring 'em.

| Margaret | Was Allison Lane all fishermen's cottages? |
| Harold | Nearly all fishermen. All Chapel Street was. All them houses between Chapels they called Pockley Row, because somebody called Pockley had been first fisher people to go in there. There was mi grandfather's in there and Mark Major's, Albert Emmerson's father lived in there, and Albert Duke's. Allison Lane was mostly fisher people. When I look down those back ways, there used to be a straight go through ti bottom, now there's walls put up. It's probably illegal 'cos fishermen had a right of way to take donkeys and carts down. When we lived in Allison Lane it was that little double fronted one and it had a beautiful washhouse where mi mother used ti bait lines. Next to it was what we called 'ass ellum' where donkey was kept, therefore there was right of way for a donkey with lines and that would be a good width. Norah Knaggs and her mother and father lived next door to us coming up this way. |

There used to be a well covered by a big flag with a ring in and on a Monday morning, if mi father weren't going to sea, he used to lift this flag and mi mother and Mrs Knaggs used get a bucket with a rope on and get water out to wash with. Same further down. Billy Chadwick, his sister, his mother and father lived other side of us and they had a flag ti get water. If one was dry, the other used ti say, "Come and get water out of mine". And they used to share it like that, pulling water up.

Phyllis   Do you know Chadwicks had an ellum and it was beautiful inside, they used to let it as a cottage.

Harold   We did rum things like tying door handles together and got folks to run you. Things like that. At Mary Greasey's cottage once, we went wi' Sam and Tom Woodhouse – a big youth. Sam said, "She knows tha Tom". Tom says, "She won't when I've finished", and turned his coat inside out, red lining showed and took a rope and tied it round watter barrel. All of us pulled and pulled it ower and watter went all ower but we did it once too often and it broke all latts out o'barrel. It had rotted wi' been up si lang, so we had policeman up at school.

It was always upstreeters playing doonstreeters at football. Doonstreeters were mostly farm labourers' children. And we had a cap ti buy, one and sixpence was this cap with a red piece on front for doonstreeters and sea (upstreeters) had a blue piece. And old Saranne Chadwick used to shout, "Come on the sea'".

Old Veeter, schoolmaster, used to say, "When you meet Mr Hall and Mr "So and So" you say good morning". These were all school governors, you know. I allus remember somebody said we could play football in their field. It was the one at top of Carter Lane. We had to play at this end where Flamborough Football team played. Sam, ringleader, says, "We shall 'ave some goalposts to buy". Then poor old Tant Fell giv us a lot of canes that he brought off sand at Thornwick, washed up. We got them tacked with a piece across and we used them. And then it would come we'd a'ti buy boots, but they wouldn't buy boots, they'd buy shorts. So we used ti gather jam jars up at Garends – from the tip up there. Scavengers tipped everything up there y'know, before they got a field to put it in. And if you could find a Hartley's jam jar, they were grey stone and underneath 'em was a lighthouse, you got a ha'penny for them from Nelly Bayes and Jennis's, where rock shop is now. Sam says, "We'll all gather up at tea-time and we'll see what we can find ti sell to get money". There was about twenty or thirty of these ere jars; we had to fetch a bag from our house ti put 'em in. I'm in charge of these jars in bags and there were some bottles as well and they went ti pub and there was ha'penny on lemonade bottle that had a glass ally in top which you pressed in wi' yer thumb. We went round and got rid of 'em all at Tom's and we got rid of other lot at Nelly Bayes'. All except lemonade bottle and nobody wanted it, it warn't theirs, it belonged to a Brid firm or summat. So Sam said, "We'll hev a bit of fun wi' it".

So we fills it up at that tap at end of Dick Bayes' yard at comer of School Lane and High Street, presses this glass stopper and there was some people lived up somewhere North Landing way – where John Emmerson lives now – called Playfoot. They'd two brothers – one was errand boy at Sid Coates, the other called Harold, a bit younger than me. And there was Ken Stevenson and quite a lot of us, Albert Emmerson, Dick and Ron Traves, but they were only little uns agin us. There was a tin shed opposite where Ivy Leng lives, and Fred Kirby's lived up there but, before then, old Mr Atkinson lived up back of there, Robert Atkinson's father. There was this old tin shop and two old lasses that lived in them cottages, one called Mary Mallory. There used to be two or three eggs on a saucer in winder and two or three tomatoes on another. Them two old sisters went ti Wesleyan Chapel, and they wore them old Astrakan collars. There was an awd lad lived in this end un called Sparrow Checks. Sam says we'll hev a bit of fun. Sparrow Checks was an elderly man, but a good runner for his age. Sam says we'll throw bottle in ti grate. Our Tom was wiv us, there was into teens of us. I said, "I aren't having anything to deea wiv it 'cos we'll get belted at home". Dick Traves says, "I aren't either", but Ron says, "I am, who's going to throw it in?" Sam says to our Tom, "Thu throw it in, Tom", and Tom says, "No", he says to Playfoot, "Thu throw it in", and he says, "Alright then". Sam says, "When I oppen door, Sparrow Checks' wife will be sat there knitting and he'll be sat at t'other side and he weean't see thu. When I oppens door about that, throw it inti fire". We all got ready for running, Sam oppened door and lad threw bottle.

By it did crack and bang on fire and glass flew all ower. We set off ti run and he kem out, he had long hair flowing out back ere, and I'm stood watching. I'd nowt to do with it, me and Dick Traves. But Ron, wi' being littlest, he couldn't run as fast as t'others and when he got to top there, Woodcock Road end of Donkey Trod, there used to be a big blue boulder sat in road. Them boulders were to stop hosses and carts knocking corners off houses. We were all jumping ower it 'cos gate was shut, and Ron Traves jumped it just as Sparrow Checks jumped it and he got 'od of Ron by middle of his back but he had ti let go and Ron got away. We didn't know n'more, we cleared off home, but we hadn't been in house long when mi father cum in. "Now then which of you's been at Sparrow Checks?" I said, "I ain't", and Tom says, "I ain't". Then mi father says, "Now, no lies". Our Tom says, "Why I ran but I didn't throw bottle in". Father says, "Now't n'mer aboot it till timorrow when policeman cums up ti school you'll etti speak truth up there". Next day policeman, Mr Bryan, cum up ti school and them that had been there had to line up up out there – all them fishermen's sons and footballers. "Were you there?" I had ti say yes, but I didn't run, I was only watching 'em, but I gat same as them as was! "Well", he says, "Mr Mainprize – that was Sparrow Checks real name – he's in a very bad way and he couldn't go to sea today. He's split his head and all his face and nose". By, it was a mess! He'd tumbled over this boulder he'd tried to jump and missed and fell full length.

They were rotten tricks ti do really. We nivver did get any shorts, that was finish. They've nowt like that at school nowadays, upstreeters playing doonstreeters.

When Mr. Veeter came in 1923, I had one or two school prizes; he had 'em all signed. Mr Moreton was vicar and he used to come ti school and tek a class at a time. He was very strict and you had to listen and a lad sat next ti me called Dicky Tarry *[Will and Nelly Overy's brother]*, he died when he was about ten years old, he tumbled into Mar and got wet and got pneumonia. I was sat next to him and he was a rum un for talking to me and I'd ti keep answering him as he kept saying "eh" and bumping me. So Moreton started looking and all of a sudden he walked down middle and got 'odden my head and Dicky's head and he banged 'em ti'gither. By gor, I got a headache. I went home and I didn't want any dinner. Mi grandmother says, "What's matter?" I says, "I have a headache". Mi grandfather says, "Whose been hitting thu?" I says, "Parson". "Parson, what's he done?" I told 'im, and he says, "Right I'll be there". Ah says, "Thu needn't bother 'cos he won't be there till timorrow morning". Tomorrow morning mi grandfather was there waiting for him, "I'll bang tha bloody 'ead if it happens ageean". Another awd lass cum to be a school teacher, Miss Bent, she lived up where Albert Emmerson's lived agin Chapel; she was lodging there. A Miss Huddleston was there, she used to tek all school teachers in that used ti come. There was a lad in Post Office Street – Tom Cross and Ben and Grace. Tom was in same class as me, he sat in front of me, and because he didn't know, he hadn't been listening. "What did I say Cross?" "I don't know, Miss". "You weren't listening were you?" "No, Miss". "You will before I've finished with you", and she picked up his slate and hit him on head with it. There was bits of slate all ower show. By, she kem up to school did his mother and didn't half give 'er some stick. Little things you think of like that.

Old Mrs Waud lived in that comer house in High Street. She was mi grandfather's sister, they called her Mary Eleanor and they'd a fairly big family – Will, Jack and four girls. There was Beatty and Linda and there was one different from all the others. She married somebody from away called Stead. Just like her George and Vera had ginger hair but Jack were'nt. But old Will Waud had ginger hair and so did Mrs Barnes. Cissie and mi Aunt Clara and Iris Cross's mother, together you would think they were sisters, as like as peas. They were cousins. There was another one married to a coastguard called Barnes up at Lighthouse. This girl married him and they went to live at Scarborough. Then there was another one, Nellie Hudson's mother. Anyhow as a little lad going to school, about five years old, Nellie was just about my age. I lived with mi grandmother and grandfather in Chapel Street 'cos mi father and mother were at Spurn at Lifeboat Station, so I had to stay at Flamborough so I could go to school. Mi Aunt Clara used to say, "Right, we're going up Allison Lane to see Nellie and you'll be able to play with her", and mi grandfather used ti say, "Call and see our Sarah before you go up". That was in the comer, Mr Waud's wife. Anyhow I can just see it now, me and Nellie playing snakes and ladders on floor till we fell out. One thing I used to look forward to, Nellie was always a little bit chesty and her mother used to mek some cough medicine on her own, did Mrs. Hudson. I used to look forward to this cough medicine. I remember father, Walter Hudson, he comes into it in this respect. Old Mr and Mrs Nordass lived i'Allison Lane. John Nordass, well they brought him up; where he cum from I was too young to ask, but he was ever such a nice man. I remember

I joined Buffs with him and he made it very comfortable and pleasant going there. How he came into it I don't know, but he kem to live with them as a little lad and they brought him up and he went to Flamborough school. I can't think what relation Joyce will be to Waud's as her mother was a Nordass and old Mr Waud was never called Will or William he was always called Obb Waud. I think that Joyce's grandmother must have been a sister of old William Oxley Waud. The only people he employed were all relatives, relatives kem first. Our Tom asked for a job and he said, "Oh, yes you're a Stork, when do you want to start?" and that was it.

You're on about Laurie's relatives, where you live now *[Greenside Cottage]* and next to it, the Drill Hall. Then there was nothing up School Lane but a row of big high boulders and on top of the bank it was all soil – three layers of barbed wire to stop kids going ower into the gardens. It ran round where Jim Fell had that first bungalow built and to the Women's Institute and down to your house with boulders. This was called Gough Dyke after Laurie's uncle Billy Gough. Billy Gough always used to grow oats in that piece of land, they were for the horses. After he died, Jim Smith tumed it into allotments. All his mates in the village had an allotment there and then they built some higher wire round so lads frae school couldn't go in and pinch carrots. Talking about Village Green I've seen hares running across Gough Dyke coming down Dyke and across village green. Laurie's mother and such girls came from York and the West Riding for jobs as maids. George Willie Emmerson's wife, Hannah, came to Shipley's at Grange Farm as a maid. There was a Jack Mainprize, his wife came from Wales and she got work up this way and went to Grange Farm to work as well. Now then, Norah Gibbon and Annie, their mother, worked at Grange Farm, all in their turn. They only stayed a year, same as farm lads only stayed a year. That farm had sixteen horses which meant there was eight lads living in, each lad did two horses. And they always had two maids but I don't know what two were together but they left at the end of the year to go to a different farm. Mi mother originated frae Driffield and she came to Dog and Duck, barmaid cum scrubber out and all the lot, you name it, for five bob a week and her food. We get some laughs about it all because in one of those cottages round in Post Office Street was a barber's shop and I think it's the one that's Adrian Williams' side of passage. They didn't do much trade because none of the fishermen could afford to go there and get a shave in them hard times. Anyhow he did a bit of hair cutting and shaving with old slasher and they called him Mr Tunnicliffe, but he was no relation to any of these Tunnicliffes that originated in Flamborough. Mi mother said, landlord said to her, "Go round to Post Office and post that letter, and on your way back call and ask Nimrod if he can cut my hair at two o'clock", and she says, "Alright". Nimrod was nickname for him and he didn't like it. Mi mother called at barbers and said, "Good afternoon. Mr Osgood of Dog and Duck wants to know if you can cut his hair, Mr Tunnicliffe?" He was kettled up half of time, and he says, "What did he say to you?" She said, "Go and ask Nimrod can he cut my hair at two o'clock". "Nimrod!" he says, "What are you talking about, my name is Tunnicliffe". You know you had to be careful with names. When we first got married, I said to Phyllis whatever you do be careful when you're talking ti folks, they're all related to one another.

There was a semi-circle of old cottages opposite school, right up to the stile you got over to walk across that field to Lighthouse Road. I had a walk round recently and I had to come away from hedge, a different way from what it used to be. They are bound to leave a way. The way the farmer's left it, it's bad walking; instead of little bridge there used to be, there's a couple of planks put across. Violet Dowse and her mother lived there right bang opposite school. There was just two cottages together and some people called Wise lived there. Old Ted Wise was a shepherd, and his wife and Frank and Robert lived there. There was a girl called Winnie but she went away, and Robert went to Australia, but Frank stayed here. Then you came to those cottages where John Stork lives. They were Coastguard cottages belonging to Coastguard Station because then I should say there were six or eight coastguards in Flamborough. Only two lived up at Lighthouse as there were only two cottages up there then and they added some more later. There was a little paddock behind the cottages and it belonged to John Hall. He used to have Royal Mews. There was nothing but horses in there. He had two white horses for weddings and two or three black uns for funerals, no cars you know. Leaving there and coming round, there was cottage where Chapmans lived. They had a big family. There was three or four girls, one them was Walter Shipley's wife, Jinny, and another one married and went to live at Bempton; there were three girls altogether. Then there was Jack, George, Fred and Will Chapman. How they all lived in that cottage I don't know. Then there was Violet's grandfather and grandmother lived next door and then a bit further on was a big gap and it led into a yard and Rob Leng, Alfred Leng's father, kept horses in there – a white horse and a brown horse. He pulled boats up at South Landing with them. When fishermen landed he used to be down there with horses and chains. At stern of cobles there's two rings and he used to fasten chains to boats, then fishermen used to put skids under and that's how they pulled boats up. The next cottage after those stables was Violet's mother and father. They had two girls, Violet and another; they were twins, but one of 'em died. In those days, if they couldn't afford a hearse from Hall's Mews, lads used to carry 'em on their shoulders and I've had that job – me and Albert Emmerson and Sam Chadwick. Threepence each to carry a coffin on your shoulder, four or six of you.

They were happy days though. After Violet's mother and father's house was an old lady and two daughters, and we called her Mary Greasey. I don't know what her proper name was. There was Lizzie and she married a chap called George Claxton, he was frae Grindale way and he had scavenger's job. They were all earth closets then and he had a horse and cart, emptying all closets – terrible – coming up Allison Lane with a bit of hill, water dripping out of cart! I always remember 'cos when Atkins' Blue Buses started in 1926, I got a job with 'em. I was hired at North Landing, at North Star and Ernie Collins got me a job with conducting and George Woodhouse was a driver, and his brother, Herbert Woodhouse was too. I always remember George saying, "Come out and go on bus with me up to Lighthouse". And when we got round Lighthouse Corner he used let me drive up to Lighthouse to practise my driving. I remember us coming back and we were a bit late and on the bus we had three or four people who worked in Brid and one or two who worked in the village. Now then: Arthur Wiles' mother, (she was from somewhere down south, near Portsmouth way and his father was a coastguard, and she got a job at Readhead's paper shop and that's how she got on with Jack Wiles), with him being on buses, she was on this bus. I wasn't driving, thank the Lord, and as we came past Allison Lane, George Claxton came out with scavenger's cart and went broadsides on to the bus and tipped all out on ti road. Ooh!

He nearly got the sack did George Woodhouse and it warn't his fault. Old George Claxton wasn't too bright, he was a bit short of a shilling, and he just came straight out, never mind looking either way. Bang into George! Bus was buckled up, but we got to Brid alright.

Behind Mary Greasey's and three cottages was all green fields, and fencing it off was steel bars and wire threaded through 'em as also was opposite Dog and Duck back way. From the end house to Post Office corner and then right down Carter Lane to the very end was a good big wide verge, and fishermen used to take their donkeys down there and fasten 'em to these rails to eat grass in summer.

When Mar was there full of water it was alright, but in summer when it dried up there was nothing to see but old bike frames. And in winter when there was plenty of water, they used to say there was a spring under as well. If it froze ower and you went skating you had to mind you didn't hit anything or you were down.

It's all altered has Flamborough. I can only go back to about 1914, but the population would be no more than six or seven hundred. I don't know what it is now. But that's why when you talked about one you talked about another, the population was so small. It was made up of farm labourers and fishermen, apart from the odd tradesman, you see. The main diet was fish. It's no disgrace, isn't poverty; it's nothing to boast about either, but at the same time you had to go through it. I've gone to school wiv a pair of mi auntie's shoes with high heels chopped off.

I remember a schoolmaster after First World War called Mr Potts. He introduced football games. We used to ask Mr Woodcock if we could use his field and he warn't a bad awd stick, he let us. Every time I kicked ball, up into air went mi shoe as well. "I think Stork", says Mr Potts, "You'd better go in goal".

Now, round here in bad weather, seasons have altered as well, because beginning in middle of February right through till end of March, there was nothing but cold easterly winds and snow and they couldn't get ti sea to earn a penny. Some wouldn't borrow and some got groceries on tick until they could pay for it. Now then, mi father once cum in and with me being oldest of four of us, I got all the mucky work every time. "Go when you leave school up to gamekeeper's with this bass here [a woven *straw bag]* Wait at door and the gamekeeper's wife'll give you it back. I was to go up to gamekeeper's at Danes Dyke house, that was a chap called Freeman, and that was when Bolton had Danes Dyke but he didn't used to live there always. There was always someone who kept it going all winter and he used ti cum in summer. He was a bachelor and he'd bring his nephews with him and that. When he kem, he had to be captain of cricket club just because he was Lord of Manor. I used to tek this bass, knock at door and wait. She used to say, "Wait a bit sonny", and she used ti give you a bun and a drop of milk and when she kem back a couple of rabbits were in bass. That was because we'd had fish Sunday dinner previous ti that. We'd had a little cod baked in a dripping tin and a few roast potatoes to it, and that was your Sunday dinner. They would throw it at you today.

Bolton owned most of Flamborough – all Allison Lane, all Chapel Street and most of the farms. He had two gamekeepers and he used ti cum occasionally for a shoot. He'd come about a fortnight, before Christmas, to have a big shoot, and there was plenty of game. When he had this shoot, one of gamekeepers and a woodsman kem down with a pony and trap and all on bars across of trap was hung rabbits, hares, pheasants and partridges. And they'd say, "Here you are, Landlord has sent you a Christmas box". All of a sudden, in 1926 "Have you heard the latest?" "No. What?" "Bolton's gone bust". I think what happened – his brokers transferred his shares from tea into rubber and within six weeks they went wallop and he was sold up. Some chaps cum round and we moved from Allison Lane into Chapel Street then, a'gin one of them passages, that one nearest the Chapel. We lived in first house on right of that passage. I was born in that house 'cos we'd lived in it before. Now Bolton sent two solicitors round, "You'll have heard about your landlord? He's giving you first choice to buy your house". Chapel Street houses were £75, why, we hadn't 75 pence! There were six of us and you did well to live, nivver mind buying houses. Mi grandfather and mi uncles lived in that house where Bond's lived, coming down towards Primitive Chapel and they were £100. Jessie Woodhouse, school teacher bought ours and we had to pay rent to her. It was only about two shillings a week.

When I was twelve years old, I had to get up at four o'clock in winter, pitch black dark and there was no electricity then. You had a paraffin lamp or a candle in a bottle and mi mother used to say, "Gan along ti thee grandmother's, she'll be waiting for you". There was a big enamel bowl full of mussels and a knife and a little basin or a colander – that was best 'cos water drained away, and there was a big tub. A grape barrel was favourite that you begged frae greengrocers'. You used to have it near fire and these old rugs. You used to mek 'em in winter, one clipped old clothes and t'other had an old clothes peg, poking the clips into sacking. They used mussel bags washed out, and another one to back it with.

"Here you are, there's a bowl of mussels, get on wi' 'em as fast as you can 'cos your mother will be waiting for you". I used to plug in, opening these mussels and chucking old shells into barrel and steam used to be going up chimney. Mussel shell barrel used to smell! When you'd got your colander full, you used to put mussels into a bucket half full of cold water to steep, wait a minute, and I used to go inti kitchen and get a lump of prune pie or apple pie and a mug of cocoa. I'd get that down and I used to be coming home to mi mother's, quarter past to half past five. I used to get back home and mi mother had another bowl full there already waiting. Not satisfied wi' that, if I went fast, I got another half bowl to skein. I've been running up to that school as bell's been ringing and I've had all black marks of mussel water all round mi wrists, smelling terrible. She used to say, "You needn't keep looking at clock, it isn't nine yet". I've been running up there as fast as I could to get into line as bell was ringing and a bit of breakfast in mi hand. They don't know they're born today.

It was even hard when we got married; wages were only twenty-five shillings or thirty shillings a week.

Phyllis   We didn't have a mattress when we first got married. I'd saved up for sheets and other things like pots and pans. I got eight clean sacks and I washed them and filled them all with straw, sewed them all together and we slept on them. My bottom came through latts 'cos they were latts (laths) on the bed in those days.

You know them old chalk cottages on the Green, Major Cross' father and mother and them all lived there. There was an old lad lived on there called Ralph Lowther and somebody says, "Mrs.Cockerill's flitting". That was Jack Cockerill's mother – she couldn't look after herself. "She's going to live with them, so her house will be empty, go and see about it". So I went to see about it, one and six a week, alright. The old lady left us an old rocking chair and a few oddments. Of course it was a home. Mi mother kem up – she was a bit "umpy" when I left home 'cos they missed your bit of money. She says, "If you mix some paste I'll bring some wallpaper, a big bowl full". We mixed it and put it on pantry floor while next morning and when mi mother cum next morning it had all gone, rats had eaten it! There was nowt but paw marks and mucky black marks in it. We had no more money to buy any more, so anyhow a neighbour who lived up there, Alice Scotter, says, "Worried wi' rats up here, lad, I ought ti have telled yer". Oh dear, what a start ti married life! Mi mother says, "I'll mix some more". Nellie Bayes had that shop opposite Rose and Crown, so I had to go to Nellie Bayes' and have another start. We papered it and everything and we were saving up for curtains, and in the end we got saved up. Anyhow toilets and everywhere were alive wi' rats and there were cats galore but they couldn't keep 'em down.

Harold
"Never mind lad", said Alice, so we put Phyllis's new mackintosh down to block the bottom of pantry door to stop 'em coming in. They chavelled it all away! "Never mind, lad things'll mend", says Alice, she was a jolly soul you know. "Just before bedtime, give us a knock and I'll bring our old tabby in for you", so bedtime came and in Alice comes wi' this tabby cat. Off we went to bed wi' candlesticks, but during the night there was such hullabaloo as you never heard. Phyllis says, "What's happening?" I says, "Either cat's killing rats, or rats is killing cat". I lit a candle and cum downstairs and I could have cried. It's a wonder I didn't kill it. All cups were knocked off table, all was all over floor, and cat was hung in curtains, which were ripped to pieces. What had happened, cat had been frightened being in a strange place. All he'd been trying to do was get out – he'd been frightened, too many rats for him! Well the rats used to sit at the fireside with old Mrs Cockerill. Jossy lived up there then and Hetty and all of them. Freddy Atkinson's mother as well – I'd think that youngest lad, Jim, would be born up there at Highlands. You see all that lot has been pulled down.

It isn't Flamborough as it was. You've got to see it on photographs. Fred Chapman would be a year younger than me and Albert Emmerson. Albert and me played together. Chapmans lived over there and they were a real big family, Fred was youngest but one. There was only another lad called Will younger than him. I can just see old Mrs Chapman, Mary Ann, come across – Albert and Fred Chapman would be cousins – with newspaper and three pieces of apple pie wrapped up in it. "He's just starting school this morning, look after him won't you, lads". "Yes, alright we'll see to him". "I'll come across this afternoon and see him again". Fred says, "You'll come and see me, won't you?" She did and apple pie again. Happy days! It has all altered, it's hard to believe.

Same down behind Church you know, that was all fields and when you go across Maitlands to Dykes, that's another right of way and should never be done away with. It belonged to Woodcock, Rex Stiles' granddad. And on the left he used to let cricketers have it. You went through that big gate behind Hartendale Farm and the cricket pitch was on the left. Tom Woodhouse's father and George Bayes were very good cricketers and your grandfather, Rita, George Cross, he witnessed same thing as me 'cos he umpired regular. Tom Woodhouse was a walloping big man and when he hit a ball wi' bat it did go a long way and wi' being big fields and long grass, balls took some finding. He hit a ball one day when they had just turned hosses out and knocked a hoss eye out. They had to have vet come out on his bicycle. I think they lost this hoss at finish, so he stopped 'em playing cricket.

Then of course Mr. Woodcock got a lot of land belonging Bolton. He was bailiff for Bolton and he had first chance and bought Hartendale Farm and Ocean View Farm. With him being bailiff, any farmer that wanted a new gate on a field or a barn repairing, he told them to go to old Oxley Waud. There was another joiner working in village, Bill Sunley, but he was only in a small way working on his own, but Waud's had two or three joiners so all farms that needed repairs, Waud's did them and bill went into Mr Bolton's solicitors and they checked them. And they've never looked back.

We'd nothing to start us so we couldn't mek any progress – too much competition when we started. There was some funny laws in them days.

Now, as I've said South Landing, always had a big gate went across and they always said it belonged ti Council and the road down belonged ti Council. Tom Woodhouse kem to me one day said, "I've been told that you worked on that road with the steamroller man, can you tell me what year it was and for how long". I said,

"Yes I could, it was in 1929". I'll tell you how it kem about, I was out of work and I dropped in for old Mr Woodcock one day. Atkins Blue Buses, later bought by East Yorkshire, wouldn't tek you on as a driver unless you were twenty-one and I was two or three weeks short of twenty one, so what happened, I got sack. Cum when I was twenty-one they'd take me on for summer, but this was winter when you wanted work. Mr Woodcock asked me what I was doing, I told him I'd got the sack and why, and he asked me if I was looking for work and what kind did I want. I told him I was not bothered what, dustcart or anything as long as I was working. There were a lot of us at home and they were always at you, you had to be bringing something in. "Why, ger on your bike and go down to Brid to St John's Avenue and see Corrie Johnson and I'll give him a ring in meantime". Corrie Johnson was architect. "Yes, I have a job for you; Mr Woodcock's told me your name etc. There's a steamroller coming into station at Brid here on a goods truck, coming from King's Lynn, Edison Steam Rolling Company. We'll let you know what day he's coming, then you come down to Brid on your bike and you can get fire going and steam up, then you'll have him to flag all way to Flamborough." Bike tied on back and an old caravan pulled on back – by, it did tek us a long time. It was dark when we got to Flamborough. We parked the caravan near Waud's shop on that bit of grass at side of school. The steam roller man says "You'll stop with me from now on".

He hadn't been in Flamborough long before he got friendly with Jimmy Kingston and Jim and him liked a drink. Jim used to sit with him on a night in caravan, they were real good friends. He says to me, "When's this road starting", I said, "What road?" and he said, "I've come to roll a road down somewhere". Woodcock Road it was but they were keeping it quiet, that it was to be called Woodcock Road.

"But first job I have is for a Mr Burton up at a farm. He's leading a lot of chalk off the beach with horses and I have to roll it in when they get it cracked, and bind it in with some smaller stuff. It's a weekend job, it's got nothing to do with steam roller company – it's extra beer money for me. You can come with me and make some baccy money. It's for Saturday afternoon and Sundays." We rolled all these barns out; they'd been old wood and soil. We rolled 'em in and following weekend they got smaller stuff in. And that's what we did for first three or four weeks.

Then they cum and said there's a job for you at South Landing, starting at that big gate that opens right down to bottom with your roller. Old lad frae Bempton was foreman over roadmen around here, parish council men. They called him Mr Horner. They stuck some iron bars in with teeth on and they called it 'scarifying' and job I had to do was at back of steamroller. As he went on wi' roller I had to turn a wheel and these teeth fell down and pulled the earth up loose. Then he rolled it down and levelled it. It was a silly job because he made 'em blunt after two or three hours and they had ti tek 'em ti Wiles' blacksmith shop for them ti sharpen but nobody bothered. We started again the next morning then when it got on a bit longer he says, "There's no more work for me now for another month, but I'm leaving roller and mi caravan here and Jim's going to look after it for me. I'll be back again in a month's time when they get this road marked out." Nobody knew what this road was or nothing.

One day and mi mother said, "Mr Woodcock called and you're to go down and see him". He says, "You're not out of work you know. Your pay goes on as usual". I'd already had a fortnight and done nothing, but cheque was only three pounds for two weeks' wages. Anyhow to cut a long story short, he says, "I want you to meet a Surveyor at ten o'clock on a morning, he's coming on from Beverley to stake a road out. I've heard they're going to call it after me. He'll stake the road out so you'll get a few more weeks work." I staked all that Woodcock Road out. He held chain at one end and I had to go across with chain under mi arm and, when he said 'RIGHT', I knocked a peg in and walked on. We went round in a circle and right away till we got down to where it turns for North Landing. On one side was Cowling's house, they had the end house, and on the other was a white chalk wall, with a letter box in it, and next to it was Alfred Leng's father's. When we got to there he says, "We're in trouble, Harold. You know these people, you'll have to take me to them, I want to talk to them. I want so much of the land from both of them". I thought there was going to be trouble 'cos Cowlings had a bit of a shed on their bit of land and they kept a cart in it. They had a pony and a cart to tek their lines and crab pots. He wanted two foot inti where this cart was and I thought maybe he won't have much bother, but if they tek two feet they wain't get cart in. So next day comes and he goes to Rob Leng's first. Why, there was trouble there straight away with Rob's, it hadn't to be touched until he got Solicitors onto it. There again, you couldn't do what you liked wi' your own property. They said, "It doesn't matter if he's Rob Leng or who he is, get the two feet taken off". So where Iris Taylor's bungalow is built we took two feet off. The old chalk wall had to be pulled down and the letterbox pushed further down.

Now, a fortnight ago, I was up that way taking John Emmerson's car back and he said to me, "Can you solve an argument? Some of 'em say that letter box was further up". I said, "Yes, it had been moved from the comer when road was staked out. It had to be knocked down and they kem on frae Brid did postal people and they fixed it into a wall further up". It's about fifty feet further up.

Now Cowling lost his foot of land, they brought the architect, a big fish. I don't know about aught else – they made it one foot! He was a nice little chap and he used to call at our house at ten o'clock and mi mother used to mek him a cup tea. She used to be baiting a line or skeining mussels. He said, "I like to watch you". If it was a rainy day, we had to sit in his car. I used to get frightened I got the sack or somebody reported me. He said, "It is nought to do wi' anybody, I'm your boss while you're here". Mi father was on one day and the architect asked him, "How much fish do you get from a big long line like this?" They got talking and mi father told him donkeys carried it up cliff in baskets. He said he would like to see that, so mi father said, "They'll all be at sea tomorrow – it's fine weather. If you come to North Landing you'll see 'em getting fish and washing it, putting it in baskets and lifting 'em up on to donkeys' backs, and leading it up". At North Landing there was some stands about that high (2ft 6ins) and every buyer had one, they were just high enough to pull rulley up or horse and cart up and tip your box of fish on. All of them stands are down now, aren't they.

We lived in North Star. When I first left school I went to Sid Coates as errand boy at thirteen and a half. If you had a job to go to and a letter ti tek to schoolmaster, you could leave at end of term. I left at thirteen and a half and went as errand boy with Sid, five bob a week and a joint at weekend. When Ron was born, Sid's son, he was born at Doncaster at one of Mrs Coates' sisters so she could look after her y'see. In meantime, Sid had an old motorbike and sidecar and he also had a box you could fix on instead of sidecar so he could tek meat out in it. There was another little butcher further up, called Newbold and Walter Redhead, he used to have a little motorbike to run all over taking orders, and I'm struggling on a bike. I says to Sid, "You ought to learn me how to drive that motorbike, no wonder he's teking all trade off you". He, Newbold, used to get all visitors' trade; he sent Walter up and he got all their orders. Sid goes ti Doncaster weekend to see his wife and baby, and he went on train. Monday was scrubbing out day, nivver opened, only for scrubbing all out. I thought to missel, 'I'll be around early and get all scrubbed out, and I'll have a go on that motorbike'. I got motorbike out and it had box on side. I got it to kick start and I gor it struck up and all of a sudden somebody shouts, "Hello, thu'll ger inti bother". Dick Traves was errand boy at Bee's baker's shop just ower wall, Copperfield's it is now. Anyhow, he says, "I'll come round a bit later and I'll have 'er". He used to come round when we were killing a pig or owt like that. In t'chained big doors, there was a hole in each to thread chain through – I didn't bother putting wooden bar on as well. Motorbike started up, you didn't go very far down to gates before I had ti stop and turn her round for going back again. I kept getting faster every time and then what happened, clever man me, took his knee to knock it into next gear as I'd seen Sid do, and I knocked it into next one after that and it gave one big jump forward. Smash bang! Through gates, it sent chain and lathes of wood all over. I skinned every knuckle on that hand on wall as I went down passage and I ran slap bang into footpath dead opposite, where Chris Young lived. He was a tailor, married one of Mr Waud's daughters, Beattie. Jack Bailey cum out, he was a good sort, grocer next door to butcher's, "Thu's for it now. What's thi going ti do?" "I don't know, I'll have ti tell him. Get it pushed back". Front wheel was just catching a bit, they weren't very strong. They weren't much stronger than a bicycle. We get it pushed back, and he looked at gates did Jim Bailey and he says, "I'll soon put that right for thu". He put gate back and made it alright. Then George Thompson, Sheila's father, cum, "Thu'll get into a row now. What's thi going to do about it? "Can't do anything about it can I? I shall etty tell him". "No, we'll fix it. I'll go and get mi tools". He took front wheel out and he had spokes 'cos he med bikes and light motorbikes. He put three or four new spokes in and straightened wheel up and you couldn't tell owt had happened. What happened later on, they opened their mouths and told him (Sid Coates). "You didn't tell me you'd smashed my motorbike up", but after that he said, "Now you've had a go, you'd better get it". And that was it. Five shilling week and a joint.

I remember one week, it was before motorbike, we had a pony and trap and he used to go up to Lighthouse with it on a Friday. They all got their meat off him on a Friday, all coastguards. We used to go right to Foghorn Station and then we used to go across field to that farm which Waines have now, but Sid's uncle had it then – old Willy Coates, he was a bachelor. It was a windy day and that field has a lot of ins and outs. They allus said after a big flood it had been left like that. We were going up and down over these ruts, both of us sat up there and he put reins over one hand to strike a match to light his pipe, and at same time a bird flies out of grass, and she shied did pony. She set off flat out and pulled reins out of his hand. There used to be a big hole up there and a square built all round it. It was where wireless first started, some wireless men lived up there. She just missed that. He was clinging on and then he shouted to me, "Jump", and I jumped off cart and caught mi knee on the thing you put lamps in. He rolled over the other side and do you know that pony never stopped at gate, it jumped that gate with cart hung at it and it got half way across and gate collapsed at finish, and they all came running out to see what was up.

On days that they were threshing you know, they used to tek some extra meat out to thresher men. They used to give them their 'lowance' [refreshments] at half past ten and then again in middle of afternoon. Miss Butters, the housekeeper, used to bake and they were just like lumps of concrete. Have you heard about 'em? You couldn't get your teeth in 'em. She used to give me two or three wrapped in a bit of newspaper. When I got on mi way back doon ti village I used to pelt 'em over hedge.

I'll tell you who brought us down ti village, Matt Major, Dorothy and Christie Major's father. He had a little Ford, a Tin Lizzie Ford, and he'd been bringing stuff up to that little cafe where he sold ice-cream. You see Sid had to go down to hospital to get his ankle set. I had a week at home wi' me knee all bruised and swollen. Sid stopped in hospital a week afore they let him out, and that weekend his Aunt Helen came down to look after shop. She lived opposite Miss Sunley's shop, where Ada Coates used to live, that belonged to old Helen Coates. All Coates's had a bit of money and property – Willy Coates, her brother at Lighthouse and Dick Coates had Thornwick Farm. Helen Coates also owned that field that school's built on in Carter Lane. It was called Camp Field – reason was it had troops in it in First World War. They camped in there in tents as they were training for ti go abroad. Helen and Sid kept a lot of chickens in there and there was a big gate to go through and some old barns. Happy days!

On Bonfire Night, nobody could afford crackers so they used to roll sacking in big balls and tie it, soak it in paraffin. Then dip it in tar bucket and thread a piece of wire through it. They set fire to it and when it got going, swing it round and round – in Chapel Street or High Street. There used to be lumps of cloth dropping off it still alight, it's a wonder they hadn't set village afire. Then policeman used to come and they all run away and left him looking at it, and trying to trammell *[stamp]* on it and got tar all on his boots. We did some rum things!!

When they first started with engines in cobles, that would be 1920ish, previous to that it was all pulling on oars and a bit of sail. Then during the war so many of 'em had to go into Navy – into minesweepers. So many of 'em that didn't pass the Grade 4 had to go to fixed coastguard stations or to fixed lifeboat stations. There was more than one fixed lifeboat station besides Humber in those days. While they'd been out on these jobs and other lot had been on minesweepers, rest that was left had made a fortune. Fish was rationed and fetched big money. When engines kem out they were able to afford engines and get out ti sea when others couldn't. They kem back to cobles that had rotted at beach at South Landing and North Landing. Most of those Emmerson's didn't go to First World War, and they all had money to buy new engines in their boats. In the end, mi father was going to sea wi' Sam Chadwick's father John and Albert Duke. They were paraffin engines but they had to be started on petrol and then switched over to the other tank, to paraffin. They always carried a spare can of paraffin and a spare can of petrol. Sam had been to North Landing and took a can of what he didn't really know. He took this can of fluid and put it into coble. Johnny says, "Which has thu took, paraffin or petrol?" Sam says, "I don't know". Johnny says, "Where's the other tin?" He says, "In wash house", Johnny says, "'We'll have ti find out, which it is, paraffin or petrol". Nowt n'more was said, and all of a sudden, BANG! Dick took lid off and struck a match, up went tin. There was a mess, burnt all his hair off. It was petrol.

There was three men in a coble and they worked two lines each, six lines. I remember mi father only had one line; those that could afford worked two. Whilst they were at sea, they had two lines at home that their wives could be baiting, but such as mi mother was sat waiting for old line coming back before she could start baiting. Well, it wasn't they couldn't afford another one, it was that they hadn't sense to get two to begin in the first place. Same with skids to launch cobles down, they used to buy lard from shop ti grease the skids, they hadn't sense to get dripping. Billy Collins used to bring it from Brid in lartle bread tin, and they used to rub all these skids with it and boat went down on it's own nearly. Butchers gave dripping away or sold it for very little.

We are Storks from one side and Nordass's from the other, and Nordass's were bricklayers or labouring, and the other Storks were joiners. Now there was a little man related to 'em and he was mi grandfather's brother. They called him Harry Stork. He would be brother to Sara Ellen, old Mrs.Waud, and he lived in Tower Street, somewhere about second or third house from the railing. He was a joiner and one of his daughters, Nellie, was Edwin Bayes' wife. Clara Stork, and Lillian Stork, Arthur Stork, Stanley Stork – they were all related to Wauds. Arthur went to Waud's to be a joiner, learnt his trade with Stores's cabinet making, then walked straight into Waud's. The big house at the corner of Allison Lane and High Street was built for the eldest of the boys, Will Waud, and his wife, when I went to school, was caretaker of school. I remember he had job lighting streetlights. They were square but I can't just think whether they were paraffin or there was a candle in 'em, or what there was. Acetylene, that's right 'cos he used to use a stick.

It was fourpence to go into pictures. We'd ride down to Brid on our bikes. Now my bike, I bought it off Tom Hindle's, a brand new Fleet, twenty-six inch wheels. Three pounds ten shillings it was, one and sixpence a week and I got into bother wi' it, 'cos you had to have a paper signed by your father or mother and I'd signed mi father's signature. I did get some hammer. We used to go to Winter Gardens but they used to call it Coliseum, and we parked our bikes up a passage. What a going on sorting 'em out, one fastened in wi' another. But what tricks some of 'em used to do. They'd turn your water on in the acetylene bicycle lamp and it slecked all your carbide that was in and you couldn't get a light, there was a jet when you turned your water on. Same with Institute, two billiard tables were covered in blacks that had dropped off acetylene burners. Old Tacey Robson used ti look after Institute, and there was a load of carbide in a big container and water dripping inti it, and it gev off that gas. It was a beautiful light. We started tekking our lamps into pictures wi' us.

When Atkins Blue Buses started running, it was a shilling return to Brid. It was a kind of reddy-brown coloured ticket and if you could find one in bus that had been used, when you got down to Brid and went into pictures, you gave her the old bus ticket, she would tear it in two and give you half back and show you to your seat. You'd get into trouble today wouldn't, you?

When shown an old photograph of fishermen outside the Rose and Crown, Mr Stork identified some of the men: John William Bayes at the left end of the photo and 'Pod' Cross next. He then went on to say that Edie Morgan's mother was a Cross related to the 'Pod' Cross in photo. The only way to distinguish people was to give each person a nickname. There was so many Crosses, Majors, Storks, Emmersons, Mainprizes, Chadwicks and so forth, and sons were called after fathers and daughters after mothers that it was necessary to give them nicknames. If you had to describe a certain one, John Major, it was no use just saying John Major because there was maybe four or five of that name. Same with Crosses; there were umpteen Crosses, so if you said, "Which one?" They might say "Pod Cross". They were described by their nicknames. The next photograph which evoked Mr Stork's interest was of the present Co-Op shop taken before 1909, showing a horse and wagon delivering goods. He had had an argument with someone that the present entrance was not the original one.

Harold   Door was at the corner when I went to school. I was living with mi grandfather's and grandmother's in 1914 -1918 war because there was no school at Spurn, and the sergeant, schoolmaster at Spurn, used to take us on a morning from eleven to twelve o'clock. The Army had barracks at Spurn and they used to reckon it was the last call they had before they were sent over to France. They had a dug-out and trenches all round the point and we used to play in them trenches. Wire meshing all round and they had rifles pointing through, and they had some dummy stands on the beach wi' bags of straw and old men's faces marked on 'em for 'em to charge, but they used to practice firing at them first. When we knew they'd gone and we were waiting for next lot of soldiers coming, we used to run and play in there wi' bits sticks and shouting "Bang". This chap, Mr Skelton, got put abroad and we'd slates and slate pencils 'cos I remember mi father ask Mr Skelton if I could keep mine and he said, "Yes I shan't want 'em anymore". When I got going to Flamborough School it was all books and pencils. Games day used to be a Friday and they played in Stylefield. I'd never seen a football or a cricket bat while we lived at Spurn. That was one of the reasons mi mother and father got me to mi grandfather's. They brought mi up till I was ten or eleven years old.

On seeing some old photographs of South Landing it reminded Mr Stork of a painter [cable] which boats used to use at South Landing. This painter is still there at low tide and when tides are very heavy, and there's a big long ebb, you can see part of this thing. It was still in until about ten years ago, fishermen used to use it when they pulled cobles up.

Mr Stork, looking at a photograph of the old South Landing lifeboat...

Harold   All them men are pulling on that rope to pull the lifeboat into the sea. It's a practice day, they're not going off to anything. Now then, on a turn out to a distress and it had to go, Rob Leng, Alfred's father, had two horses – he used to pull cobles up at South Landing. There used to be twenty fishing cobles at South Landing, slightly more than there was at North Landing 'cos it was a better place for getting off. Then eventually, when horses finished, Langton, Dora and Daisy's father, got a tractor, built a little shed on left hand side, and pulled 'em up with his tractor. Herring cobles used to be painted the same colour. When they finished crabbing, they used to get set for the herring season.

Looking at old photographs of Dykes House Mr Stork remarked on the wall of the old kitchen garden.

Harold   When you get so far, there's a brick wall, we've gone over top of that wall, do you know what for? Pinch apples. There was some Siberian apples and they grew 'em up the wall and if you leaned over as far as you could, you could get them. I've been up there, leaning over picking apples, and there's been Sam Chadwick holding one leg and somebody else holding t'other. If you tummelled in you'd nivver get out again, you'd get caught, 'cos you had to go right down to house to get out.

Mr Stork looked at an old postcard of the Fog Siren and told of the family who lived in the house there when he was young.

Harold   The ones I remember mostly were Joliffe's. Mr and Mrs Joliffe and two daughters, Kath and – I forget what they called the younger one. I knew 'em by going to Wesleyan Chapel, they were very religious people. I used to love to hear that fog siren. When that boomed out on a still night you could hear it echoing right up cliff. Now all they have is a penny squeaker!! That's since radar – they don't need it. I don't know when it was altered, but in my young days at school Lighthouse used to flash two whites and a red, and it's all white like now – four whites and a break. Phyllis had an uncle in the police force from Barnsley, he came on and he said, "I'd love go on to that fog horn. Some of our chaps had been to Brid, a fishing party, a sergeant and some more of them, and foghorn had struck up when they were fishing off foghorn; they could just see it." So they said they would go and see it, and they all went up to Lighthouse next day, it wasn't 'alf foggy. They went to the Lighthouse first but the lighthouse-keeper wouldn't take them up. He was sorry but he'd just had a message that the foghorn would be striking up, and when that was blowing he wasn't allowed to take them up. So they all went down to the foghorn and there was a big wide path right round it. It struck up and some of 'em had got half way round and Mr Joliffe had had to come out and ask 'em to clear off.

I haven't been down there since I was about thirteen or fourteen years old. When I was down there then, we had an accident, we had a fresh pony and every Friday afternoon we used call for orders at Violet's mother's. She used to bring me a piece of prune pie or apple pie then, when we finished there it was straight up to Lighthouse. We used to start at this end and go on till we got to the Lighthouse and we finished up at his Uncle Willie's farm. Cuth Owen was stationed at Signal Station at the Lighthouse with another lad called Mick and two more Navy lads who used to call at Readhead's shop on the evenings when Muriel and Vivian were finishing off. Walter Readhead was errand boy at another butcher's, Newbold's, further up street. We all knocked about together, Walter, Albert Emmerson, Sam Chadwick – there was a big gang of us. But this night there was only three or four of us and we'd fetch a big nail and a hammer and knocked a nail in doorjamb. Sam said, "We want some string ti tie door". I had the key of butcher's shop so I went and got some. We tied some string from the nail round the sneck *[latch]* – this was the side door round into Tarry Row. We tied front door as well, with red and white string from butcher's – sausages were tied with it. Now William Readhead, Muriel and Vivian's father, used to get this string off Sid to tie things up in his garden. The four in the shop couldn't get out so they had to ring up home and William had come and caught 'em with these two lads. There was trouble there, he was very strict. He came down to shop for his meat a day or two later and said, "Sid, somebody tied our lasses into shop two nights ago and they couldn't get out. They had to admit there was two lads in back of shop. I've given them something to go on with and I'll give 'em summat to go on with who supplied band for 'em. Have you any band like it, Sid?" He knew very well he had! Sid says, "Yes, off Palethorpe' sausages". "Who works here who could get band off Palethorpe sausages. Thu wouldn't tie 'em in would you?" "No, it's 'im as tied 'em in". He didn't half kick me and cuff me back of ear.

Same people, Readhead's, that was them that lived in the big house opposite Victoria Club but previous to that they lived in Manor House down street. He was a big man at showing poultry. He'd three or four different breeds of poultry and bantams. And they sold eggs and garden produce from down there. Albert Emmerson left school at thirteen and a half because he had a note from William Readhead for him to look after poultry. William Readhead was away quite a lot at these shows and some were big shows down London where he had to stay overnight. He was winning prizes with 'em and people were coming and buying 'em and he was getting big money for some of 'em. Albert says to me one night, "Are you coming down wi' me to-night to Manor House. We have two incubators and I have to turn 'em up a bit at night as it comes colder". Albert had been shown how to work all these things during day. So we went down and he lit a stable lamp or two and we went round all those incubators and turned 'em up a bit and there was one with a lot of little chicks in. There was a big oval pointed thing and in the centre a thing made of aluminium with holes all round side and chicks were running in under there as it kem cooler. There was one lamp and it shone down on 'em and he had to turn this up a little bit. Next morning, when he went down, William Readhead had got home. Sack straight away – he'd turned 'em up over high and roasted all chickens. He gave Albert a belting. He was a hard man, but he was a very good man for village on Parish Council.

Harold
There was not much to get crabbing. You see how many cobles there was at South Landing and same number at North Landing. Some weeks they couldn't get rid of their crabs, markets were flooded. Mi father used to send us to Lighthouse selling crabs also he used to put some lines in at South Landing baiting wi' worms out of garden. They baited and then put cabbage or rhubarb leaves over the hooks then sacking to keep the bait fresh. It was all plaice that was caught. He used to string four or five together for sixpence, and then say, "No running off when you leave school, straight home". Me and our Tom used to thread these fish on a long bamboo cane and then we had to go up to Lighthouse to sell it. This was in summertime and there was quite a lot of visitors. All those houses and those black cottages were all full.

One day when we'd come home, Tom says, "I'm sick of this up to Lighthouse trying to sell fish". Some nights you sold the lot and other nights somebody had been before you and you were bringing half of it back again. I said, "We etti go". We got over the stile, and down that dip and up the other side and all of a sudden, "Bang"! All these horses coming galloping. Our Tom says, "They're coming for us". And we set off to run; I was in front, he was at back. I was a bit taller than him and he had all weight at back. He tumbled and I kept hold of bamboo and all fish was sliding off the bamboo into a big heap. We needn't have worried. All it was, poor things were coming to this pond for a drink. We used to catch newts in this pond with a pin, and bullrushes used to grow all round and there were moorhens' nests in among them. We washed the fish in the pond. It was alright!

Manor Corner has altered. That chalk wall used to be rounded and blue tits used to nest there where pieces of chalk had come out. They weren't like blue tits we get in the garden, they were bigger.

They were only in a small way, but there was lime burning, two lime kilns were down South Landing Road. We used to try and get in 'em when we were kids and they were all grown up wi' grass by then. There was a gateway leading into backway of John Robert Hall's and forty or fifty yards past it there was these two kilns, one aside of each other. We used to wonder what these archways were. It was where they burnt lime. They were pulled down when they built the very first bungalow down there on the right. It stands back from the road. The lime kilns were pulled down to make way for the road leading down to this bungalow.

There used to be brickworks where Jack Agar's barn is now, and there used to be one where garage at top of the hill is now. That's the reason it's on pillars. It used to be a pond and wi' tekking the clay out for bricks, it made this pond and it was always full of water. I'll tell you where they burnt lime as well. This corner house, East View, top of Allison Lane, before that house was built, it was all chalk. There was a good long way before you came to first cottage, old John Nordass and his wife Hannah lived in there. On this empty space there was two big long troughs and when you peeped in as lads, you could see all steam rising off 'em both and it was Waud's burning lime. Then old John Nordass, he was related to Waud's, he used to go in with a big rake and he used to throw these bags of stuff in, and then rake it about. It was horse hair and cow hair. It came from the knackers' yard – from their manes and tails. We used to think, what's he doing that for? If he was there he used to say, "Go on. Clear off". Tell you what it was, there was no cement in those days, it was mortar to build with. Now if you go and look at all the white chalk walls and poke, you'd be poking sand and lime. When it had all got dead, it had all finished steaming, it would be 'quick lime'. They used to shovel it into a barrow and put it into a big heap and put so much sand in with it, like mixing concrete and mixing this hair in with it. They used to lead chalk off sand at South Landing. There's that old castle at back of War Memorial, it would be built of all such as that. There was more of the castle when we were kids, you could slide down it at the back.

Ship Yard – there's some argument about that. My grandfathers and fishermen in Chapel Street, when they wanted to take their lines to sand, to North Landing, had to go right round by road. But they didn't, they used Ship Yard. There was no Woodcock Road in those days – it was a dead end above Wesleyan Chapel.

Now the only other way was Tarry Row, it was cobbled and you could get through wi' donkeys, but not wi' lines on the back, it was not wide enough.

Miss Huddleston *[Jack Emmerson's house]* used to take in teachers. George Bayes' second wife lodged there when she first came to Flamborough, and Sid Coates' wife, another teacher, did as well. You know the big rent *[passage]* in the row of cottages in Chapel Street, I was born in the first house on the right hand side of that rent. We've lived on either side that passage. When they were getting ready for crabbing, the ropes used to come; it was just ordinary rope and they used to bark it, tree bark in block form, melt it in copper, then fill up with a drop o'water. Then they put bark in an old wash tub that mother had finished with, then they fastened a piece of wood across it. Before they filled up wi' pokey *[bark liquid]* they poked one end of the rope under and out from the wood and while stuff was hot, they pulled it through. They wore old stockings on their hands, and then they used to coil them up and throw 'em on ti tiles to dry out. When the rope was dry, they used the same tub, next preparation was tar. They used to fill up with tar and pull through just same. They used to last for years. They use nylon or some such today. Mi uncle Len said to me one day when I was six or seven, "You needn't go to school today you can give us a hand to tar these pot tows *[thick rope]*. You can look after fire. I'm just going for a pipe of baccy". While he was at shop this 'ere big bucket of tar was boiling on the fire and bits kept bubbling over and dropping into fire and setting on fire. I thought it would be alright, and I was larking wi' cat. As he kem back and just as he opened washhouse door, all smoke kem belting out! It had set fire to bucket of tar. There was no taps, so we had to run to well in yard for water to slek it out. That finished tarring pot tows for day, I was in bad books!

Albert Duke's sisters and Norah, Jack Cowling's wife, they all lived down there. She was good old neighbour was old Mrs.Duke. He was from Robin Hood's Bay. She was a good old sort, "Annie, don't worry about dinner for kids today, I'm making it and you'll get a surprise, you'll enjoy it". Mi mother said, "That's very nice". So at dinnertime school bell rang and there was a mad rush for home for this dinner. She came in with it in a big enamel bowl. There was six of us altogether like, mi mother put it into middle of table and got knife to cut into it. Do you know what it was? Onion Pie! You got it down you. It was that or starve.

I remember one time I was out of work and you had go down to Brid to 'sign on' on Wednesday as well as drawing your bit of money on a Friday. It was one pound, four and threepence for a couple. I hadn't a bicycle so I had to walk on cliff top and draw my money on the Friday. There was a butcher called Argenta in King Street and meat was sixpence a pound. We used to get sixpenny worth of stew meat and that was Sunday dinner. It was nearly Christmas and Phyllis had told me to go into Woolworth's and get a shillings worth of Christmas decorations. I went into Woolworth's and picked what I thought would be alright, and when I got home I gave them to her, and she looked at them and looked at me. She had told me to get cake decorations and I'd bought decorations for a Christmas tree! She made a hoop from two hoops from a grape barrel and crossed them and decorated that with the decorations. There was no money for a tree!

We lived in Allison Lane at one time and they were all oak beams with a big hook for a lamp, and mi mother had got a hanging lamp from mi grandmother. It was one on chains and you could pull it up or down. Me and our Tom were not old enough to go to dances, but we were allowed to go and play whist. It was a shilling for whist, one and six for both whist drive and dance. We came home from the whist drive and all was in darkness and our Tom says, "Matches?" and I said, "Yes", 'cos we were smoking on the sly then. He took the lamp glass off, turned the wick up and put a match to the two wicks. He clapped glass back on and smoke went up and 'Bang', glass cracked and smoke went all over the show. Before we could get lamp down it all set on fire. I think there'd been too much paraffin in it. Mi father kem downstairs, clicked this lamp, ran into the yard wi' it and threw it into sink. We did cop it next day. We had to use candles till we could afford another lamp. That put paid to whist drives until we were older and we were allowed to go to the whist drive and stay for the dance.

I couldn't dance but I sat and watched. The dances were held in school. They used to slide the partition back making one big room and throw some stuff on the floor. There used to be a piano and a fiddle, and Dorothy and Christie Major played the mandolin and cello, and the Major boys all played musical instruments. On a Friday night mi mother used to say, "You can go to whist drive and dance if you behave yourselves, but don't be any later than twelve. Get yourselves washed and ready". She came to examine us and to see if we'd washed our necks, she was a rum un for discipline. Mi father was alright, he was easier carried on. She used to give us the one and sixpence each and there was cup of tea and a bun as well. She used to say, "Go and enjoy yourselves and I hope you win at whist, but no cheating". We used to get a proper lecture every Friday night, "And if you get friendly with any girls remember, treat 'em as you would have your own sisters treated". Some of these dances were held to buy sports gear.

Looking at a booklet produced by William Readhead in 1900, Mr Stork remarked about some of the advertisers who were still in business when he was a child.

Harold   Hannah Barclay and her sister at the Laundry, Tower Street. They did a lot of starching; poor people couldn't afford it, but larger houses such Danes Dyke House and Primrose Cottage did. Mrs Jackson, Mrs Huddleston at Grove Farm, "Five minutes from the sea", were advertising as guest houses, 'Huddleston's'. There was Ernest, he would be brother to Alice, and he was a roadman and he lived in the cottages going out of the village. Jessie Woodhouse used to dressmake. Now, Mrs Nordass at Ebeneezer House, would be George, Nellie and Elsie Nordass', mother. William Readhead had two brothers, he was the youngest. Wilf, one of his older brothers mended three-wheeler bicycles; his shop was at side of the old Wesleyan Chapel, now the garage. When the Wesleyans built the new Chapel, Wilf Readhead took it on as a workshop and George Thompson took it off him

Phyllis first came to Flamborough to work at Danes Dyke House, when Dr Woodhouse was owner. Walked her up to Danes Dyke House one night, I thought to myself, "I don't want to be doing this every Friday night". We've been married for sixty-three years. There was a housekeeper and a cook, three housemaids, two girls in the kitchen, a boots, several gardeners, a woodsman, two gamekeepers and chauffeur, when the Lord of the Manor, Gerald Bolton, lived there before he went bankrupt. He owned all the farms and nearly all Flamborough, and all the land from one end of Dykes to t'other. A lot of people who had a bit of money saved, did very well when the land and properties were sold, some of them were very cheap.

Nellie Almond

Daughter of a farmer, she married a farmer and lived on a farm her whole life until she and her husband moved into the village to retire.

Mrs A   I was born at Hill Farm, where camp is now, in that house up there. It was a shame it was pulled down – it was a lovely little house. It was as dry as a bone; there wasn't a damp patch in it. When you cleaned that house, you washed it from top ti bottom 'cos it was all lined wi' grained wood and it shone like glass if you washed it with a drop of vinegar in your water. The only bit of walling was joining the stables and pantry – it was only outside back door and the rest was wood lined walling. They were lovely buildings.

Mi father was a farmer, mi granfather was a farmer and I expect mi great-grandfather. Mi father kem from Hull side – Brough, agin Hull. His father and mother was farming up there, but there was twelve of 'em in the family and he was towards the eldest. He was brought up by an aunt in Brid and that's how he kem to be this way. And eventually he worked for his uncle at Sewerby, at Charity Farm, and I think he made his home there, until he got married. And then they got married and went ti Hill Farm and we had twenty-two years there, and then moved across to Wold Farm, and that's where I was married from. I was born at Hill Farm but I was married from Wold Farm.

I was related to Nicholson Hall. He got the name of Nicholson 'cos they called his uncle Nicholson, and they put his name with James so he was called James Nicholson Hall. He was my Father. Mr Longden *[local grocer]* and my mother were brother and sister.

It was a nice little farm. There was no tractors. We used ti keep six field horses. They ploughed all by horses then, worked it and drilled it, did it all by horses – reaper, binder cut it with horses, everything. Mi dad didn't employ any men. When it was fine, mi mother and I, when I got older, had ti go out and help – we made one man! When it was wet we had ti do our cooking and housework. That was during war. We used ti keep about six cows, but we allus had four in milk. And when I was a girl, from being ten year old, me and mi brother, we had four cows ti milk before we went ti school and we had ti walk from Hill farm down ti village ti old school. We used ti reckon we'd done six miles a day 'cos we allus went home for our dinner. Mr Rawnsley was school master then, and he used ti let us out a few minutes before the others so we could get away. It made all the difference 'cos we were half way home before the others kem out, 'cos you could hear 'em shouting.

When it was bad *[in winter]* – but it had to be bad – mi dad used ti cum up and fetch us. He used ti put a bottle *[bundle]* or two of straw in bottom of a heavy cart with a heavy horse and he used ti cum and fetch us. He used to mek corn sack pixie hoods for us ti sit and cover up with. But it had ti be very bad. Well then there weren't 'ni Wellingtons, I used ti wear boys' Sunday boots and gaiters and I allus used ti change 'em inti some dry shoes. I allus had a pair of dry stockings in mi bag for if I got damp.

Margaret   Did any kids come up to play with you or did you come down to the village or not?

Mrs A   No, they nivver used ti cum up but Lewis's and Cowlings – Tom Cowling used ti set us down so many fields because there was some Irish bullocks in these fields and we had ti go through these bullocks and we didn't like it. Then we had a policeman who had two sons and two daughters, Parker, PC Parker. They lived just at the bottom of field there in one of them cottages, and they used ti cum with us, and then cum back down fields. And they weren't afraid but we were. Why, you see, they were older than us. Lads thought nowt about chasing 'em; up with their tails and off they used ti go. They used ti like that but I didn't. They were good old days.

Margaret	You'd do reading, writing and arithmetic at school, did you?
Mrs A	That was it, and that was your lot and needlework. You made aprons and pillowcases and such as that. But you had ti do a specimen one before you were able to do aught and you had ti tek your own materials. I had two or three aprons I made, and they were all done by hand. Mrs Rawnsley used to teach us and if you weren't doing it right she had a pencil and she used to knap your knuckles. As long as I went she came to school, and it was always Mondays and Wednesdays afternoons after about two o'clock. She used ti come while leaving time. Boys used to etti go inti another room, when you had your sewing, and they used ti do Geography and such as that and Mr Rawnsley used ti tek them.
Margaret	How did you do your shopping then?
Mrs A	We had a horse and trap – to do shopping – and we nivver did much at Flamborough. We went to Bempton and Hardwick's in Old Town. They lived on corner there opposite bank, and when I got grown up and had a farm I used ti tek butter and eggs there. Mrs Longden used ti get so many eggs and butter and Hardwick's used ti get the rest. And after mi mother died I used ti go and do mi dad's butter. They used ti mek butter, and I've made ovver a hundred pound up in a day. I used ti get up at five o'clock and do mi own and then go up there and do their's. We had ti put it down, cover it with muslin and stick it down well to mek it stiffen up to mek it work, 'cos it was always cold down there. You didn't put it inti water, you just hung it.
Margaret	Where was the well at Hill Farm?
Mrs A	In the kitchen. There was a flag in kitchen and that was well. You used your water for domestic work, but for drinking we used to lead it in a water cart. It was five hundred gallon tank on wheels and they used ti fetch it from water-works for a long time. Then they stopped us 'cos we were at Bempton. That was after I was at Butterick's so we used to go to Bempton tap *[pump]* for it.
Margaret	That would be the water-works at Wold Farm, would it?
Mrs A	That was it, down Wold Farm Road.
Margaret	You know I've heard mi father-in-law, Jim, he remembered when they struck water, they had to leave all tools 'cos it kem up in such a rush. That's what he used to say, and that it was lovely water.

Mrs A	Aye, it's milky on a morning sometimes; you have to run it for ages. I think it's something they put in it. I never use water without boiling it. I drink a lot of water, but it's always boiled.
Margaret	So you would marry Mr Almond from Wold Farm?
Mrs A	Yes. I was married from Wold Farm but he kem from near Garrowby. His father was a farmer down Garrowby way. It was a much bigger farm. Why he came this way with his father and mother, there were eight of 'em and so he was one of the eldest. Well his eldest brother had to go to war. And, when he got his demob, he didn't like the idea of not being at home – there wasn't work for two of 'em and his father as well – so he said he would go out and earn his living 'cos his brother had had four years away. And so that's what he did. Well he did two years out that way as a beastman, and then they had a family that grew up and they didn't want him so mi aunty (who was married to one of the sons) wrote to mi grandad to ask if he wanted a bullocky, 'cos if he did there was a good one leaving. He said, "Yis, he was looking for one!" And that was how Henry kem to Wold Farm ti mi grandfather. And then when we left Hill Farm and kem ti Wold Farm he stayed on as beastings 'cos we had ti have some help and that was how I got on with him. We were courting seven years and then I wouldn't get married till I'd somewhere to go to.
Margaret	Did you have to look after the chickens and all that sort of thing?
Mrs A	Chickens, geese and ducks. Latter part of my time there, we used to get turkey chicks and rear them for turkeys for Christmas – and geese. And when you started about a week before Christmas, you couldn't get naught. Before then, you had to prepare a lot of stuff – food – so you could do naught but pluck, pluck, pluck. I've known when we've had thirty geese and ducks all on boards and dishes down on floor in pantry ti keep cool.
Rita	Praying that it didn't come warm.
Mrs A	Aye, that was just it, though you never knew it warm at Christmas. We got snow then and we didn't like too much frost 'cos that could tonn 'em wrong. If they were only there three or four days it was alright, but if they were there longer and all dished out....! It was hard going but it was lovely – I wouldn't have nowt any different.

Margaret	How did you cope when it came snow? That bit of road from Bempton Dyke to where you lived – it always seems to block up first.
Mrs A	In 1947- 48 they used to send German prisoners of war to cut it out. When you were going to Bempton you couldn't see nought but snow piled up at each side of you. I know it was that bad at one time, we let 'em in one end of our field and they kem out t'other, and they missed the dip you see. They come on hedge side and there wasn't much snow, it was sheltered there, it hadn't drifted over. If they got stuck, you had ti tek your hoss oot and sometimes you wanted one in front of t'other ti pull 'em out.
Margaret	Did you ever go out dancing to Brid?
Mrs A	You never wanted to go dancing – you kept working while you were tired. You were glad when it was bedtime. And right up to me wedding, I was twenty-eight when I was married, I weren't allowed out after ten o'clock, unless it was by permission and they knew where I was. And they were allus waiting for you coming back. They knew you couldn't slide up to bed, there was no fear of that.
Margaret	Did you do knitting or sewing or didn't you have time for that either?
Mrs A	I used to do a lot at part of time. I started to crochet, My aunts taught me, 'cos they were both good crocheters, both mi Auntie Clara *[Mrs Longden]* and Aunt Lilian *[Mrs Leeson]*. They used to do a lot of crocheting for blinds and such like. I said to mi mother one day, "I think I should like to crochet", and she said, "You can't crochet", and I said, "I'd like to try". And she said, "Why, I'll soon get you some cotton and a hook", and she did. I was fumbling about and Mrs Longden's husband used ti work for us at that time. I couldn't follow to read it out of a book and so, if I saw a pattern, I could do it. Anyway, he used to read it out of a book, and I used ti do it as he read it. And I still have a bit of insertion – about that long- the last bit of crochet I ever did. I've crocheted miles. I've done fifteen tablecloths, a yard square. I have one on now on way. I have two lots on way. *[Mrs Almond showed us her work.]* I was only ten or eleven when I first started but I didn't do nought like this when I first started. But I've done all family one and all grandchildren one. This is just a long runner, for a Welsh dresser. I like ti have two or three lots on go; I can't sit and do nothing – I mek rugs. It's surprising

how many hours they tek, and it isn't only that, it's Hessian to do 'em on. Then it's clipping of the old clothes. I'm busy doing that when I'm at work. I have a box full there ready for clipping. I allus pull 'em to pieces you know, so I've nought to do but just clip 'em up.

Margaret   Where did your family go to school, Flamborough or Bempton?

Mrs A   Bempton. In war time they were going to Bempton, and anyway we used ti get allowance for tekking 'em when they were little. They would measure from Bempton to our gate and from our gate to Flamborough to see which was nearest. Bempton was nearest but only by a few yards, so we were glad 'cos we hadn't 'em to change. They would just have gotten nicely settled in at Bempton and they would a started again at Flamborough. I know I remember when they were on about it. They called policeman then Colley and he used ti cum up to our place a bit. They were on about allowance for petrol for tekking kids ti school and Henry said, "If I used what I have for business, you'd nab me", and Colley said, "No I'd jump ower hedge and swear I'd never been near". I don't think he would have reported us, but sometimes you had ti use it to tek 'em to school 'cos you didn't get enough to tek 'em. You got so much for business and so much for tekking 'em ti school 'cos they sent this man from Beverley ti measure it!

Margaret   When did you get rid of your horses then? Do you remember when you got tractors?

Mrs A   We had two horses as long as we were farming, but we didn't use ti work 'em a lot. One of 'em was there for as long as she lived 'cos she was an old favourite. She was same age as I was so we couldn't part wiv her, and anyway, when she did go she got so bad she couldn't get up in her stable. She had to go then but Henry allus said, "As long as she can stand and walk in and out, she'll stop". When she couldn't he said, "I'm not going to see her suffer but I deean't want to see 'em when they fetch her away".

Margaret   Did you have dogs up there for shepherding?

Mrs A   Oh yes, we used ti keep about three dogs, sheep dogs.

Margaret   Did you breed your own?

Mrs A   Yes, we used ti 'ave one and it was a black and white collie and a good sheep dog, and we had other two off it but we didn't keep puppies of them. We used to part with 'em, give 'em away. You didn't sell 'em in those days, you give 'em away.

Margaret	Did you have to go to church on a Sunday when you lived at Hill Farm?
Mrs A	When mi dad lived at Hill Farm and I was at home you had ti go to church or there was trouble. We managed with once a day and it was generally on a morning – Sunday morning – and you were back for your dinner. Mi mother had dinner all ready. And I know when we used ti go ti school, Friday nights was hot cakes *[bread cakes],* and fried ham. We very near run all the way home 'cos mi mother used ti mek bread – nivver bought bread in those days.
Margaret	You'd kill your own pigs and cure them, didn't you?
Mrs A	We used ti kill three pigs a year when we had men in house, and we allus used ti keep a big ham for Christmas and just curr *[cut]* it in half, and purr it in copper in copper house and boil it, great big lump you could cut at.
Rita	Yes, and it would taste good.
Mrs A	Yes, it was ham, with a bit of fat on it – cured with Demerara sugar and saltpetre – you used to stuff it in their legs. Shove steel down then put a bit of saltpetre, demerara sugar and salt down and then do same ovver again until you'd filled this hole, then you laid it flesh downwards on slab. We allus used to do 'em in pantry and it had a slab floor, and you allus put a thin layer of wheat straw all drawn clean and lay 'em flesh down on that. And next day you used to turn 'em over and sprinkle a bit of salt on, and do that for three weeks.
Rita	Did you make sausages?
Mrs A	Yards and yards of sausages, and we used ti 'ave black puddings. We used ti put scraps in, put 'em through mincer – that was rendered fats – and we used ti put a bit of meat in. We nivver made 'em without a bit of sausage meat in and then you put your rice and blood and that; and you had to be there with a basin with some salt in and a fork to stir it up so it didn't clot. Those were the days. There was a lot of cleaning up and siding up but mi Uncle Bob, Robert Towse, he used to be a very good hand at killing pigs and dressing 'em, and he was so particular, there wasn't to be a hair left on. We used to scald 'em, and scrape 'em as you were scalding 'em, then put 'em in a tub. And you used to have a chain and do all way on the back with it, so you got all the hairs off. You had ti tip that lot out and have another go. We allus had ti 'ave copper and pans and kettles all boiling ready.

	I've said ti John sometimes, "If you had pigs, we could have killed a pig", and he's said, "I sudden't know where to start", and he wouldn't.
Margaret	He probably wouldn't be allowed to these days.
Mrs A	No, he wouldn't, not unless he got a licence.
Margaret	And you used to make braun with the head, didn't you?
Mrs A	Aye, you used to chop their head up, put it in pickle as they called it and leave it for three weeks. Then tek it out, wash it and stew it for ever while it tummeled ti pieces. Then pick it out and mek braun with it, and press it into braun dishes. Pork pies – stand ones. Used to purr 'em round a stone jar; but I wanted a smaller one or two, I used to purr 'em in a glass – three pound one – work 'em round. Then you had strips of white linen and you had ti put that round – you had ti pin it with a safety pin then. There weren't ni sellotape to hold 'em in position if you hadn't them loose bottom tins. I had half a dozen of them but I had ti mek twenty or thirty pork pies, different sizes. This body wanted one and that body wanted one and you soon got rid of 'em.
Rita	And what kind of an oven did you have?
Mrs A	Just an ordinary fire side oven, coal oven. When you were busy with that you had to have plenty of wood piled up in corner 'cos you had ti keep shoving wood under it and great lumps of coal, but you can't get 'em today.
	In 1947 mi aunty died at Bempton, Walmsley House, and we went night before, and we got through alright wi' car. She had a wedding cake to do and she hadn't finished it, and mi uncle said would I finish it and would I cater for funeral? And I said, "Yes". I couldn't do ni other, 'cos I'd nearly gone there ti live and allus helped. We went on and carried these baskets of stuff, tarts and buns and things and we were going to take rest next day. We had ti walk. We couldn't get through wi' car, and I had Wellingtons on, and there was so much snow that it had gone into top of mi Wellingtons – I was walking in water by the time I got to Bempton. But I was prepared; I'd taken dry shoes and stockings. If we'd not taken most of stuff day before, we should have been stuck. It was very bad – snow was up, you couldn't see aught but snow either side of you.
Margaret	It used to be like that more often before the war, didn't it?

Mrs A	And during the war, 'cos they got German prisoners-of-war to cut it out, they kept Bempton road clear, but they let Brid road block. They kept a road through Bempton to Brid. They said it was easier to keep clear than Brid road. German prisoners had cut it out and next day it was all full up again. It had come some more snow and they had ti cum again. And I know that year, government gev you a rule, you had ti put so much potatoes and so much sugar beet, and we did. The acreage they'd allocated - we didn't ger our seed back when it cum to harvest it. And so Mr Almond rang 'em up at Beverley and told 'em, and they couldn't believe us but they'd send a man out to see. And they did, and he said he quite agreed with Mr Almond and he'd go back and give a report, and he did. During the following few days there was a letter cum: 'If you can't sow potatoes and sugar beet put so much more acreage of wheat in.....' But that didn't bother us 'cos it would grow wheat, so we had that proportion of wheat instead of roots and sugar beet.
Margaret	So they controlled what you had to grow.
Mrs A	Oh, yes. They told you what you had to plant; you couldn't do as you liked. You had to give an account of all your stock and corn. We used ti go Medforth's, Harry Medforth and Ken Medforth. You had to sell your corn and that through them as well, you couldn't sell it where you liked. It had to go through a professional dealer.
Margaret	How did you go on before the war, Mrs. Almond? Did you sell to anybody you liked then, sort of thing?
Mrs A	Yes, you'd more liberty then before war. But before First World War come they put these restrictions on and they never tuk 'em off, not altogether. They released some on 'em. There weren't as much paper work before the war but you had ti keep counts of stock and that – what you have and what you bought and what you sold – but that was about it. Corn and that – and what acreage of each kind of corn and how much you sold off it – they weren't as tight as they are today.
Margaret	Did you used to sell eggs or chickens to the market or anything?
Mrs A	No, they used to go to shop. Eggs and butter and if I had any fowls ti dress, they'd tek 'em at shop and then I'd finished wi' 'em you see. Then I used ti go and stay with Henry's mother and father, they used ti stand in York market, and they used ti do 'em and tek 'em ti market and stand in market all day long. They

	used ti go from Garrowby to York wi' 'oss and trap and they used ti come back same way. Them left at home had ti 'ave hot mash, bran mash, and this pony had ti ave hot mash, when she came in and they got her rubbed down.
Margaret	And they got fed before you?
Mrs A	Oh yes, it didn't matter about you. It was a long way with a horse and trap ti York, but anyway it was nice. It was nice going; it wasn't so good coming back. After standing in market all day – you were tired. They went just once a week on a Saturday and they had to be there by ten o'clock. They were getting up at five o'clock, loading up, tuk your sandwiches and flasks. You could go and get a cup of tea, but they never used to. Driffield market and Beverley market was nearest round here. At one time there used to be one at Brid, cattle market up in Old Town. He used to tek his stock in there, a long time ago.
Margaret	Was Mrs Longden in that shop when her husband was alive?
Mrs A	Yes, he died there. Do you remember Stan? He was two years old the day his father died.
Margaret	I remember going to the shop when she was there when some gypsies came into the village. They walked up the street as far as the fish shop, crossed the road and walked on the side opposite. She said, "They won't come in here 'cos once they did, begging bacon bits and saying I had a lucky face. I said, 'You know as much as I do about that' and they've never been in since!"
Mrs A	I can just imagine her doing that. She had to stick up for herself. She had a long time on her own bringing up those two lads. She did marvels really. She looked after the shop and home-baking as well, to make ends meet. And Charlie was a handful. There's only John left now.
Margaret	When you were at Butterick's, did you have to bring your water from Bempton?
Mrs A	Until they brought it on to Flamborough, we had to lead our own for drinking. I can't remember when that was but I know we had to pay for it bringing down the road and putting in. It was after we bought farm, after Mr Lloyd Graham sold all his farms and you had to buy or get out.
Margaret	That was 1926, Laurie said – that was when Dad bought that shed. It would be a godsend, wasn't it, when it was on tap?

Mrs A	You didn't know you were born – instead of leading it and purring it in boiler at side of fire!
Margaret	Washing day would be the old dolly tub, was it?
Mrs A	Aye, peggy-stick and dolly tub, then I got a washer with a peggy-stick inside. I had that as long as ever I had a washer.
Rita	Washing took practically all day.
Margaret –	Did you have the things on the ceiling, a pulley and that for drying things in winter?
Mrs A	No, we never had a pulley but we had three rails, two up and one a bit lower down, and we allus put them up there on a washing day night. They were all filled rails. We never used to put 'em up as long as you were sitting in.
Margaret –	What farms were there before the war? There was Hill Farm – was it a working farm after you left? Did Lounts go on after you?
Mrs A –	No, Mr. Lount died there. Shepherdsons were there in between us and Lounts.
Rita –	Who did you take over from – one of my great aunts was there? One great aunt was at Hill Farm and another was at North Moor and my great grandmother was at Ocean View. Aunty Polly was married to somebody called John Bielby.
Mrs A	Now, I think that Bielbys were at Hill Farm.
Margaret –	Who would be at North Moor, North Landing, when you were at Hill Farm? Would it be Bayes?
Mrs A –	Langtons: Daisy Langton, Lily Langton and Edith Langton.
Margaret –	And did they used to go home for their lunch?
Mrs A –	Yes, they were in with us [at school] and they used to walk. There was them and Stonehouses at Lighthouse Farm.
Rita	Willy Coates was at the other farm at Lighthouse.
Mrs A	That was Will Coates and t'other was Charlie Coates.
Rita	He was at Thornwick Farm.
Mrs A	Aye, and I've heard him shouting and beealing. You could hear him out of our pantry winder if you had winder open. And chasing Mrs out onto field, if he'd had a few drinks.
Margaret	Oh I see. He was a bit merry like, was he?
Mrs A	Poor awd lad, he warn't half a bit. Still he was a nicer man as ivver walked when he was clear of drink. Henry used ti cum in

and say, "There's awd Dick been on the razzle ageean". And if you were in our pantry you could see right down in their grass, and he was shouting at Mrs and she was shouting back. Generally on a market day he got ower much, and that was only time. Still, when he was alright, you never met a nicer man.

Lily Leng

Sister of Albert Duke, Lily stayed home to take care of the family who earned their living fishing and helped her husband with his fish business.

Lily   Mi dad and our Albert were fishing and mi mother weren't very well so when it came my turn to leave school – I was eight years younger than our Anne and Norah – (they were at Woolworth's) they said to me, "You'll have to stop at home and help us". So that got my lot. All I had in mind was going into a flower shop. I'd gotten the gardening bug then, I think, and I was going into a flower shop but anyway I got mi mind changed for me. You daren't say in them days that you weren't going to do it, you know, you daren't say 'no'. You didn't get asked what you wanted to do, but that was that.

                 I've been looking for photos. This is when they spread fish at North Landing. These were fish buyers – there was George Bayes up there, there was John Willie Bayes, Bessie's father, down near the bottom, there was Vicky Bayes down lane and I don't know if Bob and Micky used to do a bit. There was him and his sister wasn't there? Now, that was one of Alfred's uncles in olden days and Tom Cross, but that's in Hull, they used to sell fish off a cart you see. He was Lizzie Kirby's father. That's Ruby's father there with mi dad, he's the one at yon side.

Rita   Did you have your own boat?

Lily   Well, eventually they did yes. They had one and they called it 'Eleanor Norah' I think. And when they got saved up plenty of money, they'd earned a bit, they bought another one. I'd got well grown then, and they named it after me you see, 'cos I can remember, when it got built, going to North Landing to see it come in. I mean they didn't have them christened or ought in those days. It was built in Scarborough, I was about fourteenish or maybe just under. I can remember going with mi dad to see it getting built and this little snicket we went up – down at bottom of Westborough. But who it was I don't know.

Going back to 1914 war, things were bad in Flamborough and a lot of them went to Hull. Mi uncle, Lou Knaggs, he went to Robin Hood's Bay or Whitby or somewhere. Mi dad went ti Hull and lodged with mi aunt and he went on lighters, as they called them, ships of some sort.

Rita   Weren't lighters the ones that brought coal down the coast? They brought coal down from Newcastle to London.

Lily   Well, they might have been, but that's where they went. It was very bad and they didn't come back ti Flamborough until things were better you see. And they would get a house here, I think Chapel Street would be first one, and that's where they went. Our Albert got to be leaving school and they didn't want him to go to sea, so he got a job at brickyard – on top of Dykes there. But he didn't like it, so all he done was natter to go sea. I think when he was about seventeen, they let him go with mi dad you see and from then on he was going to sea. And then, of course, all he got was crazed to go in lifeboat. Aye, that photo was South Landing lifeboat, rowing boat that was.

Rita   We've seen that photo before. There's Mr Stevenson and Mr Warcup.

Lily   Oh aye, an' there's mi dad and our Albert and then all the rest are either my uncles or Alfred [Mrs Leng's husband] that's why I keep it. Our Anne had it when she died. So I said "Don't do anything with that photo" – when they cleared out – "I'll have it."

Rita   There's Tommy Dust and Kenny this is a lovely photo. Who's this tall one with the beard?

Lily   Don't you remember mi Uncle Bill Tuff? He used to stand at Post Office corner and direct traffic right i'middle of road. He had a big lump above his eye. I could show you a better photo of him than that.

I have a photo of North Landing when the lifeboat was a rowing boat. That was when that boat kem ashore and mi Uncle Tom jumped overboard to see what the situation was. And he got crushed between packet, as they called it, and lifeboat. He hurt his ribs you see and he never did aught good after that and kept having strokes. But that's when that big hole got put in lifeboat. There you are, 'Rowing Lifeboat at North Landing' mi Uncle Bill Tuff, somebody Mainprize, our Albert, one of Alfred's relations, do you remember Mr 'Artley – school teacher? That was a chap that lived on here before it was all pulled down. That would be either Tommy or Kenneth Stevenson, and I don't really know who these are.

Rita   That one behind is Bessie Bayes.

Lily   If that's Bessie, would it be Cameron or someone like that? Do you remember Jennis's shop?

Rita   Yes.

Lily   Well, that was Mr Jennis.

Margaret   That one with the cigarette is Dick Cowling isn't it?

Lily   Yes, it will be. Now then, this is Alfred's mum and dad, and that would be Alfred (as a child), and this is when they kept a horse for pulling up. Alfred's dad – I think he had a job pulling boats up for 'em you see, and that was when they used donkeys to pull up at South Landing.

Margaret   Did Alfred go to sea then?

Lily   No, only in bits, when war started he had to go in the navy. *[Looking at another photo]* There's John Willie Bayes there and that'll be Tom Woodhouse. I think that will be Will Cross.

Now this one was 'ighland. That was at back. You went up a row of houses like at side where Jack Stevenson lived, round about there where this lot is now. They were all fenced and that, but of course they've all been pulled down now. And then there was this row of cottages at back where mi aunt lived, mi mother's sister, and we used to go up there. It was a treat to get a walk up there on a Sunday night.

Margaret   What you did for treats in those days!

Lily   Aye, they were few and far between. Now, you know Rose and Crown here? Well old chaps used to sit behind wall. They used to gather there and at Post Office corner.

Another photo is Tom Cross, Alfred's uncle, Lizzie Kirby's father. Now that is where aud carry cart used to come. I don't know whether you would remember it Rita, I just can. You know it used to come with pots and pans and things on they carried all sorts on. It was summat like a Rington's tea cart with all sorts on, you see – like a travelling hardware store. Now, this photo is when pierrots used to come on Brid sands. You can see the sea. Mi dad is by the stage. They must have had stalls and things. I can remember mi dad tekking me to see them when I was a kid, and they were all dressed up.

Margaret   What did you used to do when you were at home? You'd have the washing and all to do. Did you have a weekly timetable or what?

Lily   *[Laughing]* Oh no, you couldn't stick to a timetable. You see, they used to be baiting and skeining mussels – baiting lines. Sometimes you couldn't start baiting lines while they fetched 'em home, you see, because they couldn't afford ti have that many. So you used to have to wait till they kem home. But they used to be skeining mussels. Mi mother did them. You won't have heard anybody talk about Fanny Kane, Mrs Pilmore they called her. She used to skein 'em a bucket of mussels. She lived up here *[at North End]* somewhere, I think. Then they used to be skeining fit for 'em baiting lines when they kem home. I used to ha' to do housework – this was when I left school – keeping tidy and get meals ready. That was where I got chucked into cooking. You used to ha' to fettle a meal, bake and do like that you know. Eventually I learnt. And then of course you had to help in with all sorts – go to shops, fetch errands. Before I left school, I used to be pals wi' Doreen Shepherd but I got told, "Come straight home as there might some errands to run". So anyway Doreen and Betty Bancroft – they used to get larking and they lived across the Green where council houses are now. And then I used to go round there like, and we used to be round about in summer. But in winter, it was a full time job, it was baiting and skeining and by the time you got finished, it was bedtime. And at one time, before they got electric and that – do you remember it coming?

Rita   Yes, I do.

Lily   Into shed outside, you used to have to bait in kitchen of house. Oh, it was a going on. All I can remember of that, was water dripping off boards, plonk, plonk, plonk it used to be going. I was a kid listening. It used to be like a tune, and that's what I can remember.

We used to get a trip, I don't know whether they still had it when you went to school, Rita. They used to tek us to Lounge Cinema about once a year. We went to Lounge for tea and that was a treat for us. It was school trip, I don't know who paid for it, but they took us from school. I mean we all couldn't go; it would be the older classes. Then of course, we had a day out to Scarborough from Sunday school, and that was alright. It was all we got.

Major's had a big family. I used to lark wi' Billy. We used to be skipping when it was time and then there was whip and top. Before it [the road to the Institute] got made, Woodcock Road got on the go. But before it was made, it was alright because there weren't no traffic. Then we used to go into entrance to Victoria Cottages when it did get done. But I can remember it getting made, and oh, it was a rough road. There was great big stones on it, and there was a cottage next to Freddie's garage. Is it still there?

Rita   Yes, it's still there.

Lily   Oh I forget, anyway Abe Trowel lived there – Alfred, Leonard and Amy. And I used to lark with Amy. We had an old bike what we found and I can remember Amy falling off this bike. Oh, she had a knee, from these real rough stones you know. They were just mekking it then, 'cos there was nothing but field at top you see.

So that was all your school days. There wasn't anything else but out playing and that like. When you got older you had to dig in and help at working, you see, if they were fishermen. And eventually of course, I got learnt to skein mussels and then I had ti help. You were glad when summer came and they were packing up, and then you got a bit of quiet, leisure time. I took to gardening myself to get out of cleaning up and cooking, and that was all there was to it. It was like a job at first, from bed to work in the winter 'cos days were short, so there wasn't much else. Your highlights were a concert at Chapel if somebody put one on, and then of course there was Anniverseries when you went to school.

Margaret When you had to learn your pieces?

Lily   Oh, I used to hate it, I could never remember. Anyway, eventually I did used ti learn.

Rita	Did you go to Wesleyan's or Primitive's?
Lily	No, Primitive's and then of course there was Wesleyan's and Church. But I can remember there was that many on Primitive stage, if you got ti end you were frightened of shunting off – I was only timid in them days.
Margaret	Did you have a new frock for it?
Lily	Oh yes. There was a little shop up here *[North End]*. It was Miss Rushton's. It's where Mrs Holme's cottage *[Puffin Cottage]* is now, and there was a middle one.
Margaret	That one that used to be cobbler's shop?
Lily	No, it would be next to cobblers shop, and she opened a little drapers shop. And I can remember coming up there for a new frock for Anniversary. It was a blue sort of material like. It weren't allus they could afford a new one you know, because there was shoes and everything. But they tried to get you one. There weren't much money in them days you see, they didn't earn a lot in the winter. If they got crabbing when crabs were dear, they used to get a bit you see, but in winter you had to save for a rainy day. 'Course sometimes there was plenty of them. They couldn't go if it was bad weather. No, there was plenty of days when they couldn't go. Oh, it was a job.
Rita	Did your mum knit?
Lily	No, she was ill Rita and she couldn't knit. She told me how to do 'em. She says, "I can tell you what to do but I can't do 'em". So we had a jersey, I don't know where it would come from, that was knitted and I just picked it up, you see, from there. But I've knitted a few and I've knitted them for Alfred an' all. But the last one I knitted, I was getting a bit dim in sight though and it had to be a light coloured un, it was like a fawn colour. You see, needles – they shine especially in lamp light, and you couldn't see to do 'em.
Margaret	Did you just knit them for Albert when you were at home?
Lily	I once knitted one for a chap, they kem and saw it, and he wanted one, and I said well I would knit one. But they used to tek me about a year to knit one, some folks did 'em less and a few weeks maybe, but they did 'em on big needles and they were loose you see, but a proper jersey is real fine.
Rita	Yes, I've still got Auntie Ginny's needles and they're fourteen's aren't they?

Lily	Yes, they're real fine.
Margaret	I mean they never wear out; only the elbows get a bit of wear.
Lily	Well, they used to sleeve them and I got where I used to knit welts and turn 'em upside down. I don't know whether it was Dorothy what gave me that wrinkle, and pick 'em up from bottom. Then when bottom frayed, you could knit bottom off again easy, so you could repair 'em that way.
Margaret	What was your main diet?
Lily	Well, I don't know really, they used to like dumplings and stew and rice puddings. I used to make a variety when I got to know what to do. But I mean there was plenty of meat to be had. There were no scares about meat, of course, that was till war started. Then of course you were rationed but there was plenty of meat and I won't say it was expensive. There was Jack Agar on go then and who was the other one?
Rita	Sid Coates; Jack Agar was with Chew up there, wasn't he, to start with?
Lily	There was another one started in where Lilian Warcup's father lived, or was it Cross's?
Rita	Leeson.
Lily	You had to spread your ration books, two at one and two at another. You thought you got a bit more like.
Margaret	Yes, Laurie used to say your mother was very superstitious, 'cos I've heard him say he used to come round to your house and he'd stand up and then say, "Well, I'll be off", and your mother would say, "Sit down lad". He would say, "No, I haven't time, I'll be off". And she would say, "Sit down lad, will you". He used to do it for devilment; he knew he had to sit down before he went out.
Lily	Well, that is one thing that some folks are still like it now, if you go out of house and forget something, come back but before you go out of again you sit down, so that was how it kem in. If men met nuns or women, though women weren't so bad, going to sea, or if you mentioned rabbits or whatever when they were baiting – oh, you did cop it. Sometime you slipped and didn't think, you know, they were ever so superstitious. Mi mother was an' all, I don't know what else there was, all sorts.
Rita	Was she superstitious about knitting, because Auntie Ginny would never start anything on a Friday.

Lily	No, that was another thing, our Albert was like that he wouldn't start aught on a Friday. But knitting, they wouldn't wind wool in lamplight, they reckoned it was unlucky. I don't know why, maybe summat had happened when somebody had done it and they blamed it.
Margaret	Of course it would be in hanks then.
Lily	Yes, it was in hanks. Even when I knitted, it was in hanks. Miss Sunley used to sell it, and then I got some in Whitby once when I think she'd given over selling it. I think I got one lot there with Alfred. We used to go to a little shop on corner just over the bridge. Mi Uncle Henry lived in Whitby. When it was bad i'winter, some went to Hull and some went that way. Well, mi Uncle Lou went to go with mi Uncle Henry you see. They got that job of mekking all boats and they got 'Easter Morn' *[a coble]* out of it when they paid 'em for mekking film 'Three Fevers'. Well, they used mi Uncle Henry's boat – I think it would be the old boat – to mek it like.
Rita	Yes, and it's his hands in the film isn't it? His hands doing things but they put the film star's face on.
Margaret	Did Alfred say much about going with fish around the countryside with his dad before the war?
Lily	Yes, he would 'cos he learnt to drive on an awd Ford motor he used to say. He would go round with his dad in his teens, and of course they used to go around the countryside selling fish. His dad said he'd stood and watched him many a time to see he'd got across the road alright 'cos he'd set off without looking left or right, 'cos the traffic was terrible i'summer. No, it was a job in them days; I wouldn't like to see them come back.

Olive Traves was supervisor in Marks and Spencer and I got a job in there one summer. I used to be mad 'cos I couldn't go to work. Anyway, I got this job but when it come ti winter I was gunna have ti leave, and she begged me to stop as it was good wages. They allus paid more than Woolworth's or anyone else i'Brid. She said, "You are silly." But I said, "It's no good you had to help in winter". Another summer, when I managed to get a job, I was i'Woolworth's but that had to go when it cum ti winter. So that was my lot for work. |
| Rita | Did you go on the bus or on a bike? |

Lily	Oh yes, I used to go on bus, but there was a bus strike while I was there. I had a bike and I went on seafront on this bike and I gets ti work – oh no, it was after, when I was at Dewhirst's. I gets there and they used ti have a handyman and of course I went on Garrison Street never knowing ni more and not riding bike much, no car in them days. And he says," Hey, do you know you've just come down a one way street? You deean't seem bothered". Anyway, I didn't do it wrong on the way back. When you look back, it's only them things that lightens your life a bit.
Margaret	You didn't go to whist drives or aught like that?
Lily	No, 'cos you never had chance to go. And dances, well, there was such a carry on when some of 'em start to get drunk and that. They wouldn't let you go when you were young and when you got older you didn't bother.
Margaret	Did you get to pictures often or not?
Lily	Well, not often – it just depended how tight money was. You see you didn't used to get any wages or aught like that. No, it was a treat ti get ti pictures – you know – if it happened to be bad weather on a Saturday night or aught like that and that was it.
Margaret	That's where I first saw your Albert, with Alfred. Laurie had got to know me at Flamborough station and I was in digs at Brid one winter. I used to go home to Filey some weekends, and he would meet me off the bus. I used to get off the bus in the bus-station at far end and there'd be Albert leaning on a window, Alfred leaning on another window, George Noddy (Nordass) and George Major. They'd be saying, "Hello, Hello, Hello" all the way along.
Lily	I could show you some photos of 'em all, you see, they were all pals together and at one time they used to go egg climbing. Alfred could talk about egg climbing. He never went down. He was one of haulers up at top. And he never liked pictures in summer, he used ti say he'd far rather go up on cliff top wi' gun or summat, than go queuing up to sit in pictures.
Margaret	Ah well, it was winter when I used to see them, 'cos I was at Brid in the winter and summer at Butlin's.
Lily	Yes, that was what he used to do but they were pals and I have some photos of them where they're all laid out on cliffs at Lighthouse – you might have some.

Margaret	Yes, I think Laurie took some of them – all in their navy blue suits.
Lily	Aye, in their best suits. Our Albert once went to Lifeboat in his best suit. Oh why, we couldn't say aught about him. I think Dick Cowling was coxwain then, and he was at Brid I think. Anyway, he was dressed up i'Sunday suit, and he went straight ti Lifeboat and, by, it was a mess. That was end of suit of course but he'd have ti have another one like, but I don't know how. They used to ha' ti drop all and go you see when the rocket went off. I remember one night sitting nearly all night wi' mi mother, 'cos if they went off i'lifeboat she would sit up all night. We could get 'em on radio. She would listen while they got back again. We'd daren't go ti bed. Anyway like, our Anne had ti go ti work so I said I'd stay up, anyway we listened ti wireless. Do you remember Majors going adrift? I don't know where I've seen photograph, I thought we had it, of lifeboat with Majors in boat, towing 'em into Brid harbour. They were out every bit of night. This boat – it weren't theirs. It belonged ti somebody else and they just went in it. There would be Ted – Billy didn't go ti sea – Bob and young Allen, and they'd no flares, no nothing. They were just going with bare essentials. Oh, it was awful. They were doing well but I don't know if it came in foggy or what but they'd got lost and had no means of attracting attention to get back. By, that was a night, just sat listening to that thing. They used to have Humberside radio then you know, and they would be talking to the lifeboat and then to the boat and then back. She used to sit with her head ti it and I'd say, "Come on let's go ti bed". And she'd say, "I in't going while they ger 'em".
Margaret	Did your dad die before your mother then, Lily?
Lily	Yes, he didn't live long after he stopped going ti sea. He got ti be sixty-five and coming on pension and of course he was going ti pack it up. There was a lifeboat do. He walked ti lifeboat. They used to go and get what they called a jacket *[in order to help the launch]* – they got so much. He walked there and when he kem back he sat with his feet up on a chair and when he wanted ti put 'em down he says, "Oh, my feet – they are numb like". He couldn't walk, if he stood up he couldn't get set off, you know what I mean. They never told you what it was, they just gi' you some pills and that was it. And he never did ni more good after that. He did get pension but I don't know for how long, it weren't

much in them days only thirty bob, a pound for a man and ten bob for the wife. And one reason you had ti stay at home was he used ti set off for a walk up fields above us, never thinking he had ti come back and he used ti go as far as pump and he had ti have a sit down. Many's the time our Albert has had ti go, when we've said he hasn't come back yet, to look where he is. And Fred Atkinson had got car out, gone up Woodcock Road through gate and straight up field ti camp. He used ti be sat i'v hedge waiting ti come back, and he used ti pick him up and bring him back. We'd say, "Don't go any more as far as that; just think you had ti come back". But he weren't exactly soft.

We used ti go for a walk ti allotments when I was gardening. He couldn't do aught like but same as I say, he would stand up in chair but he couldn't get set off he'd shuffle like but that was how we were. You know it was sommat like Alzheimer's, I suppose. That curbed us going out as well you see. Because I mean if we weren't there – me and our Anne – our Albert had ti be there. Either one or t'uther of us had ti be there in case he got up and took hissel off.

But he just went out like a light when he did go. I remember John Major was in our house, he'd got drunk once, I think mi mother used ti tell us, on rum. By, she said he was badly and never took ni more. Anyway, he was in and mi dad said, "By, I could do wi' a pint". So anyway, we weren't used ti going inti pubs where you get pints and our Albert weren't there, so John Major says, "I'll go get you one". So John fetched him a pint and I don't know how long after it was, but that was all he wanted, a pint. And it weren't long before he died. It was funny because he never drunk or anything you see, he just fancied it. And he just went ti bed and mi mother shouted us out, "You'll have ti get up, there's summat wrong with him". We had a bed downstairs i' front room and he was all of a shek you see. And he says to her, "Stop shekking bed". And she said, "Why I in't shekking bed – it's you". Anyway, it had been him and I reckon it had been his heart and he just laid back and when we got down, that was it – he'd gone.

Margaret	Did Albert go to the Institute a lot?
Lily	Alfred did, there's two cups he got in there. Yes, Albert went. He was on committee I think. It was when Mr Wall was there you know and he wanted ti alter it, didn't he, and I don't think they

approved, but anyway they got their own way i'finish. I know they didn't want a bar in it 'cos I think it was a Temperance do. I can allus remember mi mother saying she signed Pledge. It maybe warn't there, it might have been a men only thing, or it might have been that one over where garage was, but it was a working men's club.

Rita   Mrs.Crake at Marton Hall gave a lot of money so there was a working men's club and a Reading Room.

Margaret   To keep the boys of the village off the streets.

Rita   Sort of to teach them to read if they couldn't read.

Lily   Aye, he used ti play billiards did our Albert and Alfred. They used ti go in at Christmas Draw or whatever it was and Alfred had got them two cups. He used ti go through ti Brid with 'em. I used ti say to him after we got married, "Go ti Reading Room", but he'd say, "No I aren't going, not now I've gotten wed. I can sit at mi own fireside". He wouldn't go. I couldn't shoo him there. Alfred was more for outdoor, like as I say, going roaming about, than he was for sport. But he used ti be up at four o'clock in a morning. I mean he was oft gone from here at eight o'clock. After mi mother died, I got a job at Dewhirst's for a bit. Then I turned sick of that and I went ti clothing shop on Hilderthorpe Street, Fairest's, and Mr Acey used ti be there. He used ti say, "Your young man – I saw him at yon side of -I don't know where – a long way off – before eight o'clock time." And they used to be out late and it were still same. When I went wi' him, we used ti go on a Wednesday. We used ti set off from here and go all on Queensgate. And from there, it got ti be dinnertime 'cos there was some Flamborough folks wi' relatives lived on there, and she used ti keep me chattering – wanting ti know all the news and that. She used ti tell me things I didn't know that went off i'Flamborough, and I used ti ha'ti go hesserling after him then on Queensgate. From there we used ti go to Haisthorpe then Burton Agnes – right ti yon end and that's where we turned round ti come back. And as like as not, it would be six or seven o'clock by time. Then course he'd got all washed down – he believed in washing down while he couldn't smell fish, wi' water like, and then of course he had van ti wash out. Then sometimes he would say, "I think I'll do a bit of filleting fit for morning". I mean them were long days for him. Sometimes we've been having dinner at nine o'clock.

Margaret	He used to keep nice fish did Alfred, I used to come on a Friday and get fish nearly every week.
Lily	Aye, Fridays. Well, his dad had a bit of a stroke you know one Thursday morning. They used ti go round by Wetwang, – that was a long day. So anyway, he fetched me and said, "He's had a bit of a stroke or something you'd better ring doctor". We didn't know what ti do. He said, "Well, we'll ha'ti bring him on here". So Art and Alfred pushed and shoved him somehow into Art's car or else van and took him on there to our house. But as you know Alfred's mother was a bit awkward. Could we heck as get her to go. It weren't while quite a while after, that she condescended ti go and live wiv us, so anyway we said, "You'll ettie go, you can't stay on here on your own and especially on a night". She said, "Why folks'll be coming for fish". Alf said, "No they won't, 'cos it'll be locked up while I'm at home, you see". And of course he used ti stop at the cottage a bit. And then we got her persuaded ti go on and do you know after she got there, she was a lot better in health – with the asthma – than she was at the cottage. It was funny, whether it was because they were higher ceilings and there was more air or whatever, I don't know.
Margaret	Where did you live on there?
Lily	"Briarfield" – yon side of Daisy's *[Cowling]*. Well, it was Anna Overy's. After she condescended to go she was a lot better. Times change.

Dick and Ron Traves with Dick's wife, Miriam

Dick and Ron's father worked at Danes Dyke House where they both also worked. Later Dick went into the grocery trade and Ron became a motor mechanic.

Dick's wife, Miriam, is sister to Mark Major and was born in Flamborough.

Miriam	I often think now, I could have asked mi mother things about the past. Mi grannie used to be full of old tales. George Waud knew all the old fishermen and that. Yes, you know, we used ti go down to Ron and Dick's every Christmas. I used ti go with mi grandad for a Christmas tree, 'cos they worked at Danes Dyke and they used to get us one every Christmas, didn't he? I allus got on with Mr Traves.
Ron	Your (Miriam's) grandad could be a case an all. I know when I fost joined band. He says "You're George Traves' lad, aren't you? He used to be in band, he used ti play drum; he still has mouth piece!!" I allus remember that. We used to live at Manor Cottage then. And I worked at Dykes House for six months when I was seventeen. I had ti go and work somewhere or go back ti school.
Dick	Aye, butler, Will Forms, left and I went for six months when Dr.Woodhouse was there, after Lady Cottrell-Dormer. Then I went back to Co-op. When mi dad worked at Dykes House, in beginning it was John Upton, he was there. He was landlord then, and then Bolton. Mi dad worked for both of them. Also for so long he was junior engineer for electricity.

Ron	They had an engine up at farm, old paraffin engine. He used to start it with a blower and there was all batteries. Then next door there was an engine that drove a dynamo that made electricity for Danes Dyke House. And also down at house there was a well, just through the yard going to back door. There was a well there 'cos mi dad used to go down to pump water to a big tank. There was this big tank on top of house and it had iron railings round it, and he used this engine thing ti pump water up into this tank. They had running water in the house and that was his job. Then he was gamekeeper and woodman. I've often looked for this well *[at Danes Dyke House]* because he had a flex with a bulb on it and he used ti lower it down – when all packed up and that – he had that flex. And the things that flex did when electricity came to Flamborough. He really shouldn't have used it 'cos it really warn't strong enough to tek it. But mi mother wanted electric kettle in her bedroom, so she could mek a cup o'tea, and flex up through kitchen floor. I allus remember when they put electricity in oor house, Butte Stacey did it – he married a lass frae Thornwick pub. They gor it down the wall, he gor it in and it was hanging down the wall, ready to put a switch in there and of course he finished that night. Well mi mother started round with a duster, and she turned it up. He says, "Who's done this?" and mi mother says, "I did, I didn't want it running all over carpet". Not long since, a woman in Flamborough, I can't tell you how, every time she pulled plug out, she stuffed it wi' cotton wool to stop electricity leaking out. When they switched light on mi mother says, "I thought I'd dusted" – she was used to oil lamp!
Dick	Mi father was gamekeeper and woodman. You know when you go in Villa gates, this end – the wood on the left – did he plant them, Ron?
Ron	Yes, mi dad and Dagleish. They had a forestry that grew trees and it was at Market Weighton, and when we used ti go to Estrick in train you could see it. There was acres and acres of saplings growing. And he used ti cum and stop at oor house and they put it either side of Villa Road – they planted them trees. A few years ago they sorted 'em out a bit and I was told about it. Ernie Dickinson and me went up and he was saying to fella that was cutting 'em down – he was marking 'em – "You can knock that one down and that one, firewood and good logs". And I says, "It is funny, I was only a bairn when mi dad planted all these". He said, "Did he?" I said, "Yes, we used to go out and watch him".

Dick	Your mam would remember them being planted, Rita.
Ron	I used to spend a fair bit of time at your house, down there at Sparrow Cottage. There was Mary and Ethel and them, they took us to school, they were good. We went when we were three.
Dick	Ethel and Ida took me to school for three or four years. Aye, Ethel was a great pal of mine. Aye, after we had electric in, when we went ti bed you'd hear noise and it was rats knocking bits of plaster off that workmen had left, running down sides.
Ron	Manor Cottage was all under-drawn with wood and you could hear 'em trying to ger up into hayloft. You took it for granted.
Dick	You can't imagine tekking visitors in with an outside toilet these days, but then it was across the yard, next door to pig-sty. We once had a black un. By gum, it was fat. Mi dad had two pigs a year. He sold one to Rushworths and killed the other and hung it up. Most people kept pigs.
Margaret	You were telling me about being in the choir, weren't you?
Dick	Yes, we were the first two servers. We were in the choir until we were fourteen, with Harold Playfoot; he used ti live at North End. And Bob Sunley and Bert Redhead, they were both choir lads, they could sing allus full of fun. We had a choir then, you know, fourteen or sixteen lads and at least ten men.
Ron	I was telling you about every harvest, they put that sheaf of bread at the lectern just before you went up to choir stalls, and we used ti tell younger choir lads to pick it up and tek it to vicar. But of course they couldn't, 'cos they got a knee up their back from men in the choir 'cos they weren't supposed to touch it.
Dick	We used to go to church once a week and had slides on various religious people. Tom Woodhouse allus called 'em funny names and had us laughing at 'em, didn't he Ron? He had cane more than any other kid in school. He was a very intelligent fella and he was very big in all ways. He allus had blue serge trousers on, long short trousers, they cum down ti just below the knee. I've seen Veeter, schoolmaster, give him twenty on each hand, not once, scores of times. Davidson used to say, "Sit in that corner", with Cathy Major's sister, not Bertha, the one that did London, Annie Major. And Tom Woodhouse and Annie Major used ti stop in a corner out of road.
Ron	Do you know he could talk broad, a bit like Dick Bayes, and then as posh as you like, 'cos he was organist as well.

Margaret	Did you pump the organ then? Laurie used to say that somebody used ti pump the organ and it would go "whee-ee".
Ron	Yes, there was a leg, and when you got it pumped up it would squeak and all sorts. I used to do that; it was nice ti ave a squeak going off.
Dick	Aye, we did that and we did serving at least once every Sunday. We used ti go ti church eight o'clock and nine o'clock, eleven o'clock, Sunday School, and half past six. We had ti go, it was only way we could get out at night, to go to church.
Ron	We lived at Manor Cottage and mi dad could see straight down that path. In summer we missed church at Matins, 'cos we had ti go to Communion or there wouldn't have been a server. We used to go straight through church yard and on to South Landing. It was summer holidays and it always seemed to be good weather. We used ti get a bottle of that kaylie powder and mi mother used ti give us some sandwiches, and when tide came up we used ti go on to Roger Sellarslate's at right hand side, and we used ti fish off there. There hasn't been many times when somebody hasn't fallen in. None of us could swim then.
Dick	We used to wait till fishing boats kem in and get those what we called Tell-pies *[whelks]* for bait. If they didn't have any of those we used to have to run down home, dig some worms, and then run back. We mainly caught eels.
Miriam	You had to make your own entertainment.
Ron	Then during the week at Wesleyan Chapel there was allus a concert of some sort. Silver collection, threepenny bit and if you could get through without, well that was it. And there used to be a lot of Flamborough people. Marjorie Bayes was a good singer, Dick Bayes was a good singer, big Dick.
Dick	Bempton lot were very good, weren't they? Concert parties used to come from all ovver.
Miriam	We used to go to Wesleyans. But mi granddad always went to church, you see. But then Sunday School finished at church It came up to ordinary school, so we started going to Wesleyan Sunday School. I remember this, when I was five, Connie Cross said she would take me to Sunday School – Primitives. She called for me and took me. When I got home I said I wasn't going there any more. So when she called for me the next Sunday, mi grandma says I didn't want to go there, and I went to Wesleyans.

	I didn't tell her for a long time but I said, "I don't like that lady, I'm not going with her any more", so we went to Wesleyans and stayed there
Dick	Do you remember a few years ago when they closed the old school and all the old pupils were invited one afternoon? They were reading the old minutes in 1922, and where the class were shooting blotting paper pellets dipped in ink and they were stuck on the ceiling. Well I got caned for that. Spit on blotting paper and roll it, flick it with your ruler
Rita	We were still doing it in 1939 'cos I swear Sallie Bayes could see even when she was facing the blackboard. She must have been able to see through her glasses or something 'cos she could turn round and she knew who it was that had done it.
Ron	Miss Chadwick was nice; I allus got on with her. Charlie James was decorating on Christmas and there was a piece of holly, a long piece, and Charlie cut all the little bits off and took the stick to Miss Chadwick and said, "I've brought you this". "That's just what I could do with". And she used to swish the stick and try and frighten us. They were very nice people, you couldn't fall out with 'em, could you?
Dick	She used to have a real thimble on her hand and tap you on the side of your face. Miss Bayes was very severe; you couldn't kid her on aught.
Miriam	Miss Chadwick's father was coxswain of the lifeboat, you know, and lifeboat used to go off and she used to get all het up, and of course our fathers were fishermen too. But poor Miss Chadwick used to cry. Iris [Cross] used to say to me, "I remember you at school when the lifeboat went off with Miss Chadwick's father, and you were crying 'cos your dad was in it". And I said, "No, it wasn't me, actually it was Norah", 'cos I was never in her class, 'cos I'm a bit older.
Ron	There was two classes in Flamborough; there was Upstreeters and Downstreeters.
Miriam	Fisher people and farmers.
Ron	Downstreeters were from Ned Taylor's corner down, opposite Seabird's, and Upstreeters were from there up. So there was always some competition, and they'd say, "Why, he's a downstreeter".

Miriam	They (meaning Ron and Dick) were downstreeters, I was an upstreeter.
Ron	But when Chris Hartley came *[school teacher]* – he'd have 'em 'Land and Sea'. And the boys, 'Sea-men', they wore a cap with a light blue trim round, and the land uns wore a cap with a red piping round, and they used to be a lot of competition from that. I often wondered who bought caps. I don't remember being given 'em but I've often wondered.
Dick	There was always something going on, even in wintertime. You were always playing wi' marbles or booler
Ron	Well the year was sort of turned round. Spring you got whip and tops. You used to chalk on them all colours. Then you used to get Ringtaw *[marbles]* which you had at Post Office corner or any street corner or footpath. You just used to make a ring then put marbles in centre ring, then you had a shot alley and you used to stand maybe twelve foot away, and you used to shoot at them. If you had mates, like if Dick and me were playing tigither we'd try ti put our shot alley at front o'the ring so the others didn't pass you. And then you'd throw one right into a corner. It's a bit like bowls. In school – lads' toilet, they used to come off wall like that *[it formed a right angle]*; you'd throw one into that corner and you'd have no opposition.
Dick	Sam Chadwick and Tom Stephenson were real crafty. They used to get the biggest alley they could and smash all the marbles, 'cos the marbles were only clay. Sam was a real one for that.
Miriam	We played Hopscotch and we used to play Marbles and Jacks – you played it on your hand. I couldn't do it now, I don't think. You never had time to spare – you always had something to do.
Rita	We missed out on Jacks, they weren't around when we were at school, but Louise played it. They must have come in again because she still has her set of Jacks.
Ron	Square things, coloured, you used ti put six on your hand, throw 'em up and catch 'em on the back of your hand.
Rita	Those hoops – they were marvellous. You used to go and get them from Matt Major's. They were hoops from fruit barrels.
Dick	We used to have steel uns. Mi granddad was a blacksmith in Tower Street. He would mek us one and then we had a stick, and we didn't think owt of running to Sewerby wi' 'em and watching 'em play cricket. There were some good players in Flamborough, your grandfather *[George Cross]*.for one

Ron	If you were going to South Landing you went with your booler and hoop and you run there and you run back. Do you know piece of ground opposite John Brown's and cricket field? We used to play cricket on there and Tower Field.
	After the war there was a lot of coastguards, youngish fellas that had been in the Navy. They were there wireless training up at Lighthouse and they were good footballers. Talking about church and that, with the Reverend Moreton, he was a footballer. He played goal, they used to play in where George Sunley built his bungalow up Bempton Lane, and he was goalkeeper, was Moreton. And we had Boy Scouts, and when Harvey came we had Sea Scouts. But Boy Scouts, to get uniform for them, I used to clean Reverend Moreton's ducks out on Saturday mornings, once a week. And then I used ti do any gardening he wanted doing. I was only a kid so he had ti tell me what ti do. And he used ti put money, whether it was sixpence or threepence, whatever it was in a book. Then when I could afford a shirt you know and a hat, the proper hat, that's where I got my uniform and socks with a little green tab on.
Miriam	It was wonderful when they all got their uniform. We used to have Guides up there as well
Ron	Scout House was that Parish Rooms when you go back way of vicarage to garage, it was over there. There were two rooms. And first vicar I remember here was Rigby, and he was a very severe gadger. He always had leggings on, and I remember, I don't know if it was for choir, but you always got a prize. You went ti school for it and you got a shirt, didn't you? And shirts for a lad, and of course they were shirts for you, but they would fit your dad. And as soon as we got out after meeting or whoever it was, purr our shirts on and went running round frightening people.
Margaret	There wasn't much money around in those days, was there?
Ron	No, but it was funny what you could do with it. You got tuppence a week and there used to be four of us, Dick, misself, Arthur and Stanley Stork. And we could go to Tant Cross' and get 'aiporth of something, then we could go ti fish and chip shop, Jack Major's fish and chip shop in Ship Yard, and get a pennuth of chips and a bit of scrap, and get inti trouble for being in that back place where they used ti chip chips. And we used to play Zip. One lad stands against the wall and all the others bend on him and the other team jump on his back as far as they can. You'd maybe

have as many as ten, five each, and one stood against the wall and the others jumped. Fost jumper had ti jump far enough so the other four could ger on his back as well. Now it wasn't an easy thing; the end one put his hands on his back to get a bit of leverage for his jump. If you didn't all get on, then the other side took on, and when you did all get on the fella agin the wall, he put his hand up and said, "How many fingers have I put up?" And you had ti guess and whether you were right or wrong.

Dick   Well, I'll tell you a story, I shan't mention any names. A farmer med his daughter marry an old parson, he was a lot older than her. When the wedding was on, Flamborough people, the rum uns, the terrors pelted him with grass sods when they came out of church. It's true, mi grandma told me that. I won't mention names.

Miriam   That was one of John Willie's tales, wasn't it? He used ti tell us all sorts of things.

Dick   Our George and Richard, they wouldn't go anywhere until he'd been. Every Saturday night he used ti cum inti shop for maybe an hour and they would sit listening to him.

Ron   By gor, I could tell you some tales. Mi mother used ti go to church on a Sunday night and this was before I was in choir, so I was very young. Mi dad used ti tek me ti mi granddad's. That was shop in Tower Street, just past Wiles'. Mi grandma used to walk down to our cottage and go ti church wi' mi mother. Then there was Tom Traves, Dully, George Thompson's father; there would be Matt Bailey and a few on 'em used ti go to mi granddad's, and the tales they used to tell. They could go on and on telling tales. And then when they'd been there about an hour, mi granddad used ti say, "Who's going?" stick in the pitcher, mulled ale. They used ti drink it out of cups 'cos there warn't the glasses in those days. By, they did used ti tell some tales!

You had to be in at eight o'clock, or seven o'clock, in winter and if you weren't, well trouble! And you used to play cowboys, a gang of you, and catch one another with lassoes, 'short ower', 'dogs can't talk'. And when they got hit, move on, and so on until policeman saw you. Policeman used to have one of them canes, and he used to use it an' all.

Dick   Do you remember running up the hill where oor bungalow is now?

Ron	Aye, he hit me on mi back with it. We were going to form a football team, and older lads than me, we used ti go and play in that field just across there. Woolworth's had just about started up in Hull and one of these older boys says, "My uncle goes ti Hull and you can get football jerseys and shorts, and they're only threepence a piece". So we would collect for 'em. So we went home and collected what jam jars we could and empty bottles. Jam jars a ha'penny, or big two pound jars a penny, and lemonade bottles. Not that you had any lemonade but you used ti get kaylie purr in, and we got rid of 'em, all but one bottle. I should think there would be twelve or fourteen of us, and I should think me being youngest or smallest. We filled the last bottle, which we couldn't sell, with water at Dick Bayes' tap, on High Sreet. It's still there. Then we went up street and went down the Avenue and second door down Avenue there was an old fisherman – he was sat on a stool wi' door oppen and somebody threw bottle in. I was at the back like. It wasn't thrown at him, just in. He got up and run and I was last, he must have tuk his slipper off or fell, or summat, he stumbled and knocked me down. And we were frightened 'cos it was a serious job but I didn't know what they were going to do, but I was there. So I went straight inti mi granddad's blacksmith shop and he was working, and there was an awd fella and they were talking and I used ti sit at back a fire and pump it up. And he says ti me, "You're all of a flush, what's up wi' you, what have you deean?" "I ain't done anything". I wished I hadn't done anything 'cos we could get belted. Policeman kem ti school next day and they had us all out of class. Of course, silly me, I went an' all and he'd told us that we had done a very serious thing and we'd get into trouble for it, but we had to go and apologise. So at dinnertime off we went and apologised. I'll tell you what – I didn't go up rent, I was only on street running through. I allus remember that.
Miriam	I remember Bessie Bayes and Sylvia and me and one or two more went to Guides once and we went on a track thing, you know, and we left some gates open at Woodcock's. We had to go and apologise. It was first time I'd been in that big room, he was doing nothing but laugh at the time; we were frightened. We had to go in and say we were sorry, some animals had got out.
Ron	We used ti get an empty jam tin, tie a string round it, fill it full of water, purr it on a winder sill, tie it to a door knob and knock on door. That was one trick. Then there was a button and pin, to

	tap on winder. Then there was 'devil up spout'. That was just put a bit of rag up spout, light it and it used to boom up spout. Those were just regular things you allus did.
Dick	They used to tek post to Flamborough Station every day, and old Billy Harris was driving and he had one of these caps with a peak on. Me and Walter Readhead – he got on one side of churchyard and me on the other side with string, and as he came trotting by we fetched his cap off.
Ron	Another thing we used ti do. Crofts Hill, there allus used to be landaus and parties and horse and trap coming from Brid and what have you. They used to tek 'em up to Lighthouse and North Landing, and we used to stop at bottom of Crofts Hill. They used to have to walk up hill, so we could run and sit on axle and have a ride up ti top.
Dick	When Bill Sayers was driving Blue Bus we used to have a sledge behind bus, and he used to pull us up to Lighthouse and then down again on this sledge.
Ron	Just with back door open. He used to put a piece of wood across door and tie sledge on. When I started on Blue Buses and left Danes Dyke, I got a job of a mechanic apprentice. And I saw Mr Atkin and he said, "I'll have to see your father", and I thought that's done it. Anyway I went home and told mi dad, and I gor him talked round, and I said Mr Atkin wanted to see him, and you can have a free pass on the bus. So we went and we saw Mr Atkin. He, mi dad, didn't want me to leave Danes Dyke. He was charging batteries for electric and pumping water to top of house for ever and then that would be my job. The most mi dad ever had was thirty five bob a week, and I got six shillings a fortnight, that's what I had. I got the job on Blue Buses and I left school at fourteen, and got the job on the twenty first of February. Johnny Traves was there – he was a bit older than me then, so I would do the next year. Mr Atkin cum ti me and said, "Ron, how old are you?" and I said fifteen and whatever it was and he said, "You're sixteen now, go upstairs and Mr Coates will fill a form in and you'll get your driving licence". So I got a driving licence, and you know Beck Hill, our buses were right at the bottom there – Sawmill Yard. We had so many buses in there and you could get over a wall to it. That's where everything was done. There's many a time we got drivers, come to work for summer and couldn't back a bus out of the garage. You see you

had to back up a hill and come out inti Beck Hill. Johnny Traves used to back 'em out, and I used to back 'em out, and we used ti get threepence or summat like that; that's how good they were. Anyway I got mi licence and I got driving. And Billy Sayers, he used ti get off at nine o'clock, and they lived in Dog and Duck Square. So Billy used ti ger off and have his supper and I used ti tek his bus to Lighthouse. There was no restriction on age and that was a very good thing because it was nearly every night I used ti look forward to it and it was good training like. Then when it got nearer into summer I had ti drive in mi spare time, and it was wonderful to me 'cos you don't know who to go with. I used to have cushions ti sit on, and I had a cap you know, you had to have a cap to drive in, it came right ovver mi ears.

Dick   In winter it was good on our sledge up ti Lighthouse, but we never had any accidents.

Ron   In winter we used to get a lot of snow and ice. The Mere was full in winter and a lot of folks had skates: and especially on a Sunday when we left Sunday School, we used to start running on it, a whole gang of us.

Rita   Yes, playing Tewey.

Ron   Aye, you know, it used to move in waves, you had to keep running; if you stopped you fell in. But it stopped all people who had skates, they couldn't skate and they did go on! Margery Bayes got hold of me and she said, "Ron Traves, if your mother knew she'd be very annoyed", and slapped my hand. Margery was a very nice person, why they all were as far as that goes. But the first school teacher when I went ti school was Miss Woodhouse, Sid Coates' wife, Ron Coates' mother. She was a nice quiet woman. I thought she was a lovely person; she was real kind to us, you know, she had no badness in her. I allus kidded Ron Coates when I saw him, "Don't get cocky lad, thu's second". There was only two Rons in Flamborough, I was first and he was second. They called me Ron because they were going to call me Donald but there was Donald Wiles.

Miriam   I remember Miss Woodhouse being at school. I remember when she was getting married, we gave her a present. I was only an infant then, its over sixty years since.

Ron   Why, weren't she Infant teacher? I remember Mr Rawnsley, he was at school when I first went there.

Dick	Mr Rawnsley was coming out of Post Office and somebody says, "Now Mr Rawnsley, how are you?" and he said, "I'm alright but I can't get this hand to go. It won't go at all". And he died next day. I allus remember that. A grand fella: he taught mi dad. They went ti school when they felt like it, didn't they?
Ron	He allus reminded me of King George V, he had a beard like him. If ever we went to choir on a morning or anywhere, mi dad would allus ask us when we came in for dinner, "What was the collect for the day?" Didn't he? I'll tell you what; they knew the collects for the days because you were brought up on church. You went to church oftener than you went anywhere else, so we had the prayer book out.
Dick	There wasn't the badness in the village in those days. Mischief yes, but no badness. We used to flick bits of paper across to one another when we were in the choir and sometimes they landed on the heating grill or something. There must have been a right old heap in there by the time they cleaned them out.
	Do you remember when Moreton had hiccups that Sunday, he was trying to stop his hiccups and he was, "Ooups, ooups", I never heard owt like it, we all laughed. You know white wall round by Manor House. Well it's low now but it used to be high. And when they fetched it down George Sunley's dad, Albert was knocking it down, and there was a bald head built into the wall! I can see it now.
	We had pigeons, and I was main pigeon man. And that very day we were racing from Peterborough, and Albert Sunley says, "there's a pigeon just landed on your loft", and I went and it was blue and white one, and I got first prize, one stone of corn.
Ron	And as soon as pigeons come we used to run it and position ourselves; one would run it as far as Ned Taylor's corner and another one would tek it on a bit further. There was three of us, 'cos we hadn't a clock in those days. We got the ring into their clock, you were allowed so much depending how far away you were. Clock was at Drill Shed. Sometimes you got half a stone of flour. You didn't get any money or owt like that, and there was only the one clock at Drill Shed.
Dick	Don Wiles' brother, Will Wiles, was a special constable and he used to be at Post Office corner. When Freddie Readhead came up on his bike, he would stop him. I really loved keeping 'em.

| | Matt Bailey used to live in Dog and Duck Square, you maybe knows where, when you turn first right to go round. He was a cobbler, shoemaker. That was the place we always used to go to if it was wet, cold, or owt like that, and Matt Bailey was making big fisherman's boots. We could allus go to Matt Bailey's on a Sunday night, and he was allus telling us something. He was a nice awd fella, he didn't mind. . |

Dick   You would know mi uncle Robert, that girl of Major's used to go with him. She used to leave him at our house while she went down for milk. Him and mi dad allus used to argue about how to cut apple pie.

Ron   I remember that, we were having oor teas but he wouldn't have any tea, but he'd have this apple pie. And he was blind but he'd argue with mi dad how to cut it. He used to get a suit from Bradleys from Leeds. Bradleys used to come and take Manor Cottage for maybe all August. We used ti sleep outside in a tent and we allus got a suit, mi dad got a suit, Dick and I got a suit and Fred Atkinson used to get a suit, and old man Atkinson. I reckon they would get more for suits than they would pay for cottage. Then they took Hawthorn Cottage after that, didn't they?

Dick   Yes, do you remember that robin nesting in the watering can, just at back door at Hawthorn Cottage?

Ron   And we used to have a band. I played cornet.

Dick   I tried to join but Miriam's father wouldn't let me. He wouldn't have me, wouldn't Mark; I was always taking the mick.

Ron   He was a good player, was Mark – he played with Jack Cowling, cornet and Tom Cowling was band-master. But when I fost joined, just after First World War, Mr Bee, he was band master in Army, and you had to start at beginning and play for him and he'd give you a position in band. He could play everything, every instrument, including piano. Mi mother had a hymn book with music for piano and we used ti get that and tek it into tool shed and blow hell out of it in there. We used to play for Fisherman's Sunday, February Gale 1871. I was in band six or seven years. We started at Cenotaph and then played up to Priory Church.

Dick   Tell you who I always admired in band, George Colley: euphonium, he could play it.

Ron   We were playing this time and films had just come out, and they used to tek films of us, and there was one right on where the signal box is at station, at level crossing. We'd just finished playing – we'd played from cenotaph – and George Waud, he played big Bass and he'd spotted 'em being at front. He tonned round and said, "Come on, play up you buggers". We couldn't, you had to get right music! We used ti go to Danes Dyke wi' choir at Christmas, mince pies and ginger wine, and then we used to go to Cliffe House.

Margaret   Did you go on the cliffs much playing? I remember Laurie saying he went down somewhere but they played hell up 'cos his suit got mucky on a Sunday.

Dick   Old Fall. I used to go poaching rabbit, I always had a ferret.

Ron   All night we used to go four or five of us, Walt Readhead, Dick and myself. We'd always be in the fields there and we had some nets and a ferret, hadn't we? We used to muzzle the ferret and a piece of string tied to his bottom and bring it up tied to his top, so he couldn't eat rabbit. We used to get quite a few rabbits.

Dick   Walt Readhead and I went one New Year's Day. We went with a ferret to Hartendale Goat, and there wasn't any, but six rabbits ran into some Hawthorns across on Zedman's, and we thought we'd put ferret down there. We must have sat for two hours and nothing and then all of a sudden they started running about and we caught six. But just before that had happened it was the general 'Shoot' day and there was shot and shell and we were poaching and we had six rabbits! We daren't show ourselves above hedge top and there was shot and shell all round.

Ron   I know first year I was at Dykes, first Christmas I had to help the butler, I had to clean shoes. They had one of those things you stuck knives in. It was sort of a drum with slots in and inside it had Shinio, and knives used to stay put. Every now and then you were messing about and turning real fast and all bloody lot would fly, then there was trouble. And while they were having breakfast I used ti tek coal into the bedrooms.

Then, when I'd got all these chores done, I used to go on to gardening with Johnny Robinson from Sewerby and Tom Cowling, Laurie's father. When I'd finished breakfast, I used to look across yard and if there was a jug of tea there that was it. It was there for you. When they'd finished, we'd go down into the boiler hole. They had a boiler for heating the greenhouses, and we used to go down there and we hadn't any cups or aught, so we used to drink it out of the jug. And Johnny used to say, "Aye why, is she quaffable?" And he would have a sip and I was last. "Aye, she's quaffable, in fact she's quizzable". You know you'd sup it all. It was just nicely after the war and Johnny had been in war in France, and he'd got a Military Medal and he told us all about it. Tom had been too young to be in war and when conversation was getting to end and jug was empty, Tom used to start with something else. It was nice and warm down there, instead of going up there and digging the garden. Aye, he got Military Medal, he was a Lewis gunner and he said they were absolutely in the mud and that. And there were seven at a Lewis gun: there was a firer, the loader and what have you in the gang. And second day he was at it, he went as No 4 as firer. The others had been killed. They got a shell which absolutely smothered them with mud and all that. Then the ones that weren't killed retreated and they realised that they hadn't got a gun, so Johnny went back, fetched the gun, cleaned it, and they held their new position. He told us how he got it, called out and given the medal. It had been a bravish thing he'd done.

Margaret	It's a long time since you started in the shop, isn't it Dick?
Dick	Your mother-in-law made me some money. She came in often when I first opened, and after about two years she said, "I hear you're going to boil ham to sell in the shop. And I said yes I was going to and she said, "bring it to the boil and then add either a handful of Demerara sugar or a small bottle of Guinness; boil it up again and let it simmer for four hours, but don't let it boil again". That was a fourteen to sixteen pound ham and it was beautiful. She said her mother worked in service in Scotland. She, Mrs Smith, used to check up on me and I used to give her a quarter now and then. 1948 when I went there – the shop – November 1st.

First complaint I had about it, Boy Brown's wife said that the ham was lovely on the outside but it wasn't ready in the middle. Four hours, and Richard still does it, 16lbs ham, put in this big pan, bring it to the boil; you put your Guinness in it straight away, or Demerara sugar and let it simmer for four hours, its perfect for the hotel. ['Thornwick Private' – now 'Flaynburg'] And all the sausages we made!

Rita	I used to love those herb sausages, they were good, and that ham was good as well.

Dick	I used to make forty pounds on a Monday and by Tuesday lunch time they'd gone. A bit of seasoning in – marjoram.
Margaret	Mother-in-law was in service, I think. We never knew much about her family, apart from there was a big family of them at York, but she never kept in touch with them.
Dick	Her mother was a cook in Scotland. Every Saturday I used to do a full ham on the bone and one to slice on the machine, and two thirty pound turkeys on a Saturday.
Ron	I wish they had it today, Dick, at the same prices. You never went asking for a shilling or half a crown 'cos they hadn't it, had they? Mi mother used to go out when Jo Rushworth's used to come from Brid, on a Friday, for Sunday joint, and the arguments she used to have. "No, well thu can keep thy meat then!" and it was only for a penny or tuppence, and she'd get it. Jo used to say, "I shall have to mek it up myself".
Dick	And she used to say, "That brisket you sent us, it was all fat". "Well did you waste any of it?" "No we had to eat it", maybe sixpence a pound. Another thing, when it was school holiday at Christmas time we used ti go to North Landing, about when the fishermen used to be coming in, and we used to help 'em to spread all fish out on the sand for buyers to see. There was always a lot of fish that wasn't cod or haddock, such as gonnets and all sorts. They used to give us some and we used ti tek 'em home, and mi mother used ti clean 'em, and she used ti mek bread or those scones and gravy. She allus used ti bake it. By gor it was good; I wish we had it now.
Miriam	I remember when they used to spread all the fish out. When we were at school, from being about seven or eight, we used to spend all summer holidays at South Landing. It was always fine. We used to pack up, pack our dinner and tea, jam sandwiches and that. I think we used to have had it all by about four o'clock and we were all ready to come home. I always had family with me, younger kids to take with me you know, I think nearly everybody went – children – when they were young.
Dick	There was always a lot of sand and it was always fine. You always enjoyed yourselves. I don't think anybody locked their doors; we never did, Manor Cottage was never locked. It's a different world all together now. When I was fifteen, I went to Escrick, to my uncle's, butchering for three or four months, and every Monday he used to tek us to York Market, horse and cart, me, and the lad,

	and we had to ark two bullocks and six sheep back every Monday night, rain, snow or blow, six miles from York to Escrick. We never complained about it. Every Saturday morning boots were out and cleaned.
Ron	Didn't get owt for it either, did you? They used to put beef into salt brine when they killed, and you had it for dinner.
Dick	No, we got nowt for it, only a big fat lamb chop for your tea. We ate all the rough stuff, you never saw a bit of steak.
Ron	I went ti mi Auntie's quite a bit when I was stationed at Richmond, Catterick. Saw Laurie there, and Eric Major and quite a lot of 'em one Saturday night; we all had a drink. I went first to France when I was called up, and I went to Catterick when I came back from France.
Dick	I went there for mi demob, before mi demob. No, it was Strensall.
Margaret	We went up a couple of summers ago. Laurie kept on about the Green Howards' Museum at Richmond, and I said we'd have a run up. He was in the Green Howards. He was driving a Bren gun carrier, but he wasn't called up till after Dunkirk.
Ron	I was back in Catterick from Dunkirk, when I saw him.
Dick	It's a wonder Mark Major hadn't got hold of him being a Green Howard.
Margaret	Well, sometimes when he's seen him in the Club, he's chatted to him about it. He said, I'd love to go to Richmond" so we went up one day and we came back through Catterick Camp. "See that tree over there? That used to be our aim for firing and it's still there, nobody blasted it quite away". He was in Bren carriers, because he said, "I'm going to have something I can ride in. I'm not going to walk".
Dick	Aye, Bren gun carriers, he'd be in "D" Day then.
Margaret	Yes, he was in France then or Belgium.
Ron	I had ten months in France before war started. I went out in September 1939. I joined Reserves in 1938. I joined for fifteen pounds a year; it was a suit, a pair of shoes and a shirt, I never got it though. The only reason I joined, after the First World War I used to be absolutely sick of people falling out. "What did thu do i'war, then?" They all used to be at Post Office corner and Ship corner, all working men out of work, 1938 and 1939 and right from War. I remember searchlights. I should be six

	when war finished and I remember mi dad gerring us up to see something.
Dick	Was it that sea-plane that landed on that laure at South Landing there?
Ron	Why there always was sea-planes there, Italian sea-planes; there was about four. That was what Roger Sellarslate's laure was made for.
Dick	Near where that water runs down, Bob Chapman blew it up, don't you remember? Roger Sellarslate's is just to your right. It was made during the war – First World War. Before the Second World War they blew it up – Bob Chapman and his son.
Ron	Then come real rough weather and he couldn't do it, and he gor away with a lot of it.
	Mi dad always used ti goes for a walk to Lighthouse every Sunday night. There used to be him and Matt Bailey, Preddy Readhead, Dulley and Mr Thompson, and they used to be right across road. They used ti set off about 10 o'clock and road used to be full walking abreast. They used ti go to Banks' gate, that's first gate agin awd lighthouse, and odd times I used ti go, because I was very young. And once when we went one Sunday night, we went across Ned Taylor's to cliff, and there was a battle at sea and the lifeboats were right in the bottom of the cliff – I remember that. All this battle was sort of going on, and some had got ashore or had been washed up and had got ashore – I couldn't tell you what battle it was. I also remember one Sunday an aeroplane landed this end of golf course and I should think we were first there, two or three of us.
Dick	Dulley, he was in charge of the road men, and he got a man started work, roadman – ex army – and he wanted to know his particulars, where he was born etc, and he didn't know. "Well, George, you have neither home or habitation, you were born up a haystack, and cows have eaten your parish". And that is absolutely true. He didn't know where he was born or how old he was or anything.
Ron	You see there was never any traffic on roads; you could walk on roads and be safe. In fact when I worked at Bridlington you could come up Fortyfoot and turn right into Long Lane, as we called it, Martongate as it is now, and you never looked left to see if there was anything coming from left.

Dick	I started selling fish in 1948 and a lad from Hull had introduced me to Johnsons, where I got mi fish, and they were here for the week-end at our house. So he said he'd come with me this Friday night delivering fish. Coming back from Brid – it was still daylight – and coming up Fortyfoot to roundabout turning right for Flamborough, he says, "You never stopped and looked did you?" "No, 'cos there's never anything coming", I says. That was Ken Doings.
Ron	I'se think you can remember, Rita, at Fortyfoot – that ring; you never went round it when you were in buses and that, you went to this side of the roundabout. You just turned right to Sewerby. There was a bus stop at other side of road. You had respect for everybody, hadn't you? I'll nivver forget our Richard at shop; and George Robson and Florrie our Richard was serving. "Now then, Mr. Robson", he said – and I forget who it was in said, "Dis thu call him Mr. Robson?" "Yes", he says, "He's older than me and I've been brought up to respect age". When I was working on mi own there, I always called mi customers Mr.
Dick	When you hear now they're calling their boss by his first name. Nobody ever called me by my first name when I was in charge.
Ron	No, when I first went to work for six shillings a week, and, when I went to Blue Buses – five shillings a week practice. Second year, Johnny had been there a few months longer than me, and he kem to his second year and he give him ten bob. I should have got seven and sixpence but he gave me ten bob. When I cum out of Army there was Holtby and White's wanted me, there was Saville's wanted me. And I says on mi embarkation leave, I would go to Saville's and then I went to Holtby and White',s and I've never forgotten – one and ninepence an hour.
Dick	Why, builders were on sixpence an hour, weren't they?
Ron	Jim Smith – I allus remember him in Rose and Crown – was a fella I allus respected, his age and his knowledge and what have you – and his bluntness! He wouldn't cut any corners. If he had owt to say to you, you'd get it.
Dick	Do you remember when we played darts, going to Filey with Jim before the war?
Ron	Cigarettes went up to two an six a packet, and he got a packet and a box of matches and Jack Craven, landlord, said he hadn't given him enough money, as both cigarettes and matches had gone

	up. "Tek 'em back", he says, "I'll nivver smoke another bloody cigarette", and he didn't.
Margaret	No, he didn't, but he had a packet of cigarettes when he finished, and they were stuck on the mantle-piece for years. Robbie Traves was working for them and he said to Dad, "Can I go to shop?" and Dad says, "What for?" Robbie said, "I want some cigs". Dad says, "I have some you can have, instead of going to the shop". And he got these cigarettes but they were very dry and Robbie says, "Where did you get these?" "They've been on the mantlepiece for years, lad".
Ron	I allus had cigarettes in mi pocket after I stopped smoking, 'cos you can allus tek packet out of your pocket and put it back again.
Dick	Old man Knowles wouldn't supply any sandwiches when those fellas kem from Filey, so we had to tek 'em. And when we went to Filey they allus gev us a good "set to". He never could get on with him, couldn't Jim. That was just before the war.
Ron	He would allus go if there was a whist drive and dance. He would allus tonn up at dance. He didn't dance but he always had a bottle of something with him. If he hadn't, somebody else had!
Margaret	I've heard him a time or two on about a coal agent who used to come up during the last war from Hull to Flamborough, to the Rose and Crown. Dad used to get him eggs, and this time he got these eggs and boot of the car was full of eggs. *[This was illegal as eggs were rationed at this time.]* The policeman kem out of pub and says, "Now what have you got in there, Black Market stuff?" And he says, "Aye, that's right", and policeman just walked away. They were quaking in case he'd made them open the boot!!.
Dick	There was a lot of that going on. I remember a sergeant in Brid, and he was telling us where he'd been and caught so and so. This lady had put on a meal of lamb chops and all this, and they were talking about this Black Market as though he wasn't bothered. It was Abraham, he was court usher, and Arthur says, "You've got an easy catch there", and he says, "Not likely, you don't bite the hand that feeds you". Old Scrowy, PC Scrowston, was watching me sometimes at 44 Council Houses and her father was helping me. Scrowy was at Billy Sayers' corner and he, Miriam's father says, "He's watching thu, let's put these back", so we put them in Wilkinson's straw stack.

Margaret	Did you know anything about somebody tekking wheels off policeman's car once? I've heard Jim on about that. They jacked his car up on bricks, then when he wanted to go, he could'nt. But I can't remember who it was.
Ron	What we used to do: them Jowitts – on the road – they just had a little hole for exhaust in middle. We used to get a cork and stick it in. And then – when they started it up, or it wouldn't go – they used to keep revving and they did get cross. They didn't pinch things like they do now. I don't know how they get away with it, by heck I don't.

Nellie Gardham (née Taylor)

Nellie was the daughter of a farmer and was brought up and worked on the farm as well as delivering milk round the village.

Nellie	We lived at that farm was just on the corner across from the Seabirds. Rita and Les used to come across for milk didn't you?
Rita	Yes, we did – a penny a glass.
Nellie	A penny a jug. I'll tell you who used to come for milk when they were here in summer, Althea, and it was milk then weren't it?
Rita	Yes Althea Stipetic. And sixpence in a glass jug on a Sunday, for cream, for tea.
Nellie	Mother used to make curd and all.
Rita	What did you take the cream off with?
Nellie	We never had a separator. Wilkinson's had a separator on Church Farm. Well, you used to separate that to make butter you see. Then, when cows calved, mi Mother used to make pans and pans of curd 'cos you couldn't sell milk for so many days so you can make curd. We had what we called 'biselins' – the first milk *[after calving]*. You could make curd and it turned straight away for the curd. Some people turn curd with Epsom Salts don't they? Mi mother always used alum, but Epsom Salts makes real nice curd. Then we used to sell it 'cos Walter used to go round with cans of milk.
	I used to come to Laurie's Mum and Dad with milk, before you were married. Then I used to go across to Bessie's, Bessie Bayes,

	through that side and she used to say, "Go in then, get a jug, put kettle on. I'm just going ti tek mi Dad his breakfast and then we'll have a cup of tea". She was a good sort.
Rita	Did your Mum sell butter as well, because I can't remember buying butter off you?
Nellie	Well, as I said, when we had calves she made curd, and we had a churn and could mek it. But no, she didn't make a lot – more or less what we used ourselves.
Margaret	That was hard work wasn't it 'cos you had to keep turning it. I can remember from when I was on a farm during the war, when I was evacuated, they used to make it. We used to go and turn the handle.
Nellie	And generally, we used to kill a pig at Christmas. Stan Wilkinson down at farm – d'you remember Stan and Clarr at Church Farm? Well, Stan really was a butcher by trade, and he used ti come 'cos mi Dad was always friendly wi' Wilkinson's and he used to come and kill a pig. They allus said you could use everything on a pig but it's whistle! But you could make braun and black pudding and everything. Then mi Dad used ti cure bacon and ham and it got hung up in farm kitchen – there was hooks like – and you used ti rub salt in...We used ti put saltpetre in the veins. Oh, it used ti mek your hands sore.

I used ti come ti Laurie's Mum and Dad wi' milk like you call it Greenside – well, we allus called it Back Street Hill didn't we? Me and Anne Major were allus friends and she lived up there 'cos mi grandmother lived next door ti Anne's. There were three cottages up there.

Margaret	Yes, that's right, Warcup's lived in this end one, George Warcup lived in next one. There was two brothers and then the one that got married lived in second one so did Anne live in next one? Then there was two or three lower cottages.
Nellie	I don't know who lived in next one, but Sam Woodhouse lived in first of the smaller ones then Dickie Major's and then mi grandmother. Mi Uncle Frank Taylor was very friendly with Jim Smith and they used to clock pigeons in at Drill Shed – they'd come running wi' pigeons.
Rita	How many cows did you have then?
Nellie	I don't remember how many mi Dad had, but Walt had about fifteen, and we had pigs and sheep as well. There was two houses

	here and we were nearly going up to South Landing, and mi Dad bought these, you know when the estate broke up in 1926. Then we had some land up Lighthouse Lane that we called 'Ringeralls' and the little field down Lily Lane as well, and a field opposite Thornwick pub. All the land to this 'Ringeralls', it really belonged to a church in Manchester and it was charity land and we had to send the rent to this church because it had been left in trust and it was supposed never to be sold. Maybe in time, eventually, they must have decided to sell it to him 'cos our Walter used to keep calves and lambs in. And then we rented what we called 'Town End'.
Rita	It would be where houses ended *[in Chapel Street]*.
Nellie	Mi Dad worked the farm apart when he was living and there was the lad lived in, what you called 'hired'. Les Burton lived with us, he was four years with us, and then as Walter got older, he helped mi Dad. Walter went ti fields, ploughing and that, and mi Dad and me went round wi' milk. We had a pony and cart to go round wi' milk. Neither of us got married till I was twenty-four and he was twenty-eight, then I used ti go on mi own with pony and cart.
Margaret	How far did you go round the village, Nellie?
Nellie	Oh, I used to go down to Farrington's *[bungalow set back from road at bottom of Croft's Hill]*. It's a right pull up that hill. I know many a time in bad weather, when I've been going down, I've nearly slipped down and landed in mud. I tell you who worked there, was it Violet Mainprize and May Hall.
	I was allus at home up to mi mother dying 'cos I helped ti nurse her. Mi Dad he suffered with rheumatism as well, he was never very strong you know. Walter's more like Stonehouses. He was like mi Dad but mi Dad was much taller. Both of us were dark like mi Dad, very dark. We kept chickens in a big black shed up at 'Ringeralls'. And they used to come over, so many years, from this church and they'd see it all and maybe it was five or six years you sent your rent to this church. So, however, Jack Agar took land up at Wold Farm and he got that field at 'Town End'.
	Oh, there was some prime customers when I used to go with milk, 'cos you see there was some cottages next to Seabirds, do you remember them?
Rita	Yes, I do, I can remember Bluett's living up there and Chadwick's.

Nellie	There was two and then a smaller one and then there was a rent *[passageway]* to stop anyone. Aye, well, they lived down the front. And Billy Beall was there and Aaron Bielby. Do you know, he'd put his clothes on table and brush 'em, shirts and all such as that. I mean this day and age unless you had a washer you couldn't wash properly. Two different ones lived in the next one but Bluitt's lived in the bottom one.
	Bess used to sit and tell fortunes you know and that chap they used to call him – they all had nicknames hadn't they? I think they called him 'Dunc'. He used to come across and help mi Dad a bit. Billy Beall lived in the bottom one and then who lived on where St Quentin's lived, would it be Lockwood's?
Rita	No, Lockwood's lived at the other side, didn't they? I can't remember them living anywhere but the other side.
Nellie	Oh yes, there was four cottages, I think, and they pulled them down and built 'lectricity *[the electricity showroom that used to be on Tower Street]* and that house. There would be Tant Traves lived there, and Pinder's.
Rita	Yes, that's right, Clifford Majors lived somewhere down there when I was young.
Nellie	Yes, Clifford Major's lived where the rent is, they lived in there and then Traves' lived in the next one and then Pinder's.
Rita	Uncle Arthur Kingston lived somewhere down there.
Nellie	That would be in next block and I tell who was living in one – Tom Freeman lived in that end one.
Nellie	All up Allison Lane like, they were more or less fishermen. When we went with the milk we used to go into one house maybe Binnin's, they allus lived in the back. And I used to go through Knagg's and mi Dad used to say, "Go in at front through back to Binnin's". I went to nearly all the fishermen with milk.
Margaret	How did you meet Jim then, was he Flamborough born? Were you younger than him then because you aren't on that picture are you?
Nellie	No, I'm seventy-seven, he would have been eighty in February.
Margaret	What did you get up to at school then? Mischief?
Nellie	No, Sarah Anne used to live with Mrs Kind. I believe she lived here, with Mrs Kind. Sarah Anne was a good teacher though, but, by gum, she used to shout. I mean you learnt all your tables

and that, didn't you! By gum, she made sure you did learn all your tables – over and over. Her classroom was very dark wasn't it?

Rita   Oh yes, it was.

Nellie   And then, when lifeboat went off, and Sarah Anne went home like we went to Sally Bayes's. She was a good teacher too, wasn't she? We did sewing and knitting. She was very nice was Sally Bayes. In fact, when we left, she asked us if we wanted these photographs, so I fetched these photographs. I never really knew which was mi Dad's likeness, anyway I took this photograph to Women's Institute and Sally Bayes was there and I said, "Can you tell me which was mi Dad?" She said, "I'll tell you them all Nellie", which I should have wrote on the back of them but I never done it. I can remember quite a few of them, like there's mi Dad, Jack Stephenson, you know called Fatty Stephenson and George Leng, Jack Waud, George Bayes, Tacey – do you remember Tacey? I was telling John Waud one day about the photo 'cos it would be his grandfather.

I tell you what when mi Dad was living with us, mi Dad had Rocket Cart you know and he had two horses to pull Rocket Cart. Mi Dad had job to tek Rocket Cart and they had a team – Jim Smith, Jack Waud, Bill Waud, Tom Chadick, and did they call him Coll?

Rita   Yes. Ellen Coll, she had a fish shop hadn't she?

Nellie   Yes. They had a team, you see, with this Rocket Cart and they had two horse. And when they fired the rockets, the horses looked – they were set to go like. Mi Dad took 'em and they used to have seventeen and six *[17 shillings and 6 pence]* was it for a practice and five pounds if it was a actual call out as you might say. When 'Rosa' came in Rocket Cart went and when they fired line across right on that corner, mi Dad used to take hosses out and tek 'em away from where gun was going to fire. I allus remember him saying it was really foggy and he was going to tek hosses away and Laurie's dad said, "Where's thu going?" He said, "I's going to tek hosses out o'road", and he said, "Thu silly bugger. Thu's gonna walk o'er cliff, go t'other road". It was so thick. Then, was it night 'Skegness' kem and he kem under Bempton cliffs didn't he? I allus remember me and Elsie went to see 'cos they were all lost weren't they. And we went on bikes to see. It was a Grimsby trawler wan't it 'Skegness'?

Rita	No, it was a Hull one.
Nellie	Oh, it was Hull trawler. I thought with it being 'Skegness' it was a Grimsby trawler. If it was hard going for the Rocket Cart and they had to go maybe up Stonepit or Wold Farm – roads were very bad – they could go and they couldn't refuse to lend 'em a horse. They'd to call at Shipley's to get another horse. But it was too hard work for 'em and then Laurie's dad would start to tek it with his coal truck up to where they had a practice. I tell you who was one of 'em – Herbert Gibbon, Herbert's dad.
Margaret	I have some photos of them.
Rita	I can remember mi Grandfather Cross – he used to say about the horses having to go across the fields.
Margaret	They used to have big boxes with the ropes in didn't they, and they were heavy.
Rita	Well, I mean the cart itself wasn't light was it. It was a very solid cart, and you see they all got sat on the cart on the sides.
Nellie	I tell you who lived up there. They called her Janie Youngfield. And Billy lived 'ere and I'll tell you where he went to live. There were some cottages up where they built flats, Preston Flats. He died up there or mebbe went into what they called the Union, didn't they? Did 'e come and 'elp his auntie – Billie Beale? He liked drink! I've seen him come out of Seabirds and he would nearly miss rent-end. Did they farm Noth Moor?
Rita	Yes, one of them did. Would his father be married to my great-aunt? She was up there, at North Moor and I'm sure it was a Beale. [This turned out not to be true. He was married to Great-Aunt Kate and lived at Hill Farm.]
Nellie	Could 'ave been, an' they called him Billy Beale, didn't they?
Rita	He must have taken after her then 'cos didn't she drink? I think she drank herself to death.
Nellie	And then some relation of yours that would have 'Ocean View', wasn't they?
Rita	Kingstons had 'Ocean View' – that was my great great grandmother. And he went and broke his neck riding from North Moor, on a horse. It tripped in one of those dyke things they used to have for rainwater.
Nellie	And James Woodhouse at Croft Farm – were they some relation?

Rita	They were cousins of mi grandfather's. And Aunt Kate was at where Lounts were, Hill Farm, but I don't know what her husband was called. It was Polly that was at North Moor and the other one married old William Readhead and they were at Manor House. They used to have quite a lot of land, didn't they? At 'Ocean View' there was a nice bit of land. And then there was Lighthoose Farm. Mi grandfather, Stonehouse, they were at North Moor. Now, did Waines take over from Stonehouses? I can remember meeting one of Stonehouse girls and Ethel Wise knew her. Ethel was married to Frank Wise and my Auntie Elsie was married to Tom Wise. And he used to come every Sunday night for tea, did Ted Wise, when we were little, you know. He used to go to Church and then come over. And Aaron Langton used to come Saturday night. 'Im and mi dad used to go to Dog and Duck and have a drink. Women never went ti pubs then, like. Mi dad was really a nice singer.
	There were dances at the old school. Ethel learned to dance.
	She was a real good dancer. I remember she used to teach me to dance and honestly sometimes you had to hold her up.
Nellie	I know. I know! But she really was a good dancer. I used to go around with your Aunty Elsie, Rita. Elsie was a year older than me. Now, who was it? She'd be yer mother's auntie. She lived at Unamby. *[Hunmanby]*
Rita	Auntie Aggie?
Nellie	Yes, Auntie Aggie. We wouldn't be that so old, mebbe twelve or thirteen, we'd go to see this Auntie one Sunday. We were told to come home before dark. We must have stopped longer than we should have done and it sort of fell dark as we were coming back. We were coming on to Bempton, from Bempton to Flamborough and we only had one light. Going past Buckton Hall, we saw lights coming the other way and we stopped and let these lights go past. When we got to Chapel, mi granddad was standing at Post Office corner. "By gor, you'll koppit. Your father set off ti meet you. Where ivver 'ave you been?" It was mi dad we'd passed at Buckton Hall!

Nora Brown

Born in Filey, Nora lived in the village from the age of five and later catered for visitors.

Joyce	Were you born in Flamborough?
Mrs Brown	No, Filey. I was about five when I came to Flamborough. I'd just started school in Filey. We lived opposite Grapes Hotel; it's been pulled down since. Mi mother used to tek people in. It was a cottage but it had an entrance and a room and a big kitchen and it had a big garden. It went right down to Ravine you know, where you go down to beach. I always remember there used to be old men come round with bears and they always used to sleep down Ravine. There was a walk right down there. I don't know what they were. They used to do anything in those days – tramps, people sharpening knives or scissors.
Joyce	Do you remember a man who used to come round? Mi grandma always used to call him Russian Jew and he used to have a suitcase with him and he used to have all sorts like – aprons, bits and pieces.
Mrs Brown	There used to be a lot often come round. My cousins had a big drapers shop in Filey. They used to come round in a van, selling clothes and things. You could order sheets and things.
Joyce	There used to be a traveller from Carlton's come round, didn't there as well. I think they called him Ellis.
Mrs Brown	They used to be from Cousin's and that other shop come round for orders. They brought your things on Fridays and then you

paid next time when they came for your order. They used to come from shoe shops and Kidd's – he used to come round to see if you wanted anything. They came round every week and there was old Chew, he used to come round with horse and cart with meat. He used to come from Brid.

[Mrs Brown continued talking about Flamborough shops.]

I know Martindale's used to have where Adrian Williams [Co-op] is now. They used to sell materials and that. One of Smith girls used to work in it, Honor Smith. *[It was actually Ada Smith.]* Jennis used to live where Shipley's used to live, just round from Post Office, next to Fred Kingston's, 'cos they were big Wesleyans and they used to come a lot to mi Grannie's. Down near Sarah Barclay's, there was Mrs Brownley's – she had a few little things in the house. They used to mek men's shoes, Woodhouse, next door. He used to come round didn't he, with a sack on his back mending shoes, he did mend shoes there. He lived with his aunt. That was Tom Woodhouse's and next was May Woodhouse's and she used to let it.

Joyce   I just remember two ladies living there.

Mrs Brown   Johnson's, they were friendly with her at Thornwick Private – Doris Walker – she went to live with her brother and he mended shoes and she used to let that. They had it for years and then it was sold. They used to let in summer. I'll tell you who had it, flats are called after him, Preston, 'cos I've photos with Mrs Preston, they used to tek our kids ti Thornwick with 'em. Next door, was Miss Fell. She was there from 'em being built, they were built for her. I always remember 'em saying her brother was a builder frae Scarborough and she had so many girls and she used to live down in village. Her brother built these for her, the four houses and they only cost one thousand pounds – all four of 'em building. Of course there wasn't a bathroom and they had bathroom put on afterwards.

Joyce   I know she had a daughter called Fernanda, didn't she? And then there was Florrie, she lived with her and Tant.

Mrs Brown   When they came in, it was just before First World War. There was very poor doings at farming. They lost their boys, they died, and there wasn't much doing on farm so they sold up and kem in here. There'd only been two people in, I think Woodhouses, man and wife, when they came in and I've been in seventy-one years. I was twenty-two when I was married and I'm ninety-three now.

If he'd lived another two weeks we'd have been married sixty seven years.

"Sunnyside" was built after these 'cos Nordass built them. I worked for 'em you know. Nellie, Tom's mother was a friend of mi mother's. She was always coming down to our house. She lost her husband. *[He was drowned off North Landing. She married a Cowling.]* I don't remember that with only being young then, but she used to bring Tom with her. They used to tek visitors in. There used to be her and young Tom and her mother and father live there and Jack. And I used to go and help her in summer time. And then when she was poorly I went and helped 'cos she was in bed. She had cancer, had Nellie. Our Nellie was called after her, Elizabeth Helen. And then I worked there a bit and mi mother used ti cum and black-lead fire-side in that little place, not the big kitchen. Every week she did that and then they got in Frances Fell, a cousin of mi mothers. They had a farm before that.

We had a baby but we lost her, she would have been older than our Nellie. We called her after Frances. We looked after old man and lad.

Joyce	Do you remember Mr Nordass' wife? Iris used to say to me that we were related.
Mrs Brown	Just can remember. She's one of Stork's, she's Iris' grandmother's sister. Waud's you see; another sister married one of 'em. I just went in holidays, with visitors. In them days you did owt ti ger a copper or two. I was there when Nellie died.
Joyce	Did you ever live in Fairholme? Next door to mi grandma's.
Mrs Brown	No, she always lived with her grandma.
Joyce	'Cos there was her house.
Mrs Brown	They were all left one weren't they? Maybe she had that left. And there was one that was lame, what did they call him? He married a Filey woman.
Joyce	John Willie.
Mrs Brown	Aye, John Willie, he had that little un left and he married a widow from Filey.
Joyce	That's right, her daughter married a Waud again, Jack Waud.
Mrs Brown	And then there was one that lived at Hull.
Joyce	That's right and he fell out with his father and that's why he went to Hull. He married somebody from Flamborough.

Mrs Brown	I ought to know 'cos I've walked to Brid with her many a time, Maud Headley. She used to come and see me when she comes to Flamborough, but she's older than me you know. She and her brother lived in that little cottage where you went over stile to Lighthouse, where they've built council houses. She was related to Elsie Cross.
Joyce	Did you ever belong "Bright Young Things"?
Mrs Brown	No.
Joyce	Dicky Bayes used to belong and Sylvia Readhead.
Mrs Brown	Sylvia's father got one up and Peggy belonged them.
Joyce	Oh, you're talking about during the war, F.A.D.S. – "Flamborough Amateur Dramatic Society". I remember that.
Mrs Brown	Then there was another un – Sykes from Brid.
Rita	That was "Flamborough Original Players".
Mrs Brown	Aye, that was it.
Joyce	I was thinking before that though. It would be in the twenties, they used to have do's in the old school. I've heard mi dad talk about going dancing.
Mrs Brown	We used to go dancing – ti school and we did have dancing lessons 'cos Sally Bayes took 'em in Victoria Rooms. Once a week we used to go. I remember that, but they always used to have whist drives and dances in school.
Rita	A lot of them used to cycle to Brid, to the Winter Gardens, to dance there, didn't they? Mi dad and mi mam used to go there.
Mrs Brown	I've never been to Brid to dance, only in war time when there was a 'do' there and there was bombs then. I don't know who ran 'em.
Rita	I remember there was one big one each year for Conservatives.
Mrs Brown	Yes, because Peggy and Jean Hindle used to do a turn.
Rita	And Faith Burnley used to sing, didn't she?
Mrs Brown	Yes, she did, she was a lovely singer. And there was a Fancy Dress. I remember Laurie Cowling wanted to go and I said I had a pig outfit. And he put it on and he won it and Mrs Woodhouse from Danes Dyke House presented the prizes. I don't know what our lads went as but they wouldn't have the pig outfit and it won it. And then soldiers used to have dances in Village Hall didn't they?

	But first bus that got to go ti Brid, Boy *[Mrs Brown's husband]* took it and then Matt Major had it. It was a waggonette and it was a shilling. It used to go Wednesdays and Saturdays and then on Saturday nights if there was ought special. You had to book it, it wouldn't hold many.
Joyce	That was before Archie Robinson's, was it?
Mrs Brown	Oh long before they started, it was first bus of all. You had to walk. There wasn't a bus at all. You used to go to Brid Fair, there used to be streams of us. Our mothers used ti tek us and we used ti walk there and back. Then John Halls', they had a waggonette. Matt Major's must have been more money, and he went there and they used ti tek a load and then come back and tek another load. And we used to go to a café next door to Brunswick Hotel at top of Queen Street for a rabbit pie supper. A shilling it was. Billy Collins and Sarah Batton and all of us used to go there after we'd been to pictures, or somewhere. Nobody had cars and there was no buses then. Then they started White Buses.
Joyce	And you always got a full bus, did you?
Mrs Brown	Oh yes, 'cos it would only hold ten or twelve or summat like that. It was long and you sat at side like, it wasn't like a bus, you didn't sit forwards, you sat sideways. Matt Major started that and Boy drove it for him. He used to bring a load and if there was more than a load go back for them.
Rita	My Uncle Fred worked for John Hall; he used to go up to Flamborough Station, didn't he?
Mrs Brown	Yes, with a pony and trap.
Joyce	So that would be before Billy Collins and his carrier cart?
Rita	Yes, 'cos Barclays used to do it.
Mrs Brown	Aye, Billy was older than me, but Barclays and then Screeton and then there was someone who lived next to Chadwick's. They lived there and they called him Chadwick and I'll tell you where he used to keep his horse – up in a stable above where Preston Flats are now. There was a row of cottages up side 'cos we used to live there.
Joyce	Yes, they were still there during the war, 'cos Doreen Coward used to live there.
Mrs Brown	Old Gilbert used to ride, do you remember him? Before then, Jack Barclay and this Chadwick, 'cos she allus used to work, she was very friendly with Mrs Hall, big chapel people. Then

Screeton took it off them and I'm sure there was a Sunley, I can't be sure. But there's allus been two when somebody's finished.

Wages weren't very much in those days, and he – Boy – went to Woodhouse's for what was considered a big wage, five pounds a fortnight. I don't know what year he went to Dykes, I know Peggy was a baby. He went as chauffeur there after we were married.

Joyce   That would be before Marshall was chauffeur?

Mrs Brown   Oh yes, a long time before Marshall 'cos Boy was there fifteen years. It was only after they got four cars to look after, that Marshall went. And of course Marshall went with 'em, but we didn't want to go 'cos we'd bought this house you see. They went back to a place that they had before, just outside Hull [Cottingham].

Joyce   Would that be when the estate was sold up?

Mrs Brown   Oh no, that was before the war, you know when Bolton lost his money – in India or somewhere and they all bought their houses, farms and that – before Second World War. Three kids and no child allowance, but we always had plenty and managed. You wonder how you did manage. He used to go on a Sunday night with kids if there was ought at pictures they wanted to see. Walter Hichen made radios. Before we were married we used to go there on a Sunday night and we had warmed up vegetables and cold meat. Always we had that at home as well when we were younger.

Rita   We always had cold mushy peas with vinegar and cold meat with bread and butter on a Sunday night.

Mrs Brown   We all did on a Sunday night but all that stopped at war. Why, you could get a good joint for two and sixpence.

Rita   Sixpence worth of fry on a Friday.

Mrs Brown   Aye, I know when we were first married I used to have sixpence or threepence of meat to mek a pie with taties in. You had ti mek money go round. And I know mother used him, Mr Taylor, you know, next to shop opposite Rose and Crown, used ti hawk fish and crabs. He also had a stall in market [in Bridlington] and when he used to have a wuff, he used ti send Arthur round with it you know – "Tek that round ti Gran's". And she used ti skin it in boiling water and do it and the meat was as white as white and it used ti drop off bones. We oft had that wi' roast potatoes on a night for supper.

You know where you go round Rose and Crown end, there's another door. Well, they *[grandparents]* lived in that part. You see they only had mi mother and that's where they lived. Then they went to where they built flats. There was a row of cottages went up with herring spots at top. And they used ti go down ti Robin Lythe Hole and he used ti sell fish at corner.

Rita   He's on that photograph I have of fishermen at Rose and Crown. They used to congregate in front there.

Mrs Brown   He was called Overfield. Mi mother, she went to Filey ti work and that's how she gor on wi' mi dad. She worked in one of those big houses on the front. They used ti tek lords and that in, and of course they all had maids. After we kem up here and we went to stop in Filey wi' relations, we allus went to see the old lady where she worked and she allus gev us sixpence. And we thought it was ever so much, you know. Then they lived in top cottage, Cameron and Betty *[Atkinson]* lived in it.

Joyce   Didn't Brian *[Mrs Brown's son]* used to live up there?

Mrs Brown   Yes, he lived in old Sam Chadwick's and then the next door one was empty so he got that and knocked two into one and so they had two bedrooms and a room and a kitchen. They did it themselves.

Joyce   There used to be a few places in Flamborough where cottages went back, instead of going along the pavement, like just below Nellie Tom's.

Mrs Brown   Mary Mallory, she had a shop in there in the last one right at top.

Rita   Can you remember two old ladies called Miss Hope living up there? Because when I was a little girl mi grandma Cross used to send me for bread, and she always used to say, "Go to Miss Hope's for my bread", and I used to go up there.

Mrs Brown   That would be Mary Mallory's and they had a shop at the end and it had a little garden in front. It was only one that had. And toilets were all right at end. They all had ti come out and go right across in front of other houses.

Rita   Bob Atkinson used to live there when Gordon and Dorothy were little.

Mrs Brown   Yes, his second wife, Renée. First was Lily Langton and she died. They lived up there before they had house and garage built.

Rita	I can remember that being built, but Cameron lived with his grandma didn't he?
Mrs Brown	Yes, he went down and she lived opposite Ship, didn't she? Then there was Ada Coates an'all. Things have altered haven't they? Woodhouses lived in where Tom Cowling lived. *[North Marine Road]* Christie Woodhouse, she married and went to live at Brid. There was a lot of Woodhouse lads.
Joyce	Who lived in the last one where Miss Postgate lived?
Mrs Brown	I'll tell you who lived there at one time, a girl called Rachel; she was a rum un. Her father was lame and he danced over a broomstick. What did they call him?
Rita	You don't mean Jimmy Robinson do you?
Mrs Brown	Aye. He used to go up to Thornwick 'cos we used to go up at weekend and he used to go up and dance ovver a broomstick. And he had a girl, Rachel Robinson, and fellas were always running after her. Then they went ti live ovver Green, in one of them coastguard houses. Then there was a girl and her mother at the end house, and she looked after Tom's mother, 'cos she was there when she died. She was a nurse and she used to come in and dress her and that.

I can remember 'cos I was there then. There was ever si many lived there. Some of 'em were teachers and they were teaching at a school and used to bring these kids here in the holidays 'cos their parents were abroad. 'What do you call her' was friendly with 'em, she lives in flats – Hannah Mary *[Traves]*. Then Woodcock's had it in wartime, bookies. Two or three of 'em were teachers, 'cos they used ti cum and ask Peggy if she was going for a walk ti Thornwick with 'em. They brought mostly lads but some girls, every holiday she used ti bring 'em. Then there was a couple 'cos when we went to pictures they were there, we always had same seats at front. It was agin harbour. |
Joyce	Going down this way past Hopwood's *[Oakwood House, North Marine Road]* – who used to live in that house next door?
Mrs Brown	Woodhouse, May Woodhouse. Her sister was a teacher. She married Sid Coates. Her father lived there and they had both of them houses.
Joyce	Then Miss Steele, she lived down there didn't she?
Mrs Brown	And Sarah Leng, she lived there.

Joyce	Wentworth's – didn't they live somewhere there? Two sisters, used to ride these 'sit up and beg' bikes, and their old father.
Mrs Brown	Yes, that was in the other house, the other side of the passage. They used ti cum from Brid and they used ti let it sometimes. They had it let in wartime, to an Air force fella and his wife. He was looking after those boats at Brid. I can remember he got up two bus loads and tuk us to that old place, Alexandra. We went to that pub near and Gertie Redhead was there and you know what she was! She gor her arm round a bottle and she was full of fun. She'd only had one drink but we couldn't get her away. We went back to dance and I know we'd just got back when Brid was bombed. And you see it was all free with these buses.
	Nancy Stork's mother – her mother's mother bought 'Uplands' and she came to live with her little boy. They had it built. There was her and two daughters and of course Nancy's mother. She was married and she had a little boy and she lost her husband. Peggy used to go and play with the little boy and he died. They wouldn't have doctor. They didn't believe in doctors, they were Christian Scientists. And that's who had that built.
Joyce	I can only remember this old lady standing at the gate. Peggy?
Mrs Brown	Cockerill, and she had one up here, one of those first ones built from those big stones from North Landing.
Joyce	"Olicana" or "White House"?
Mrs Brown	Then she came down here when they sold it. She was a big Wesleyan.
Rita	They had some sort of school didn't they? Because Mavene Bailey, Bob Bailey's daughter, used to go there you know. At "White House".
Joyce	"White House" had the underground air raid shelter in the back garden that Pockley's built during the war.
Mrs Brown	Air force had an air raid shelter built in garden at back of us. It was all boarded out, walls and that and electric light, and they were never in it. It flooded when it rained!

Lilian Bond

Born Lilian Warcup, Mrs Bond travelled the area selling crabs and fish and helped in skeining and preparing lines for her father. This piece was written by her for her children and grandchildren.

I was born in Flamborough village, a small fishing community on the North East Coast. At school we always had to put "Flamborough is a peninsular sticking out into the North Sea". I say born, as the village had its own mid-wife whose family had done this for generations. Not only did she do her job, but also brought along her daughter who took charge of any other children in the family. No one went to hospital unless any bad complications arose as the Doctor had to be paid and money was very hard to find sometimes. The fishermen being Self Employed had no means of "Dole", as it was termed; consequently they very often put out to sea in very bad weather conditions in order to support the family.

My father was a fisherman who went to sea in sailing coble days. They had a large brown sail put up when the wind was a suitable way, but most times rowed by the crew of three as a rule, no hauler in those days, which meant fishing lines. In the summer, crab pots all had to be "shot" and hauled by hand.

Getting back to village life, the cottages were mostly kitchen, parlour and two "chambers", (bedrooms). We had three so my brother and I always had our own rooms. There was no electricity until I was around twelve years old, no gas, so everything was cooked on the fire. You had to let the fire burn down low and then fetch the "Grid Iron" (which hung on a nail outside) and lay across the bars to support the frying pan. Kippers were just laid across and tasted lovely. A big pan with a steamer on top for potatoes cooked all the veg, a wide variety, as we had a large garden and never bought anything in the way of garden produce. The only means of hot water was from the kettle, a large copper one on the front of the fire, always on ready for cups of tea etc at any time. The kitchen always seemed warm as the oven was on for meals. I can also remember a huge "Keel Pot" which produced lovely soups and stews. It was always warmed a second day and hung on what we call a "Reckon", over the fire.

The lighting was provided by means of an oil lamp in the kitchen (living room}. We had one that hung from the beams supported on four chains to the lamp itself, narrowing to a smaller circle at the top to a large ball coming down the middle. This let the light up or down, as you needed, when pulled. It was all done in golden gilt; my mother used to guild it (paint} from time to time, we had a stand lamp in the front parlour. You carried around a pretty piece of pottery with a glass globe (I still have it), otherwise you carried a candle in a candle stick up to bed, being warned every night not to put it near anything. I remember getting a "Kelly Lamp"; it had a small round bottom, which wouldn't tip over, it rolled back upright if pushed. A great improvement, it lasted much longer than a candle.

The village then was small everybody knew each other and more or less were related. Fishing and farming were the two industries. Thinking back, we had a good supply of small shops. A Drapers run from the house in Tower Street, a Cobblers shop, a Grocers shop and Co-op shop in Dog and Duck Square, a really old fashioned Sweet shop at the bottom of Alison Lane which made trays of home made toffee with chocolate on top, broken by a hammer. You could buy ½d *[half penny]* of bits left in the tray, sumptuous. She used to seem to be always standing outside in a long black dress, white pinny, white hair done up in a bun. "Post Office Corner" shop sold sweets and home cured ham, lovely carved straight from the bone. She was also very prim and proper, old fashioned and always polite. She also made teas from her room for visitors in the summer. There was also the Post Office and General Store. We had a Wheelwright's shop, who made the big wooden cart wheels, a good Bakery in Chapel Street, who would deliver you anything by means of his motor bike and side car, (a big box with trays in). Coming up High Street, we had a Fish and Chip shop owned by the Brewery, (which incidentally, my father and mother at one time rented and I worked in, in my teens). It has since been pulled down to make bigger access to Ship Inn Car Park. Next door, an old man had a Cobbler's shop and sold boots and shoes, then there was the local Butcher, another little Grocery shop who baked buns and cakes, the Plumber next, another Grocery with Café which is now a Fish and Chip shop. Kippers, home smoked were sold from a cottage, another Sweet and Grocery, then a Wooden shop, I seem to remember it being a Butcher's a while then changed to Fish and Fruit. Next we had an open piece of land call Tarry Row, we always played there as children – ball games, whip and top, taws *[marbles]*, skipping, hop scotch etc. Sadly they were allowed to build on this and Central Stores *[now the pharmacy]* stands on it and what used to be the Paper/Drapery shop etc. Across the road was Fruit and Veg, next came a Cobbler shop, a very low dark building, you could hear him hammering away mending shoes as you walked past. A Doctor's Surgery came next; a little old lady let her two rooms to Dr Watson from Bridlington two afternoons a week. We lived next door, I remember him driving a big "Sunbeam" car, a lovely model my brother and I used to love to admire.

At that time my father and mother sold ropes, lines hooks, tar thread "Pokey" to bark lines, marlin for crab pot nets, all sorts as an agent for a Scarborough firm of Ship Chandlers. I have an old photo with a board advert sign "Rope Stores". Next door was a Sweet/Groceries, you could go there any time, get your mother's apron full of slightly damaged fruit. Crossing over again was the main Sweet shop we all spent our ½d on the way to school. An old gentleman, a real Dickensian character, with a hard black hat used to sit at the door, he would take a sweet from his pocket and give it to you if you looked in the window and hadn't any money. His name was "Tant" and everybody for years remembered it as such. The lady who carried on *[Miss Edith Sunley]* sadly died this year so I would think it is finished as a shop. *[It is presently an off licence and grocery.]* A small Supermarket is now where the "Tinker's" shop was. He sold cycles, spare parts of all sorts and crockery etc and, I suppose, quack medicines. If you were poorly you got a "Jug of Water" from there which cured everything, you told him your symptoms and he made it up; it was only 3d *[three pence]* a time. The cure for a cold in those days was onion gruel taken as you sat with your feet in a mustard bath (bowl on the floor). For a bad headache and stuffiness you sat with a towel over your head over a jug of boiling hot Friar's Balsam.

Talking of baths, the "Copper" in your wash house had to be filled with water, a fire lit under. A big tin bath brought in front of the fire in the kitchen and hot water carried in buckets to fill it, which was quite a operation, as to nowadays turning the hot water tap on.

The Copper was used for wash day, also clothes were soaked in a "Dolly Tub", turned round with a "Dolly", a kind of small stick with four legs, a long stick up the middle into which you pushed a "Dolly Stick" through a hole and turned round in half turns resembling the movement of later day washing machines, then into the washing tub and thereby scrubbed towels etc before putting all fast colours and whites to boil in the copper. So wash day was hard work, not forgetting the huge old mangle, which took a tremendous amount of energy turning. It was of course, all followed up by ironing. The "Flat Iron" was put on, or balanced in front of a bright red fire, you had to be very careful or everything was scorched. Later on you could buy a "Shield" like a bright bottom of today's iron, you put the iron on and clipped it over the handle this saved getting smuts from the smoke.

Getting back to High Street, we had two houses selling milk. You took a jug and had it measured out. They, along with about four local farmers, delivered this by horse and cart. Another Butchers and another Grocery at the top, two places you could buy fish, but fishing families always had plenty brought home in the lines. There was another shop you could buy almost anything edible, a really old fashioned lady had this, and always had a starched white pinny and she wore a white frilled cotton cap also. I think they owned "Mill Yard" which was an old road going up to where there had been a mill. Behind the cottages is "Mill Hill", this old road came right through to Mereside. The cottages alongside now pulled down were called "Burdsill Row", at the bottom of which was another old shop, a store run by an old man call Pat. Outside two big stones stood, one a flat stone cob we sat and played on, the other a blue colour oblong one, these were called "Pat Stones".

Towards the bottom end of village, down Tower Street, (incidentally, at school there was always friendly rivalry between "Top Enders" and "Bottom Enders" depending on where you lived) we had a Blacksmith's Forge. Donkeys had to be shod there and I loved to go with Father into this creepy dark place, lit up by a huge open fire. A big anvil stood in the centre and sparks flew up as shoes were placed on it, red hot and hammered into shape, occasionally plopped into a cold water tub which sent out a sizzling noise. Two white haired old men owned it and reassured us the donkey couldn't feel anything, it was frightening at first, but you stood there fascinated.

Behind the Church at the bottom of the village was the house where we got corn maize and wheat for the donkey and hens, we kept the donkey to take the fishing lines, crab pots, etc to North Landing, the hens for your own supply of fresh eggs. This was always known as "Haunted House", you never ventured past the threshold and didn't go past after dark, they must have threshed the corn there as the big barn was full of machinery banging away. Father used to hold a sack under a chute, then carry to the weighing machine and bring home on his back.

At the bottom of Croft's Hill was a water pump where in days before piped water, supplied the village along with another one on the village green. I've heard say an old man made his living by selling water in buckets from the cart he filled up from the pumps. Behind this one is a field call "Maitlands", there used to be about three large ponds with grassy banks between trees hanging down all around, (we played there along with down street friends). They were fed by springs which continued out onto the South Landing beach.

At the foot of the cliff's highest point Beacon Hill can still be seen there at low tide bubbling up, hence its name of "Springs" for that part of the beach. These ponds were filled in and trees cut down, but later on when new bungalows appeared further down, they had trouble with flooding until it was drained away.

We had two big Chapels in Chapel Street, Primitive and Wesleyan. The first one on the corner (now replaced by a smaller one) the second, although newer, was also demolished, as it was too big to keep going for the smaller congregation. Across the road was the fisherman's institute (now renovated and run as a Club); it had been given at some time to the young fisherman of Flamborough for recreation (so the old plaque said) and it had a large billiard table etc at one end and the village library hence the name we all called it "Reading Room".

The road as such ended at the Wesleyan Chapel, just a cart track followed known as "Gar Ends", possibly because the gardens of High Street went right through and finished there, this led to "Crow Field" only, later on a road was cut right through into North Landing Road, called "Woodcock Road", which now takes most of the traffic, missing the High Street. We had one garage selling petrol to the few cars, owned mostly by businessmen, and his work was mostly mending punctures and putting second-hand bikes together for sale.

The two coal dealers had horses and carts, later replaced by lorries. There was also a carrier with a horse and trap who came around the streets in a morning and he would get you anything from Bridlington. The shops there would give him things you asked for, if you needed shoes, they would send 3 or 4 pairs to choose from the same day, you paid the next day and sent the rest back. If mothers were busy, a sweeping brush was pushed out of the front door that meant you wanted him to call. A well known person was the Village Crier (bellman), whatever was on, a jumble sale or any meeting, you gave him a shilling and he would ring the bell and shout at the top of his voice all round the village. The school was used mainly for any function. There was a "Parish Room" but it was over the old stables at the back of the Vicarage, you went up some very rickety stairs to a long low room, heated by an old stove, which always seemed to be smoking. We went up there for Brownies and Guides, and I remember the floor used to bounce when we all ran around, this was pulled down when the Vicarage was updated.

The wives took a big part in the work to be done each day, three piece lines had to be baited, that meant Mussels and Flithers (Limpets) and sometimes whelks were used. The mussels all had to be skeined by means of a knife which cut on each side, you had them made at the blacksmiths, he then fitted the blade into a wood shaft, which fitted neatly into your hand. You then had to get out each mussel without "ragging" it; you soon learned the art and started helping at a very early age. It was all done in the kitchen, clip mats at the fireside were rolled back from the brick floor, a large drum – I suppose tar had been bought in it for tarring the lines and ropes – was put in the centre of the floor and you sat around it balancing a bowl of mussels on your knee with the rim resting on the drum. You threw the empty shells into the drum and put your mussels into a basin. Two or three of you would sit around and when enough had been opened, then a bait table was placed over the kitchen table, this had a border round to stop water going anywhere except through a little hole in one corner under which a bucket was placed, a piece of wood was put under the top end and so all the brine ran down into it. The lines were on "Skeps", a circle of woven willow basket, the empty lines were put on your left and you worked it over onto the right skep as you baited each hook. These were set at about 4 inch intervals, five or six mussels filled a hook and were put at the front of the coil so you ended up with a full mussel face at the front, this was covered with wet sacking and put outside to go to North Landing, carried on your donkey next morning. Usually two sometimes three had to be done each day. Father would come home from sea, have a warm meal, then help to finish the baiting, then of course the floors had to be scrubbed and all put back neat and tidy, that was the best part when the fire was built up, the grate shining from being black leaded, and all cosy and warm

In the "Front Room" as it was always called, we had an old fashioned grate with an iron casting around, which had petals standing out. Above this was a mantel piece with chandelier ornaments, which dangled and shone in the light, over the mantle was a lovely mirror with side shelves built in, we had little ornaments on each shelf. On the hearth was a brass fender and fire irons polished every week. I remember that in the kitchen the "Tidy Betty" which stood in front to stop the hot ashes dropping down, had "Grace Darling" in a rowing coble going towards the lighthouse, raised up on the front of it, (this was sent to Bamborough Museum later on). The furniture was very different from today, two armchairs in the kitchen, and a " lang settle", a long wooden seat with arms, back and underneath three big drawers to keep all your clothes in, a small chest of drawers and the table. The washing up had to be done on this in a bowl and baking, ironing etc. In the front room was big horsehair chairs, a leather sofa, another pair of big oak fancy drawers, later taken up stairs, and replaced by a mirrored chiffonier. We had a lovely organ with mirror and fancy patterned wood. My mother exchanged this for a "wireless" (radio) when a man in the village started making them to sell, we all regretted this later on, as my brother, who was five years older than me, started first to make "crystal sets", then wireless sets. We had always been brought up to sing round the organ so it wasn't long before we acquired, from somewhere, an old piano. Mother and father used to sing away as they baited lines, the men all sang at sea in rhythm with the oars pulling, an old favourite was "Pull for the shore sailor" and "Throw out the life-line across the dark wave". We were taught all the Great War songs, "Dolly Gray", "Two little girls in blue", "Daisy Bell", etc. All the able fishermen had volunteered for minesweeping in the war. Mother used to tell us how Zeppelins used to come in and go out using Flamborough Head as a landmark. I wasn't born then but my brother was a baby and they all used to run out into the fields and lay in the hedge bottoms as these big Zeppelins came droning over very low. She said one night she couldn't find Grandad who lived with her, apparently it was Sunday night and he had gone back to change his best trousers, saying when he arrived back, "I'm not mucking my Sunday trousers for no Jerry". We all spoke broad Yorkshire at home and at play, but at school and Chapel, etc, we always spoke "properly", as it was termed, hardly anyone except old Flamborians use the old tongue now. We had a very nice Grandfather clock and it used to be in the front room, then because of it continually stopping due to the vibrations from solid tyre double decker buses, it was moved into the kitchen, it struck every hour and you could hear it all over the house. It didn't bother you by its chimes all through the night yet I always awoke upon it striking eight for going to school.

My mother was the youngest of seven, and so we always had Aunties and Uncles around, one auntie in particular used to take us, along with her family and a few more to the beach. Banana sandwiches packed up and Spanish water to drink, (you bought ½d of spanish, poured water over it and shook it up, then bottled it), doesn't sound too tempting now but we loved it then. Another auntie who hadn't married a fisherman used to come and take me to her house whilst mother did the baiting, this was in winter and I liked her house as she could always have it tidy. She knitted "Ganseys" for fishermen in 5ply worsted wool on 5 needles, so it is all in one piece. I used to watch her and soon picked up the art of knitting them at quite an early age. All fishermen's underwear was knitted in creamy coloured "hob" smelling greasy at first, the idea was as they were always wet sitting in the cobles, this kept body heat in. When Princess Mary opened the Parade at Bridlington, she heard about these gurnseys and my aunt was asked to knit a Yellow one for the Prince of Wales. Fishermen never wore a collar and tie always a best gurnsey for Sundays, they had strong views about Sunday, you weren't allowed to knit on Sunday or play in the street. They were also very superstitious, if they saw a pig on the way to sea, they turned back, or if anyone stepped over a rope or line that was very bad luck, and at New Year a shovel of coal was put outside the door for the first person in to carry luck in with them. I well remember one Sunday morning a knock at the door brought in three farmers from the

West Riding wanting to be took out fishing for the day, they tried all ways to persuade Father, even putting a big white £5 note (which I had never seen before), on the table, it represented a lot of money in those days but nothing would move him, he wouldn't desecrate the Sabbath as he put it, nor would any of the other fishermen.

Almost every fisherman had a donkey, "ass" as he was always called, some owned theirs, others had them from Scarborough after the summer was over, (they were used on the sands for donkey rides all season). You could have one all winter if you kept it in good condition, this was their way of not having to find winter accommodation for them, an old man used to walk them from Scarborough, a distance of 20 miles, breaking his journey overnight. We had our own "Old Bob" as we needed him in the summer as well, but a neighbour across the road got one and she always got the man something to eat, one day he came un-expected, and I was sent to get a quarter of ham, she called later and said "I was ashamed of that ham, he put it on the end of his fork and it was gone, but I gave him some pie", I was teased about this for years, it seemed I had asked for ounce not a quarter of a pound, which just shows you could buy small quantities of anything without question as money was scarce.

The fisherman's year was divided into two seasons, line fishing in winter, crabbing and taking visitors round the caves or private fishing parties in summer. All this was done from North Landing, about one mile from the village, hence the need for donkeys in winter, they were sure footed to bring the fish up the slope, then mostly hard packed mud and stones, (now all concrete} from the beach to the cliff top, as well as taking and bringing the lines home. In summer the crab pots all went down on fish buyers' lorries and were used all season. We had four local buyers who bid for the fish in auction each day. As the cobles landed, fish was spread out on the " loar", the hard concrete where the cobles were pulled up out of reach of high tides. It was laid out from each coble in layers of "Codling", the smallest, "Sprag", the next size, then "Cod" the biggest. There would be more than a dozen craft working from North Landing, so this was a sight worth seeing if you could stand the cold. Winters then were always high winds, rain and after Christmas, snow. The Lifeboat was at North Landing and was always being called out to the local cobles, and if you weren't at school when the Rockets went, you ran with mother to the beach to wait for news, I hated this and shivered behind the old engine house (a fixed tractor that pulled the cobles up) many an hour vowing to mother, "I'll never marry a fisherman). This dread of the sea has stayed with me, my family will tell you it takes a lot to get me on the sea even now.

I remember the "ROSA" being washed onto "West Scar", the point of the inlet into North Landing, its big "scars" (rocks) stick out and makes entry a small channel, bad to negotiate in storms even by local men. We had all gone to the beach (I would be about 8 years old) and the lifeboat had put out. Now at that time there was Coxswain, a 2nd.Coxswain, and a Bowman but the rest of the crew to row the boat was made up of the first, I think, 10 men to get a "Jacket" (lifejacket) on, then the rest were called "Helpers" who manhandled the boat down the slope by lowering ropes round bollards then putting Skids called locally "feat-an-trees", under the boat to stop it ploughing into the sand. This particular night you could hear although you couldn't see the men crying out. We found out later that the lifeboat had been washed onto the rocks trying to get near to take the men off, but the next big wave cleared her and they did bring the whole crew ashore, it was a wonderful feeling of relief when it was all over. Next morning almost all the village folk went to North Landing to see what had happened, there she was standing straight upright between two big rows of scars just as if someone had stuck her there. It was low tide and we walked out and gazed up the huge side of her, she was holed all along the waterline with gaping holes and out of them gushed her cargo, we called them "cinders", coke is the proper word. The beach was black with them plus wooden debris from her two lifeboats, one of which was brought up the slipway and stayed there a long time. No one except officials from the Salvage Company could board her, when they eventually took anything of value away, then father took us aboard by a rope ladder. Everyone who could, collected old prams, carts, anything that would carry them did so; they supplied the village fires all that winter. She couldn't be moved, so just stayed there for years until the sea gradually broke her to pieces. One of her boilers remained for years, my own family remember "Rosa's Boiler" sticking out on West Scar. We had father's permission to look round ourselves but only at low tide. Tides could be very dangerous up there, the rocks you stand on are bare, but look towards the shore and the tide is creeping in nearer, cutting you off completely. Many visitors still ignore local's warning and have to be rescued by boat, so this was drummed into us at a very early age. My brother saw a way of getting the tiles, out of the galley (cook-house). We managed enough to make a tiled hearth at the kitchen fireplace. It looked great, a creamy brown colour; all we, and all the cottages had before was a slab of stone, you "Yellow Ocamed" each day, we were very proud of this; and father brought home the ship's iron ladder, everybody got something.

Summer was altogether different on the beach. Sunny, calm mostly. My mother started her own little "Crab" business. She would go taking me with her on the donkey up to North Landing, sometimes bidding in the auction if father was late landing. Mother was a well-known figure and everybody helped us to load up the baskets of crabs and I was sat on the top. The visitors, of course, took an interest in all this and old "Bob" made the most of it. He loved ice cream and if anyone was eating one near him, he just took it at one bite and opened his mouth for more. When we arrived home, the crabs were put into a large copper in the "Bark House", as we called it, as it was used to bark the lines and ropes. "Pokey" was put into a smaller copper, (a dark brown hard substance into which the lines were dipped). Getting back to the crabs, they had to be gradually warmed up, if you got too much heat under they would all throw their claws off, so it was a gentle heat up to boiling point, boil for 35 minutes, putting salt on for the last five. Mother then had to "Skep Net" them out, boiling hot, she did this by standing on a fish box up-turned with a long iron handled netted end in her hand. They then all had to be scrubbed in a washing tub of cold water to take off all the scum and make them presentable to sell. We learned to help to "pick crabs", meaning taking all the fish from the shell, at an early age. Mother had her own way of doing this, no fancy picks, just a spoon end. She always had the same one, an old silver one. I continued to use this and still have it having "picked" thousands, as my brother and I, and later my husband, carried on her business right through my working life until my husband had to retire. We had our own style, brown meat at the bottom covered by white meat from the claws, topped by 5 sprigs of parsley. We had a stall on Bridlington market Wednesday and Saturday, and up at North Landing on other days, so I, until school age in the long summer holiday, was allowed onto the beach in care of my brother. He also made pocket money along with more boys selling picture postcards to visitors. The shop in the village let them have them a little cheaper, so they made a few pence. There are 2 caves, "Robin Lythe Hole" and "Dancing Cave" you can walk into at low tide, usually large pools were left, so the enterprising lads made stepping stones and helped visitors across, sitting me at the far end with my upturned sun-hat to put pennies in. One time I remember somebody ran off with it, I started yelling for my brother who managed to retrieve it, he daren't have took me home without my hat. The summers were always so hot we had to wear pretty straw hats either white or pink with flowers woven in and raffia, a dangling ribbon plus elastic under your chin to keep it secure. The entrance to Robin Lythe cave was at one time quite a steep drop when you got in, this provided two old fishermen with a means of earning a little money by taking a short, probably four-runged ladder, carried on their backs all the way from the village, and put just inside the cave, and giving a helping hand to steady visitors down. This cave is very dark on entering but as you go along you can see the light at the other end, as it goes right through the cliff and out into the open sea round the corner from North Landing. At a very low tide you may be able to walk right round, but many unwary people find themselves cut off by the tide and need to be brought in by a coble, this was where Robin Lythe, as a baby was supposedly found. The cobles take people "round the caves" in summer, these are the ones where you can go inside, mainly at Thornwick Bay, the next beach to North Landing. "Five Arches" stand out in this area and can be seen quite clearly from the main road from Scarborough at various viewpoints. Coming back up a quite steep slope from the beach at North Landing, you come first to the Lifeboat House which is straight up and has a hard cement run down with a channel in the middle to take the boat straight down into the sea at high tide, from here to the top of the cliff in those days was a rough hard padded path (now a proper road) which runs parallel to the beach, to the old engine house that hauled the cobles and the Lifeboat at that time, and from there it runs directly to the top to a line of wooden shops.

The one right at the seaward end sold postcards, fancy goods, sunhats etc, the next sold fruit and ice-cream, the next was a cafe with ice-cream and sweets etc at one end. It was always busy in summer with lots of day trip coaches, in fact there was a policeman at that point, as we always had an "extra" all summer who lodged in the village to help out the local policeman. Usually one stood at Post Office corner at the busiest part of the day, that was before any "Halt" signs at major roads came into force. Coming along the road from North Landing you passed "fish stands" at the side of the footpath, each buyer had his own built up to possibly 3 feet higher than the road, here the fish was transferred from donkeys and ponies, weighed out into fish boxes and then taken by lorry to Flamborough Station to be sent all over the country. The station was about 2½ miles from Flamborough at that time and was quite busy as all the mussels came from Morecambe and Lincoln to bait the lines in winter. In summer fish came from Hull Docks to put in the crab pots and it was brought by train then delivered by the two local coal dealers who also brought everything from the station to your homes and shops. Down the hill from North Landing you come to the Thornwick Hotel, alongside which runs the road to Thornwick Bay, there are two ways onto the beach known as "Little" and "Big" Thornwick, these are totally for pleasure, no boats are able to land owing to the big rocks and currents all around the area. It's a very pretty place, paths go down to"LittleThornwick"and take you on to the "Amphitheatre", a huge white chalk piece of cliff with ledges all down one side, you can climb down to the lower rocks where there is a gully known as "Iron Hole", as anything from broken up ships and loose cargo washes up there. My brother had taken me up there one day on the crossbar of his bike, supposedly going for little bundles of firewood, but he spotted this long plank and decided it could be split and made into a wireless aerial to get better reception on your wireless. With a pole in your garden and an aerial to your house, the higher the pole the better the sound. We had to tie a rope round one end and struggled to pull it right over the peak at the top.

I don't think we would have managed it if a man walking his Alsation dog hadn't spotted us and helped to pull it over, when we finally got to the top, up another slope, it had to be tied to the bike and we walked it home. Needless to say, we ended up with the highest pole around and got very good reception. "Big Thornwick" is mostly full of rough gravel and sand with huge rocks you could jump over from one top to the other. A local man used to bring sand and gravel up from the beach by means of a horse, dump it into piles and the local builders paid him for doing this, then made cement and mortar with it. This was finished when a firm started up a sand and gravel pit at "Beacon Hill" overlooking South Landing. One incident stays with me about Thornwick, before I was old enough to sit still at Sunday School, father used to take me up there as the sea was always rough in winter and you could always find a few coins washed into cracks between the rocks. You had to scratch the bits of rock away with a little knife and lever out the farthings. sixpences and shillings, mostly washed from some ships that had broken up. Father left me to get out what he thought was a halfpenny piece, when I pulled it out and rubbed it clean I saw it had on a horse, I shouted "it's got a galloping horse on" and he came running back, it was a sovereign, I'd never seen one and it's the only one I've ever touched. We rushed straight back home to show mother my find, even then they were paying more than the 21 shillings so I suppose it would represent enough to keep us for two or three weeks. From the cliffs north of Thornwick there is a path to the village, still there to Woodcock Road, we called it "Rotherhams", these paths were very rough in those days but now the Heritage Coast workers have done a great job and you can walk it comfortably with steps etc. provided. You can go right round the headland from Thornwick to North Landing, then on to the Lighthouse passing "King" and "Queen" rocks, two large pieces of rock standing out from a cove: one has since been washed away as has one from "Adam" and "Eve", two more rocks nearer the headland, then round to South Landing and from there to Danes Dyke. We as teenagers did these walks regularly and enjoyed it; I think we knew our Flamborough much more than children today.

The roads from each beach centred in the village, you pass bigger houses coming down North Landing lane, all at the one side of the road facing towards the Lighthouse. These took in visitors, many families came regular each year. My fathers' older sister lived here, and until she married, had taken on the role of mother when their mother died and being older than father and us not having any grandparents on either side, we looked upon her as Grandma and spent a lot of time up there. We were allowed to play with our cousin's things, he had a lovely Hornby train set with loads of lines and carriages, Meccano, and lovely big reading books and annuals. When we were old enough to take some of them, they were passed down to us and in turn we passed them to other cousins, that was really the way you got toys for Christmas and birthdays. My cousin was a very studious boy and he won a scholarship from the village school to Bridlington school from there he was taking exams for Cambridge, when suddenly his mother, our Gran, died and to make it worse it was Christmas Day. I was seven and the first we knew was when my brother and I were sent suddenly off to another auntie's for Christmas Day. It made a big mark on our young lives, going to their house was never the same again but our cousin won his place, and I think he was the first to go to Cambridge from Flamborough School and I don't think many have since.

Father used to tell us about going to the Vicarage when he was a youngster, with his sister to help make soup for needy families one really bad winter when the cobles couldn't get out to sea and earn money. He told us about putting turnips through a "turnip cutter" the ones farmers use, then chopping them up to make soup which was then put out on a big table at the back of the vicarage for anyone, the "soup kitchen" it was called. To get to the road to Flamborough Head, you pass where the old cottages stood which were condemned and pulled down and new council houses built. "Mereside" was where my mother was born in the one nearest to the "Rose and Crown" public house, there was also some more houses behind called "Highland", I had aunties all over this area, it was a great shame these were not preserved as most were whitewashed and picturesque. They presented a backing to the Mere, mother told us that when she was a girl it came almost to the road, it was still quite big when I was little, almost everybody around kept ducks and geese, you could find duck eggs at the edge any time. The grass around was a play area, you had to watch the geese as they could knock you down and be very nasty. The water tap, which provided everybody around, was also the cricket wicket, a big cast iron one; folks getting their buckets filled would shout at you to wait a bit. The Mere was most fun in winter, it froze and we had snow every winter then. We built big balls of snow by rolling a small one to start with, then placed three around to make igloos, these lasted for ages. The Mere wasn't deep, a grown up would test the ice to see if it would "bide", then we all went on, the bigger boys had skates, and as the thaw set in we played "Tewy", all link arms and run across, it sort of lifted up and down with the motion. It was great fun which ended up with a few getting soaked but by being all linked together no one ever went under. There were a number of ponds in the fields around but no one was allowed near them as they were deep in places, so were dangerous as well as the fact that farmers had to keep breaking into them for cattle to drink from, so some parts could be deceptively thin. At one time I can remember the headmaster, Mr.Artley, took the two top classes to dig out a moat all round as local builders began dumping their waste rubble, but in the end they won and years later it was decided to drain the water away and fill it in, this was a great shame, it should have been preserved. The Mere and the whitewashed cottages around would certainly have been preserved today, but at that time, new council houses were the big attraction and the biggest part of the area was cleared and it is now an open village green. To the top end were cottages, St Oswald's school, this was demolished in 1991; everyone in my young day went to it until 14 years old. The secondary school at Bridlington was built around 1936 and takes children at 11 years from all the neighbouring villages. My father told us he left school to go to sea with his father at 12 years old. We had 4 classrooms; the infants had a big fireplace in as had Standards 1 and 2, as well as large pipes run from a big coke freestanding boiler which was in the top class, Standard 6. In the main building were Standards 5 and 6, separated by a huge glass folding screen which was put back on any big occasion and made one big hall. Personally I enjoyed school, mother had taught us to read and write before we started. Three of the teachers were local ladies, they taught us everything really in a way that it never left you. I remember being very proud of the first pair of pillowcases I took home for mother and as we progressed we made our own simple clothes and cut patterns from newspaper. Knitting was the same you started off with socks and went on to jumpers and pullovers. The local lady teachers were Miss Sally Bayes, Miss Sarah-Ann Chadwick, and Miss Mary Bayes who married and became Mrs Ned Cross, who incidentally, is still living In the village at a big age. Mr William Ralph came in from Bridlington and later moved into the village and taught my children, Mr Hartley was Headmaster and taught Standard 6. Miss Chadwick's father was the coxswain of North Landing lifeboat and her brother the bowman, so when the maroons were let off (large rockets), to summon all the helpers, it was a very anxious time for her, usually in pouring rain and ferocious gales of wind, Mr Hartley would assemble us all, as many classes as could get into the main building, and we sang our hearts out, all the sea shanties, "Pull for the shore", "For those peril on the sea" and everyone you could think of. I can see him now conducting us in a way that kept us all going until someone brought the news that the boat had landed safely. He'd pat Miss Chadwick as she shed tears of relief, then we would sing "Jerusalem" and get back to normal again. I would think about half of us were from fishing families, so most of us had fathers or brothers out at sea. We kept "May Day" celebrations, St George and his men would be chosen from the top class boys, and we made their costumes from dish cloths (grey knitted ones) and cardboard painted with silver paint. They rode ponies from Dick Bayes, fish buyer, through the main street and on to the village green where a May Queen had been chosen and there was Maypole dancing, Morris dancers with bells round their ankles, the Flamborough sword dancers in navy guernseys and long white trousers, accompanied by a tambourine and melodian, and all the floral dancing etc. Everyone was in high spirits and all your Mums gathered on the Green, and everyone had a good time.

Hetty Mainprize

Born into a large fishing family, Hetty worked for many years at the Thornwick Private Hotel (now the Flaynburg).

Hetty started by telling us about people who lived on Highland, which was to the north of the village green behind the cottages still on that side.

Hetty   Pat Lord lived up there. He had a little shop. Olive was at shop – they had a good trade there. Old Fanny Emmerson, lived at end house you know, them biggish two, why they weren't ni bigger than ours but were taller, she used to go there a lot, and she said ti me one day, "Hey, honey, just go ti Olive's and get me a quarter o'tea and some same". I thought, why she means same tea. So I went ti Olive and I said, "Fanny Emmerson wants a quarter o'tea, two pound sugar, that was it, and 'same', so she means same ageen". Olive said, "No, she means lard". Well, I said, "I've nivver heard of it. My mother nivver said naught like that". Olive says, "Well she does". I went home and told mi mother. She said, "Oh, that'll be one of her sayings".

Margaret   That would be with it being pork would it? Weren't they a bit superstitious about pigs? It was taboo to mention pigs: would it be connected with that?

Hetty   You hadn't ti say ought about pigs when you were baiting, and that. You hadn't ti say rabbits nor nought like that, pigs and rabbits and things when they were baiting fishing lines. And they didn't like parson calling either. My granddad, he hated if parson called. Parson went one day when they were baiting fishing lines. Well, you see – two of 'em bait, one clears what you say 'clearing hooks' – putting bait on – and t'other's building it up at side. So this parson kept putting his hat on line and every time mi granddad did a coil he knocked awd hat off, you know. So mi granddad got fed up on it and he says, "Looks thu, if thu puts thy bloody hat on that line again I s'all chuck thu and it oot". He was sick on him 'cos every time he made a coil and he put it on, hat flew off, that was parson! He said, "Oh Mr Mainprize". He was a rum un mi granddad, he was straight. Granny was a little woman, ever so little; they called her Mary.

Margaret	Was she dressed in the usual black?
Hetty	Yes, like satiny stuff, I can just see her now, she had some artificial flowers, pinky coloured really. Me and our Gertie, when we left mi mother's, she wouldn't let us put powder and stuff on, and we used ti get this stuff and wet it and then put a bit on. Mi granny found out and she says, "Now then, I've found you two oot – leave my flowers alone". And our Gertie says, "Why, you're like mi mother, she weean't let us put nay powder on". And she says, "Nay, and I'm not gonna let you put my flowers on". That was rude, she said.
	Aye, there was some do's i'them days. Everybody helped each other. If one hadn't, t'other would help, you know, and if anyone was poorly they were there ti give a hand. But nowadays things have changed; it in't like it used ti be, is it?
Margaret	What happened when any of them had babies?
Hetty	Oh yes, there was an old midwife, Mrs Thurlow, she lived first house where her two nieces live now. *[Victoria Terrace]* She brought hundreds of babies inti world.
Margaret	What did they used to wear, binders then vests, nappies and thick nighties?
Rita	I mean they were sort of wrapped and sewn into their vests, weren't they in their winter vests.
Hetty	Yes, they kept 'em on.
Rita	And they kept 'em on, because that was why they had lice and things.
Hetty	They used to get them. Mi mother used small tooth combs. Every night she combed our hair with this comb, nivver found any. She was allus washing our hair but there was a lot had 'em weren't there.

Rita	Oh yes, even when we went to school.
Hetty	Mi mother used ti get awd washing tub, it used ti be lasses fost and lads next, bathing us when little. And then we got bigger ti do oursells like. She used to plait our hair.
Margaret	Oh aye, every body had long hair then didn't they? Very few had it cut short, I remember we had long hair.
Hetty	Oh aye, right down here. Doris Walker had hers put back in a great plait, didn't she? We all had plaits. She used ti wash it ivvery Friday night, it was bath night. By gum things has jumped frae then, haven't they, you wouldn't believe it, would you?
Margaret	I mean, then you had a tin bath in back, you used to bring in and fill with water, didn't you? And she'd need it with all that lot.
Hetty	Yes, now you've plenty of water inside, in't there? You had ti fetch it all. I know on washing day we used to fill that big barrel for mi mother. There was a lot of undies; she used ti hang 'em from winda there ti corner. That's all drying we had, like. The other four houses had a garden a piece but we hadn't a garden. But Joss bought a garden belonging somebody that wanted ti sell it, and we had that but we never put a clothes line 'cos it was behind them other houses where Burtons lived. There was like gardens up there, weren't there? And he just set tatties and vegetables. Then he sold it, somebody wanted it and he sold it.
Margaret	When those houses were knocked down you would come into this one, did you?
Hetty	Yes, just a year before war, and a bomb dropped on those three in Stylefield Road. There was an old man and his dog in middle house, Janey Major and her mother and father in another. There's old fella and his dog and he was killed, warn't he? Oh, Pockleys lived in the other. Pockleys, Joe Roe's, you know, Grace and Joe, 'cos little lass Doreen, and Grace was in. They were up at Thornwick pub and somebody had gone up on a bike and told 'em they'd bombed these three houses. I was coming down from Mrs Walker's and I got t'top – just a'fore I come ti George Bayes's bungalow, and these two men were sitting in gutter there. One of 'em says, "Eh honey deean't go doon there. They've bombed Council houses", and I said, "They haven't", and I could see all this dust, and there was horses gotten out o'field somewhere running up road. So he says, "Stop a bit honey, will thu? Let awd thing get o'er". And it was flying was plane, you could hear it. And he says, "They might drop another". But he didn't, he went

out ti sea. I went down and the cars that was there with all their lights on pulling 'em out o'rubble. They said awd man and his dog, they think he'd been wi' door open. But somebody said they reckoned fighters was after him and he'd wanted to get rid of the bombs.

One night airman said ti me, "Come and have a look at this light over yonder", so I said, "Why, it isn't Council houses, it's too far over". He said, "Well Jerry's just dropped some bombs". He'd dropped 'em on a boat and we were stood there, and these fighters come over and they fired and knocked him doon in Thornwick. But, do you know, it seemed to touch o'er top o'Thornwick Private 'cos it's a tall spot. I said, "Oh I ought ti have been inside wi' Mrs Walker and them two 'vacuees. She had two 'vacuees". They said, "Oh they're alright, he's well away. He's gone that one". These airmen [*who were billeted there*] was watching him, that's when he bombed these trawlers or summat i'bay. But I can remember that night they bombed Pockley's and them.

Margaret	Did anything get bombed here in the First World War then, or not – in Brid or anywhere?
Hetty	Hull mostly and cities. We nivver had 'em here. We had old Zeppelins and that come over.
Rita	Scarborough got shelled.
Hetty	Yes, he came in flying British flag and fired on Scarborough. He hit sea front, didn't he?
Rita	Yes, I found some old postcards the other day and one of them was the damage at Scarborough.
Margaret	You would have a range in the old house, didn't you?
Hetty	Yes. Aye – the old fire range – wrekins and chain to hook on, awd grates and white hearth – we used ti whiten hearth. Our Beattie was doing it one day and she was writing her name, she didn't know mi mother was watching her; she was writing her name with whitening. Mi mother said, "That in't way ti wash hearth, get it done". Beattie said, "Oh I didn't know you were there Mum".
Rita	You used to do doorsteps and everything, didn't you?
Hetty	Oh yes, I remember in awd houses we hadn't ni carpets. We used to prick hearth rugs. Mi mother used ti sit clipping 'em and we used ti mek a middle, mebbe black or coloured, and coloured

round edges, and sit doing them on a night. And I can remember mi mother getting it all ready for us to prick it. And then we used ti have ti wash floor, and then we used ti get red stuff - I've forgotten what they called it- and then redden it, but there weren't ni carpets.

Margaret	It would be all tiles, would it?
Hetty	Yes, tiles, little squares; it was a rare awd job, and step yellowed.
Rita	Holly stones.
Hetty	Aye, we used ti call 'em 'beaver' bricks. I remember when I first went ti Mrs Walker's, a great long passage and we had it ti wash and do edge about that wide all round with this yella stuff.
Margaret	You'd have oil lamps then, did you?
Hetty	Yes, oil lamps. I have one upstairs with a globe and a glass, you know.
Margaret	You maun't break the glass 'cos you can't get 'em now. Did you used to do embroidery or sewing?
Hetty	I used ti do a bit of sewing and knitting.
Margaret	But when you look at the light you wonder how you did it.
Hetty	It was only a lamp, an oil lamp or a candle.
Margaret	Did you ever do any crocheting or anything like that?
Hetty	No, I nivver crocheted. I could sew and knit but I couldn't mek a jersey. At school we just did writing and 'rithmatic and all things like that. Miss Chadwick shouting, and awd Sammy Rawnsley wi' his stick; some of lads rubbed their hands wi' onion so they'd break his awd stick.
Margaret	What if they rubbed their hands with onions?
Hetty	If they rubbed their hands wi' onions when he put it on, it broke his stick. They did some rum tricks i'them days. They were all innocent bits of fun really.

Rex and Jean Stiles

Rex attended Bridlington School as a boarder and his grandparents lived in Flamborough. He farmed at Hartendale for many years.

Jean was the daughter of a farmer and married a farmer. She was a member of the Flamborough Amateur Dramatic Society and performed as a principal in many productions.

Jean   I was born in Bempton: you know the Green – where the pond is – the long white house is where I was born. Then we moved to Wilsthorpe and Dad took on a small-holding: it was also a caravan site but he rented it and then we moved to Flamborough in 1933. We moved in the April and Anne was born in the June – she is younger that me. What I remember more than anything was the donkeys that used to go down to North Landing with the big baskets on for the fish. Our road wasn't a road as such, it was a track and I've known mi mother and me when we've caught last bus – we've maybe been to Chapel or Anniversary – one night we got off and it was thick fog and we could not find our way home. We didn't know where we were it was such thick fog and with it all being a cart track and fields. We had to shout for someone to find us and take us home.

You see the Signal Station and the Lighthouse had young girls on them and they all used to come and play down at the farm and the Coastguards as well. They used to come down on a night-time and our John made a trapeze with a stake and two ropes and we did all sorts. We made a big table and they all used to bring food or something down and mi dad made drinks an' that. We'd also bales of straw – this was in the barn – now then the walls were a terrific height in that barn, what we did was the lads put a pulley in the corner, and the bales were round three ways and then there was the wall. We had to go up these bales and there was a hole at the top and me, I would show off. I don't know if you remember Mr Wadsley who married Miss Wentworth? Well he came in and of course, clever me, said "Mr Wadsley, come and have a look at this." And I went up the bales of straw got hold of the rope, got the wrong end and fell top to bottom, my back, every bone hurt 'cos I caught the wall. Mr Wadsley fetched mi mother and they had to pull all the bales away to get me out 'cos I was right at the bottom. They fetched me out and mi mother said, "For goodness sake don't say anything to your dad" – 'cos you know what mi dad was like; we were all terrified of him. I was sat in a chair – I couldn't hardly move 'cos I was stiffened up and he says to mi mother, "What's matter with her?" Mother says, "Well, she's fallen and hurt her back". He looked at her and she said, "I may as well tell you." Father said, "Right, you lot into that barn. Put all those bales away; get 'em all put back where they should belong." So barn was banned – we did used to have some good times in there. Do you remember the field called 'Numbers' – going across to North Landing from North Cliffe Farm? It used to get frozen up – well, it was always flooding. I don't know where we got these ice skates from – I think somebody had left 'em – and we used to go on 'Numbers' ice skating. I'll tell you what else we used to do: we had a little round bath sort of oval shape and our Bill used to tie a rope on it and we'd get on it and he'd pull us round the pond. A fella called Roger had left his boat up in our granary or barn for winter, so we got it out and got it on pond and our Billy says to me – 'cos I was always trouble-maker – "Let's get Clarice onto it." Clarice Traves used to work for us. We shouted of her and he says, "Come on Clarice have a ride on canoe" – as we called it. "No, because if I do you'll mek it tipple over." And we said, "No, we won't honestly." As soon as we got her on we went like this, [rocking it] and over she went. She was shouting, "Help, Mrs Waines, help!" Her feet were stuck in the mud and we didn't realise that. I can see mi mother now: she came to the back door and tears were running down her face with laughing 'cos Clarice couldn't move her feet.

We were into so many things but Billy was always the root of everything. Another little incident: Christmas time, Mum always used to buy us those little pink and white mice, do you remember them – with a bit of string for a tail? Well, there was one each put on the tree for the six of us. However on Christmas Eve we found that one's head had been bitten off so mi dad had us all lined up. We had to open our mouths – "No it isn't you." He came to our Billy. He says, "It's you, you little bugger." And it was: his teeth were exact dye.

Auntie Dorothy had come to stay with us and she'd lost her wallet with her train tickets and everything and of course Bill was blamed. They got onto him so much did mi dad, "Now where have you put it?" He said he'd put it in box aside fireplace. Well, they looked and it wasn't there: then he said he'd put it in rainwater tub but it wasn't there. Auntie Dorothy had left it at Grandma's and poor old Billy was getting blame for everything, but he is always so happy isn't he? Full of it – teasing.

I loved Village Hall dances though, they were lovely. You would go to them, didn't you?

Margaret	Yes, one or two, after we were married.
Jean	Did you Rita? I remember my Mum used to help with the refreshments in the back.
Rita	Yes, especially when they were for the British Legion because my Mum and Dad were in it and they had to go to help so we went.
Rex	Before the war it was Major's band wasn't it?
Rita	Oh, yes.
Jean	Oh, didn't you think it was marvellous in that school? I can remember Bessie Bayes and Bertha Langton – do you remember Mrs Hoyles, postman's wife? She used to sing, 'Walter, Walter lead me to the altar'. Bessie Bayes and Bertha used to be sat in the school window and they used to be helpless with laughter. Then Mr Hoyles turned to mi mother and said,"What did you think to that then, wasn't she good?" Real chuffed you know and mi mother said, "Oh very good." And we were all in tucks because she warbled, you know, she really warbled.
Rita	Yes, and there was Faith Burnly but minds't you she was a good singer, wasn't she? She used to sing at Conservative do's.
Jean	'Shirty' Hoyles used to come, deliver post on a bicycle and he used to ride up to Lighthouse and then he used to cut across

fields to North Landing and sometimes he would be absolutely wet through when he got to our house. Mum would put his coat on a chair in front of fire and he'd sit and have a cup of tea; then he used to cut across fields to go to Dick Hoods and then the rest. When you think about it – it's in a van now and some people complain about it being late.

It was Mr Fussey that started the Flamborough Amateur Dramatic Society. We used to have rehearsals – I'm not sure if it was mainly at the Village Hall: but when Mr Sykes took over – was it at Rock Shop? Brenda Gouge was with us in show.

Rita   Yes, Brenda Gouge was from Bridlington. Her father – was he a barber?

Jean   Yes, and it was "Red Riding Hood". I was Red Riding Hood; Brenda was the Prince and mi cousin Catherine, who was only a little tot, came to see it and when the wolf was chasing me she started screaming and shouting, "Mummy, don't let it get her". We could hear in the back – I've never forgot that! Then I can't remember whether we took the concerts anywhere else but we went all over when Mr Sykes took over. We went to Filey, the Spa, and the Pavilion at Bridlington. All the money went to charity.

Rex   Oh, you went all over at nights

Jean   Yes, because your father came with us and old Mr Scrowston – he used to come with us. Ruth Wilkinson was in; and Ruth and me – I'll never forget – we were at – what's that place where you always sing 'This is my lovely day' when we go past?

Rex   Boynton School.

Jean   That's right. Well we were there and there was a concert and Ruth and me got up in one of the rooms and could see on the stage. It was wrong of us and we shouldn't have done it. We were pulling faces at them on the stage. Well, Ron Coates came through and said, "Bloody well get down". I said, "Don't you dare speak to me like that." I got a bit on mi high horse, "Don't you swear at me". He said, "You heard what I said." Anyway we got down. I think you said something to him and he apologised, he said, "No I shouldn't have sworn at you", but it was all over in a matter of minutes you know.

Rex   Weren't you in plays, Rita?

Rita	Yes, I was in FOP, Flamborough Original Players you know Mrs Weatherall started that.
Rex	Well, didn't Fads and Fop run together for a while and then they amalgamated?
Jean	It would be Jean Hindle who was principal.
Rita	Yes, she was principal girl and I was only in the chorus, until one year – it was when Nancy Hudson went – I took over as principal girl just the one year.
Jean	We did have some good times, didn't we! When you went out into the country you used to get some lovely suppers and you used to put some in your pocket. Scrowy used to come and sit near me on purpose and say, "Come on then give us a sandwich" – 'cos he'd seen us, you see.

Jean then proceeded to show us photos of the players and named many of them and said how some of the main players were handed flowers at the end of the shows. Looking at one photo, Jean said how one lady who lived at 'Treetops' on North Landing Road sent her a fur stole with tails dangling down. She thought 'How am I going to get out of wearing this? I'll look a right Charlie in it!' So she put it over her shoulders for so long then whipped it off.

Jean	Of course, all the soldiers and the Army were stationed up there and I would only be about fourteen or fifteen. I was embarrassed 'cos they were in our barn and sat on the granary steps – I daren't go to lavatory!
Margaret	It would be an outside loo was it?
Jean	Yes, and to go and catch a bus or anything, I really was embarrassed – just at that age. They would be sat on granary steps and I'd get on my bike and get up as much speed as I could before I got round corner. They used to whistle and I wouldn't dare turn round or look or anything and they used to say when I came back, "Will you meet me?" I just hated it. Mind, when I got older I appreciated it. Mi mum was ever so good when I think about it 'cos they'd be in our back porch, in our kitchen, in our front room having a sing-song and she'd be giving them all a drink of tea and baking, you know. Mi dad used to say to one or two of them, "I'm on duty tonight so keep your eye on 'em". There was one called Ron Durman and he used to sleep on settee and of course he thought it was lovely – he had his feet under

table 'cos they were in barn and there was rats and goodness only knows what was in there. The officers were in caravans. Some of the caravans were beautiful inside. They were railway coaches and they were beautifully furnished.

One day, there was the Royal Fusiliers and the Durham Light Infantry and they had a scrap. The officers fell out, and they were firing live ammunition from the Durham Light Infantry which were at Head Farm and – I think they were Royal Berks – at Northcliffe Farm where we were. Mi dad said he'd never seen anything like it. "Get inside all of you." We were sort of watching, you know!

We had a little hut and this fellow used to make ice cream. He had a bicycle with a big box on the front – what did you call it?

Rex	Eldorado and Walls used to have them – 'Stop me and buy one.'
Jean	He used to do those that were green and in a paper – I used to love those. He used to sit the boy, Derek Smith he was called, at the bus stop and catch people as they got off the bus, you see, and catch the soldiers if they were going on the troop.
Margaret	Your father had the farm down here hadn't he Rex?
Rex	No, mi grandfather was there first: he was born at Flamborough Head on Head Farm. His father died when he was only in his forties, and mi grandfather's eldest brother, he farmed there for a while, and then he left and went to Bessingby and mi grandfather took Hartendale.
Jean	Mi dad was Thomas William Waines and we were going to move across there only mi mother had cancer and I nursed her for a year at home 'cos there was no going into hospital or hospice then. Mi dad had a terrible accident moving a caravan: he broke his leg in two places. I had both in bed together and then men living in and them at home like Richard, Bill and Ken,. I'd everything to do and no modern washing machine – dolly tub and a wringer Then wringer conked out so you were wringing everything out by hand. When you think back to the work folk used to do....
Rex	Tell them about the money.
Jean	Oh I got ten shillings a week till I was twenty-one, and I'll tell you what, it was work there.

Rex	When your mum said to him, "I think it's time our Jean had a bit more money, don't you?" He said, "What the hell's she doing with it she's getting ten bob a week?"
Jean	I remember buying a pair of shoes and they were six and six, and the bus fare was one and six. If you got on White Buses with Gilbert Readhead, he never charged me.
Rita	I used to go up to Ruth's to play at the farm. I walked up and then mi mother always used to give me a penny to come down on the bus, and he used to say, "Keep it in your pocket honey for some sweets".
Margaret	Didn't your brothers go egg climbing?
Jean	Yes, they did – Billy and John. There was collectors used to come round and they would look at them and say, "I'll have that one", maybe a pound, which was a lot of money in those days for an egg. The basket used to be quite big and it used to be full of eggs. When mi dad and them come home we used to get frying pan out and fry 'em – I could never fancy 'em. Minds't you, having said that, they were supposed to be a delicacy, weren't they?
Rita	We used to have 'em boiled. Mi mother always used to think that they were too rich for us to have one each so we had to have half each. You boiled them a long time so of course they were set so she just used to cut them
Jean	Yes, they were big weren't they? I remember I used to pester mi dad to go down the cliff and he wouldn't let me go. Anyway, this time he said, "Right, get yourself ready; you can go down this time". Our John just says to me, "Whatever you do, Jean, don't look down". I got to end of Barmin's, ready to go and looked down and I says, "I want to come back". Oh, what a height it looked! But our John was brilliant; he used to go in and then swing right out and mi Dad just knew what to do by John pulling on the rope how many times, maybe two to go further down, maybe one to stop and maybe three to come up.
Margaret	I think it was one of your brothers; did they used to be in the LSA, the life saving company?
Jean	Yes, they did, they saved a lot of lives and they were never mentioned which grieved me 'cos they were my brothers.
Margaret	Yes, I think it was one of them – they were doing a night drill on by Brayle Newk and mi Dad came on with Old Martin, the Coastguard District Officer. They put a Coastguard over from

Filey; he'd never been over the cliff and they put him over on the rope ladder. They called him Jim Sweeney, he was only a little bloke. Mi Dad says, "You'd better go down – you've never been down the cliff". So he goes over – there was one of your brothers with 'em. He got near to bottom and the rope didn't quite reach. I was on the cliff top and mi Dad played hell with me that night for where I was standing, and when they brought Jim back up one of your brothers just went and felt his trousers 'cos he'd been that frightened.

Jean   What did they call them that lived at Redcot, the little bungalow in the corner near Hartendale? She was a Flamborough girl and her and this soldier used to get up at Village Hall and, by, couldn't they half dance – she went to live at Filey.

Rita   Doreen Pockley.

Jean   That's right, Doreen Pockley – and her daughter lives in this house. Well, when we first got married we went there – he was a collector for eggs. He said we could have his place to let. Anyway, we went out this night to pictures. I hadn't time to wash-up or anything so I left pots on table and tablecloth – everything just as it was; put mi clothes-horse round the fire with all the washing on. Our Anne had come down and said, "I'm going to pictures are you coming?" We all three went and she stopped the night. When we came back and got off bus at corner, I just said, "What a smell of burning, wouldn't it be funny if our house was on fire?" It was! Oh, the stink and when you opened the wardrobes they were full of smoke. All the floorboards round the fire were burnt out. I had a ring – I don't remember if it was my engagement ring – but I had some weeny candle-sticks and it was on one of those: it was covered in red wax – it had melted. All mi clothes were burnt. I said, "What is Mr Rickaby going to say? You ring him and tell him, I daren't". Rex rang him and he said, "Don't worry about that, I'm insured. Get it seen to." So we did. Then we could only stay so many months 'cos they were coming for summer, so we went to 'Uplands', the house on the hill, next to Croft Farm. I don't know how long we were there and would you believe it, we had another fire. Rex was working that weekend – milking and I thought, 'Saturday afternoon, I think I'm off to pictures'. I'd forgotten I'd put a frying pan on: you know, bacon – that great fat stuff with a bit of lean. And of course, I'd put it on and didn't turn it off, then went to pictures. Our Kenneth was staying with us then because him and mi Dad didn't get on very well and he came and stayed with us, and there was a letter on table when I come in which said, "Sorry, but it was like this when I came in". And he'd gone. What had happened was the shelf just above the cooker where all my pans were, the wood shelf got on fire and burned everything. We were going on holiday within a few days and I'd washed everything. Rex's mother had made me some beautiful white gauntlet gloves with rabbit skins. There was a rail in the kitchen, it was a real big kitchen and it was like a round rod across. I used to stand and throw things over to air, just sling 'em, I must have got on a chair 'cos it was so high: these gloves were there and they were stiff, just like boards. I thought, "Oh no, I don't believe this". Well, then Rex's Mum and Dad went away so she said, "Will you come down to the farm while we're away and look after things?" Yes alright. We went down - it was threshing day and we had a special big can with tea in and we used to make sandwiches, cakes or pies. I was baking and I kept thinking 'there is a smell of burning' and I kept opening mi oven door and no everything was alright, it was Triplex fire place with two ovens wasn't it, and it was the top oven. When I opened it – 'WOOF'. I'd all the clothes on the line, they all caught fire and I ran out and shouted, 'HELP! House is on fire'. Captain who lived across the road came running. He got mi bucket of tea that was left and slung it. Well, he couldn't have done anything worse! Rex came running in - "What have you done this time?" I said, "I haven't done anything: your mother had left a load of drying cloths and towels in that top oven and she'd a big dripping tin of fat on the bottom and the cloths and towels on the top - well, it just went up in flames." I thought, 'Oh no, I don't believe this.'

I can remember I was going to a rehearsal that night, at the Rock shop, and as I walked in, "Here comes fire king!" I tell you what, I'd never been used to electricity which we hadn't at the farm, and I put the kettle on and it hadn't a plug on, so I just stuck the wires in and it sent me reeling right across room. Well, you see, I was ignorant about electric. Money – I hadn't had any money to do house-keeping. Rex used to give me his wage and I used to think 'by gum this is alright I'm well off'. Then about end of month he would say, "Have you put money away for electricity and coal?" "No". "Well, you'll have to do that". I did a chicken once and left it's innards in and when we cut it, all corn flew out its crop! And you know, trying to do things properly – like his mother would. Well, I thought they were soup spoons but they weren't they were ladles so I put them on table when we were having soup. Rex said, "What are these for?" and I said, "They're for your soup, aren't they?" He started to laugh – and there's me trying to get it in mi mouth – and he says, "They aren't soup spoons; they're ladles for ladling it out". I did make a few mistakes but three fires – it was unbelievable, just as if I was fated, I couldn't believe it the third time. Of course we had to tell his mother but she was lovely was his Mum, really.

Do you remember Miss Woodhouse who used to live at farm? You tell them, Rex, about Miss Woodhouse's sister who married the vicar. You know – Miss Lillian who was at Hartendale with us, her sister. Maud, was it? Or was it May?

Rex	No, she was the one that lived at Chantry Cottage. But there was another one and I think her name was Kathleen or something like that and they used to farm at Croft's Farm and I'm not quite sure what her name was. Anyway, this one, she married the local vicar: she was seventeen and he was about seventy. And when they came out of Church they stoned them. John Willy Bayes, he used to tell this tale – it was all like a monologue; it sort of went summat like this:-

> *She was seventeen and he was seventy.*
> *When they come out of Church, they stayned 'em.*
> *And Nell Sugar, she was there.*
> *And she was ambidextrous.*
> *And if thu deean't know what that means -*
> *She could swear with eether hand.*
> *I always remember him saying that!*

Jean	What about that woman who was a bit of a prosi?
Rex	Yes, I once overheard a couple of men talking about her, when one said to the other – "Can thu still get leg o'er then?" and he said, "Aye, but it's a bugger getting it back again!!"

It reminds me when we used to go to Pocklington – we used to go swimming every other Friday. There was Taylor Fussey and Sylvia, us, Herbert and Lily Gibbon, Sheila Freeman, Ida Mainprize and Jennifer used to go sometimes; anyway, we used to go to Pocklington swimming pool. We used to get there for eight o'clock; we used to swim from eight to nine o'clock and when we came out of the pool we'd get dressed quickly and go to the pub, across the road. We'd drink in there till ten o'clock then rush like hell back to Driffield and get fish and chips.

Jean   And tea and bread and butter. Sylvia Fussey always used to take a jar of marmalade to have our last half slice of bread and butter with – to 'take the taste out' she said.

What are your memories of Flamborough Rex? You went to school here and then you went as a boarder at Brid Grammar School.

Rex   Well, mi mother was from here and mi father came up here during the First World War and that's when he met mi mother. He was stationed yon side of Brid and they used to patrol on the cliff. If it was a bad night they used to get as far as Brid and then they used to go in the nurses home there. Then when they come out they used to go to that horse trough – do you remember that horse trough that used to be opposite Lloyd's Hospital? – they used to go there and chuck water over each other so it looked as if they'd had rain all night: that's how he met mi mother, you see. He was from St Ives in Huntingdonshire; they were a biggish family and he went away to sea. He got to Canada and he deserted there and was over there for a couple of years before the First World War broke out. Then he came home on a cattle ship and joined up, came up here and met mi mother. He was a prisoner of war during the First World War and after the war they got married. The family business was bakers and confectioners in St Ives. He went to some friends and family at Newark as what they called 'an improver'; stopped there a couple of years and then they bought a business at Thame in Oxfordshire and that's where I was born. Anyway, after I was born mi mother was quite ill with a miscarriage and scarlet fever and one thing and another so, when she was off form, I used to come up here and stay with mi grand-parents and go to Flamborough School until I was eleven; then I went to board at Brid and I used to come to mi grandparents. I only went home once after I was eleven, why, like down south.

Jean   So really he's more of a Flamborian than I am in a way.

Rita   During the war I often used to walk by myself down to South Landing. I can remember walking up and just getting to where those tank traps were across at the top of the first hill and I thought, 'There's somebody watching me' – you know how you get that feeling. I looked round; I couldn't see anyone and I walked further up. It was these two escaped prisoners; they would be in that block-house that looked down the ravine.

Jean
Yes, well there was one, I'm sure he'd got an RAF uniform on and mi Dad says, "Keep inside all of you".

When we used to have our school dinner, we used to have it in Auntie Sarah Anne's classroom. There used be all the Halls; David Button – do you remember him from Lighthouse? – he wore a big boot; and there would be the Green's; there was Flo Green, Elsie Green, Ben Green; there was three boys and I think two girls; Ben Fluke, he was in the RAF. Do you remember Auntie Sarah Anne? She had a little round mirror and she used to stand it on the desk and we were all chittering away at her and she'd be titivating her hair up. There was a little hole in the floorboards but we made it bigger. We used to put our crusts down, and Auntie Sarah Anne would be saying, "Who's been putting the food down the hole? There's mice down here and it's encouraging the mice". "Not me, Miss." None of us had done it but the Hall's used to bring fig pie wrapped up in newspaper and they used to say to me, "Change us a bit of your ground rice cheesecake for a piece of fig pie". And I used to think, 'Oh golly', because the figs were in among the newspaper 'cos they'd squirted out. I think she used to feel sorry for you, Auntie Sarah Anne, because she used to say to me, "GO into Mr Hartley's. DO as you're told; GET into Mr Hartley's". 'Course I'd have a tear in hope and then maybe, "GET sat down in your desk", and then she would say, "Go to that little medicine bottle and fill it with water" – for her plants and you would get tuppence. It was as much as to say, 'Oh, I shouldn't have talked to her, I shouldn't have done that, I'll reward her, let her go and fetch the water'. And you had to go round to the tap and fill this little medicine bottle. But she was a good old soul. If it hadn't have been for her, I would have been pretty short – she used to give me half a crown every week. She used to buy me 'Girl's Crystal' and, after Mum died, she came up once with two jerries (chamber pots) in her bag. I just happened to say, "Oh, I've broken another one", she'd catch the bus down, be back on next bus with a couple of pots. She took me to Brid and I tell you what she bought me: she bought me what was called 'knap' cloth, navy blue coat, a navy blue rain coat, two pair of shoes, one for school and one for best, brown woolly stockings, liberty bodices, knickers, vests, a pair of leather gauntlet gloves for best and a pair of woolly ones for school, a navy blue beret and three dresses. They were all from Machin's opposite Binn's. Then she took me down to Marks and Spencer's to buy me nightdresses. It was most embarrassing – she would get me to hold it up here then she would walk and stand back and say, "Do you like it? Now, you're sure you like it? Will it fit you alright?" She would go on, and I'd say, "Yes, I like it Auntie; it's lovely. Thank you ever so much, Auntie." "Now, you're sure, you're sure?" "Yes, Auntie." "Well, pick another one then". And she'd get me maybe two or three and she bought me all those at one go. I mean she was marvellous with me and she was with our John and our Billy.

Rex	Your Kenneth lived with her for a while, when your Mum was poorly. It was that winter of 1947
Jean	Maybe, I can't remember. You see, I had mi Mum in bed for a year with cancer of the breast; she was terribly ill and then mi Dad as well. Dad was in bed and he was on crutches
Margaret	And there was not much medication then.
Jean	No, it was funny because she'd got up one morning – it was just after Christmas because I was rehearsing for pantomime – and she just said to me, "Can you feel anything there?" Do you know my stomach turned over when I felt it? I said, "Oh Mum how long have you had this?" "Well, for a bit". So I ran outside to mi Dad and said, "Will you come?" He said, "We'll have to get doctor". The doctor came – it was Dr Gordon Taylor – and I heard him say "Oh, you have been a naughty girl. Why didn't you come to me before?" Then I heard him say to mi Dad, "I'm afraid there's nothing we can do". I mean it just about broke my heart did that, and I went to our Kenneth – he was milking – and we both had a good cry. Then mi Dad said, "Can't we send her anywhere, isn't there anything we can do?" A cousin had said, "Aren't you going to Leeds, to the Brotherton Wing for treatment?" So they went and they rang up; we had got the phone in by then, we hadn't electricity but we did have the phone. They rang from Leeds to say there was every hope and I was just washing mi hair so I got onto my bike, I was that so thrilled, came down to Auntie Sarah Anne to tell her. It cost of course. She was in an awful mess underneath her arm and I'd to dress it. She had long hair – she used to have it in a plait right across top – and I had to cut it: I hated doing it. She was ill just over a year: she was poorly

before but didn't say anything, and as the doctor said, "You've been a naughty girl why didn't you come to me before?" It was too late. It was awful 'cos she'd worked hard all her life. Just when she could have had things easy: the family was all growing up. Mi Dad was the old fashioned hard sort – as far as money was concerned. He never gave her any money you know. She had to get all from Co-op. If she put biscuits on her order, he'd say, "You can cross them tea toy things out." You can't believe it, can you?

Rex   She used to get her cigarettes there but they always went as something else.

Jean   Oh yes, she liked a cigarette – Craven A. The manager was really in favour with Mum and he used to say, "I've put you some cigarettes in under self raising flour." Mother had to go quickly into pantry to get them. She'd say, "Oh, I hope he's not put me any cigarettes in this time: if your Dad goes in there'll be trouble if he sees them." She used to keep them under the mattress, under her bed; she was frightened to death that he'd see them and she always kept a little flat bottle of brandy on top of the wardrobe for medical purposes only.

I'll tell you about another incident about mi Dad. It was when Mr Scrowston was here. We'd gone to the Spa on Christmas Eve and we were just dancing there when I said, "Oh, I've left turkey in the oven." I was partly cooking it for Christmas Day you see; so I said, "Oh, what can I do?" Rex says, "Well, your Dad'll be in the Dog and Duck: ring them up." I rang Dog and Duck up, mi Dad says, "Oh, we'll sort it out." He was half slewed anyway and Scrowy would take him up: they ended up eating half of it! Mi Dad said, "By, it was just ready to a T." When I looked at it I thought 'What's happened to it?' and he said, "By, we had a lovely meal; it was just ready." They'd had nearly all one breast. He must have thought we were daft, mi Dad, because – you know in your room you had those cloths on your table, what did you call them? It was a big one and it was maroon and like a velvety material.

Margaret   Chenille was it?

Rex   Yes, they had tassels all round.

Jean   Yes, that's it and you had a plant on the middle of the table – he used to keep his booze underneath there! I mean, when you were playing hide and seek, as a kid, it was the first place you'd go under

	as it went right into the wall. But also we had two front rooms, you see; we lived more or less in the living kitchen. One was 'first' room and the other was 'best' room and we had incubator in there, you know, where we used to put eggs: however, there wasn't any in, and mi Dad had put in five hundred pounds in cash.
Rex	Five pound notes, them old fivers, you know.
Jean	He went for it, it was all in crumbs, a mouse had been among it. It was like confetti and when we said, 'Serve him right!' He went mad.
Rex	I was on school governors with him and on Lifeboat as well; and at Christmas, in those days, they used to have the do at Village Hall, for the kids, didn't they? You know – a concert and that. As governors, we were sat on front row – he's sat next to me – that great big top coat on, he got it from Leven, (he got me one as well) he'd got muffler on – you know how he used to be. First half was over: all floor was bare and he just leaned forward like this and a bottle of rum dropped out of his pocket and it rolls across floor and he says to me, "Ger it lad, ger it". All the dignitaries were there.
Jean	Connie Cross, Tant Cross and all the dignitaries were there. Well, I've never seen anything so funny because everybody was sort of looking at it and it kept rolling and rolling and you sort of looked and thought, 'What are we going to do?'
Rex	You know the boards are sort of worn – it was going 'bump, bump, bump'.
	We were up at 'Uplands' and it was when he'd been in hospital I think. He used to come and see us on a Sunday but with him being poorly, he used to come at other times; we were just going out and we gave him the key. We said, "Help yourself, you know where whiskey is." He'd gone in and gone into pantry; he hadn't got his glasses on, he got what he thought was whiskey and it was a vinegar bottle.
Jean	It was a vinegar bottle and he'd tipped it up. He said, "Bugger me, I didn't expect ti be drinking vinegar". Do you know, he used to come up here every Sunday; he would start off here, get his whiskey here, a couple; then he'd go to our Anne's. Well, I sometimes hadn't any, I mean in those days you didn't keep booze, it was unheard of, and I shouted to Anne, "Have you any whiskey 'cos mi Dad's come and I haven't got any?" So she

rolled it under the fence to me, poured him one, and then she said, "Let me have it back for when he comes", so I rolled it back underneath the garden fence. He went there and then he used to go to our Billy's and get one there; then he used to go to the Dog and Duck, the Rose and Crown or whatever. Our Billy used to say, "He's pie eyed". I kept finding whiskey bottles in our garden and I kept saying to Rex, "Do you know it's folks coming down from Timoneer; they're slinging their empty bottles over here." Our Anne says "It's not folks from Timoneer; it's mi Dad!" He used to get them from all over – admitted he never drunk when Mum was alive, not that I know of.

I remember Mum used to be friendly with Mrs Johnson who had the Ship. She was from Bempton and we'd gone there; it was during the war and I'd wangled mi way into the parlour – they were sat in the kitchen, you know, mi mother and Mrs Johnson, having a cup of tea. A couple of these blokes from the Army were in there and they shouts, "Give us a song then, come on". So I got up and sang and mi mother and Mrs Johnson came in and said, "If your father saw you in here singing......" It was something about 'Red Sails in the Sunset' I think or something like that. I thought afterwards how I dare do it, I do not know – in a pub of all places: oh, mi mother was crazed! Another time, I don't know where we were going – in this taxi, there was Stan Wilkinson, Ted Lunn, Gordon Scrowston, Geoff Scrowston, me, Ruth, Mary, Margaret Walker and we hired Johnny Traves' taxi; we all put maybe half a crown – I don't know – to go to a dance, in a pub in the country – I can't remember where it was – maybe half an hour out of Brid, and by, it was making a row was this tin shaker. Stan drove and he went all the way with brake on: it was smoking. He kept saying, "There's smoke coming from somewhere." But we couldn't care; we got there and they says, "Come on in for a drink." We thought we're alright with these lads, Ted and Stan, I mean we're safe enough with them, and they bought us cider, well, of course, when you're not used to drink – cider....!!!. Well, do you know, I can see Mary Wilkinson now. You know the signs that say 'Bridlington, Scarborough' – she climbed on top of there and she was singing at top of her voice. Well, we went to the dance, came out, got into car again, how we all got in I do not know, and we'd only been going about ten minutes when she conked out and it would be maybe, I don't know, twelve or one o'clock, and we were near a farm so Gordon and Geoff went to the farm and said could they ring their Dad.

Building Flamborough Village Hall
a. Back row: unknown; George Sunley; unknown; Tommy Dowse; Tom Cowling;
b. Front row: Bertha Langton; Vera Waud; Cyril Sunley; Bessie Bayes; unknown

Filling water carts at the bottom of Crofts Hill to sell to villagers

Flamborough Village Band, approx 1907.

Cart going to Bridlington at Danes Dyke 1907.

Sword Dancers outside Willowdene on High Street.

Matthew Middleton Lifeboat at South Landing,
a. from the left back row, Kenneth Stephenson, young Tom Stephenson (Dust),
Lew Knaggs, Tom Stork, Albert Duke, Bill Mainprize, Jack Cross,
b. front row, George Stork (Walsh), Tom Stephenson, Jack Stephenson (Fatty),
Chad Knaggs, Bill Stephenson, Lew Knaggs, old Albert Duke

Robert Leng's grandfather with crab pots on the Green.

Visitors Watching Crabs Being Boiled.

Jean Stiles (nee Waines) on the steps
of a gypsy caravan.

John Longden on his horse in Austria,
one of 300 he looked after.

Cath Chadwick Skeining Mussels

John Chadwick senior baiting in
his coble.

Outing coming home at the bottom of Crofts Hill.

Top Class, Flamborough School, 1928
a. from left back row, Ernest Sunley, Cyril Pickering, Mr.C.Hartley,
Stanley Waines, Cyril Sunley,
b. front row, Bertha Langton, Lillian Stork, Sylvia Readhead, Linda Langton,
Millie Stork.

Wilkinsons Harvesting, Late 1930's, Joss Mainprize on top and John Longden on the ground.

Flamborough Original Players in their production of Simple Simon from the left, Mary Waud, Gordon Scrowston, Ron Coates, Mary Kemp, Ruth Wilkinson, Jean Waines, Frank Woodhouse, Eric Lount, Jack Jessiman, Doris Woodhouse, Kath Lount

Flamborough Original Players
a. backrow, Mr.Scrowston senior, Ron Coates, Bob Sunley, Frank Woodhouse, Gordon Scrowston, 1 unknown, Jack Sykes at back, Ron Williamson pianist, 1,unknown Eric Lount, Basil Scales
b. middle row, Rachel Pockley, Eva Sykes, Edith Jane Waind, Mary Waud, Mary Kemp,
c. front row, Margery Emmerson, Anne Pockley, June Major, Glynis Needler.

Robert Leng with wife and son, Alf with the horses used to pull boats at South Landing

South Landing Ravine, Early 1900's

Tom Cross, Alf Leng's Grandad, at North Landing on fish stands.

Alf Leng (with his father) on a horse at South Landing

Lighthouse Area Early 1900's

Steen Knaggs on a Sailing Coble At North Landing

Fishermans Return, North Landing

Selling Fish at North Landing Market

George Major, George Nordass, Bolton Warcup, Laurie Smith, 1940

Flamborough 1947

Cottages at the back of the Mere.

Co-Operative Store on The Corner Of Dog And Duck Square

Donkeys on the Little Green looking across to the Mere

Observer Corps
a. from the left Mr. Wall, George Cross, Frank Wise, Mr.Southwell,
George Thompson, Tant Cross, Gilbert Readhead, Reg Stiles, unknown.
b. Front row, Mr.Gardner, John Waines, Bob Edmond, Fred Freeman.

North Landing, Early 1900's

Flamborough Life Saving Apparatus 1947
a. From the Left, back row,S.Coates, R.Whitehead, W.Chadwick, L.Smith, J.Smith,
W.Woodhouse, H.Readhead, T.Cowling.
b. Centre row, R.Major, D.Wiles, S.Woodhouse, F.Freeman, T.Stork, G.Langton,
D.Sayer, W.Sayer.
c. Front row, T.Wall, T.Cross, H.Gibbon, G.Waud, Coastguard Inspector,
Chief Coastguard, J.Waud, District Officer Martin, Station Officer Sambourne
d. in front, P.Wiles.

Highlands showing the shop.

Flamborough Fishermen outside Rose and Crown.

Fishing Lines drying outside a cottage with Robert Leng's grandfather

Three Generations of
Chadwicks, Dick, nephew John
and grandfather, John.

Fish Buyers at North Landing from the left, Tom Woodhouse (Morse),
John Willie Bayes and fishermen.

School Photograph with Teachers Sally Bayes And Mr Davidson

School Photograph with Teacher Sarah Anne Chadwick

Jim Fell and a friend coming up from South Landing

Climmers at Bempton
Back row: Bill Major, Major Leng Major, Jack Major
In front: Smiddy Fell

Chadwicks coming home from Sea

High Street early 1900s

High Street early 1900s

High Street early 1900s

Lifeboat in Bridlington Harbour

Post Office Corner 1946

Old Flamborough Lighthouse

Flamborough Carrier
Sarah Barclay and brother, Jack

Donkey at North Landing

Sword Dancers at Danes Dyke House

Jim Smith on Back Street Hill
(Greenside)

Chapel Street before the Memorial

Chapel Street after the Memorial

Flamborough Postlady –
Mary Collingwood

George Major, Charlie Cross, Alf Leng and Albert Duke on the cliffs at Lighthouse

6th West Riding Infantry marching into Flamborough during the First World War

Local Midwife Thurlow

Local Midwife Thurlow

Fishermen at the Memorial

Irene Stork, Olive Stork, Bessie Bayes, Jean Stiles, Sarah Anne Chadwick,
Violet Dowse, Unknown, Margaret Smith, Elsie Longden

Aerial photograph of Flamborough 1934
showing Highlands on the right of the Mere

Flamborough Fishermans Club

They rang Scrowy, policeman, and he wasn't at all pleased, but he came through, got me and the girls, Gordon and Geoff and left them lot. Whether the farmer gave them some petrol to see them home, but they'd used so much petrol with going with eight in and brakes on. Mr. Scrowston rang me up at home; I don't think he was too pleased either. I tell you what he did do, we'd all been at the Spa hadn't we, and we were going to the midnight service, Christmas Eve, and you know how it's all lit up at Church on the path and whatnot; one of our lot was pie eyed, and what had happened was someone had dowsed his drink, we don't know who, and going up the path all of a sudden – blurgh, I said, "NOT on a tombstone for goodness sake".

Rex   I says "Hey up, it's Auntie Sarah Anne coming".

Jean   I was really upset, I thought if me Auntie Sarah Anne sees us like this there will be trouble: she would have been absolutely horrified. So I said, "I think you'd better go home." I didn't want him going in Church; I thought if he starts that in Church..... Well, he got a bit further and blurgh: I got him to the back gate and left him and went into Church. I thought, 'Heck, how am I going to get home to Northcliffe?' Mr and Mrs Scrowston were there so I went up to him and I said, "Mr Scrowston, can I ask you a favour? Would you run me home please?" I must have looked pathetic, and he said, "On one condition, you come with us we're going to the Seabirds." So I said, "Oh, alright then". He was pie eyed and we got in there and poor Mrs Scrowston – she always wore hats – he kept going like that and bringing the brim down over her face; and all she kept doing was putting it back – never saying anything. I thought, 'I don't know if I feel safe with him.' Anyway, I got in the car; he had one eye shut and he would go one way and then the other and he says, "I'll run you down the road". I said, "No, it's fine, I'll be fine thank you very much, Mr Scrowston; it's very good of you". I thought if mi Dad sees him and me getting out of car, he'll swear there's summat going on.

We hadn't been married very long and his Dad was always cadging cigs from me and in the end I said to him, "Look, I can't afford to be keeping you in cigarettes." He got hold of me and put his arm round me and says quietly, "I tell you what, if you'll give me a cigarette, I'll buy you a packet tonight". As he did that, mi Dad walked in. Dad's face was like thunder, you know, 'What's going off here?' sort of thing. All I says is, "What do you think,

Dad, he's cadging my cigarettes and now he's just said if I give him one he'll buy me a packet". Well mi Dad's face changed but I'm sure he thought 'What's going off between these two?'

Mark Major

Born into a large fishing family, he was an electrician by trade and was very involved with the Green Howard Association.

Mark   As a little boy, mi granddad taught me, if you want to grow up to look after yourself, visit as many trades people as possible – he meant trades workers – so I used to go up to Mr Hopwood's a lot. He would send for me especially when he was going to steam wood – to bend it in his steam box. He used to use elm for the gunnels of the boat. They were steamed to bend into shape because if he didn't they were putting pressure on the rest of the coble, you see. Anyway, he had this great big set copper and he had this box running from the top with a lid on, a lovely lid he'd made, with an opening that the box fitted in. And the box went right the full length of his workshop and he used to put timber in there to steam. He'd chippings of wood all over the place 'cos he used an adze, and I used to get a great heap up against the copper. He filled the copper with water as I was only a little lad and he hadn't a tap there, and I'd get it boiling. Once I'd got it boiling, I'd to keep it boiling and keep topping it up. Then all of a sudden he would shout and he would open the front of the box where it was hinged, throw the front up, and he would get the timber. Then he would put it onto metal to the shape he wanted, with pegs in for the timber to fit behind. He'd force it round, you know, and then put it back in.

He once sent a message, could I go with him, he had a repair to do at South Landing. It was to a coble, 'True Vine'; it was George

Hotches at the time. It had been damaged and he wanted a piece of this elm bending. 'Course he couldn't do it at home; he could have made a template, I suppose, but he didn't do like that. He borrowed Bill Sunley's hand cart – Bill Sunley the wheelwright. The first thing he put on, a five or six inch piece of cast iron fall pipe, then his timber, his tools and a bag of shavings and chippings to get it started. When I got there, he'd made a plug of sacking, bunged into one end of the pipe, and he propped his barrow handle between two bits of crossed stick. Then he says, "Fetch us some water." And I went and got some sea-water, and he poured it in. "Now then", he said, "Make a fire down here; keep clear of the wooden props and keep clear of the bottom because of the wooden plug." I made a fire there and when the water got boiling he shoved his timber in. He had it tied at the top so it didn't go right into the water, threw an old sack over the lot to keep the steam in, and I just kept it going till he knew it would be ready and he could just bend it to the shape he wanted. That was things I learnt as a boy.

He used to say, "Are you coming harvesting with me?" He used to go to all the plantations, where he had permission, up the hedgerows and plantations. And all the trees, he'd let them grow to shape, you know, a branch with a side branch. And if he marked them, when they were cutting the hedges, they never touched them. And he let them thicken up then when they were big enough and you could see the shape – well, very often, they weren't flat they were rounded, because they'd grown like that. He cut them down and he got two out of one. They were hung up all round the workshop for seven or eight years to mature and dry out. When I was going, he was using stuff his dad had hung up. Another thing, when there were any ash wands, as he called them, young ash growings, straight up or a cross bit, he used to tie them in position; maybe find a long straight bit of any old hedge or any old timber, and tie it where this was, and he'd bend it round and tie it alongside this, then bend it in a nice curve at the end and train it back and it would grow. Then when we went back the next year or year after, there was a piece like half a trombone. He cut it off and when he got it home, one bit straight to put a knob on and the other bit with a curved handle for walking sticks, and he'd put a ferrule on the other end. He had standing orders with different shops to supply them. I used to love to go with him, but it was hard work because we used to

	cut a lot and we'd put five or six pieces together. Then, when we'd finished, we had to gather them up and sometimes we couldn't carry them – we had to go home and come back again. Still I didn't bother.
Margaret	I've heard Laurie say that he would start with a bit of wood, and he'd no template or anything, and he would just cut it with his adze and get it to the shape he wanted.
Mark	Oh yes, he did. Bill Sunley was the same with an adze, you couldn't hardly take anything off with a plane. Marvellous. He was the wheelwright on Chapel Street, right opposite mi mother's, next to Institute, where Sunley's workshop is.
Rita	He lived next to Aunt Ginnie's. *[Ogle Cottages]* Where Keith Sunley's house *[Priory House]* is – that was all his garden.
Mark	There were two blacksmiths down Tower Street. There was Wiles's then a bit higher up, there was Lockwood's.
	Mi granddad went to the night classes run by Mrs Crake at Marton Hall, but he didn't leave fishing. He used to be helping her to teach others and when she died he was given this certificate – I don't think there was many given out – from Louisa Francis Crake. She was the one who donated the Institute. Now, her son married the heiress to the Rawcliffe estates near Goole, and it was a bigger estate than Flamborough, so the title changed to Crake's of Rawcliffe and Marton. And Mrs. Crake, his mother, lived at Marton with her daughters while he lived at Rawcliffe.
Rita	Can you remember Billy Gibbon?
Mark	Yes, I can. I remember him coming out of his bedroom window and running down street. *[He had pneumonia and was hallucinating.]*
Rita	Yes, he would have killed himself doing that, wouldn't he? His wife was my godmother.
Mark	Ginnie Major.
Rita	Now, were they related to you, 'cos they were cousins to Matt Major weren't they?
Mark	Yes, they were related through granddad and mi granny as well in some way. You know a lot of people didn't know who Billy Gibbon was. It was in the Institute one night, and I'm not sure if it wasn't Laurie who said, "Well, come on let us in on it, who was Billy Gibbon?" I said, "He was Melsh Gibbon's brother". Melsh was a local preacher – I've a photograph of Melsh. He was on

B.B.C. – it nearly made a big rift. Rob Leng, mi Uncle Charlie, Melsh Gibbon and Jim Cross, and they, used to take Bob Otch – *[when they went around to different chapels preaching and singing.]* He didn't preach but he was a good singer. And do you know, they asked Rob Leng to stand down, his voice wouldn't record properly on the radio. But Rob was a good singer, a tenor singer.

Now, here's something will interest you, you may know about it, Shrove Tuesday in Flamborough, do you know another name for it? Well it was Kepping Bowl Day. What happened on Kepping Bowl Day – the boys got up and they went straight off to the wheelright, the joiners' shops, the coble builders, collecting sawdust. Meanwhile the girls got busy with cloth in little panels and sewed them up to be a little boat, kept the tops open and filled them with sawdust the boys brought. They sewed them up and there were several games they played, but only one I really remember mi grandmother telling me about. The girls formed a circle with so many of the boys inside it, and passed the balls from one another either around the circle or over the top, I can't remember which, without the boys getting them. And as they passed them, I think the boys counted and the girls said their prayers. I said, "What prayers?", and she said, "You fathead, the Rosary of course". She said all these things came in after the Reformation. I mean she was a big Wesleyan but she said they used to recite the Rosary, those who wanted to try and keep the Catholic religion, and she used to say, "But be quiet. If anyone hears us we'll be bont at stake". But when you come to think, her granny lived in the time of when they would be. She used to tell me that they always made these balls on Shrove Tuesday and nearly all Saints days they had some game or something they played as an excuse to saying their prayers. But she never held it against them, you know.

Margaret	What did you get up to as a kid at school? What games and that did you play; what mischief? We've heard about putting bags on someone's chimney!
Mark	I'll tell you the only two games I ever got up to – I was that busy going to these workmen, honestly – I never played a lot,
Rita	I don't think you did play a lot 'cos you hadn't time, you had to help out.

Mark	Well, you had and being brought up by mi grandmother I had an old head on my shoulders, I accepted responsibilities that I shouldn't have known about. I used to play "devil up spout", have you heard about that? Everybody's fall pipe finished this high so that you could get a water butt underneath you see, and you would stuff paper up, not too tight, and light it. By, it didn't half roar away. Anyone in the house wondered if a train was coming.
Rita	We used to do it at Matt Bailey's, next door to us.
Mark	Any strange lad come to live in the village, we'd say, "Can I come and play wi' you?" "Yes. We're going to play fox and hounds." And – you know where a lot of houses had two doors together – we'd tie him between the two doors and then knocked and ran away. One woman shouted "Let go" when t'other one shut her door, then opened hers and give him a great clout – he couldn't get away.

As for going "trotting" – I went on mi own to South Landing when I was 10. I went off like that, any hour; didn't matter what time was low tide, I went off. And I didn't know until after I left school, but mi grandad used to wait till I was out of sight, then he would get dressed and come after me. He'd wait among the cobles at South Landing and when he saw mi lantern coming off the beach he'd clear off home. I ought to have known, because when I come to think, teapot was always warm when I came back from "trotting" – he'd had a drink.

I was never afraid of the dark. I could somehow always find my way about, and that served me well in the desert *[in the Army]*. You know I never got lost, but it let me in for a lot of jobs I didn't want! I remember one particular night, we were surrounded in this box, and we heard a great load of armour come smashing past the front and go up one side. Then it stopped and we knew they were digging up for the night. So muggins was sent with some men, to identify them. If it had been Germans I don't suppose I'd have been so keen but it was because I could find my way about in the night. I met a Bridlington chap, a fisherman, a Flamborough fisher lad really – he was out there in the tanks. I said, "Now then, how's things?" and we had a chat. I said, "One thing you'll be alright, you won't get lost". He said, "Mark, I've never found mi way here; I can get lost coming out of garth. I can't find mi tent or mi dugout where I'm living".

I'll tell you what mi granny used to do – she made all mi dad and mi granddad's oilskins. She had this heavy sewing machine, it was; she made the coble sails as well. She made the oilskins, I can see her now, great big doppers; you know, the ones that came down here. She'd put a broom shaft through them, knock head off a brush, put the shaft through and hang it up on clothes line. Then she'd paint it with linseed oil, about seven coats to make them waterproof. For doppers they used heavy cotton or something, I've got it down here. What did they call it-duck!

She would make sails out of, generally, cotton. She knew what type to ask for and everything. And mi grandad could draw them out, a lot of people thought they were just a shape, but they aren't straight down like they look when they're out. They have to have a bag in them. It's a big thing to understand, this sailing. The sails have got to be made so that when the wind hits them, if it's a side wind, it hits them and if they're set right. It's the force of the wind slipping off that sail, having a quick vacuum, which draws the boat and doesn't push it. The old square sails, old Norman galleys and Danish galleys and that sort of thing, the wind pushed them on. But sailing like a sailing coble, and like a yacht, it's the action of the wind. You've got to have the sails so that the wind hits it and slides off, and it's the air rushing into that vacuum that pushes the boat on. It's like aerodynamics, the way they're set. There's a lot of pressure one side and nothing much at that, and it draws it on. It's a great thing when you can understand it.

Now then, full length sea boots, the last pair mi grandad got was in 1922 and they were £2-10 shillings at Tanton Chadwicks. I went to Tanton Chadwick's helping and sweeping up for him, polishing boots he'd done. One day he was mekking a pair of seaboots and he reckoned to prick his finger, and you know he got a bit of big puffball mushrooms; they all used to have that for stopping blood you know, did you know that? All the workshops had it. He said, "Oh dear and I did want to get this finished". I'd watched him sewing and I'd done him lengths of what they called 'waxed ends'; you know, Rita, don't you? You used to cut the cotton into lengths and pull it through a ball of wax. And he'd started this sewing, a needle on each end and you pass them through the same hole, you know. So I finished it for him, ten or a dozen stitches. He examined it, put his hand in his pocket and gave me a penny. Mi grandad said when I went home and told him, "You passed your test then". I thought it was great.

Do you know it came into wonderful use in prison camp. I was at a prison camp in Italy. Before the war, all the hospitals were staffed by nursing nuns and there was a lot still there but there was a lot of medical orderlies – you know – Army lads. A nun came once to talk to one of our regulars and her shoes were dropping to bits. It was snow on the ground. She hadn't come far I know, because we were between the convent and a big military hospital. Anyway, I asked the sister, "Can I have a look at her shoes?" She took it off – they were felt uppers and leather soles. I thought, 'This was easy' so I said, "I could repair those. In fact I could remake them if I had some tools". Next morning, she never said anything to the sister. I was sent for from the office and when I got there the admin officer said, "What do you know about shoe making?" I said, "Where I live, Flamborough, inshore fishing people, you had to be self sufficient – able to do anything and everything. When we couldn't afford to take shoes to the shoemaker's I repaired them for the whole family". And he said, "What do you want?" I said, "A sail maker's kit for these particular shoes and a good pair of scissors". "Oh, sister will see to that for you". And do you know in two days they had a sail maker's palm and needles there. They brought me this woman's shoes and I took them all to pieces and made cardboard templates. The sister brought me a great big piece of felt as big as this table. I cut them out and sewed them and where I was having a bit of difficulty getting them to lay flat, she was there with her flat iron, a great big thing like they use on a billiard table. It took me about three days but I didn't mind. A perfect pair of brand new shoes! We had slippers called 'shabats'. I think they just had a leather sole and heel with just a little piece over your toes. It took some getting used to walking in them, but once you did they were alright. Well, I was in charge of the stores, so I used to steal some – nobody knew actually. You know, if I wanted a pair for somebody I just went and got a pair. I would cut the piece of toe off – well, I would unstitch it properly – then I made the sister a pair of brand new shoes. Well, do you know, I was at Palma in North Italy, and I think all the nuns in North Italy wanted their shoes repairing. Anyway, I got out of it because, after a while, they had a cobbler at the convent, but he was an old man and he died. Their shoes wanted repairing but he'd been ill for a long time, then he died and they brought me all his gear. I thought – "I'm here for life!" And then a Moroccan came. He'd been fighting for the French and he said "Do you want any help?" I said, "Do you know anything about cobbling?" And he said, "I joined the French Army as a cobbler, I'm apprentice trained and I can both hand and machine sew". I got permission from the sister and gave him the whole lot.

Anyway I think I've got the names of the cobblers in Flamborough. There was your granddad – George Cross, Rita; Jack Cross in the little shop, Matthew Bailey, Tant Chadwick and Mr. Gilvey.

Now, horse hair was used a terrible lot in the fishing industry: for snoods – that's what the hook fastened into – for place lines; it was all horse hair and Granddad taught me how to spin horse hair.

Margaret   Was that what covered the hair?

Mark   No, the snood's what the hook fastened onto.

Rita   'Sneds' we called them, cotton sneds.

Mark   One way we used it was when it was bad in winter – you might have heard this – we used to eat sparrows and starlings. You know sparrow dumpling and starling pie – just the breasts. And to catch them, this is what we used, what we called a 'gilldit'. You had this netting on an iron hoop off a whelk pot and then you fastened horse hair to it. I've spun it thick and thin, thicker like we used for snoods.

Rita   And where did you get the horse hair to do it when you were young?

Mark   Well, I used to go to Sam Duke. You know all the ponies for fetching gravel up off the beach, they all had good tails. Now then, I did that in prison but I couldn't have a hoop. I didn't want one. I wouldn't have been able to hide it. I just made a square piece of netting. I went one day to the cookhouse and I said, "Any stores coming in today". It was when things were really bad, we were starving; and of course the cook started off with, "There'll be two or three half beasts coming in, peas and all sorts". But then he said, "As a matter of fact, with a bit of luck, there's a load of potatoes coming". When it turned up, it was a driver I'd dealt with. I was one of the chief barterers in this camp – he was one of the Germans I'd dealt with. Poor old lad – you know he nearly wept, I gave him a cigarette, he didn't want to take it – "Nix, nix" he kept saying – he hadn't anything to barter. I got a Scotch pal who could speak German, "Hey Mac, come here. I want you. Tell him all I want is some horse hair from a horse's tail". He thought I'd gone off my nut! He said "Help yourself" and brought me about sixteen, the first time. I said, "Bring me some more tomorrow", and by, he brought me a bag full. I made a square piece of netting and these little sneds and I found some bits of wood to make pegs. The next morning, I was at the gate to the sports field, which you weren't often allowed on, but a cigarette did wonders. The Germans who were stationed at home, they got down to soldiers issue, one a day; they were worse off than we were. Anyway, I gave him a cigarette and he let me through into the sports field and I went to the far corner where there were no-one nearby, and the old lad with the horse – I'd told him what I was going to do – he said, "You'll want some of this" and gave me some oats out of the horse's nose bag. So I put mi gilldit down and put some oats and in no time at all, I had about thirty birds. I just nicked the skin and pulled the breast out and buried the rest of them. Then off I went and got a fire going and cooked them. There was chaps coming past nearly crying. A lot of them used to say, "That b--- so and so – I'm sure he's in with the Germans". I was always cooking something. I was always bartering and I got one or two good friends among the Germans, they were older chaps who were in the First World War. One particular one, funny enough they called him Walter Kemp, and he lived about eight miles away and he used to get home for a weekend now and again, maybe once a month. When he came back, he used to bring a couple of eggs or a few vegetables, and I remember the last time, he was nearly in tears, all he could bring me was half an onion. They were starving. Then of course we were put out on the march. The big men – they couldn't let them go. They'd been so long with practically no food their legs wouldn't carry them. I weighed six and a half stone and was passed as fit to march.

I was in Germany, then in Bavaria. I got to the dizzy heights of lance sergeant and they couldn't make me work, so I was a non-worker. But we suffered for it as we only got one meal a day, that was at half past eleven; one or if you were lucky two slices of black bread, only from small loaves, or three little potatoes – what we called pig potatoes, and a spoonful of scullywort. "Scilly" we called it – I think it was water heated up and a blob of margarine slung in to make it greasier, and that was it. Of course Red Cross parcels were stopped – while they were on the go, we could manage. And we went down and down and down and then they took us out on the march – it was cruel, wicked.

A lot of the prisoners I was with at this camp were taken prisoner at Dunkirk. George *[Chadwick]* was taken prisoner at Dunkirk, but he was a young man. These were old soldiers, they'd come home just before the war to get discharged after twenty years service. They were turned forty then and they got sent to France and taken prisoner, so by the time I joined them they were forty – five or six, some older. And having to go out and march, well it was cruel. One old feller, well two, of the Northumberland Fusiliers who were in the hut I was sent to – tell you what they were like, they had waxed moustaches! They hadn't even had battle dress issued and they were prisoners. I thought I'd got into another world when I saw them, and I said I'll never complain again not ever, and everything I bartered, everything I got, I particularly shared with these two old lads. One was called Finnemore and t'other was called Matt. I kept in touch with Matt till he was over eighty and he died. Finnemore died of cancer at seventy five.

Now then, you know about the lantern for the cobles don't you? They were made of metal; they'd a blank side at the back, and then they had a white glass and a red glass and green. They had shutters to shut them down. If you wanted to, you could just show a white light to sea from one position. But they were mounted on a hollow metal tube and that was to fit over the tholl pin, where they put the oars in. When they were shooting lines they put one on the tholl pin so they could see what they were doing, otherwise, when they were sailing, it was hoisted up on halyards.

Rita   Were they just candles inside?

Mark   Oh yes, mostly tallow candles. And when I mentioned those young fellows going for their own sailing colliers, a lot of them couldn't write you know. A lot of their teaching – navigation – was taught in poems. There was one mi granddad taught me when I was only a little lad. He used to go off in herring season. When they were coming back from Kings Lynn, almost opposite out at sea, was the Dungeon Lightship, and it said:-

> "First the Dungeon then the Spurn,
> Flamborough Head coming next in turn,

Flamborough Head as you pass by,
Filey Brig is drawing nigh.
Scarborough Castle stand out to sea,
Whitby Light bear northerly,
Huntley Foot that very high land,
Is five and twenty miles from Sunderland.
And our old men say if things go right
We'll be in the Tyne by tomorrow night".

This is how they were taught. He used to tell me all sorts. When he was herring-in', they used to pull into harbours, Whitby and that, and if there was a lot of wind, they sent them up into the inner harbour 'cos there was that many cobles and herring boats of one kind or another. And he said there was an old lad, he'd been on sailing colliers, then he'd married a woman from Culler Coates and she wanted him to settle down, so he became an inshore fisherman, but he went on herring boats in the season. He didn't drink, the old lad, but he'd come round from boat to boat and sit and have a cup of tea with them and sing to them or say poetry. And he used to sing a real doleful, sorrowful song, a lovely tune though it had to it, about the mine disaster at Hartley Colliery near Blythe in 1865. Two hundred men and boys were lost, the big beam holding the winding gear and everything gave way and everything crashed down into the shaft, trapped the fellows and they either suffocated or drowned. I won't try and sing it, it was a lovely tune though, but the words were:-

A miner was leaving his home for his work
When he heard his little child scream.
He rushed to her bedside, her little white face,
Oh daddy, I've had such a dream.
I dreamt I saw the pit all afire
And men struggled hard for their lives,
And then the scene changed to the top of the mine,
Surrounded by sweethearts and wives.
Oh, don't go down the mine daddy,
Dreams very often come true.
Daddy, oh, daddy it would break my heart,

If anything happened to you.
So go and tell my dream to your mates.
For as sure as the stars that shine,
Something is going to happen today.
So daddy don't go down the mine.

There are two more verses to it and I wish I'd written them down. I've written all over to get the rest of this because I'd some of the lads in my section, they were nearly all Geordies or Tees-siders, they used to sing this. And whenever they got the opportunity they always sang this. And by, it did make a party for them; give them some NAAFI somewhere or maybe a big tent and a piano and they'd get cracking.

I wished I could play the piano, but I could play cornet and sometimes I got somewhere where I would play the trumpet, but on it's own it's no good.

Margaret	You were in the Flamborough band then?
Mark	Yes, I was in from being a lad – on the bugle.
Margaret	How long did it go then?
Mark	Right up to the war. Do you want to know the history of the Flamborough Band, then? It started in 1859. The Government called a muster for troops and volunteers all round the country – they expected an invasion. At Flamborough, they were volunteer artillery, and there was that many volunteers – Beverley was the county town – they could neither pay them when they went for drills nor give them uniforms or find them weapons. They had two thirty pounder guns; they found a third one and said you must have two crews for each gun. And still there was a great load of spare men. They gave them all the rifles they could, and they said "You'll have to ask the rest to leave". Well, no one dare ask them to leave or the lot would have gone. And Northallerton got to know, it was the county town for North Riding. They said, "We'll lend you all the uniforms and weapons you want", so they did this, but there was still spare men, so the Army did a wonderful thing. They sent a load of instruments to Flamborough and they sent a bandmaster or musician as they were called in those days. He was billeted at Bridlington, and he walked on to Flamborough three times a week to teach them. And mi granddad said there was only one man in the band could read or write and yet in six months they could play marches and hymns, simple ones.

The artillery band went on till 1908, and then there was a complete reassessment in the Army. The old volunteers were disbanded and the Territorial Army was started, and of course when the volunteers were disbanded the instruments had to go back. The fishermen, they were all fishermen practically, were absolutely lost, so they got together and said well what would it take to buy some. Old Will Hall was the tailor in the village at the time and he was a keen bandsman. He said, "I'll put some money up"; and I don't know who the other two businessmen were that put up the money, and they ordered a set of instruments. Then they had concerts and collections and all the bandsmen paid a shilling a week towards the instruments. Mi grandmother often told me, "Your dad would join". And sometimes two shillings a week was a lot of money to find. Anyway, this is how Flamborough band came into being, through that. It's a shame that something hasn't been done by now because those instruments were publicly subscribed instruments. And they should all be collected in and a decision made whether to try and form another band or sell them and give the money to charity or something.

Margaret   Where will they all be now?

Mark   Well, they are all over the place, I had a lovely new silver cornet.

Margaret   They used to practise up above in the Drill Hall.

Mark   Yes, I loved it up there.

Margaret   Well, there was all those hanging lamps, wasn't there, and chairs all round. I've heard Father say that it was taken over by the First Aid during the war.

Rita   Yes, because mi mum used to go up there.

Mark   The lamps wouldn't be there then.

Margaret   Yes, they were there until the First Aiders finished with the room.

Mark   Because I wired it all out with electricity, early on, 'cos I worked for the electricity company that brought electric to Flamborough, you know, and I wired the band room out. But the lamps would probably be there, I've no doubt.

Margaret   Well, whoever was there when they went out last, the lamps all went but one and we have that one. And Father said the others just vanished; where they went they just all took them.

Mark	It's a shame because they were great big ones, and old Tant Fell used to polish them up. Another thing about Tant, he was the finest kite maker anybody ever saw. Any lad that wanted a good kite, go to Tant and he used to say, "Right, thu be at band room at six o'clock on Tuesday night and I want thu with some coal and firewood, I'll mek thu a kite". And Tant supplied all the stuff for a kite as long as the lad fetched a bit of coal for the fire. Tant was like that. He wasn't having the band paying for coal which he was having to make an hour earlier than need be. He made some beauties.

Funnily enough, I copied him in prison camp. I got telling some lads about him, and they said, "You do tell us some tales". They used to call me 'god' because I could do nearly anything, so I made one and it was very funny. Just at the time I made this, we decided to have – in the camp – an Arts and Craft exhibition. All these do's we used to put on were because we had some escape plan going on, or there was something we wanted, or to distract the Germans. The chap making the models of all sorts – it was marvellous what they could make – they wanted paint. So I got mooching round. I used to go round the wire every night. I never slept a full night, and you weren't supposed to be out after dark. I met a chap who said he had a friend, who had a friend, who was a traveller for a paint firm, and he could get me some sample tins. So I said "Right – but he'll want something down" – they always wanted cigarettes, something beforehand so I risked it and gave him some cigarettes. Well, the night I was going to do this exchange, by, the heavens opened. It did rain and the bloke wouldn't come out. He was there but he wouldn't come out in the open, and in the end one of the guards said, "Look, come back in an hour and we'll change guard by then and I'll come back whether he will or not, and I'll make sure you get something". Well, he fetched a great box of paints and I'd to go over the trip wire and reach right through – there was loads of wire – he passed it through, a tin at a time. Then he threw the box over the top and I got them back, and I said to old Mattie Forester, that was the name of the sergeant-major – he could speak German, I said, "Matt, come and have a look at these and see if I've been done alright. I think they'll be dried up and no good." But they weren't, they were smashing. There was one, the biggest of the lot, tallest but narrow, and it was a luminous paint, so I stashed that out of sight. We'd double tier bunks. Mattie slept on the bottom one and I slept above him and everything I had, I kept under his bunk.

And I made this kite, and as soon as I tried it out, within a few minutes there was German guards galloping all over the camp, so I got it out of sight. The only time I could fly it was after dark, and then I had an idea. I used to get these silly ideas; it's a wonder I hadn't been shot! I got this luminous paint and painted a skull and cross bones on it. The next night, two of these lads, that wanted to see it flying, came and I said, "Now stop here", and they stopped in the entrance to my hut. There was a big look-out on stilts, you know, and wind was blowing straight down there. So I walked right down there and I started to let the string out and it took off beautifully. Then I tried to pull it down. Two of them nipped out and said, "Oh you're about three yards short of the sentry box". So I let some more string out. Then I had another idea. Do you remember we used to send "travellers" – put things on the strings? I put some on with mud stuck on – it was all clay was the camp – and I cut some bits of cardboard, cut a slit in and I clapped mud on, and I brought the kite down. I couldn't have done it better in daylight. Apparently the tail scraped over the top of the hut and one of them looked up and saw the skull and cross-bones. By, I did plague them!! Two of the chaps got put in jail for being drunk – they maybe had a little drop that was issued.

When I got a bee in mi bonnet sometimes I used to do all sorts of tricks, you know. Do you remember that cigarettes used to be in packets and then there was like a greaseproof paper wrapping, not like the cling film nowadays? Well, we got that we could undo that carefully, take the cigarettes out, and I used to fill 'em with slices of cardboard, then seal them up again. I did that with some Germans. I wanted some balls of string. They sold me some and it was all short lengths tied up together. They said "Well, your cigarettes was non existent!" And another time, I noticed on tins of coffee, they were the highest price of anything you could exchange or barter with, the bottoms were pressed in, sort of crimped – one place on the machine didn't flatten them properly. I had a piece of iron with a tag on like a scythe, and I could get it underneath and gradually work it round, take the disc off the bottom, empty the coffee out then fill it up with sawdust and paper and all that – the same weight. I got three tins of coffee out of one – when they opened it and took lid off, it was coffee there.

I did this several times. I once did a big deal -sixty cigarettes for woollens (though we reckoned not to sell wool unless it was for a particular purpose). There wasn't a cigarette in the packet; they'd copied me and put cardboard, so we called it quits then.

The thing about all was, it sounds so funny and I can laugh at it now, but all this was being carried on when you were nagged by hunger twenty-four hours a day and never knew whether you were going to get any rations tomorrow; never knew when you were going to get another letter from home. It was all going on, like, all the time. One thing I missed was privacy; you were never alone. But I will say the Green Howards' were second to none, in fact other people called them the second Red Cross. For every Green Howard that was a prisoner in Europe, the regiment sent two hundred cigarettes or the equivalent in tobacco, every month. The Flamborough prisoner of war thing sent me Red Cross parcels – personal ones, just like we got issued with, but with mi name on. I got every parcel that was sent to me, I kept account.

I know I told you about having to go out on the march, well, two days before we went, there was a big buzz around the camp; cigarette parcels have arrived. There were five and there were five thousand in the camp, and two were for me. Next morning there were three came, and one was for me, and the morning we left there was one, and it was five hundred Woodbines from mi sister, Norah, in Leeds. I daren't fetch that on mi own. Nearly the whole sort of street went with me! Well, some would have cut mi throat for that many cigarettes. I set out on that march with eleven hundred cigarettes – I always say it saved my life. Of course I'd stopped smoking long ago – I preferred to buy food, well buying food I could share with mi mates as well. I was in one camp with two mates and two chaps had been sent to a working camp from next to us and there were some men mooching around, "What's them after?" "Oh they're in transit and the engine's been taken off the train". The Germans used to run short of engines. No matter what was on, if they wanted an engine for summat, they'd take the engine and leave the rest of it in a siding, you see. They said, "We can't go 'cos the engine's been pinched". And they'd come here for a day or two. There was three shelves in this stables, sleeping like herrings we were, on top shelf. They were looking round and one of them come up the ladder onto this top shelf, he shouted to his mates, "Come on then we'll be alright here". I looked at mi mate and we made room for the third one. I got tea on straight away, gave them a cup of tea, and I said, "What made you say you'll be alright here?" He said, "Because I saw your cap badge and we've been in two camps where a Green Howard quarter-master has been in charge of the rations". I said, "Who was that?" and he said, "Honest Pat". I said, "It wasn't CQM Lewis, was it?" He said "Yes, it was". Pat Lewis, the insurance man, from Flamborough, he wouldn't take a crumb, in fact sometimes I think he went short himself to give a bit extra to someone else. He was in the Green Howards' with me and the same unit.

| Margaret | Laurie was in the Green Howards'. |
| Mark | Yes, he trained in the Green Howards'. I always wanted him to come and join me at the association at Bridlington, but I never managed it. It would have been worth it. I'm Chairman now, I have been since 1989. I can't get rid of it, but I enjoy it. |

Do you know anything about 'Whelkole' at Flamborough, South Landing? Do you know what they are? Well, they were long rows of stones, different to any round here. When I was at school, a professor from Sheffield University came with a gang of students and they started taking chippings. And one of these days, mi granddad, at dinnertime, he whispered, "Nip down to the wharf", and I said, "Yes". He knew where I used to hide so that mi granny didn't know – she was stricter than him. I got mi dinner and then said, "I'm off now then". Off I went and waited for mi granddad to come. And we got crabbing. Over in Whelkole we could see all these lads, and mi granddad went across to the man in charge, this professor, and said, "Have you lost something, sir? He said, "Oh, you wouldn't understand, old man". "Oh", he said," I won't bother then", and off we went. When we got round this East Newk corner, one student had detached himself quietly from the rest – he says, "Him and his old stones. I don't know what he'll do with them. I want some fossils". Mi granddad said, "Oh, I'll show you a place where you can fill your knapsack in ten minutes". At 'Sandole' there used to be a lot in cliff bottom. So mi granddad said, "What's going on then?" The student said, "Well, he's doing a paper on the movements of things in the ice age. He found some stones in Cumberland and he's traced some odd ones down here and there – right onto the Yorkshire Moors. If these match up with them then, he can give the direction of movement of everything". Mi granddad laughed his hat off. I didn't know what it was all about. That day, after we'd had our teas, mi granddad wrote a note. He said, "Here, take this down to schoolmaster". I think the professor was staying with Mr. Hartley; he was there anyway when I got there. Mi granddad had said, "Unless the professor wanted to make a fool of himself, tell him to forget about the stones at South Landing". By the next morning, Hartley did give me it at school. Anyway, in the evening, going for a walk with mi granddad, we met Hartley with this professor, and mi granddad said, "Now then, what d'you want to get onto him for, it's me you want to get onto – I sent that note – he didn't write it." And this professor said, "Well, what do you know about it then?" Mi grandad said, "I know exactly where those stones come from because I helped put 'em there". "What do you mean?" "Well", granddad said, "Every herring season we mostly finish at Kings Lynn and when we were coming back home, with a great big forty-five foot herring coble, we needed some ballast. We took them aboard and when we got to South Landing, we went up in that corner and chucked them overboard". He dropped his paper and said, "That's where they came from".

Rita	But Sir Marmaduke Constable had a harbour built.
Mark	Oh, there was a harbour. I think the Romans built the harbour in the first place.
Rita	And it was a bigger harbour than Brid harbour, when Sir Marmaduke Constable built it.
Mark	And I'll tell you another thing, Mr. Bolton that went bankrupt, he was going to build a pier there. It was all planned, they'd even had permission to put buoys up and everything. All it was going to be was a big pier pointing towards Barmston from East Newk there, it was going a bit outwards so that it would get deeper water. And they were going to make the road up Brig Hill, you know where I mean, going to Lighthouse, then turn to your right cut across fields and just past Cliffe House, then start to go straight down. Mi granddad's shown me a plan of it many a time. Mi granddad was one of his generation who could read and write, through Mrs. Crake, and they made him secretary for all sorts.

Mark showed us various photos and documents with his granddad's name on. One of them referred to soldiers who were at South Landing over one Christmas and the fishermen had a whip round and gave them £5 towards their Christmas dinner in 1917. Another showed how little the authorities knew down in London. It said, "The Board of Agriculture and Fisheries are informed by the Admiralty that fishing vessels with aliens on board will no longer be permitted to call at Orkney".

Mark   Now, fancy sending that to Flamborough! Here's another letter to Flamborough Fishermen's Society for a year's rent for North Landing, ten and sixpence, and South Landing was half a crown – that's all they used to charge them. Mi granddad kept a lot of these because he said people would not believe, when fishermen wanted to do any work, say concreting chains in to put their pulleys on, that they didn't just help themselves to sand. Sam Duke had the right to lead *[convey]* it – they helped themselves but they always paid Sam Duke.

Another document showed "Names of the Fallen".

Mark   You know here there's Charlie Major and then there's a George Drake. Well, George Drake married one of mi Uncle Charlie's daughters. Charlie Major, her brother, was doing farm work like all fisher lads did before they went to sea, and he was with his brother-in-law at the same farm. They went and joined the Waggoner's Reserve. Charlie wasn't old enough but he joined. They both starved together in a prison camp. They died in October 1918.

One day, mi Uncle Charlie and his two mates were coming home from hauling his lines and they come across a trawler ashore. Weather was fine; the sea was pretty calm so they went to him and said, "Can we help you?" "By yes, would you like to take us a couple of anchors off – when tide comes up we'll be able to pull ourselves off". So they made a bargain with him, took the anchors off for him and that was that. The thing pulled itself off, and then they got an award for it, salvage, and he went to Hopwood's and ordered a brand new coble. He called it "Golden Era" after the trawler and he wouldn't use it. He kept it for Charlie when he came home, and he never come home. Eventually he sold it, and a couple of brothers from Redcar bought it. They came and set off to sail it home; a bad squall hit them off Robin Hood's Bay, overturned it and they were both drowned. And that was a brand new coble never earned anybody a penny. Charlie was lost and the two men who bought it was lost. People say, whether it's superstition or what, Charlie himself wouldn't use it till Charlie come home. You never know if ought might have happened if he had, and in the circumstances it was as well.

Cathy Chadwick with Bernard and Olive Traves

Cathy Chadwick was born in Flamborough where her father was a painter and decorator.

Olive Traves came to Flamborough to marry Bernard who was a painter and decorator and part of a very large family.

Cathy began by talking about the field on which the council estate is built.

Cathy	Mi dad used to say when I was a little lass, "Why, maybe I shan't be here to see it, but on that playing field" – this was a field full of buttercups and daisies and I mean full – "There'll be houses built in there where you play, and you'll have pictures in your houses". "Why", I said, "Don't talk daft, Dad". But it's true, isn't it?
	Sam and Dick got a lorry and started on their own, and Sam [*Cathy's husband*] led bricks here. And he said, "Well I hope if we get a council house, we get one right opposite school, where we went to school". And we did get this one, what nobody else has been in. I've always loved it 'cos we get sun all day.
Margaret	What did you used to do about fishing?
Cathy	When Sam's dad wanted him to go to sea, he fell ill, did his dad. When I married Sam he was a long distance lorry driver. I used to go all over wi' him mi self. And he bought this boat. Nivver thought I would skein mussels. His says, "Why honey, thu wean't be a fisherman's wife if thu can't skein. I'll fetch a few in a bowl and see if thu can do 'em". Oh dear! Mi hands

were bleeding. "Oh", I says, "I'll nivver do 'em". But I kept trying and didn't I do some mussels frae then! And then we started baiting when his dad didn't go. I says, "I'll nivver bait a line". I did cry that first day. But I thought, well, l should have a go and there's an old table in there. There's a bit on end of a mussel that you've ti put on last ti keep it on hook, and I was doing it, and I was laying it. In comes awd Lew Knaggs, Norah Knaggs' father. Comes in with his apron, "I've come to help thu honey". "oh, you are a good un". I didn't really want him to fall – he'd had a black out a fortnight ago. "I'se auright honey", he says, "Thu can lay line as good as anybody I've seen but thu hasn't got knack of putting them mussels on". He was with me all day. And then I started two bags of mussels a day. I often think about Laurie Smith. l often said to him, "You can tek 'em away, I nivver want to see another." And he did laugh.

Margaret	How long did it take you to do a bag, Cath?
Cathy	I used to start in a morning and finish at tea-time. I've just forgotten how long it used to tek me – there's a lot in a bag you know. By gor, it was hard work. Mi dad hated aught to do wi' fishing 'cos he worked at Waud's. He was a painter and decorator. He used ti work wi' awd Bill Waud. And he once says tiv us, "Why, we've been papering at somebody's house and you'll nivver believe it but Bill Waud is putten paper wrang way up. I always remember 'cos we used to play in that yard you know, Waud's yard. They used to have a saw-pit – what they used to saw wood in; it used to be a big deep pit. We used to have a swing and Jack Waud, George Waud's dad, used ti 'ave a paint-shop. And you could tek a tin and you could get any colour you liked and he would mix it, would Jack Waud. The shop was up a lot of steps. I've been up there many a time with Norah mi cousin, when they used to be working. Mi Uncle Harry worked there an all, mi dad's brother
Margaret	What you did do before the war?
Cathy	We lived down Allinson Lane, and mi dad was at Waud's. Mi brother, Eric, was in Green Howards in the war, and I've even found a letter from wartime. He says, "There's folks flying about in their nightgowns. It's been terrible, bombing every night and we have a lot to clear up." They couldn't tell you where, it was wartime.

Now about these houses when we first cum in – five shillings a week in1939.

Bernard	Aye, old cottages were one and nine a week, top price was two and sixpence – like those in the High Street, Allinson Lane and Chapel Street. You see they couldn't put rents up for some reason. And they couldn't turn 'em out 'cos they'd been in so many years. They still paid same money.
Margaret	Who was schoolmaster when you were at school then?
Cathy	Mr Davidson, but headmaster was Mr Veeter. Mr Davidson thought the world of our Eric.
Bernard	Aye, Veeter, but they used ti call him an awd German, he was a bad un, and Hartley was headmaster after Veeter left. There was Sally Bayes and Miss Chadwick when we were at school, as well as Veeter and Davidson.
Cathy	I'll show you this. *[photograph]* Bessie Bayes, Vera Waud, Rhoda Langton, Nellie Hudson, Stella Stork, Dor Taylor, Lillie Waines, Margaret and Harriet Duke, Syb O'Brien, Bertha Langton, Violet Mainprize, Olive Stork, that was Dorothy Tindall – mi Aunt Lizzie and mi Grandad Hall adopted her – Florrie Sunley, Norah Knaggs. This is Lizzie Dixon, that's Esmie Cross, Sam's cousin, Edie Sunley, Christie Major, Somebody Stork and that's a Taylor from Lighthouse, Vera Stonehouse – she lived a'back of church – and I think that's Vera Stonehouse's sister – our Bertha used to be friends with 'em and Margaret Warcup. And there's Millie and Mina Stork, and that's Florrie Pillmoor. It would be one class, I couldn't get in, I'm stood in the step.
Margaret	There's forty-three people, so they were big classes then. When you were there, did you have slates and pencils, because Harold Stork said they did when he was at school?
Bernard	Aye we had slates and pencils, we had them in the Infants.
Rita	I can remember we had them in the Infants. Now do you remember if there was a gallery still, when you were there? Because Mary Bayes said there was a gallery in the large classroom when she went to school. She started when she was two and a half and they put youngest children in the gallery to make them behave. If they didn't behave they might have fallen out of the gallery.
Bernard	No, there wasn't a gallery. I'll just tell you summat now. You remember that little classroom? Mrs Kind was teacher in there – so that was five teachers.
Margaret	And did you stay with the one teacher for English and sums and everything?

Bernard	Yes, but you moved up when you were old enough. Miss Chadwick, she used to say, "If you don't behave I'll put you in the Black Hole of Calcutta" – in the corner. But if you were really bad she'd stand you against the glass panelled door into the headmaster's room, and if he saw you standing there he would bring you inti his room and you got the cane.
Cathy	Sam used ti rub his hands wi' onions so that if he got cane it wouldn't hurt. He used ti tek mice ti school, him and Tom Stephenson. They used ti put 'em down holes then put cheese down, and then they used ti pop out. Saranne Tuck (Miss Chadwick) used ti play hell. Tom Stephenson was a mate of Sam's – they were always together were Tom and Sam when it came to mischief then.
Bernard	Mi Uncle John used ti have some sheep in a field at end there, and that field next ti Tom Stork's, that was his as well. That field used ti have half a day's threshing. And in barn there we used to go before school and get little mice and tek 'em ti school. Pur 'em in your pockets and then put 'em down and lasses used ti scream. Then as time went on Miss Chadwick would say, "Now lets all be quiet and listen to see if we can hear a pin drop". All was quiet and mice would pop up out of this hole and all the girls would scream. There was a great going on.
Cathy	Big Tom Woodhouse was about same age as Sam. He used ti bang on piano when we were marching in – "Pom, Pom, Pom".
Bernard	When a ball went over wall inti gardens next ti school he just used ti pick you up and over top you'd go ti get it. He was always big, he once kicked headmaster in shins.
Olive	Tell them about when church choir went on that trip to York.
Bernard	Oh aye, Church choir once went ti Harrogate – your Eric was in choir. We went in this spot for a meal and Tom Morse, as we used to call him, *[Tom Woodhouse]* turned to Eric – who had exhaled rather badly – and said, "What's matter lad?" And Eric said, "I'se FTB." And Tom asked, "What's that?" And he said, "Fit ti bust". He did laugh did awd Tom, he was a rum un.
Cathy	Ron Coates' mother, she was a Woodhouse. They used to have the butcher's, where Horsley's is. She used to serve in shop when Ron Coates was a little lad. Can you remember? There was a Jessie Woodhouse, a teacher, her father and brother used ti mend shoes and boots. How I remember, they lived next door to

	us and I can remember her father chasing her up and down the gardens – she did used ti scream.
Bernard	We lived in the High Street, next ti old fish shop, we were all born there. Nobody was born in hospital. Old Mrs Thollow (Thurlow) was midwife, Millie's aunty. She was a grand old girl was that. Owt wrong – send for Mrs Thollow.
Olive	They used to take traps to Flamborough Station, didn't they?
Bernard	Aye, mi dad and our Rob used ti tek letters from Post Office ti catch train and if there was any parcels they'd bring 'em back. Our Rob went this time ti get coastguard. They brought some parcels as well and he stopped at a cottage near awd lighthouse to deliver this parcel. There was a lot of wind, a hell of a gale of wind. Time he was inside the cottage, hoss set off with the coastguard inside and just before they got ti gate, awd Crutch, the gatekeeper, had it was shut. The coastguard jumped out and hoss jumped ower gate, tuk shafts wi' him and left landau behind. They had ti go to cliff top ti catch im. It was a war-hoss and it was stamped WD. It was a great big un. It was frightened of wind but it must have been used to jumping. That fittled awd Crutch, as the gate had been wrecked. Trinity House decided not to put up another gate as it did not bring in much money. Crutch asked if he could pay for a new gate and still collect the tolls as it gave him a living. Trinity House agreed to his request. Bill Robson was nicknamed Crutch 'cos he had a crutch you see. There was some cottages near Seabirds. There was Billy Beale, Dump, Ned Pippin, one or two of 'em.
Cathy	That's how Mere used to be. *[Showing a picture]* Mi grandad lived there, that was his sheds. He used to have a coal business and he used to have a horse in there called Prince. We used ti etti tek him up ti Lighthouse in that field there. Me and our Bertha always got job of tekking him ti Lighthouse and when we got ti top of field here we used ti give one another a leg up to give each other a ride. And that, look, is a flat cart wi' a shaft on and I'm sure that's his cart and there's somebody standing there. And Fred Atkinson lived in there and there's where cottages used to be agin Rose and Crown. They're all pulled down now. We always used to call it Back Street Hill where you are, and it's now called Greenside. We used ti go skating on the Mere as kids, didn't we? And played 'tewey' and got into trouble when we fell in and got wet through. And then when it used ti dry up i'summer we used ti

	put tins across so we could walk across. It was all wet and muddy and there used to be ducks and geese. There was a pump here somewhere, where farmers used ti cum ti get filled up before we got water-works. Grandma Chadwick used to have surgery, Dr Watson's surgery. When our John was about a year old, I used ti lock house up and go and stop there 'cos Grandma used to go ti Hull and stop with her daughter after she lost her husband. I was telling Dr Allen *[Watson]* and he said, "You're talking about a long way back".

Bernard   We used to have ducks at home and we used ti tek em to Mar every day when we were kids. But they always kem home on their own, about five o'clock at night outside front door. I'summer visitors used to stand amazed. We opened door and they used to go straight through back door and into yard. They never made any muck though. They used ti kum down Back Street Hill and down that way.

Cathy   That's our John, 11 years old, with his granddad, and Dick with the donkey. Do you know I used to love to be in bed in early morning and hear donkeys go pit-i-pat.

Olive   Did you ever see the ghost when you worked at the Timoneer?

Cathy   No, I don't know where they've got it from, I nivver heard it when I was there. It's just to get folks to go there.

Bernard   There has been a ghost a long time ago. When they had guests there in Room 4, an elderly couple, the old gentleman complained he'd seen this ghost and the next morning they took their bags and went. Do you remember Daddy Cliffe, first body who had that spot, Cliffe House? Wintertime he used to come down ti village with a horse-drawn sledge when we had snow. It was before Burtons lived there when I was a school kid. Archie Burton was on council warn't he?

Olive   You used to go Christmas singing up there with Church choir every year, didn't you?

Bernard   Aye, I used to be in church choir when I was a lad. Woodhouse was last call at Danes Dyke; we used to get mince pies and coffee. Then I got to lighting candles, then I changed frae that to purring numbers up and there was Tom Cowling's father gor on ti me. He said I put wrong hymns up. I said, "I didn't put wrong hymns up, I put hymns up that was on there, its parson that's put wrong hymns down there". And awd Cox, he was at Flamborough School when I was in choir, and he sat at that side, like I was eating a goody; so he kem and fetched me out. I was mad, so I nivver went n'more after that. We used ti get tuppence or thruppence for a choir practice if we went during week. I'll tell you who was in choir then, Matt Major, Bill Waud, Jack Langton. He'd come away from farm by then, he was where John Waud is now.

Matt Major had an allotment there and every Sunday morning all his best cauliflowers had gone. This morning he decided not to go to church and as he was going past his allotment he see'd Jack Langton's wife walking down a cauliflower row to see where best cauliflower was and cut it. He waited till she was near, stepped out and says, "Now I've caught you at last", he says, "You'll have to pay for all them that you've had before".

I remember when they were up at that farm North Moor, and an awd Ford car he'd just getten, he couldn't handle it very weel and when he went up ti farm there, he ran straight inti pond! Then there was Dick Bailey, he had an awd Ford truck thing like. He used ti tek folks ti Brid on a Saturday night. Mi mother was one of 'em like, when they were lasses and she allus said that it got away from him down Crofts Hill he couldn't hod it.

Cathy	We used ti go to Wesleyan Chapel. You know it was a great shame that they pulled Wesleyan Chapel down 'cos it was a lovely chapel. Mi Grandad Major was choir master there. I used to be in choir with Lily Cross and Eileen, Marjory Hopwood and your Blanche *[Bernard's sister]* and Olive Stork and Eva Bayes. We were all in choir and we used to go to Bible classes on a Wednesday – we were always at chapel and Sunday School. John Lewis' wife, Ella, she was in choir as well. Harold Stork used ti be behind organ at back of that curtain at Wesleyan Chapel, I've bumped him many a time. We used to have all sorts of pantomimes and things there, you know. Awd Maggie Booth, she lived opposite Dog and Duck, that first house at end with them steps up. Do you remember awd Tacey Robson, he lived next ti garage in Chapel Street? Awd Tacey, he used ti chase us round chapel.
Bernard	Victoria Club, it warn't Victoria Club then *[Reading Room]*, he was in charge of it and if anybody got on table ti knock a ball he used ti knock 'em with awd cue. And he used to say to us kids, "Neea subscriptions, outside dus th'see bor". I'll tell you a tale about him now. There warn't many cars about then when we were school kids, maybe one or two – you could go anywhere in the streets. We were playing doon Carter lane and this car

comes up and so I chucked a stone at it. This fella went up as far as Monument, tonned round and cum back, jumped out and after me. And I set off to run and awd Runty Hall was stood near Chapel at that entrance there. He shouted tiv him, "Stop him, stop him", but he wouldn't, and I kept going and I gor home, doon yard and there was a fence middle of yard. I got mi leg ower and got caught on a nail and I was fast and Tacey was whitewashing George Thompson's cottage and the man chasing me says, "Is this lad yours?", and Tacey says, "No, he belongs down there". He was a bit dozey was Tacey, warn't he? So our Lil was in back bedroom, saw what was happening, knocked on glass and brok winder. Mi mother runs out, clicks a two tined fork out of corner and says, "You bugger, I'll stick yer", she chases him up the yard. Sam Duke was standing at end – he had his stables there then. Mi mother shouts ti Sam, "Shut gate Sam", and Sam woddles over and closes gate but leaves enough room for bloke to get out. He's going down Chapel Street wi' mi mother after him. Awd Mrs Meggison was standing at front door, she shouts, "Stick tines through him Mrs, geld him, geld him". He went faster than ever even, jumped into his car and went back to Brid. Mi mother always said he was a doctor. Poor Mrs Meggison, she was found at South Landing warn't she? She died at South Landing, on beach. That's another tale – she used ti come to oor 'oose. She drowned herself. She allus cum doon backway to oor 'oose. We had a greyhound then and this day she cum, it gor under table frightened on her. Mi mother couldn't reckon it up 'cos she'd allus been alright wi' her. And that day she went down to South Landing and drowned herself. Funny that dog knew warn't it? She was an Emmerson, a lartle person. Mi mother was an Emmerson too.

Cathy   Herbie Major says, "I'm going ti tell a tale about Laurie's father, when he used ti go ti Hull for timber for Jack Waud" – but he wouldn't say any more.

Margaret   I know he used to go to Hull with Jack Waud for wood and he used to go into the yard where it was and it would be, "That bit and that bit, no I don't want that bit". And he said he used to load the truck up and once coming up Dykes there was ovver much on the back wheels and the front wheels lifted. So whoever was with them, maybe it was Herbie, but whoever it was, had to climb onto the front of the cab of truck to weight it down to get 'em up Dykes.

Bernard	Another time mi brother went to station wi' letters and 'oss set off, frightened like, and me brother borrowed a bike ti chase it, and he didn't catch it while he got ti Dykes and it had brakes on! If brakes hadn't been on the hoss would have gotten home. It passed Billy Sayers driving Blue Bus to Brid and it went by him and he says, "I thought old Jack's giving him some stick tinight!" It just went by him as though someone was driving it. They were clever osses in them days, they knew where to go.
Margaret	I remember Father on about a horse. He'd got one out at Pickering or Kirbymoorside and walked it home. The bloke said he'd never mek owt of it 'cos he hadn't been able to. Father worked it and he said as long as you treated it alright, it was alright. Then he sold it for some reason and he told the bloke that bought it, "Don't ever put a whip or a stick on it or you'll get nowt done". Anyway this bloke took no notice. He kem back to Dad 'cos it wouldn't do nowt for him. But Dad said it worked for him because he'd never used a whip on it.
Bernard	Horses is like dogs, they can sense if you're frightened of 'em. You see mi dad had a strong voice and he could mek 'em do owt just shouting at 'em. Mi Uncle John had 'em before us like, horses, about a dozen of 'em. There was one called Billy Biter. If anybody went up to feed it, it crossed its legs and kem ower ti this side and wouldn't ler 'em ger out without biting 'em. And this fella was shouting and mi dad went up and he just shouted, "Ger up there", and it just cum back and just stood straight.
Cathy	Can you remember when lifeboat went over, Brid lifeboat? Turned over three times in Thornwick. I had some visitors in, and I always remember that little girl, Madeline – they'd gone for a walk on cliff top and the little girl said, "Look, boat's gone over", and her mother said, "Don't talk so silly, it's the waves". But the mother said afterwards, it had gone over. It turned over three times and landed in Thornwick, and oor John and 'em all were there at Thornwick. Of course Mr Readhead drowned through all that. But what I could never understand, our lifeboat was away gerring repaired so Brid lifeboat had ti cum to Thornwick to get two girls who'd been swimming. They'd be already drowned wouldn't they? It was their last day, they were in a caravan and their mother had said, "Don't go swimming because there's no boats out", and they took no notice of their mother. They went and she followed 'em and she heard 'em screaming and she

thought they were laughing but they were screaming in horror. Waves were carrying 'em away and they would be dead. And poor Mr Readhead, Norman Readhead's father, warn't it? Eric Woodhouse was swimming out to him and this wave kem and took him under and he died on his way up. Awful weren't it, when you think about it? Well you know them visitors was ill; they didn't want a meal that night. They were too upset about it.

Bernard   That's the trouble you see, won't tek n'notice what parents say tiv 'em. You know they'd be bashed ti pieces before boat got right frae Brid ti Thornwick. It would wi' them waves, it used to break right across North Landing and Thornwick.

Cathy   There was once a ship kem ashore between Lighthouse and South Landing and Sam and all of 'em went down. They were hours and hours and I thought all sorts of things and we went down to see and what do you think they'd done? It was right under cliff and they got 'em on board for a drink. And tide went down and they had to wait for tide to flow again before they could get off. They'd been too busy drinking and playing cards to notice!

Bernard   It comes in a lot sharper in some spots than others. Some cinders come in once, that was awd Rosa on West Scar. We used to go down and get bags of 'em and awd Tant Fell reckoned to be leeaking after it. There was all sorts pinched off it, all them cinders washed up I remember.

Cathy   Why, 1947, wasn't that an awful year? I remember I had mi mother poorly here and we couldn't get n'coal, they couldn't get through. And me and Sam went with a paraffin lamp thing, and our Johnnie got it across road and we went to South Landing – you couldn't see hedges for snow and ice. We had a little black dog and mi brother says, "Its too bad for you to go". But I says, "I'se well wrapped up", and we went at midnight and at left hand side there waves was just coming and bringing coal right in front of yer. We got a bag of coal. I heard 'em say when I was a kid, snow was that deep you couldn't see hedge tops, and you couldn't in 1947.

Rita   No, mi grandfather Kingston used to say when they were up at Ocean View, they brought horse and cart over hedge tops some winters.

Olive   It was Amos Frankish who used ti come on thrashing machines, wasn't it? Used ti cum to Marton, and mi cousin Jack Keen

	married Sally Overy. He was driving for Green buses and then threshing men kem. They had to come in for their meal and mi cousin was there as well, and what a going on they had. They used to dance mi mother round kitchen and such a going on. 'Home in Passadena' – do you remember that song? They used to wind up gramophone and play that song.
Cathy	I remember a ship that kem ashore under Speeton cliffs, the 'Skegness'. Bob Atkinson – I believe he was skipper – anyway he used to go out on lifeboat. I used to live next door to Renee Atkinson then, and me and Renee could pick it up on wireless and they kept saying, "Hold on lads, lifeboat's on its way". Then, from the 'Skegness': "Well, they'll have to hurry up 'cos we're going to jump for it". And one lad had his leg sawn off and he was only nineteen years old. They didn't get anybody off. Lifeboat went on it and off it. *[The rough seas washed the lifeboat up on to the deck of the trawler, then off again.]*
Bernard	Rocket cart was there an all and they wouldn't come off. They were going to stop on and they were all drowned. Mi dad was on rocket cart wi' Jim Smith and mi Uncle John. They used ti tek osses, didn't they?
Cathy	Mi dad used to go with rocket cart. There used to be gun on Green in front of Dot Overy's. *[The gun fired rockets into the air, to warn the men who manned the lifeboat that their services were needed.]* When we were kids, we used to play on it. They used to set rockets off in it, didn't they? Like a big square with a big gun stuck out, and rocket cart was in shed on there.
Margaret	Did you used to take visitors, and did your mother take visitors before the war? Was there a lot of that done here in the village?
Cathy	Mi mother-in-law used to tek 'em but mi mother – no. I used to tek 'em here, but you had to have a form to fill in if you took visitors in a council house. They didn't charge extra rent or anything.
Bernard	Mi mother took 'em before the war because that was the only means of visitors staying.
Cathy	Oh yes, they used to knock at doors a lot of times, holiday times. They don't now, but I've even had lasses sleeping on the floor in sleeping bags.
Bernard	Mi dad went ti Hull and he took Bill Sunley wiv him to fetch somebody back in a coffin, and Bill nivver spok a word all way.

They got to Danes Dyke and mi dad had a strong voice like and he shouted, "What's matter wi' tha", poor awd Bill nearly jumped off waggon. He says, "The dead can't talk, it's the living that can hurt tha." I allus remember them mekking that coffin for Georgey Gibbon, he lived ovver there in Burdsall Cottages and he *[Bill]* nivver med n'more after that. It upset him and he couldn't stand it, they reckoned he got a germ up his nose or summat. He was going ti school when I was like.

Cathy   You remember outings when we used ti go in waggons ti that first farm, Almond's farm, on Bempton road? It used to be a great long farm waggon wi" sides on and that, wi' 'osses, and that was oor outing. Tea party and play in barn and that was it, oor outing.

Margaret   When did they start going to Scarborough for the Sunday School outing?

Cathy   Oh they started when we got older and we started going by bus ti Scarborough, when buses started of course. Before that you had to go by train.

Bernard   They were happy days. Charabancs started ti come to Flamborough and we used ti jump on step at back and yan of lads would shout, "Whip 'im on", and the driver would whip the horse up.

Cathy   They were happier days really, we had very little but all folks were poor, but they were happier days than they are now. I used ti go wi' flat cart wi' mi grandad and hold coal bags while he filled 'em at back of yard. We had ti 'ave a bit of pocket money.

Bernard   You had ti do in them days. They made you work in them days. As soon as we left school, we were in them allotments of Jim Fell's lifting taties and that.

Cathy   I was at Ship in summer holidays frae school, before I left school. I was working wi' Lizzie Bonnie, Miss Elizabeth Chadwick. I used to be helping her ti mek beds and washing up and doing vegetables. They wouldn't do it today, would they? Lizzie Bonnie worked there, 'cos when we had our dinners like, we always had lemonade ti drink and she used ti sup, gollop it like, and it used ti mek her sneeze, and I used ti laugh, and that awd Mrs Threllkeld, they called her then, used to be mad at me 'cos I was laughing at Lizzie. Oh dearie me, its nice ti talk about awd times.

Bernard   Awd Tant Fell, we used ti go ti Chapel on a Sunday night and he'd be there and then we had a prayer meeting afterwards and us lads, we used ti stop y'know. Tant would mumble, "And the law said unto Moses", you couldn't tell what he was saying and he kept going on like that! We did used to deea some tricks. There was awd Nell Sugar. Awd Bill Sunley used ti gan ti chapel when he was younger, always had a clean white collar on and Nell Sugar used to sit at back of him and spit at his collar. Seea he got on ti mi Uncle John Hall, superintendent of the chapel, about it, 'cos he was sick of it. "Why lad", he says, "We can't dee nowt about it, else neeabody'll cum". I allus remember one fella frae Brid, he had a grocer's shop, he used ti cum and preach and then he used ti sing, "I Like Apple Dumplings, I Could Eat Them Every Day", I allus remember that.

Cathy   Mi grandad Hall used ti preach a lot at Bempton you know. He allus wanted me to go with him, walk there you know. He used to say, "You can sit i'pulpit tonight". I used to say "No, grandad I'll sit in front seat , I arn't going ti sit in pulpit with all folks looking at you". I used to be worried stiff about walking back 'cos I used to think Ben Gilson would be drunk in gutter. When we got to Bempton Dyke I used to say, "Can I put mi head under your coat", he used to wear a long black coat, and I used to. And one night he, Ben, was drunk in gutter and I was frightened and you could hear money rattling 'cos he was headfirst in gutter drunk as a lord. And what did they do to him. On a motorbike, Pam Lord's mother, when she was courting, they was on this motorbike and mi grandad stopped 'em and told 'em to go and fetch a cart to fetch him, Ben Gilson. I allus remember that.

Bernard   He used ti come in horse and buggy sometimes and get drunk and awd 'oss used ti tek him home. They used to chuck him in back and 'oss used to tek him back ti Bempton.

Cathy   He was awful. When we were up at Avenue, you know, he used ti thump on the door, him and George Waines – after we'd gone to bed – knocking for Sam ti tek 'em home. "It's no use" Sam used ti say, "I'll have ti ger up and tak him". We used ti have a little car with a dicky seat and he got Ben in the back, and. he kept on, "Where's wheel?" We've had some do's.

Bernard   Awd Tant Fell, you know when he was at heeam *[home]* – he was having his dinner at Christie Woodhouse's. He'd had it and he was quoting Bible like and he said, "The Lord said unto Moses, deeant chuck that rice pudding out Chris, I can eeat that". Dis thu remember when Lizzie Greasy and Mary lived ower there?

Cathy	Oh, they amused me 'cos Lizzy Greasy used to go and wash for mi Grandma and Grandad Hall. She had a long white settle and she used ti pull drawers out and pull cheesecakes out. Drawers with cheesecakes in!! And they lived where Norah lives now. *[A row of white cottages behind the village green, which was pulled down and council houses built on the land.]*
Bernard	Them allotments of Jim Fell's – he had some banties there. And there was Bill Robson and one or two of us comes ower to Lizzie Greasy's. They were sat in front of fire in winter time and you see there warn't any electricity then. Yan of 'em clumb onto cottage top and put a banty down chimli and they blacked 'em all out, both of 'em. And they cum fleeing out, "Cat bogglers". They were like a couple of black women!
Cathy	That's what Sam did. What did they call them? They lived in that bungalow as you go up to Timoneer?
Olive	Shaboo.
Cathy	Aye, Shaboo. They were all laid on floor or summat and they went and put a bag down chimney and she chased 'em with her nightgown on. Now what a trick to do.
Bernard	Aye, if we saw Shaboo in street we used ti say, "Now Charlie it's a shabby day", and look up into sky, like. He used ti go to Pudsey's when Sid Coates was there and awd Sid used ti chase him with a knife. Amos Frankish used ti play some tricks wi' him when he used ti go thrashing; he did all sorts wi' him – Shaboo – he used ti go to carry caff *[chaff]*.
Cathy	You know Sam's dad, when he was retiring, he sold his coble "Unity", and Sam bought "Ocean Gift" 'cos he was going to tek Dick and our John. "Why lads", they'd gotten it up at North Landing, "I'll go wi' ya, it'll be last time I go to sea, we'll all go and tek it ti South Landing". A storm blew up and it was awful. I used to ride a bike then. I allus remember Christy Major's dad coming round with fruit then. "Oh, Cath, lifeboat's gone off ti your's, hasn't it?" I says, "I hope not, they're all there." He says, "Why, it has gone off to yours." So I went across ti Sam's mother and she was hysterical with her hands up, she says, "They're all there". Before I got ti end wall there, his dad was walking, he had his sea-boots on and he was all of a sag. And I says, "What's matter with you? Where are t'others? You've nivver walked frae South Landing have ya?" He says, "Yis, I couldn't let 'em come Cath, because sea would have tekken their coble away. It's that

bad". They'd gone round from North Landing to South Landing and they'd got ashore, and they'd to hold the boat or sea would have tekken it and smashed it up, and of course he died within eight weeks. Well he went into toilet and he was in a long time and then he shouts, "Has Cathy gone yet?" "No, what for?" "Tell her ti ring doctor up". I rang Dr Watson and he says, "Get somebody to bring him in, get him here as soon as you can, and be prepared to stay in". I knew he suffered with his kidneys and often passed a lot of blood. He went into hospital and he was in eight weeks and died and that was his retirement day at seventy. It doesn't pay nobody to work till they can't work no more does it? He never saw a bit of television or anything you know.

Then I went in. I was thirty eight when I went in for operation and they were putting new fittings in Lloyd's and it was too much for me – it made mi temperature go up. It was an awful row, them digger electrical things. I remember Herbert Zedman's wife kem in at same time and Matron says, "We're going to put you downstairs, it's too much for you". And they put me in same room as Grandad died in. And Mr Sears, who used to look after fellas, says, "What are they putting you in there for?" – 'cos he was a real jolly fella. "Why", I says, "I don't think I'm going to die." And the nurses used to say what a jolly little fella he was, Sam's dad. Bairns' ward was next door and they used tek bairns to sit on his bed. He used ti love bairns did Sam's dad, and that was it.

Bernard   Awd Billie Beale, he used ti cut grass on roadside for mi dad – 'osses like it you know – and he was allus going ti pub, Seabird. And he got drunk yar neet and your Norman and somebody else purr him ti bed. And about twelve o'clock at neet they went again and got him out of bed and said they were two policemen, and they'd come 'cos he'd been drunk and disorderly and causing trouble and 'had ti cum wiv us'. So they walked him and got ti top of Crogg's Hill you see and they started ti laugh and he realised who they were and pelted 'em wi' steeans.

Why, I think mi dad and mi Uncle Tom used ti go ti sea but what I was going to say, like, was that mi Uncle Tom he was a rum un. He reckoned ti have some bumbler bee honey. So there was two women at North Sea and fishermen told 'em, and they went to mi Uncle Tom – 'Cam' we used to call him – and they said, "Can we have some of that bumbler bee honey you have?" He

says, "Why, I int going doon ti village for about half an hour yit."
So they hung about, like. He went and they followed him down.
Tell you weear he was living then, with Bob Otch *[Emmerson]*.
He was a fisherman warn't he? He had a cottage next ti North
End and after a bit the two ladies knocked on door, like, and
he went ti door and they said they'd come for jars of bumbler
bee honey. He says, "Just a minute I'll see the wife."*[He hadn't
a wife!]* He kem back and says, "Why, I'm very sorry she's just
sold the last jar." Another time he was doon at Lighthouse Road
ends and there was a visitor cum by. He says, "Which is the way
to Lighthouse, mister?" And he says, "Carry straight on up there
you'll be alright." And off he went. A few minutes later the visitor
came back and he says, "Just a minute." And Tom says, "What
do you want?" And he had a bit of straw in his hand, and he says,
"Have you ever seen anything like this?" And he put it on the
ground, jumped back: "What do you think ti that?" And he says,
"Why, I'm dafter an you for coming back." Well, he used to get
up to all sorts.

Then there was a time like – there was Robert Leng, Gilbert,
oor John and Sid Coates, young Sid and awd Coll and they were
climming scout eggs. Sid was down gathering 'em and they were
at top, and he got fast i'cliff and they couldn't pull him up. And
seea oor John says, "Why, tie him a'back o'motorbike." And so
they did, and he sets off across field, like, and Sid comes straight
ower top of 'em sitting at the cliff top. He was allus getting fresh
motorbikes, you know, and all lads would congregate to see
these. "Has gotten a fresh un, John?" "Aye, dis tha want a ride?
Ger on back" – ti Albert Pinder. He used ti get going and then
stand on saddle and put his hands out and frighten 'em ti deead!
They wouldn't be allowed to do that now, would they?

Cathy   You know George Sunley, Kath Sunley's husband? Sam had
a new motorbike and he tuk George ti Hull, when there were
trams, and wheel got fast in tram side and split all his trousers,
arse out, and all his best suit!

Edith Jane Waind

Daughter of a farmer, she took milk around the village three times a day and was the organist at the Primitive Chapel.

Edith   Yes, I was born where John lives, on Chapel Street. They were mi granddad's cottages you know, those three up there. Mi granddad thought middle house would be warmer, so we moved inti middle house an' Winnie was born there. And I was seven when we kem down, so I've lived down here since I was seven. Granma died at Christmas, then we kem down in the summer to look after mi granddad. I haven't moved far, have I! I don't know whether mi granddad took milk out or not, I can't remember. But we did, not from us first coming. We were going to school when we should have the milk business; we shouldn't be very old. We used to go round wi' little cans, oh things have changed, haven't they?

You know where those bungalows were built at Croft's Hill by that garage – that was our land up there. We used to have corn up there, and turnips and different things. And there was all that paddock you see, where Beech Avenue was built. And we'd a field up North Landing Road behind "Flaynburg" – there, you know, Thornwick Private it was then, where cows used to go and graze in that field behind, and so far down to top of that little hill.

[Looking at the aerial photograph of Flamborough].

Now let me get mi bearings. That's Wesleyan Chapel, and ours is at bottom there, so we're there, and that's the paddock you see, and that's Bempton Lane. We called it Carter Lane, didn't we? Oh yes, and that belonged Grange Farm, Shipley's. Now then, this would be High Street, those were ours, well mine. That was Kirby's, and it's flats now you see. Those are where Ivy and them live and we're coming round 'ere to Back Street Hill.

Miss Waind started talking about the people who lived on the road to North Landing as this was part of the route where she delivered milk twice a day.

Edith   I liked Mrs Thompson, she liked a bit of fun. Middy Fell lived next door and Jack, who died suddenly a few years ago; he collapsed in a shop.

Jack Fell was held up as an example of hard work and application to generations of children as he ended up headmaster of a very large school, a remarkable achievement for a pupil of Flamborough School.

Edith   I think his mother was a Warcup. I know he was cousin to Lilian Warcup. Lilian's mother used to read service of song. She could recite marvellous. It was through George Hardwick coming from Brid that our choir got to Leeds to broadcast. It was Harry Hopeful's programme and we sang two songs, 'My Bonnie Lies Over the Ocean' and 'Ashgrove'. It was a lovely experience. Coming back on the bus – we got back about midnight – George was a rum un. He was only little, and had Edie Pod's *[Mainprize]* shoes on. He was strutting about bus with these shoes on, and we stopped at Stamford Bridge and he got out and we left him. If you'd seen him trying to run with those high heeled shoes on, we stopped at the other side of the bridge to wait for him, he tumbled back onto that bus. They had that shop on Promenade at Brid next to the old Lounge Cinema. It was a real old-fashioned shop.

We'd an old aunt, my grandma's aunt. She lost her husband very soon after they were married, and she lost her only daughter at eighteen, and she was very poor. And mi granddad let her cum and live with them. She was mi grandma's aunt, so that was mi mother's great aunt. She lived ti be ninety-seven. I think she originated from Filey. That's another dialect spot and, by, she did have some old fashioned names. I don't think she knew anything else but those so if she wanted ti move anything 'I'll remmen it' – 'remmen' for 'remove'. I think that's where we got a lot from her 'cos we never heard it wi' mi granddad or mi grandma, but I think we got it from Aunt Anne. We allus called her Aunt Anne and she lived after mi grandma. Oo, she 'ad some sayings. She used to wear a bonnet and a cape, a lovely cape it was and a big bonnet. She was an old fashioned 'cup of tea'! Stevenson they called her – her married name. I don't know what her maiden name was but her daughter, Sarah, she was eighteen when she died of consumption. There was no cure then, was there? She had some old sayings. If it was windy she used to say, "It's gahin ti blow a pup."

It was not long after mi mother and dad were married. They lived at Bempton, and they came here just before I was born. She came here to the house where I live to have John. Leonard was born at Whitehouse Farm at Buckton. Now there was a woman, used to come from Bempton, called Mrs Rounding, every week on a Friday with curd. And she used to call at mi grandma's where I live and they would exchange news. Mi mother would send news for mi grandma, and mi grandma would send news back for mi mother, with this Mrs Rounding. Well one morning they were having their breakfast, mi mother and dad, and mi mother says, "Oh I have had an awful dream". And he said, "What was it?" And she said, "I dreamt that I saw Nellie Nordass coming down Bempton Street in a widows' weed". That day Mrs Rounding took the news to mi grandma that Nellie Nordass' husband had been drowned. He was a Cowling. And mi dad said, "Why, it's a good job you told mi because I don't know whether I would hardly have believed her". That would be between 1905 and 1910.

Our John was born 1906 and they moved here in 1910. I was born January 1911. Winnie was born 1912. There was a year and nine months between Winnie and me. If I put a photo of me as a school girl near that of mi mother you would say we were twins. And now I can understand Mr Rawnsley. I was sixteen when he died 'cos I can remember marching down to his funeral. As a little girl, if I was up and down street, he would just stand in front of me and say, "Another Ester". And I've thought since, yes, I can understand him saying that.

| Rita | You are same age then as Stella Stork, Stella and Margaret Duke? |
| Edith | Yes. Now I'm going to tell you all about that. There was seven of us left school at Christmas. I was the youngest and Nora Gibbon was the eldest. We were all girls. Nora Gibbon was 12th |

of October – this was 1910; 29th of October Nelly Hudson and Margaret Duke; 20th of October Stella Stork; 3rd of November Nora Duke, Jack Cowling's wife; 28th of November, Bess. And I was 5th of January. You won't find my christening there 'cos it was at Chapel. Now we always went back to school after holidays on a Monday. And my birthday was on Monday. That year we went back on the Tuesday for some reason. If they'd gone back on the Monday I should've had to have gone till Easter. There's only Margaret Duke and I left out of us lot now. As far as I know Margaret's still living at Hunmanby.

Rita   Now I've found your dad and mum's marriage in one of those church magazines.

Edith   Well, I can't understand that because they were married at Central Chapel at top of Chapel Street in Brid, where it's 'Iceland' now. Did it say 'Bethel'? It was Central Chapel because I was looking at their marriage certificate the other day. It was a Reverend James Shaw that married 'em. It was a lovely chapel. There was some beautiful Chapels in Brid, look at that one that was next to the bus station. That was Promenade. I can remember Dodo and Dick Pockley being married there because we were invited. It was a lovely little Chapel. George Harvey went there latterly. He went to the one I was telling you about that was Centra,l and then he moved to Promenade. They're going on about the one in Chapel Street, 'cos our minister's having a rare job about it 'cos he has Sewerby on our Circuit. Mind you he's well educated and he's the only one that can sort things out really. They love pulling things doon, don't they. They never make things any better, it's a shame isn't it? I mean look at Princess Mary Promenade, what a mess, all those amusements; well it's same on Harbour Side, and they've pulled the Winter Gardens down. I think there was a ballroom there wasn't there?

Rita   Yes, because my mum and dad used to cycle on a Saturday night to go dancing.

Edith   We used to congregate there on a Saturday night. When our John was secretary of Cricket Club he always had an annual dance at the Alexandra Hotel for cricket, and we used to go, lovely place it was, lovely outlook. It wasn't bombed, was it, 'cos they pulled it down.

Discussion followed about the unfortunate demise of Danes Dyke including the derelict farm house previously occupied by the Raper family.

Edith	I remember Dr Woodhouse used to say, "When I look out of my front door I'm in Bridlington. And when I look out of my back door I'm in Flamborough". I remember Rapers living there. There was Brian Raper, he was on with us.
	When we were kids we used to have bread crusts and milk, it was nice, it had a different flavour, hadn't it? It was called 'Pobs'. I don't know if you were, Rita, but your brother, Les, was brought up on one cow's milk. Your mother used to get milk from one particular cow. Not all cows mixed together. I know Les had it, I don't know whether you had it.
Rita	When I was born mi mother was very ill and she couldn't feed me. And mi dad used to have to go to Nightingale's, the farm.
Edith	Yes, that's right. I was only thinking about Elizabeth Nightingale today. She used to be our doctor's receptionist, Dr Broadbent, who followed Dr.Whitehead. He was lovely was Dr Broadbent but our Winnie was frightened of Dr Whitehead. When she was three she had to have a tooth out and doctor had to be there, and it was Dr Whitehead and she allus blamed im! And whenever he came she would run under table. And I was thinking there was one time I had something break out in mi leg. Dr Broadbent says, "I'll have you tested for diabetes." And he couldn't see anything at all but Miss Nightingale thowt she could. She was his receptionist or nurse, whatever you call them. She thought she just saw a sign but he never saw anything. But he said, "Just as a precaution I'll put you on a weeks diet", and he did. So he tested me again. It was still clear and I thought what a good job. I think diabetes is an awful illness. Uncle Bob had it you know from Brid. And they loved to come for their teas, did him and Aunty Polly but, by, she did watch him. I remember he could eat bananas, what else I can't remember but she was watching. I don't know whether you remember Tommy Loft working up at Ocean View, well his sister lived at Bempton, and she had some friends come from away, a man and his wife. They came on to South Landing and they came into our shop and she grabbed a sausage roll off our winder tray. By, she didn't 'alf wollup it down, she'd gone too long. She was a diabetic and it was further than she expected, she'd gone over her time.
	Your Dad was a rum un with threshing machine, Joyce. Lizzie Collins worked for mi mother you know and, like me, she was frightened of mice, and he used to put a live mouse in a match-

box and send it down. He was full of it. He did tell us some tales about Willy Coates up at farm, and about Miss Butters. Billy Coates allus called her 'Old Woman'. She allus had newspapers for table cloth and there was piles, she didn't take 'em off, she put clean uns on top. And this is just like 'im – she had a glass rolling pin and he put a mouse in that, did your dad. When they went next year that mouse was still in; well it would be deteriorating but it's remains would still be in that thing.

John and Elsie Longden

John was born in Flamborough. His father was a farm worker who died leaving his mother to run a grocery store to support the family. John worked at the same farm all his life.

Elsie came to Flamborough on the death of her mother to be brought up by an aunt and uncle.

Rita	How old were you when you started on a farm?
John	Fourteen. For the first two and a half years, more or less, I was at Kirkwold, Kirby Grindalythe.
Rita	Who were you working for there?
John	Well, actually for John Willy Leeson, mi uncle. Mi aunt and uncle came over to Bempton ti me grandfather's, and they'd just moved from one farm to a bigger farm, an' she says, "How would you like to come with us? Come for a fortnight to see how you like it." Well, I did and I stopped two year and a half. But the second year, like frae November to Martimus, mi uncle says, "I think you deserve more – a bigger wage – than I'm prepared to give anyone in that position". So that's how I finished there. But my first wage from there for the, well, say April to May to the following November, was nine pounds – say six months. In that time what I was supposed to do was help someone to do the horses.
	Coming back from Malton market one Saturday, I was in the car, on front with the driver, when there was a motorbike came

out of a road in front of us and he hit us – turned us completely over. It was an old Ford, canvas top with wooden spokes in the wheels. He spun us completely over, round, upside down. We were facing the way we'd come back frae Malton. Well, I went out through the top; I was sat on side of driver. The driver, he was hurt, whether it was the steering wheel was holding him, he was fast from underneath. Well, I thought, we'd got a new gabble at front from Malton, a steel bar you know, to make holes for sheep nets. I got that to lift the side so that I could get him out. I was putting pressure on to him because he shouted, as soon as ever I lifted it – he shouted I was hurting him somewhere. So what I'd got to do was leave it till someone came. Anyway, we weren't far away, there were some cottages at the crossroads, and someone soon came down and two or three of us lifted it to get him up and took him up to the cottages. They said was I alright? I only went on my head and my shoulder. I was scrubbed but I was alright. They called a doctor – he had us in and checked us. The driver, he was three weeks in hospital.

Well, during that time, you see I'd got to do what he was doing, which was four horses in a stable and a mare and a foal in a box, and about thirty ferrets. Well you see there, where we were, we had seventy acre of dell and there was a rabbit warren. Anyway he came out but he never went back into the stable again. So that left me with the four horses but of course the mare and foal we could put out of the road, but I still had those four horses to do. I had to do on with the rest. There was only two on us for nine horses and two or three young uns. But the waggoner only did his own four horses; he didn't help me to do mine.

I was up at five o'clock and I had to feed the horses before I had breakfast, and I was in that stable while eight o'clock at night, for the simple reason that I had those to do. But the waggoner, when he finished early, he went. At the finish, well, it was the maid that did it actually, 'cos she asked a few questions like. I used to come in and have me supper, and go to bed, because I used to sleep up the front stairs and the other two slept up the back stairs. See it didn't suit. Anyway, the maid asked a few questions and she opened her mouth one day and mi uncle said "Are you tired o'being with us?" "No", I says, "I'm not tired of being with you but I'm sick of having five horses to do". "Oh well", he says "Leave one". But the one he wanted to leave, all the other eight horses had to go past her, so I mean you couldn't leave her. Anyway, there was no time ti leave it on a night. They used to put a stable lamp on gateways for us to see to come through. Well, we had four hundred and forty acre, and there was mi uncle, the foreman, the beastman and the waggoner, and then we had a labourer used to come frae Lund. We had no extra hands when it come to threshing day so it was hard work. And when Martimus come, you all went up to Black Lion, that's where you used ti get engaged. And you see – Nicholson Hall at Wold Farm was mi uncle. Well, his wife was my aunt – that was Nellie Armand's mother. He came to me while I was there and said, "Have you got hired yet?" And I said, "No, not yet." Well, he says, "I know somebody who wants someone." And he brought George Wilkinson to see me. At mi uncle's we allus had a bull. During the summertime when it was in the grass, I did most of the scrufflin – that's down turnip row, you know – I did most of that. Therefore, it was me that had to go into the grass to fetch the horse, and the bull was in the field, which I didn't care for. So the first thing I do when George Wilkinson asked me about coming to work was, "Have you got a bull?" He says, "No", so I said "OK." Anyway I came to "Ocean View" for twenty-four pounds for the year and mind'st you, for that twenty-four pounds you lived up at the farm, you lived in, you got kept but that was a pound less than I'd been getting at Uncle's. But you see I was at home, I could go home, I could help mi mother. So that's how it came that I came to Ocean View. I came there when I was sixteen, and I was there while I was sixty-six.

Margaret	Were you horseman up there?
John	Yes, I kem for Henry Carter, 'waggoner lad' as you would say. Tommy Loft was in one stable, and Henry and me was in the other. Well, that meant I had two year like that and I'd to do all the carrying and cleaning. Henry fed the horses and groomed his two. I had the other four to groom and all that.
Margaret	How long did it take you to groom a horse?
John	Well that depends how you groom them; I mean there's grooming and grooming. But then Henry got married, I believe was it the second year, they got that new house built across at the other side of "Ocean View". Mr and Mrs Wilkinson went across there and Henry got married and he fed us instead of Mrs Wilkinson. And I went then from thed i'stable [*third in stable*] as they say. That was where Tommy Loft was, because they finished with

Tom at November, and I went into that stable. But when Henry got married in the August – they got married August Monday – I had to tek his place and they got Tom back again, so then we just carried on, you see. I mean I was carrying corn then. Well, I was carrying before then, because I never did like carrying caff [*chaff*].

Rita   No, it was a mucky job. I used to get that job.

John   I didn't have it long, because you see we had "Ocean View" threshing and Church Farm threshing like – that was George's father, you see. And they used to come and help us to thrash and we used to come and help them. Well, old Stan and Henry used to carry corn, and I don't know for some reason Old Stan weren't carrying. Old David kem and says, "Which does thu want to do lad, carry corn or carry straw?" I says, "Carry corn." 'Cos I'd carried at fourteen when I was at mi uncle's. I carried sixteen stone barley frea mi uncle's because the lad that was carrying, he fell awkward with a bag on his back across the weigh and he hurt his side. So I just says, "Oh, I'll carry – 'cos with caff you have ti keep pulling it out." So I carried then, like. I've been at it ever sin' I was fourteen really. Well, you see I've had a lot of different mates carrying corn.

Margaret   Was it there where Laurie hated carrying because there was stone steps and they were a bit short or steep and shallow?

John   Yes, "Ocean View's" stone steps, that's right. They'd been up there a lot o'years at Church and they were bevelled in the middle, they weren't flat. But what I did, I put a ring down at the bottom of the wall 'cos at one time, you know, there was no hand rail up the other side – it was just straight over the top. So I put a ring through at the bottom, just about right height for you carrying, then I used to put a waggon band down that side and fasten it up in the granary. Mind I never used it, but all the others that carried with me did. Stan Wilkinson carried wi' me a bit, Herbert Good and George Shepherd carried wi' me, he was up at Cliffe House.

Margaret   How long did you have horses up there then? When did you get tractors?

John   Well, we had horses when I came back out of the Army, that was in 1946, I think. But they got a tractor, what year was it? Before I went in the Army, a Massey Harris. But George used to tek it hisself because we still had two sets of horses – well, three sets of horses going. D'you know Arthur Taylor? Well, Dick Hood's wife, Marie, was his sister; she used to live down at corner there. Anyway, Dick Major was shepherd first year I was up there, then he left and Arthur Taylor kem. And Arthur Taylor, when they got this tractor, well he was a bit mechanical minded 'cos he had a motorbike. He used to go down on a night, and take over from George Wilkinson and let George go round the sheep after tea. He weren't paid a regular wage, they just give him what they thought, which, knowing George Wilkinson, was on the right side. Well, he used to keep going at night. On a morning we could get up, Henry used to call him; he didn't call me 'cos I was allus up, he used to shout of us for our breakfast. Art would still be up stairs, i'bed. He could shout of Art, we could have our breakfast, and be off out with the horses and Art would be just coming down. One day, George Wilkinson wanted to be into the tractor house. Door was locked, and he went for the key. "Oh", he says, "Arthur has it." "Where's Arthur?" "Still upstairs." So that was more or less the finish, because, well it wasn't fair on the rest o'us. I mean he was working later on a night, but he was getting the handout and we were at work on a morning while he was still i'bed. Then you see, they got Tommy Loft back and we got rid of so many horses; we got down to six, instead of having ten. There were six in one stable and four in the other, and we allus had two young uns to brek in every year.

Margaret	Did they used to breed their own horses then?
John	Yes, when possible. We generally had four foals up there. Church Farm foals too used to go up there i'winter. If we didn't have two of our own, they used to go up to Ruswarp to buy. There used to be an old man come. He was a big horse man, old Dick Audison; he used to come and he would go wi' 'em and he would pick what he thought was good. And they allus used to make two for Church Farm and two for "Ocean View", so that's how it worked out. You know Tom Robson frea Bempton – he was beastman when I fost went up there. He said, "Has thu gotten hired?" I says "Yes." He says, "Where's off?" I says, "I's going ti Ocean View." He says, "Hum, thu weean't know whea's boss, Nack or Dass."
Rita	Dass – my grandfather, Jimmy Kingston.
John	He knew what he was doing, did Jim. He loved getting hold o'those young horses. We used to brek 'em in. He would tek the old un – she was a good un to bring a young un on side like. He

would drive her while we had young un tethered. Anyway, while Henry was feeding 'em, we lost one, it died. The vet kem 'course straightaway: "She's had wheat." You aren't supposed to feed horses wheat; it blows up inside 'em unless you soak it first. But that was underhand, I mean all you were supposed to feed 'em was oats. Oats is main feed for them, barley makes 'em itch in the leg, and wheat is taboo. But anyway, the vet seemed to have the idea that this horse had had wheat. She was one o' my pair. I had two that I used to tek. One of 'em used to have a young horse aside of her when we were brekking 'em in, but then put them two in the turnip cart, which was what I had to do all winter the first year. I could let them two go while I fastened the gate, and they would set theselves ti turnip house. One hard winter, when it was frozen up and snowed up at "Ocean View", I was a week leading [conveying] milk. Then Graingers picked it up in the cans – ten gallon I think it was. I was a week leading it down ti village. I used to stand i' cart and just let her go and that first horse would pick her way through all shallow spots right down Lighthouse Road. They were two good uns. Well, the one that was on first, she was on front – was 'Tidy.' It was her that was one of our brood mares. Well, she died. She allus looked well; you thought she was alright, but she was fat. 'Course Henry simply said, once the vet said that he thought she had had wheat, that the granary door was locked. George would ration the corn out for you. Well, sometimes he weren't there 'cos we used to go on a dinnertime for corn. Jimmy said tiv him – 'cos Jimmy weren't bothered what he said to him, he'd say owt ti him – "You know them lads is taking them hosses ti work without any corn, wi' nought to eat." George said, "Oh, why go on and help yoursels."

Jimmy told me many a time what a fool he was and that he should have been farming this instead of working there. Well, when I was feeding 'em we used to get cow cake. It was in bags, pellets, you see. I used to have a little bag so big, and a bag full of that used to go in with my bag of corn when I was feeding 'em. Jimmy found out. He'd gone for some corn out of corn bin, evidently, and struck a bit deep and come across this bag. "Oh", he said, "I don't mind that." He was a damn good un was Jimmy Kingston.

Rita   He loved horses.

John   He did, I agree wi' you.

Margaret	Did he have the horses that took traps to Bridlington? I remember Granddad Jim Smith saying that he used to drive traps for somebody called Kingston and Jim Kingston was a drinking mate of his.
Rita	No, that was Uncle Fred did that. Grandy Kingston had a water cart for so long.
John	We've got a postcard of when the pond was down there at Croft Farm. It was Woodhouse's, old James Woodhouse was there, and Jimmy Kingston used to live in that cottage.
Rita	Sparrow Cottage.
John	Yes, Sparrow Cottage, and we lived at the first cottage at the other side. He used to lead water, ha'penny a bucket.
Rita	You see when "Ocean View" was sold, the girls got the money but Grandy Kingston said he'd rather have two horses. So he got two of the carthorses because he couldn't bear to see the horses sold.
John	I was called up. Stan was about calling up age, you know, but somebody had to go. They wanted 10,000 off farms and I was one of them. Well, I think Henry did the horses while I was away. He got married and he went to live over at old house at "Ocean View" and George went into new un. I got "B" release to come back on land, or else I don't know how long I should have been still in the Army. I finished up as Brigadier's groom, and I'd a bobby's job.

When I finished mi Army training, like for artillery, we were just waiting to be posted to a regiment, and they says, "How would you like to go to the Pack Artillery, you've been amongst horses?" Well, that was up in Scotland, and I said, "Where are they training?" Oh, he says, "Up in these hills somewhere." I just thought – 'Pack Artillery'. If I'm right, that means going where the vehicles can't get. That means having to strip the guns, pack 'em onto your horse, and they'd be old mules, and they can be darn stubborn, can mules, they simply stand like that and you can't move 'em. So I said, "No, I'll stop where I am." That's how I got that side of it, like. I came out on "B" release to come back on ti farm, and someone told me George Wilkinson said, "I can sleep comfortable now that John's gotten back among the horses."

We were once threshing down at Church Farm; Ted Lunn used to carry with me. You know when you got a bag off the machine |

you'd got to put your knee under to get bag onto weigh. I'd to lift many a bag on for Ted, he could not move a bag; carry 'em, yes, but not move it. Anyway, I think Ted was with me that day. We were down at Church Farm – it was before we had our own machine – and we had hired machine in. Well, they're in at seven o'clock on a morning, and they finish at dinnertime. They were at far side of Church Farm stackyard, and we were carrying from there right a way round and up the granary steps. We had ti put steps out to carry up front and then up wooden steps. And when you got into granary you got a bit of corn up like that. The beams were that low you had to duck. Old David said ti me, "How much does thu weigh lad?" I said, "I don't know. I just weigh middlin, but we can soon see." Weigh was down i' barn just a bit further on than granary steps. I knew I weighed over twelve stone. I put eight stone on and stood on, and it took me and the eight stone. I said, "Oh, twenty stone." We carried fifty quarter – that was fifty bags at half day – frae that far side of stackyard up steps to granary. And for that we used to get a shilling extra. I think it got to half-a-crown that old David gave us.

I came back to "Ocean View." Phillip Grimshaw frea Brid was there. I'll tell you who was in the other stable for a bit, Percy Williamson – they used to be at Carr Farm. He was a strong little kid, he carried wi' me. I've had a lot of different mates.

Margaret	You were saying about the Tower in Tower Field; you used to keep something in there?
John	Implements. When I was a kid we used to go up on top, climb tower and slide down. It was black pitch, warn't it?
Rita	The roof outside was black pitch.
John	You could get on top and slide down one side on it, and Church Farm used to keep implements inside there.
Margaret	Has the roof fallen in there, then?
John	Yes, 'cos you see there's only, like, two sides on it now.
Rita	Did they ever keep calves in there?
John	I don't know if they ever kept calves in, but they used to put implements in.
Rita	We were always trying to get into it because we thought there was a hidden passage.
John	They used to say there was, to the Church. I've never been inside it because they had the gate fastened so that you couldn't get

	inside. But I've been on top and slid down, and I should say that at some time there's been a wall or something around. When you go round that field as we have done, hoeing nettles or such as that like, you come across a piece, you just think there's been a wall there so far, and then maybe so far that way, and then it's all filled in, like.
Margaret	Where were you born, then?
John	Wold Farm; that was where mi grandfather lived and if I'm right, by what mi mother used ti say, mi grandfather and grandmother were moving to Bempton and mi mother was helping 'em and of course taking me with her. I weren't five year old; anyway, kid-catcher came. I think it would be old Bath maybe then, anyway he kem to see why I wasn't at school. She says, "He isn't five year old yet, don't worry he'll be there when he's five." That's when I fost remember about school. About only thing I can remember about being down there – Elsie Kingston, lived in Sparrow cottage and we had a ginger cat that used to go down there and she would feed it.
John	Mi aunt and uncle used to come with pony and trap on a Saturday to Brid market. "Why, thu'll stop for thee tea", they used to say, and try and stuff me. We had some good times up there. Nellie Almond – she was mi Uncle Jim's daughter – when she got married they had the reception up in the granary. Well, I say a reception – they had a do after tea up in the granary at Wold Farm that was just stable lads. You could hear foxes in Dykes. We were there while four o'clock in morning. Then we went ti bed up there; they wouldn't let us stop up ni longer. Amos Frankish were there. Oh, he was a right one, he used to go up there a lot, rabbiting and that like. I know they had 'Forfeits' and 'Sing a song, say a piece' and 'Kneel to the wittiest, bow to the prettiest, kiss the one you liked best.' He had 'em all off, had Amos, and if you didn't, well.....!
Margaret	You had to pay a forfeit, had you?
John	Yes, oh, I know they had a do that night. I know it was four o'clock when we went straight up into bed.
	I'll tell you who used to come up a good bit, Pete Marshall; 'cos him and Stan was big folks. Pete would have four stone 'cos he was a stoker, on t' railway, and we had some big shovels for shovelling corn, and we'd see who could lift most on a shovel. Well of course, you see, Pete was used tiv it.

He was a devil for torment when they were thrashing, when lads was carrying caff, 'cos he was carrying corn wi' me, was Stan. And when lad had gotten away with his sheet, Stan would grease rake, and next time lad got hold of rake it was all grease. When they got baler, started to bale, Stan was wiring. They used to hook a needle in, slip wire through, then round and back t'uther way – there was somebody at either side. Stan would get so many pieces of band and tie 'em all together, and he would tie it onto that bale that was just about to go out, and then maybe ti baler. Fellow would get so far wi' bale, like, and keep going, and 'course bale used to drop off his back!

We had Cliffe House then, when we had baler. Well, Stan was o'er at Cliffe House. Archie Burton was a queer cus. We were once draining that field where bungalows is, and we got it down into gutter and water wouldn't get away. So I got down into gutter that went under road, like. I said, "I know why it won't go away, there's stones i' road." So, oh, we'll ha' to shift stones. Archie come, "You're not moving that stone", he said. "My car has to come down there, and it might let the road down, and that car is worth more to me than the farm is." That was his attitude. He sent Bill Hildrew wiv a little fire shovel on end of a shaft to shift it, and then he followed him up, like, but no, he says, it's no good. At finish George Wilkinson just says, "Right lads, gather your tools up; if we can't get water away it's no good us getting into gutter, and then it not getting away, like." Gutter would fill while it got ti drain end, and then stop it up and back up on land, you see. So Archie says, "Alright you can tek stone up." So we took stone up and o' course we never had no more bother 'cos we were always there. But by heck, he had Archie on a string, had Bill. If there was ought Bill didn't want ti do and Archie wanted him to do, Archie would be running around calling, "Bill, Bill", but Bill would be out next door.

Me and Stan once had to go round there and it was when it was snown up. Mrs Burton wanted to be out, and Bill couldn't get out in car. So alright we went wi' tractor just up and down that Cliffe House road, you know, while we got a road through for him. Old Bill says, "Come in lads, we'll have a drink." 'Course knowing what Archie was we thought it would be something strong. When we went into kitchen Mrs Burton was on a big Agar cooker and she says, "Here you are." A cup of Bovril! By, I've thought about that many a time – aye, Bill says, "Thu'll be alright lad", but that's what it was, a cup of Bovril!

It was Martimus week and it was when they used to fetch crabs off harbour for Vicky Bayes. And our Stan *[brother]* helped him – Jim Smith – one bit and he'd done something. I don't know if he'd sprained his ankle or something. So I said I'd help him for a week, on one condition. I wouldn't mind helping him but I warn't going on ti harbour among fish. Jim said, "No, I dain't want you to go on ti harbour." Now, we were leading straw frae Cliffe House and Laurie was wiv us. Mike Farnell and me went wiv Laurie to Wykeham to fetch a load of straw. It was under a shed. What they were cleaning it out for, was they were going to have a dance at night. There were three big corn bins like they used to have to store loose corn, and while we were getting this straw out, there were rats running round these corn bins as unconcerned as owt, as we were getting it. Now, we came back and on way back, it ud be at Seamer I think, at lime pits, I know we had to weigh this straw. We weighed it, and we were coming on and a car come by and pulled in front of Laurie and stopped. The driver, says, "Your load's leaning a bit." I think he thought we were going to loss it and you know what Laurie was like, he says, "It can keep leaning while we get ti Flamborough."

Oh, we had some fun. I enjoyed it. I spent fifty years there. I went when I was sixteen till I was sixty-five. Why, you could say more or less I was head hossman when I was eighteen 'cos I took over frae Henry Carter when he was foreman, and they went over ti uther house. We had a bit of a do then – maybe because Henry Carter's mother had been hinding *[feeding men that worked on the farm]*. And she was living up with them when they first got married – and it was prune pie, prune pie, nowt but prune pie. Art Taylor went up as shepherd. He cut into two or three pies, and they were prune, and anyway nobody said anything just then. Frankie Carter was only a lad going to school, like, and he was playing about wiv a stick and he was tapping Arthur with it. At finish, Arthur collared stick and threw it onti buildings out of way. 'Course, Frankie told his mother and there was a bit of a do o'er it. And that's how it started. He, Arthur, struck in about prune pie. I was going for hosses one morning, fetching them from across road, and George Wilkinson was waiting for me. As hoss passed the gate, he said, "What's all this about everybody wanting to leave?" 'Cos Arthur was going ti leave, and Henry was going ti leave. I said, "There's nought for anybody ti talk about leaving." He says, "Why, what's matter?" Well I says, "I'll

	tell you why trouble is. Henry's mother actually started it. it's all about prune pie. There's nowt but prune pie – that's what Arthur's firing over." So anyway, that settled that, like. But it warn't long after that, Arthur couldn't get up on a morning and he got the push. I think he went o'er to Dick Hood's. Well, that was one thing I would say, Mrs Carter was a good cook. You couldn't grumble about Mrs Carter. Whether George had a word with Mrs Carter or not, I don't know, but it was the end of prune pie.
Margaret	You weren't born in Flamborough were you, Elsie? You told me you came when you were three.
Elsie	I was three when mother died. We lived in Post Office Street, 'Wee Croft.' It was mi gran's, they used ti call it 'Lartle Hoos' and they said we can't have a name like that as somebody else has it.
Margaret	Yes, 'cos I know Father used to say that when the estate broke up in 1926, when who-ever it was went bankrupt, and they sold off the houses. Father, till then, had all that corner, hadn't he? – from our house right round, with corn for horses, and then some of them had allotments on there.
John	Yes, Bernard Traves, Steenie Cross. I should say, somewhere where W.I. is – it seemed to go up a bit there – they had pigeons there.
Margaret	Laurie wouldn't keep pigeons as he said he had enough pigeon running as a kid, 'cos he always had to collect the clocks or something.
Elsie	Oh yes, they did.
Margaret	Father, Jim Smith, said when they sold it, they offered him, what he understood was the whole lot; the land, the shed and the house for £100. And he went and borrowed it off someone, did Father, to buy it. When he went back to them, they said, well they only meant half of it – you know where the canteen road is. And of course, Father being Father, said, "Bugger you, you can keep it".
John	I can quite understand.
Margaret	I can remember him saying that's when your uncle, Jim Fell, come to him and said, "Jim, you don't want it?" He said, "No. Bugger them. They told me £100 for the lot and now they say £100 for half, so that's it." And that's when your uncle bought it, wasn't it?

Elsie	Yes, a third of an acre.
John	It was a fair piece, was that.
Margaret	That was when he had the bungalow built.
Elsie	Yes, he built it.
John	When we used to go gardening classes, Laurie used to come. He'd had to help his Dad fill bags with coal, and of course, old 'Artley, (the headmaster) used to play up about him.
Elsie	About his boots!!
John	He were on about stones working up on land, and he just says to Laur, after we'd been debating, "How does all them stones get on that land of yours, Smith?" And he says, "Why, lads throw stones up at birds."
Margaret	Yes, I believe he was a bit of a so and so at tormenting, was my husband, wasn't he?
John	Aye, he was alright was Laur, though. By, talk about figures!
Margaret	Yes, I know. Our Jim's like him an' all.
John	He would put sum down, he would put answer down, then teacher'd say "Smith how did you get this?" Why, he'd right answer. He never put workings down. He could work it out. Teacher would get us all stood up round the classroom, about quarter past three, and say, "Right, first un ti answer can go." I bet Laur was one of first to do a sum and one of first out.
Margaret	Yes, but Jim's like that, mind you. When Jim was in Mrs Byrne's class, she always used to say he was the only one she had to learn twenty-three times' table for. He got up to his twenty-three times' table and she said, "I used to have to do it the night before, because I knew he'd be coming to do some more times' tables". And now, if he gets a sum, he'll just go "so and so", and he's got it like that.
	What were you saying about watching them on ice on the Mere with car lights?
Elsie	Oh yes, Mr.Simms used to come, I tell you. He lived at Chesterfield House, up there.
John	Dinah Gibbon used to live in end un, and Chesterfield lived in next un. He allus used to put weather out for fishermen.
Elsie	And there was a Mr Simms used to come up there, and he used to have skates. By, he was good! He was on his own, and they all used to come from Brid or anywhere and shine their car lights on

	Mere, and he would skate. Of course the big lads used to make 'tewies'; up and down, up and down it used to go.
John	I'll tell you who could skate an all, Bill Major, Herbie's older brother. By gor, he could skate!
Margaret	When we talked with Herbert, he was telling us about going cliff climbing.
John	Why, George Leng used ti go cliff climbing up Wold Farm; that's where we used ti get scout eggs. You see, mi Uncle Jim, it was his land that they climbed on their cliff. He used ti bring us scout eggs down, did mi uncle. That was where we used ti get our pocket money, a penny a week, when we lived down in cottage. They used to go past there ti go to Brid, and we used to stop horse and trap. A penny a week, that's what we used ti get. I did it for years.
Margaret	What did you get for your penny a week?
Elsie	Forty Indian eyes or something like that.
Margaret	I was telling Rita you said about Laurie making those paper things in school.
Elsie	When 'Artley was out of the classroom, Laurie would get us all in it; and he would get us a piece of paper and make us an arrow, and there was aeroplanes flying all over till Mr Hartley came in, and he had to duck. And that was it.
Margaret	You would leave school at fourteen then Elsie, did you?
Elsie	Yes. I was at Ellis's, photographers, and different places – finished up at camp. I enjoyed it. I was at Readhead's; I was in mi uncle Jimmy Garland's shop; I was at Bridge Street, and I looked after it while our Kath finished and I took over; and I was at Promenade.
Margaret	You would be living with Fells when we got married, 'cos you were married after us, weren't you?
Elsie	Yes, I was brought up by mi Aunty Fell. He was a master builder, was mi Uncle Fell. He went on his own, he built all sorts. Why, he built that bungalow where Tom Hall lives at the top of Crofts Hill.
Rita	I think he built our kitchen and bathroom *["Willowdene"]* – for Rawnsleys. He was the headmaster.
Elsie	Oh yes, I used to go down there to Mrs Rawnsley, with her washing that mi Auntie Fell had washed. Well, they had to do

	something, hadn't they; but mind you didn't get paid that much, did you. People couldn't afford to pay much. My Uncle Jim used to do the lifeboats. He used to be with Harg Hopwood. If anything happened to the lifeboat, they'd get mi Uncle Jim to do it. He made that sideboard.
Margaret	There's some fancy work on it, isn't there?
Elsie	You didn't tell Margaret and Rita about your Cossack horses that you used to look after.
John	Oh why, there were about three hundred on 'em. You see I was on the invasion of Africa. We were right on top of Africa, through into Italy, then into Austria. At one time, we had about three hundred Cossack horses. By, get some of them Cossacks among 'em; talk about ride, you couldn't see them, all you could see was their arms. They used ti lay on side and just leg on top like that, full gallop. And get 'em in among them hosses, they could pick hoss they wanted. We had 'em hosses in a big enclosure and they used ti eat through railings very near every day, they were that hungry; I mean you couldn't keep 'em. When we had Gerry prisoners, each Gerry prisoner had three hosses ti look after, and there used ti be so many of us go. We used ti tek 'em into nearest of what we thought they could graze on, ton 'em loose, and Gerry prisoners had ti be round outside ti keep 'em in. We went ti one place – it was hay time – farmer was leading it in and we had a three tonner leading it out. We got one load; when we went next load, he was there with shot gun. I don't blame him, like. Some of 'em wouldn't make it back home ti enclosure. And of course we had ti shoot 'em and report and leave 'em laid. Some of farmers, if hosses weren't stamped, they would barter and you could sell 'em, and nobody knew. But they got awd fashioned because they branded 'em all. Only hosses that weren't branded like mine, what I rode – oh the times I could have selled that hoss but I wouldn't sell it. I daen't know what happened tiv 'em in finish 'cos we moved, you see, and left 'em.
Elsie	They med 'em into meat pies.
John	Oh, that's what a lot of 'em did. It would be in Austria, I believe. We were billeted in house, like, and you could see these hosses, two or three on 'em, going down road. Then you could hear 'bang' a few minutes after. There was a stream down at bottom of garden, pretty wide – you could see that running red, and then all offal used to be coming down, floating down. Poor beggars.

Elsie	What are you going to call this book when you get it finished?
Rita	'The Right Side of the Dyke'
Elsie	A good idea.
Margaret	Yes, 'cos Sarah Readhead always used to say, "They want to get ti other side of Dyke," didn't she, and Laurie used to say, "Yes, and she isn't Flamborough either!!"
John	Well, I tell lots of people there used ti be seven ponds down in that corner by 'kissing gates' at Maitlands. And sometimes, when there'd been a lot of rain, it used ti come and you'd used ti just get through gate, and you had ti go round there 'cos it used ti flood o'er. It was all grown up, thorn bushes, paths in among hands *[overgrown]* – you could run round and play hide and seek there. At one time, between last cottage where we used ti live and Croft Farm, was all allotments.
Elsie	He means where Farrington's bungalow is, on the hill.
John	It was all allotments was that. Mi dad had one 'cos that's where I got mi backside skelped. I love spring onions, y'know, and he was putting these spring onions in. I warn't very old, and I was following behind pulling 'em up and eating 'em, and throwing green away, while he caught me!!

Dorothy Waines (neé Taylor)

Daughter of a fishing family, Dorothy was well-known for her knitting of guernseys and was very involved with the Women's Institute and the British Legion.

Dorothy   My Dad was three days old when his father was drowned at North Landing. Ned Taylor was his name and Maria was his wife. She had three girls and mi Dad, but I never knew 'em, they'd died before.

Margaret   It was a hard life, wasn't it?

Dorothy   Oh aye, I've heard mi Dad say one night she sat up all night finishing a guernsey, so she could give him the five shillings she got for knitting it. He was going ti Rudston and she set him so far ti Rudston and gave him the five shillings and if he didn't like it, he was going to give maister the five shillings and come home. They could i'them days, you know. He used to say first week he was married he got five shillings. And at Christmas they got a pound each and it was all over village that they'd getten a pound each. I don't know how long he was on the farm. And then he finished on farm and started fishing. Then he had a nervous breakdown.

He was two years and couldn't work at all and then he started ti boil crabs and lug crabs and fish and go round hawking. And the first day he went ti stall in market in Brid he sold one crab and next stall there was a man frae Rudston Parva called Dickinson and he said, "How did you get on?" And he said, "I shan't come any more". And Dickinson said, "You know when I first kem, I sold one pound of butter and look at what I sell now. Don't give up." So he didn't. He kept going. Then he got another stall. We used ti go every Market Day. You know where them toilets is, near harbour, Queen Street – there was Sharpe's fish and chip shop and Ash's wet fish shop. We stood in front of them. There was two more – Bill Philipps and another man, and we used ti sell crabs there. The market went from New Inn corner right up to Woolworth's at that side and then from Stead and Simpson's right to top at other side. *[Harbour steps]* There was a Jackson's opposite us and for sixpence you could go and get a large bag of buns and cakes that were a day old, that they hadn't sold.

I used to hate going ti market. My sister, Norman's mother, used ti go till they were married and then I had ti go. And I used ti say ti mi mother, "Will you go, Mother, instead?" and she used ti say, "I can't honey, else I would. I hated it I really did. I was so shy of meeting folk and Philipps used to say, "Thu isn't half like your Lizzie". "I know I isn't", I'd used ti say. I always said if ever I had a family I'd never make them do anything they didn't want ti do 'cos I know what I went through when I had ti go.

Margaret	How much were crabs then, can you remember?
Dorothy	Yes, they were from threepence, sixpence, eightpence, ninepence and then a shilling. And what they're paying £3 & £4 for now were half a crown, and if anybody wanted 'em dressing it was threepence extra. I wish I had as many pound notes as crabs I've dressed. Mi dad used ti go round. We used ti ave two horses and two carts and Art used ti go round village wi errands on this little lorry and mule we had, and mi dad used ti go ti Bempton, Sewerby, all villages. He had a big round eventually. On Wednesday and Friday he used ti call at Marton Hall School and they wanted fifty pieces. He had 'em all ti cut up – they wanted it for breakfast. And we had three boarding houses in Brid we supplied wi crabs. My first job was ti pick fifty in lartle tiny individual shells for these boarding houses, and one you had ti be very careful, she was that particular. It had to be the right colour. I used ti get half a crown pocket money a week. Mi dad used to give me half a crown – mind you, they kept me in mi board and clothes. They couldn't afford ti give you much in them days.

We didn't have any spare time. You see I used ti go ti market – mi mother was poorly seven years before she died. Mi sister

Lizzie Readhead used ti let her house furnished in the summer, live here wi Norman and George and David, and then she would boil crabs and see to 'em while I was at market. Then, after mi mother died, mi sister gev ower coming, so I used ti kum home on bus before bus mi dad caught. Mrs. Kemp [next door neighbour] would light the copper fires, then I used ti see ti 'em. Many a time I was washing crabs at one o'clock in morning, in candlelight, so crabs were ready for stall in morning. I had ti do because mi mother used ti do 'em for us, then mi sister used ti do 'em till mi mother died.

I've lived here since I was nine. And when we got married – you know where Mrs. Brigham lives [Woodcock Road]? Two houses next door, Josh Shippey lived in one and the other was empty. George worked with him and Josh said, "Why don't you come after that house up there?" So I said ti mi dad one day, "If we move, would you come wiv us?" He said, "Wheear are you going?" I said, "There's a house on Woodcock Road, next door to Josh Shippey. It's empty, it's a nice house, would you come wiv us?" " No", he says. "I shan't but I'm not going to stop you going. If you want to go, you go by all means, but I shan't. I'm stopping here where your mother was." So I says ti George, "What have I to do?" He says, "Stop here. You can't leave him, can you?" That settled that, we stopped here. It was only rented then.

Margaret	Was it part of the estate?
Dorothy	No, it belonged to three sisters. You know Sam Duke? His first wife, Harriet – they lived where Mrs Kemp used ti live.
Rita	I can't remember them living there but I can remember Auntie Jinnie talking about them living there.
Dorothy	As these cottages became vacant they sold them and we took our rent to Mrs Gibbon, your Auntie Jinnie. Then Florrie died and they were eventually left to Mrs Illingsworth, the last sister. Eventually she wrote that she was going to sell it and she would give mi father first chance of it. And I wrote back and said he didn't want to buy it but could we buy it? And she wrote back and said we weren't the tenants, Mr Taylor was. The lady in the office at Hull came on to see us and she said, "This cottage is for sale and if your father isn't going to buy it, I shall buy it as an investment, but you must understand I can't afford any repairs as the rent you are paying is too low". Which it was, rents in those days were very low. When she retired she and her mother came

to retire to Brid. Eventually her mother died and she came to tell us she was selling our cottage and was going to live with her sister down south. She did give us a new floor. She bought the wood and George laid it, and we had a new window as well. "I'm going to give you first choice of buying it and if you don't want to it's quite alright but I shall still sell it". So that's how we got it. "I don't want ti move", he said, "But don't you want somewhere modern?" "No, I don't", I said. So we bought it. George did all the alterations himself. This rail came from a ship wreck that mi dad went to, it's part of the ship's rail.

Margaret	So George was a joiner then?
Dorothy	Oh no, he was a brick layer's labourer, but he knew what to do and what not to do and could do all sorts of work in a house.
Margaret	Did you start knitting guernseys then?
Dorothy	After mi mother died. I didn't learn from mi mother, I learned from John Kemp's grandma. You see my mother was poorly before I left school and she died when I was twenty. She was always poorly; she had Bright's disease and she was diabetic. She learned me how ti knit socks and Wadmans *[thick waterproof socks]* but not a guernsey. After mi mother died mi dad said, "I would like a new guernsey", and I said, "Well I can't knit you one." They always had a best guernsey – a Sunday one, one they changed into on a night or to be tidy – and a working guernsey. And he wanted to tek his Sunday guernsey for second best and have a new one for Sunday. I know Billy Chadwick's mother knits 'em. I'll ask her. Next day I was telling John's grandma about mi dad needing a new guernsey and me not being able to knit one. She said, "You can Dorrie. You go to Annie Tants and get wool. Your mother has some needles and I'll show you". And she did and from that I've knit dozens. I've knitted white, khaki, air-force blue for lads 'cos they were stationed here. Chapel used to be canteen – they used ti mek cups of tea and such like and I used to tek mi knitting down when I was helping down there. First I ever knitted, for sale, seven and sixpence for knitting it. I don't know how much they cost now.
Margaret	It'll be a hundred and twenty or thirty now but I don't know what the knitters get.
Dorothy	I don't know either. I've knitted one in three weeks and I got first prize and special prize at Spa once. Mark *[a young relative]* always wanted a guernsey and Susan, his mother, said he could

have one when he was old enough. I said to Susan, "I'll knit him one for his fifteenth birthday". So I did and he was over the moon. His birthday is November and he entered it in the knitting section of the Craft Show. Susan had asked me if I would like to go, and so I went and when they took me to the knitting section I saw I'd won both prizes. I made Mark go up for the prizes! I've knitted them for Women's Institute competition and you got marks not prizes. We did a sea-side exhibition and Mrs. Eade says, "Will you knit a guernsey? I'll buy the wool then we'll keep it." I got first prize for that. It was grey.

Margaret   Have you got the patterns written down?

Dorothy   I've wrote them down myself. Old lady showed me how ti do it. Then when I saw a fisherman walking and I looked, I could tek that pattern from his guersey and come home and do it.

When my sister was ill George and I lived at their house for six weeks. *[She lived in Brid.]* I did their baking and washing for a year. Billy Collins used to take it to Brid each time in his carrier cart. He used to bring their washing on a Saturday and then take it clean and ironed back. He used to take and bring all sorts to and from Brid. He used to carry dead bodies. If anyone died he used to bring 'em back ti Waud's *[the undertakers]*. He used to bring our meat from Chews before they had the shop here. If you needed any medicine, he'd bring it back for you from Mrs Gatenby's and such; if you needed gripe water *[for babies]* he'd bring that.

Margaret   How long was he doing that?

Dorothy   Oh, a long time – him and Screeton's. Then Screeton's finished and he kept on – he had carrier cart at first.

Margaret   They wouldn't let him take baking in it now, for hygiene, would they? Did he charge you then?

Dorothy   Yes, sixpence.

Rita   Threepence for medicine.

Dorothy   Yes, I knew it wasn't much.

Margaret   When you look back on those days no one had much money.

Dorothy   No, they hadn't. When we were first married, George earned two pounds and five shillings a week. He used to buy a packet of Woodbines *[cigarettes]* and then put the rest for housekeeping.

Margaret   And that was for the week for rent and everything.

Dorothy	Oh aye, all lot. Coal was one shilling and ninepence a bag and when we boiled crabs Jim Smith used to bring us five bags at a time. It was no good just getting a bag at a time 'cos we'd three coppers and the house. I allus remember a neighbour near us never got any coal in the summer, but in winter she was allus running for a bag of coal. It was rationed during war and she complained to the coalman that we had coal, implying we got more than we should have. Mr. Smith could be very blunt and told her that if she got coal during the summer she would not have been without in the winter. We used to go sticking with a cart to Bempton Dykes.
	Mi mother used to go to Brid in winter, and we lived with an elderly aunt and we had part of her house in North Street. I used to go to Hilderthorpe School.
Margaret	Did you go to dances and things?
Dorothy	I only went ti one lot of dances that was Buffs' 'cos mi brother was in it. Those dances were in the school. I never went to the Spa. For one thing I was never interested in going to those. We never went for holidays. My brother used to live in Hull and mi mother used to take us to Hull Fair and then we used to go to Brid Fair and that was about it. We used to go on Sunday School treats to Scarborough. We used to go on farm wagons to Flamborough Station and then to Scarborough on train. Then when buses started to run they took you on buses.
Rita	You started saving for Scarborough after Christmas, didn't you?
Dorothy	Yes and if you wanted a selection box at Christmas you took extra pennies each week to Pat's [*a shop at the bottom of Highlands, the row of cottages leading to Mill Garth*]. Then when Pat finished we took it to Nellie Tom's. [*Mrs Tom Woodhouse's shop at the top of High Street.*] You got a penny for sweets each week. You never did nothing on a Sunday, you know. I always remember after mi mother died I was washing step outside and John's grandma [*Mrs.Kemp*] came and said, "No Dorothy your mother wouldn't have wanted you to do it". I never did it any more on a Sunday.
Rita	I can remember you didn't knit or sew on a Sunday.
Dorothy	Oh no, you didn't and you didn't clean your shoes. Mi mother used ti cook dinners, tidy up and that was it. You used ti etty go ti Sunday School and take your frock off when you kem back until you went back ti Sunday School in the afternoon. I allus

had a new frock for Anniversary. I allus got sixpence if I didn't break down saying our piece. We allus had two pieces, one for afternoon and one for night, but I would never sing. We went to Primitives.

Margaret	When did Wesleyan Chapel close?
Dorothy	Oh, it was a long time before the new chapel was built. There was only about four folks left there and they wanted us to go up there. And when we decided not to move, the Wesleyans went to the Church. We had a brick-laying day. Bricks were a pound each. We brought some chairs as well as a book of remembrance of mi mother and father; they were trustees of the chapel. There was some rum characters here. Do you remember Merry? He used to sit on step and frighten the kids ti death. He pulled all sorts of faces.

George used to build folks air-raid shelters at start of War. A neighbour had one built in garden with steps down and everything. The wife was terrified and as soon as sirens went she had to go in this shelter. Some people didn't realise how vulnerable we were. During one raid an old lady stood in the street in a white shawl. The fisherman living near shouted at her, "The bloody gerries will see you miles off". Another person lit a cigarette whilst out side during a raid! It took a while for people to realise things were visible from the air. German planes came in low over the headland as they used the Lighthouse as a direction point. Mi father only went down in the shelter once. "Nivver no more will I go down there", was his comment.

Margaret	How long did Nellie Toms have the shop?
Dorothy	Oh years and years. You know when I was at school Sally Bayes, the shop-keeper's sister used to take us for sewing. We used to come here for anything we needed. During the war I used to work for Dick Bayes. And I used to bake for all his weddings – they used to be at the Village Hall. Icing sugar was difficult to get and one wedding they had to ice the cake with soft icing and someone built the cake up before it was needed. The pillars sunk into the icing and it collapsed. We had to repair it quickly as best we could and put the worst at the back so it wouldn't show in the photographs!!

Herbie Major and George Nordass

Herbie belonged to a fishing family and was employed as a brick layer. He and his cousin, George, were climmers.

George worked as a motor mechanic after serving in the Royal Navy.

Herbie	There were that many Richards in the Major family that they had to 'ave nicknames. I'se only yan that's left. There was five lasses, Rachel, Ada, Ede, Florrie, Ann.
George	He's 79 and I'm 83. So you're one of the youngest aren't you? I remember Florrie very well 'cos she used to be at Jane Collie's shop 'cos it was fost un down frew oor 'oose. Tom Widdus *[Woodhouse]* was about six years auder un me.
Margaret	You used to live in the cottages up Back Street Hill *[Greenside]*, didn't you?
Herbie	Aye, that's right. Annie and Frank Taylor lived right at end – he was at waterworks at Flamborough; then us and then Sam Widdus
George	I'll tell you a tale about Frank Taylor. He and Sam Widdus were in War together, and whether they'd been bugle players in Army or not but they were cornet players in band here after the War. Matt Major was in charge then, but it was Armistice and Ernie Pinder, cornet player out of Excelsior Band at Brid came to play 'Last Post'. He hadn't been in the forces during the war so they up and walked out and nivver played in band again. Eddie Pinder kem and played for Lifeboat at Noth Sea. He kem ti help us out.

Margaret	Were there many in the band?
George	Oh aye, it changed noo an' ageean, 'cos Uncle Mitt he was in, he dropped oot about time I started. There was awd Mark and young Mark Major and lad Mark, they were all three in. Then you see there was Alf Nicholson, Tom Stork, George Waud, Arthur Stork, awd Bill Sunley.
Herbie	And there was Paddy Marshall and Harold Stork and 'im that was at Noth Sea. Dis tha remember 'im – Burgin – he was trombone player. They taught him 'im in Dr. Bernado's in Hull, didn't they?
George	Aye, I just remember him. We played all ower. I was in the Sea Scouts and I was still at school, and there was a procession ti South Landing. There was awd Will Hall at shop, y'know, and ye got some laughs at 'im. There was one time, I don't know whether it was Tom Cowling or Major or old Bee in charge, and he said we'll play 'Heroes of the Mine' and awd Will Hall says, "They are bloody heroes an' all". They were on strike!
Herbie	Mi father was a fisherman and on Spurn lifeboat: it was a sailing boat. He was there 25 years. My grandmother and Robert Leng grandfather were brother and sister.
George	I remember when they kum. Your George was my age. We were in that classroom that looked out onti lads' playground and there was only George Major and me was left. There was neerbody else. They all had flu. Classes were that small that they shut school. We were off five weeks.
	There was a ship that kem ashore yon side of Dykes, filled wi' china clay and we would all gan. We set off ti go and somebody said, "She's sailed, they got off this morning." So we nivver did see it!
Herbie	I was born at Hull. I was only two when I kem here. You see mi awdest brother, Jack – his proper name was Sanderson, mi father's fost wife, she was relationed ti Willy Woodhouse, she was a Sanderson. Oor Jack was only eighteen months awd when mi dad married mi mother. She kem frev Hull and she brought him up and he allus called 'er 'mother'. And he was in Spurn lifeboat until he was sixty. There was oor Flor husband, Sam Cross, oor Bill and oor Jack and all three of them have medals. There was a lot of us in Church choir; Stanley Stork and Arthur, he was in, and Laurie Smith, awdest lad of Bill Sunley's, Cyril and Robert Major.

George	A general trick wi' lads was to stop pumping organ. They used ti send one of us oot back way to pump her up. Awd Johnnie Walker was choirmaster, and he used to stutter and all of a sudden he would start "www-wind!" We used to do it to hear him. He was a music teacher and he used to tune pianos.
Herbie	Then they had a choirmaster. He kem frae Scarborough and he played organ and he gor a big glass mirror so he could see you. Then there was them umluks [*pieces of elderberry or hemlock made into pea-shooters*]. We used ti shoot screwed up toffee papers or cattaws [*hawthorn berries*] through 'em. You could mek whistles of 'em an' all. I'll tell you what we used ti play a lot of – 'Peggy'. It was a lartle thing sharpened at both ends and you hit it with a stick, and when you hit it at end it used ti jump up in air and then you used ti pelt it wi' stones. Another game was Ringtaws [*marbles*] in front of Jack Screets.
George	I don't know whether you remember, Herbie, but at the bottom of street to Island there used to be a shop – awd Pat's. We used ti get 'taws there and they were made of clay and painted and when you hit 'em wi' shot alley they all shot in bits. Then there was a row. Aye, you know that wall facing – there was all bashed ti bits at bottom wi' shot alleys.
	Aye, I went ti school in 1917 and I can just remember a bit of War, very little. There was that awd gun at back of wall, and Bill Waud used to fill it with black powder, then dig sods up and shuv them in, then fire that off if lifeboat had ti go off. If wind was right road it all used ti kum on top of us i' playground. You know when that went, we often used ti clear off ti South Landing and we didn't go back ti school, we used ti gan 'ome. We nivver saw owt 'cos it could be miles away by time we got there.
Herbie	When Mr. Hartley was here, mi father used ti say ti me, eight or nine years awd, "Thu'll etti go ti ebb tiday". [*To gather whelks and limpets*] And I used ti 'ave ti go and ask him and he used ti give you day off.
George	He was some school master. He got in wi' Fatty Stephenson and a few mer and he used ti clear off and leave us. He gor another idea and got Wauds to put up a great big board right across wall and he used ti chalk it all up, lessons for rest of week and we nivver saw him. Sometimes he went ti other classes but he was out a lot.

The only machines I ever saw at Haag Hopwood's *[coble maker]* – he had Blackstone Paraffin band saws and he cut planks up. He was a marvellous man. He could build a coble practically with his self. Awd Bill Sunley used ti give him a hand sometimes when he was bending 'em. And he had a great big trough full of watter and blow steam. They were larch – when it was wet like, it would bend and then he would nail them together. I've heard awd Bill say, "I've gone and helped him for years but I've nivver seen a keel laid down yit." And he nivver made two cobles alike. Anybody that wanted it seer many feet he just built it and carried on fre' there and they didn't come out just same. He had his yard and then his shed. He just had these awd set o' iron wheels to tek 'em down to North or South Landing.

Herbie   I've heard mi dad say before that, they used ti build 'em at far side of Mar *[Mere]* in a yard across there and they used to shuv 'em across Mar. When he was a young lad, him and mi Uncle Aaron and Uncle Mitt got one built and it cost 'em thirty quid. It would be a lot of money in them days. I can remember when fish was two shillings a stone. I've seen it down as low as ninepence.

Talking about two characters in the village known as 'Merry' – Tom Jameson – and Pete.

Herbie   He yance saved awd Dick Coates from choking. He'd come frae Thornwick Pub. He'd tumbled and 'itten back of his head and blood was in his mouth. If Merry hadn't been there he would have choked. A few times after, when Merry saw Dick Coates in pub, he'd say ti im, "What have you been doing tiday?" Dick would say, 'We've been sowing tonnups". And Merry said, "I hope you've sown us a row or two!

Talking about the donkeys the fishermen used, they told us most of them came from Carvills at Brid and then went on to describe the animals that pulled the charabancs that brought the visitors from Brid.

Herbie   They were great awd things almost like mules, and they were double deckers wi' open tops that they pulled. We used ti catch 'em up and ger on axle underneath and ride up ti Noth Sea. Lads at bottom of village used ti jump on back step before they went back up hill and shout 'Whip beyond'. They used to have great long whips 'cos they had four horses ti ger up them hills. They had fancy names for 'em – 'Brittania', 'Majestic' – allsorts: and all painted up, you know. If you walked ti North Landing

	in summer you could hardly walk for 'em. There weren't many cars in them days – just landaus and hoss charas. Then them red double decker buses kem.
George	Aye, 'Town, Tooth and Warrington' they had where East Riding buses were. Then Archie Robinson started with charas in the summer time and then he got on ti Green Bus Company. And then Jack Wilson, he started wi' white uns and then there was blue bus company, Johnny Atkins at bottom of Beck Hill and Berry's garage at t'other side of road.
George	There was only the garage where Freddy Atkinson was *[Monument Garage]* and buses used to stop in Flamborough. They could put one saloon in there over night. And then they started bringing double decker and that had ti go on that bit of spare land Fred got – it was next door to awd tin shed where Matt Maujer *[Major]* used ti keep his bus. They used ti kum wi' a double decker sometimes and whoever browt it had ti push bike back ti Brid. They never bothered how far they went on bike. Mi granddad was a policeman and he used ti etti walk from here ti Dottrell to see Super. And he'd be out wi' his watch, "You're a minute late", like, and he'd had ti walk while Super was on horseback! Distance was no object then.
	Looking at photos, talking about Sam Leng, the famous cliff climber, and the gathering of sea-bird eggs.
George	That's Sam Leng. Do you remember when he fell down the cliff? He was on a ledge and it brok. I was at Noth Landing when they fetched him in. He was more bothered about eggs! He had a relation with Nelson. They called him 'Trap Major' because he was press-ganged out of Flamborough inti Navy. He was fourteen and he went onto ship that Nelson was on as a powder monkey.
Herbie	I used ti come and lark wi' Laurie, he used ti have a three wheeler bike, a big un. When we were kids we used ti have ti climm up ti get on. We used ti kum here ti get water from stable tap for mi mother. You couldn't get in ti 'oose on a Monday wi' washing hanging up. There was ten of us. You couldn't dry in garden because of smoke. I allus remember when I was about seven or eight years awd, I went to call for George Mainprize and I didn't know about his father. He had fits you know and he'd died cutting a haddock up for his missus. There was me and George Gibbon and his mother. She says, "Kum in". And I had ti gan and have a leeak at him. "Touch him; he wean't hurt you."

George	I'll tell you who lived on that row there was Jack Leng next tiv Rob Leng and then Jewitt's for a while. Then there was Merry. Then there was Tarrie's right in corner 'cos I went there wi' Jack Cowling and little lad was laid on couch real badly. Jack'd been doon ti Thornwick and got a steen wheel off Lyndon wreckage and he gev little lad it ti hod. His mother says, "He can't hod that, 'oney". He died not long after, and that was pneumonia. That was Will's brother. He would be about twelve, a lot of kids died young. I had a brother and sister and they were only two and they had pneumonia. They couldn't stop it in them days. We had yan who died, they called him Sam. He was only very young though.
Herbie	Mi father was a fisherman and we used to eat a nice bit of fish. Many a time mi Dad said to me, "Ger away ti Sam Duke's and ger a bloater for mi tea." Threepence ha'penny for a bloater.
George	Mi mother used ti send mi down ti Sam Duke's there. He finished up in house next ti paper shop but before that he was at t'other end next ti passage. "Gan and fetch a pair of kippers". They were threepence and if you wanted 'Norways' they were a bit dearer – when you were talking about twenty-four a shilling in days gone by. I've heard Long Tom Woodhouse, outside their shop, talking about these trawler men up Newcastle. "I don't know what they gan ti sea for 'cos they're going back out to dump it" – 'cos they couldn't get a price for the herrings."
Herbie	There was old Crawford who used ti kum outside John Willie's with a barrow. And mi father used ti say, "Gan ti awd Crawford and fetch some herrings". And I used ti gan and he would say, "Is thoo yan o' Dickie Maujers?" I said, "Aye". And he would say, "I'll give you yan extra".
George	When I worked at Holtby's, before War, you could see 'is awd cart in Palace Avenue and when it got a bit mucky he used ti paint it again but he never cleaned bits of crab shell and all sorts off. They were all painted in. He used ti walk miles did that fella pushing that barrow.
Herbie	Our Ada used to work at Tom Stork's – awd Fanny Jane's, and they used ti 'ave some folk come called Burkins and I used to lake *[play]* with David Burkin. He was about my age. We were laking in front of Jack Screet's and ball went through winder and mi brother George says "Kum on, let's run". And me an 'im ran and David got left when Jack Screet kem out. Mrs Burkin had ti pay for winder.

When we were only about eight or nine, Fanny Jane used ti be wiv awd George Stork and she sometimes used ti say, "Just stop wiv awd fella". They used to tie him in a chair with a great awd scarf and he used to have a great awd pipe. It had a great long rubber on and she used ti gi you a box of matches and say, "Give him a light if he wants one". He used ti say, "Give us a light", and we'd strike a match and light his pipe but it always went out 'cos he hadn't wind ti keep it going. There was an awd chap used ti kum and stop wi' im, a Captain Gurney. Awd woman says to our Ada, "Me and oor Fanny Jane wants ti gan tiv a concert at Chapel tineet but I've nobody to leeak after awd man". Captain Gurney says, "I'll sit with the old man". Awd woman says, "I'll give you a couple of boxes of matches and just keep leeting his pipe". So Captain Gurney kept lighting old fella's pipe and every now and then he'd say, "Give us a leet then". Captain Gurney eventually said, "Good Lord! I've struck a full box of matches over you". And the old fella replied, "Well, that's all thu has ti deea"!

George   Fannie Jane scalded her arm and it went septic and they cut her arm about but she died. They called awd woman 'Nan Turkey' 'cos they were having fish for Christmas dinner and Nan got a bone stuck in her throat and tried to make out that they had had turkey and it was a turkey bone that had stuck in her throat! Bebe, Nan's brother was best you know. I can just remember towards end of War, zeppelins coming over here and he reckoned to be warden going round. He wasn't very gentle. He used ti start cossing and ripping, "Get them bloody lights off", if there was just a bit of light showing. We had blinds then.

Herbie   When he used ti go ti sea, he used ti gan and call awd fella up – Tom and Tich's father. If it was a bad morning he used to shout upstairs, "Thu needn't ger up this morning, bad weather. It's neea good." There was always a ham hanging up and he always had his breakfast before he went home. George Widdus used to go a lot and he had one of them crystal sets. He had four ear phones and awd fella had one set on, and George wanted them for someone else so he said to Ada, "Ger us a couple of pan scrubbers". He fastened a piece of wire between the two and swapped the awd fella for his ear phones and said to the old man, "Nu then, can you hear it?" "It's lovely", he says!

I allus remember Sam Chadwick going fishing with 'em one winter morning and it was very dark. As they began sheeting lines Sam happened to look over at Tom and he said to George, "What has your Tom gor on his head?" George laughed and asked Tom, "What has thu got on thea 'eead?" "I've got mi 'at on, what's tha think." George said, "Tek it off and have a leeak." He took it off, it was Hilda's hat and it had a great bunch of cherries on it. He'd clicked it instead of his own in dark.

Awd Niggsy Chadwick was talking to me on pier at Bridlington and telling me about an incident when he was living at Flamborough during the 2nd World War. He went up to join the other fishermen who used to congregate outside a shop, Nellie Bayes', at top end of High Street. They asked him if there had been anything important on the news. At first he said no and the conversation resumed. Then he broke in saying he'd forgotten a news item, that they were going to call in all them awd green pound notes. He says, "Dis tha know within minutes I was left with mi sen". Fishermen did not trust the banks. They preferred keeping their money at home!

Whenever the lifeboat maroons were fired men rushed up to North Landing to help launch the lifeboat and retired lifeboat men would try and get there to be helpers.

George   I remember when 'Skegness' kem ashore, I went up ti Noth Landing. Boat had gone and there's your Uncle Aaron – when he got ti Thornwick he tummelled inti gutter; he was about buggered. Matt Duke an' all, he was same. I don't think he landed as far as Thornwick. By God, awd men they were. I don't know whether it was same night but there was awd Charlie Overy and Harold Cross fether *[father]* fighting ower a jacket. *[You had to have a jacket provided by the Lifeboat Institution before you could claim money as a helper.]* And Will Overy, Charlie's son was going to step in and somebody says, "You let 'em alone, let 'em sort it out." They had a bang or two then gave it up. For all that and what would they get. Nowt.

Herbie   I think they got about fourteen quid if they were on lifeboat. It was a rum old night. I went wi' mi dad for the rocket cart and he says ti me, "Keep an eye on the lifeboat. Tell us where it goes." I says, "He's still in Scarborough lights". *[Meaning the lifeboat was far enough out to sea to keep the lights of Scarborough in view.]* And mi dad says, "He'd better stop there 'cos I tell thu what, it'll be breaking from Sanwick Brigg right away ti Filey Brigg".

George	It was stupid ever going in within a quarter of a mile 'cos she was laid ower and it warn't as if she was under cliff. No wonder they couldn't get rocket lines across tiv it. I went up night after and sea was still breaking ower her. Biggest come ashore here I ever saw was 'Radiant'. She was laid right away under Bempton Cliff there. Teddy Fell had like a dredger and he used ti dredge up coal there. They reckon she had 5,000 ton of coal aboard. She was Italian.
Herbie	Mi Dad and oor Bill and them used ti gan and get coal off her when it was fine – and Matt Duke and Jack.

Looking at a photograph of a group of men in front of the Lighthouse, Mr Nordass remarked that he'd never been up the lighthouse although he'd stood against it hundreds of times. Mr Major used to cliff climb for sea-bird eggs and told about the two different methods used by the rope men to guide the climbers. One used to like the climber to start gathering the eggs as they made their descent. Another insisted the climber went to the bottom and gathered eggs as he was hauled up.

Herbie	Awd 'Hairy Jack' wanted you to gather eggs on way down. Jack Major used ti shuv you straight away ti bottom. I kept running and I kem right down onto a ledge, I could have jumped down onti gravel. That's where I got that double yoked egg so we gev it to Tommy Stork instead of keeping it and blowing it ourselves. Tommy said it did tek some blowing! We used to eat maybe two at a time. Mi mother used ti keep geese you know. She used ti run about fotti *[forty]* and send 'em to Seamer market at Christmas. She used to keep one back for hersen. That's how she used ti mek her money wi' geese. When she wasn't sitting eggs, she would say, "You'd better get them geese eggs itten". So we were used ti big eggs. One of her family, Joss, was killed climbing. He was only wearing an ordinary cap stuffed wi' grass and he gor hit ower 'eead wi' falling rock. If it had been like today there would have been safety equipment. I used ti 'av a tin hat; you need yan. I was only yance when I was really frightened. I'd getten doon to these eggs and I was underneath an overhang and I heard a row like thunder. Looked up and there was these rocks came ower me, I should think there was a ton or more stuff. I didn't know what ti do, whether ti come out or gan on.

Discussion took place about a picture of the Church in 1760. There was a road going down through the church-yard. There was also a door which is no longer there. It was two hundred years before anything was done about a tower. Another picture was of a boat in 1870, a relative of Mr Major's had been on it for 25 years.

George   I can just remember sailing cobles before they got engines. I used ti go wi' Tant Fell. He used ti go up David Lane and collect awd asses and tek 'em doon when they were landing. Teddy Fell and George Otch were about fost two ti 'ave engines – Edenrood *[the name of the engine]* One of 'em cut starn away to shove it through and tie a bit of wood and pop it through and hang it on.

Looking at more photographs, one of Mr. Major's father.

George   They used ti wear seal-skin hats a lot at one time, 'cos awd George Stork had one. He used ti sit out there when he was dressed up and he had his seal-skin hat on -- Awd Pod – he did. They'd get 'em off markets mebbe in them days.

Herbie   Mi mother used ti knit mi guernsey's, and she knit when she was eighty. She knit me two, this one I'm wearing and a fawn one.

George   I remember sitting wi' George Cross, cobbler, whilst he whittled leather up to make sea boots. "Mr Cross, how much do you think these'll cost?" Mr Cross, "I don't know. A pound a pair." All leather thigh boots. That was a lot of money in them days. Fishermen had to work a good bit to get that.

Herbie   Aye, I can remember awd Tant in that shop. He used ti mek 'em. Mi father used ti get 'em off him and they were five pund then. They used ti wrinkle up. They used ti keep fish livers ti rub 'em with and rub 'em wi' linseed oil. They kept 'em warm and dry an' all.

Margaret   Could some of the fishermen swim?

Herbie   Mi father couldn't but mi Uncle Bill, im that drowned at South Sea, could swim like a fish. But as they were taking rudder off, preparing to land, he slipped and rudder hit him on the head. He'd have rubber boots on, and they'd mebbe a bit slippery. When a pleasure boat kem out of harbour they saw a body on the surface but they had so many people on board they daren't pick it up. It was him.

Mr Nordass and Mr Major discussed the difference between kittiwakes eggs and gull eggs. Both agreed that scout eggs tasted better as they were whiter and their yokes were deeper.

	Kittiwakes had blue outer and paler yokes, more like a duck egg. They also discussed the price paid for rare eggs by collectors.
Herbie	Highest we ever getten, oor George and me, was seven quid a piece. We used ti keep 'em back and a bloke used ti kum called Rickaby and buy them. And old Luckton as well. One evening Mr Renshaw, Mr Luckton and Mr Rickaby came to see the eggs and were bidding against each other. *[A long time afterwards Mr Major saw Mr Rickaby and asked him if he still collected eggs. "Oh no", he said, "I sold them to a museum for £23,000."]*
	Fishermen were very superstitious even when playing cricket. A Flamborough side was on its way to play Nafferton and took a short cut down Well Lane in Bridlington. Two nuns were coming up the lane. Tom Woodhouse, nicknamed 'Long Tom' who was married to Nellie Bayes, said,"We might as well turn back now 'cos we shall lose today." They went to the game and lost!
Herbie	He was a rum lad was Tom, he was an' all. It didn't matter tiv us 'cos we gor a good tea wi' strawberries. We used ti stand outside their shop lots of times and he used ti get on talking and we had some laughs. He was very dry. Once when we were doon in cricket field, he kem doon and we were practising. It warn't often he kem doon. Do you remember Bernard Jennis? His father had that shop – he had bat. Three on us used ti tek it in turns bowling tiv 'im. He wanged one ball and it hit Tom and Tom turned round and said, "Bugger it all, lad, what's tha doing?" Then nivver took ni mer notice. When we built him his house up there, ye know, Tommy Leng was painting. Tom kem and then Nellie kem and then George Waud kem. And he says, "Noo then, I want ti know, where did thu want wardrobes and cupboards?" "I should like a wardrobe in here" – and she wanted one in t'other bedroom. Tom just looks at her and he says, "Hang 'ard, Nellie, where the hell are we gahyin ti put bed, that's all I'm worried about?" And when they'd gone Tommy Leng says to Tom "Why folks in Flamborough allus had great families?" "Good lord, your own common sense ought to tell you that." "Why should it?" "That's all they had ti deea." Tom said, "I've just been down to George Waud's to see about having the bungalow built and what's thu think?" "Why I deean't know." "He says, "What sort does thu want?" "I want two bedrooms, yan or two other things." "Why", he says, "Tom," he says, "It'll cost thu a couple of thousand pounds." He says, "I don't want a bloody mansion!"

When Skella, a relation of Tom's, got his arm off – caught in a pot tow *[thick ropes]* when they were hauling up crab pots at sea, with a winch, I says ti Tom, "How did thu come on when it happened?" Tom says, "I was fed up of leeaking at it. I was sat on one pot and he was sat on next pot ti me and he was leeaking straight at me." *[Mr. Woodhouse's relation was treated. He recovered and found work on the harbour despite the loss of his arm.]*

Jenny Pinder

Jenny was born in Flamborough and worked in a number of jobs in the village. She is best remembered for her time in the Post Office.

Jenny   I was born in Flamborough, in Tower Street, in a cottage there. There was Jack, Maud, Gladys, Ted, Albert, myself and Kitty – seven. We lived in Tower Street, number five. There's two and then there's an opening and then there was – do you remember Harry Hall that used to be a coalman? Well, he was at that one – he lived with his sister there, and then Traves's. And then Vic Pinder was there and then Alfred Freeman's mother was there. Annie Sunley – they lived next door for quite a while and then they bought that house of that old lady, Mrs Duke, opposite. There was an old lady, Miss Spriggs, she was from London; I think she was relative of someone that used to live at the other side of the Church. And then there was old Mrs Tunnicliffe, then Tom Traves. So that was our little lot. Then there was that little old cottage where Lockwoods used to live. And there was that little alleyway up where Nell Sugar used to live by the Seabirds. Alfred Nicholson and his father used to live up there – oh, they were the first cottage and then Nell Sugar, as they called her, and then Sawdon – he had first cottage. Robsons lived in one of those cottages before you come to the Seabirds and then Waines's were next door to the Seabirds, and Tuff was next. Then there was a passage way and then Barclay's, and then that other cottage before you come to Bailey's – that changed hands a few times, but there was Bailey's then there were Dowse. Who was in that bay winder?

Rita	Alice Chapman's.
Jenny	Aye, that's right, and that was that side of Tower Street.
Margaret	So how big was your cottage, Jenny?
Jenny	When we were on the street, we opened the door and it was straight into the little sitting room, and then behind that was the kitchen. Mind you we had no water in – we had to come into Tower Street. We got water from that tap in the street, opposite that little opening where you come through by the Village Hall. You know, the opening by that gate near Peace cottage. We had to carry water from there, so it was really hard times, you know – it was time they did something. They were putting it in. Traves's lived next door and Mrs Stevenson, some relation to Harry Hall the coalman, they got together and said, well, seeing that water was coming in so near, we'd put together and have it put in. So there's a loose tap outside.
Margaret	That was drinking water and everything, washday and all?
Jenny	Aye, that's right. The three of us in the yard put all together and paid for it to be brought in, I mean it's a good walk from them cottages to that tap, so that's what we did.
Margaret	We were talking to Hetty Mainprize last week and she said how many there was in their cottage over the Green, and we said, "Where did they all sleep?" They were big families in small cottages.
Jenny	We had two bedrooms upstairs and an attic. Our lads, three of them, used to sleep in the front bedroom, and we had a little kitchen, and we had a little old bed 'cos we were only small, one of us, and then Mum and Dad. In summer the lads used to go up into the attic and we could spread out a bit that way.
Margaret	What did your father do, then?
Jenny	Oh he was on the land. When they first came, they were in Bridlington. I think he worked for the Corporation – gardens. He loved animals and he missed them. He came home one day and he said, "We're moving". He'd got a job at Woodhouse's at bottom of Croft's Hill. And mi mother, "Well what are you going there for, what are you doing there, they have no gardens have they?" He said, "No, it was farm work, animals". So that was it. Mother said that she rued every hair of her head that they went there. It was lovely up in Old Town, nearly opposite the Priory, just a comfortable little cottage like all of them. I mean it was really hard work in Tower Street,

Margaret	You would still have earth lavatories out the back?
Jenny	Oh yes, there wasn't water closets. No, they were hard days for work, and yet they were tough, weren't they. I can see poor Miss Barclay there, going round, and if you where walking and didn't speak to her and were near, she would give you a real dab on your shoulder. And then Crofton, he used to go to Chapel, it was nice and near, he would hear footsteps and he would say, "Who's that?" and you didn't have to say anything, you'd just have to touch him and, "Aw, it's one of Pinders, who is it?". He knew if you had a sore or anything. He used to feel you and say, "Oh, it's so-and-so". I can hear him singing now; he loved a good sing song didn't he? He used to go a lot to the Primitive Chapel 'cos it was near, you see.
	We went to Church but we were such a long time without a vicar. I don't know who it was, would it be after MacLean went, we seemed as if we were a long time. And mother said to us, "Now then I tell you what, you aren't going to stop at home on a Sunday. You've always been used to going to Church and you can't go to Church now, there's no one to take you; you go to Chapel". And we went to the Primitive Chapel – that was nearest. Well, we didn't like it 'cos he shouted so much, they were 'Ranters'. The fishermen used to sing loud and I mean they kept you entertained; you were doing something, even if you were just saying your ABC's. We left there and we went to Wesleyan Chapel. It was a bit further away, still we went. Bessie Readhead used to go there 'cos she used to go to Church, you see, and as there was no Church you went there. I always remember at piece time, when you were saying your pieces at Anniversary, she was sat at the end and she got up out of her seat, did Mrs Readhead, and she says, "Hey lad move a bit further in, you'll knock our Bessie over". And you know everybody was looking and laughing, but she was sticking up for their Bessie.
Margaret	Do you mean old Mrs Readhead from down by Church, who used to get on the buses and sort everybody out?
Jenny	Yes, she did. Poor old Bessie!
Margaret	Did you have much to do with them down that end, Jenny, or not?
Jenny	No, we kept to our own end.
Margaret	What did you do for games? Did you have much playtime as kids?

Jenny	Well, yes but, "You don't go out of this yard". We had to play in the yard because there was such a lot of, well I don't know what you would say, tramps and that going about, and they were frightened they would coax us away. But no, we had a lovely time. We had to make our own enjoyment, skipping, hopscotch, and playing marbles and that.
Margaret	How did you get on for clothes – did your mother make them or what? A family like that it would take some clothing.
Jenny	Mother wasn't any good at cutting out and doing that. There was our Jack, Maud and Gladys, Ted and Albert, and then there's five years different between our Albert and me, so you see he'd started school and going alright when I was born. And then there was only eighteen months difference between Kitty and me, so we got hand-me-downs.
	You'll have heard of her – Mrs Thurlow, a relation of Mina Stork. Well once a year, they used to give the girls who went to Sunday School, a skirt. You couldn't call it a kilt, it had a top on and then you had a jumper over it and just pleats, maybe two pleats or something like that. Well, she used to make those and she used to make the boys shirts for being present at school, you see. She was a good hand at doing all that because there wasn't any dress-makers or anything in the Village. Mother was no good at making things. Mind'st you she had a machine and could run up all pillowcases and sheets and such things as that and make patches and put them on. But when it came to cutting out and making things, she wasn't any good. If she gave her mind to it she could; too many things to do. But we were alright because our Maud and Gladys used to make ours and they did knitting as well. And they also did for Annie Sunley 'cos they used to live next door to us at one time – George Sunley's sister. If they knitted us a jumper they had to knit one for Annie. Oh, it's amazing how they used to help each other, didn't they?
	I mean when Sunleys lived next door to us they had a little boy Ernest, and I don't know what it was, whether it was pneumonia or what it was but anyway Mother used to go in at night and stay the night and sit by him and help him that way. They helped each other and never saw anybody stuck or anything.
Margaret	What did you do when you started work? Where did you and your sisters work?

Jenny	Well, let's see. Our Maud used to work at Readheads down at Manor House: they used to take in visitors in the summer and she worked there. And our Gladys used to work at Wilkinson's, that's a farm. Go through Church yard and on the left, not the first house – that was Kirby's and then it was Wilkinson's – down near where Sudderby's lived. Sudderby's lived next door to them.
Rita	Grove Farm, where Robert Hall lives.
Jenny	Billy Collins used to have his horse and like a covered up thing, like gypsies used to have. And I don't know whether he had a bell he used to ring as he was coming through the Village to let us know he was coming, and he used to go into Bridlington. He used to have a notebook and a pen for writing down what people wanted. He's fetched all sorts of things. .Then there was Screeton's, Mr Screeton and his son, Gilbert they called him, and he had a pony – it was white. Perhaps he would go a little bit later than Billy Collins, catch customers that way.
Margaret	Where did your brothers work then?
Jenny	When my brothers left school, they were mad on horses. Didn't bother with cows or anything; it was horses. And our Ted, first job I think it was, he had was down at Carr Farm. I forget what our Albert did. When he was at school he didn't do much schooling. The schoolmaster sent the man they called 'kid catcher': he had to find out why wasn't so-and-so at school. Albert used to do that. There was a man older than Albert that used to go like, but the school master wanted to know there and then, sort of thing.
Margaret	Didn't they used to be a bit handy with a ruler or something at school?
Jenny	Oh yes, it was like a cane and Miss Chadwick, she used to have a book and she used to poke you in the back, "Stop that talking, stop that talking". Looking back you think, by jove, what did we learn?
Rita	Who was teaching at the school besides Sally Bayes and Miss Chadwick?
Jenny	Miss Chapman – she was there; Mrs Kind, she used to do the infants, she had a son, I don't know whether they were separated or if she had a husband or not. I never heard anything about him, but she was always addressed as Mrs Kind. Mr Potts was deputy headmaster – he was under Mr Ether. Who was before

	him? Oh, Mr Rawnsley, Sally Bayes, Mrs Kind, Miss Chapman, she used to have a class didn't she?
Rita	Oh yes, she was at Flamborough School; she was here a long time.
Margaret	What did you do after school? Did you have any playtime or did you have to go home to bits of jobs or what?
Jenny	No, we had playtime in the morning and playtime in the afternoon. I don't know how long maybe a quarter of an hour, I think. We went home for our dinner, twelve o'clock and back at one, half past in summertime I think. It was a bit later in summer, because we used to finish at half past three. In summer it was four o'clock. You see they had to get that time in that we spent at lunchtime.
Margaret	Where did you start work, Jenny?
Jenny	I'm not sure, I think it was at Mrs Woodcock's, down at Hartendale, because Rex was there and I used to play with him, take him down to South Landing and that.
Margaret	Did you go on the beach much in those days or not?
Jenny	No, Mother was one for keeping us round about home so she had her eyes on us.
Margaret	Were the boys kept in as well?
Jenny	Oh no, you see our Albert was five years older than I was and he'd left school, he was a man. If there was anything going wrong, "Albert Pinder's who did it". Any windows broken, "Oh Albert Pinder was there". Oh yes, he got blamed for everything, just devilment really.
Margaret	How long did you work at the Post Office, Jenny?
Jenny	Mr and Mrs Artley were there when I finished. Mr and Mrs Woodhouse were there when I started, they were there a long time; and then I was with Taylor Fussey. Mr Cross was there before Taylor Fussey.
Rita	Will Cross, yes, because Taylor would come out of the Army and he went back to Danish Bacon but not for very long before they bought that.
Jenny	Yes, they weren't there very long, about twelve months or something like that. Of course Mr Woodhouse used to say he was three years old when he first went there.
Rita	Were May and Lily Woodhouse relations of Woodhouses at the Post Office?

Jenny	Now then, they would be cousins. It would be like another generation.
Rita	They lived at the farm at bottom of Crofts Hill; May went to live at Chantry Cottage. Chantry Cottage used to be thatched, mi Mum could remember it thatched but I can't.
Jenny	I know when we went to school, on the Green, there used to be that boat that was turned over. "Hey what you doing in there?" she used to say. Oh, she was awful. My, we'd go a yard nearer this boat and it was nice to go behind if you were playing hide and seek. And I remember in Miss Chadwick's time, when she was a teacher, she had a little dog, a terrier. It was white with black markings and they always used to keep it fastened up. But if it had a chance, someone leaving the gate open, it would be out and it would come straight to the school to Miss Chadwick's. With me being small I always used to have my peg on the lowest one. I don't know what happened, whether Miss Chadwick went out into the porch or what, but this dog had taken hold of my coat and pulled it off the peg and it was in ribbons. Well, she was so upset, Miss Chadwick, so she said, "Whose coat was it?" I went to look and it was mine. Well, mother didn't mind so much 'cos I was getting too big for it and Mrs Thurlow did sewing and that. Well she was making me a coat out of one of the other lasses' coats. Well, poor Miss Chadwick didn't know what to do. I think she gave me three shillings towards another one. I thought then, 'By, what will three shillings buy?' After that they kept the dog fastened up. Someone had been in and left the gate open and it knew where to come.

When you come to think of it we had to make our own fun: sometimes it was really good and sometimes it was painful. |
| Margaret | Did you ever go to any of the dances at the school? |
| Jenny | Yes, we could go if our lads went – if Ted and our Albert were there. But our mother liked to know who we were going with, and if we were coming straight home, so we didn't really. We used to like to go and do the dancing at school, you know, 'Girl's Joy' and 'Gathering Peas Cods'. Miss Chadwick always used to take that dancing and Miss Bayes used to take a group, you know, all in one sort of thing, like we were dancing with someone else. In fact there used to be some photographs in school of Daisy Langton and that group. We didn't have many toys at home but you had more fun when there was a family than when there was just one. |

Rita	Did you play games at home on winter nights, like snakes and ladders or anything like that? Dominoes?
Jenny	Yes, but, "Look at clock, time you were putting those things away". Bedtime was seven o'clock. When we got older we were allowed to stay up later till eight o'clock; when we reached our teens it was nine o'clock. "Don't go far away", but we were never ones to be allowed to play out in winter time, when it was dark. We could go in Tower Field 'cos they could go down our garden and see where we were. We used to think that they were strict and that, and spoilt your fun, but afterwards you think that I'm pleased they were like that.

We were a long time before we got electric in the Village, weren't we? |
| Rita | We didn't have it when I was a kid you know, it was a great event when it came. |
| Jenny | We had two lamps. This one had a globe round it, but the other one was all brass. They were wedding presents mother had been given. We had one for the room and one for the kitchen.

[Jenny showed us some tapestries embroidered by her grandmother in the 1800's] |
Margaret	When you were little or in your teens did you do embroidery and that sort of thing or just knitting?
Jenny	Yes, I did a cushion cover in black. Granddad was a schoolmaster at Bempton School and his wife was a teacher at needlework, you see. And when she got married and settled down, she started with a family and she couldn't get enough children; she had a lovely family, and the only person she lived with was mi mother. Mother had all the responsibility of her and all the others, sisters and brothers were having a good time sort of thing. I can just remember her living in Tower Street. Mother had this tapestry rolled up in a bit of paper in a drawer and somebody said, "We aren't gonna have that stuck in a drawer", and framed it.
Rita	I have Auntie Ginny's and Auntie Annie's when they were at Flamborough School. They stuck newspaper behind them you know, to seal them in, and it's the actual date of when it was done, 1840 something.
Jennie	1849. It was Mother made this one and she had it rolled up in a paper in a drawer and we got it framed. It has the alphabet, writing and printing and then, 'Kate Hall, Bempton School, Yorks'.

Rita	When you got into Sally Bayes's you made pillow cases or nightgowns.
Jenny	And camisoles! They were to sell as well. You'd prick your finger and all blood on the thing. Poor Miss Chadwick.
Margaret	What did the boys do when you did that?
Jenny	Gardening. I know once the gardens they had was down at the side of the Church, next to the white house. A bungalow's built there now I think. Where did they go to after that, was it Carter Lane?
Rita	There some down where Priscilla's house was, back of Allison Lane, that was when Hartley was there. You see Hartley's garden went right across and part of that was the school garden, so he could keep his eyes on them and nip in for a cup of tea you see.
Jenny	There was some nice things that you made and if you wanted them you could buy them, and if you were waiting for the material to come in, you'd take a bit of your own sewing to do. I think what they sold, the money went into funds to buy material for other things.
Margaret	Church would be a lot different to now wouldn't it?
Jenny	Oh yes it was. Our Albert would be about twelve and George Waud would be about our Albert's age and they'd been fooling about Sunday School. And the vicar came with his foot and kicked him, missed the other lad but our Albert caught it right in his eye. Oh, the vicar was upset. He came up home twice that day to see how he was. The scar was there all through his life. Mother kept saying to him, "You must have been doing something wrong to have got that". No, George Waud had dropped a hymn book, our Albert bent down to get it and it was as he was getting up that the vicar let fly and caught him. Both our lads were in the choir. Our Albert and I think it was Bill Bayes got together at pumping the organ, I think they got five shillings a year.
Margaret	You would go on the Sunday School trips to Scarborough did you?
Jenny	No, we didn't, Church never went to Scarborough. Primitives and Wesleyan's did. I think we had tea and games. They did later on but we didn't at the beginning. When we first started Sunday School, we used to have games in one of Foster's fields. We had this tea and then we had games. Then I don't know if it was at the beginning of the year but the boys got the shirts and the girls got

a kilt sort of thing with white top as I told you; they were navy blue.

My father worked on the land and got thirty shillings a week.

Margaret	That wouldn't be much with seven children and himself and your mother to keep, and rent for the house and coal. It wasn't that dear but it was all expenses, and paraffin for your lamps.
Jenny	Oh yes, that's right. There was no child's allowance or anything. They used to make ends meet the best way they could.
Rita	Did you keep your own chickens?
Jenny	Yes, and rabbits and pigs; two, no more than two, if they an increase then they were sold. In the kitchen, there used to be these big hooks where they used to hang the sides of bacon. They were in salt for so many weeks and then they were all dried down and then they were all hung up in the ceiling so that we always had a bit of bacon or ham to cut at.
Rita	Did you do your own curing or did someone come round to do it?
Jenny	No, they did their own curing. Mr. Woodhouse used to come round and do the killing, Willie Woodhouse. Then we had chickens as well, you see, for eggs.
Margaret	You'd have a garden, had you?
Jenny	Yes, it wasn't a big one in Tower Street. There was two strips with a path in between and then Traves's had the same. We had chickens on half and then we had a little place where we had pigs; then all along with vegetables. But before Mum and Dad went to live in Tower Street, they were down at the bottom of Crofts Hill. Our Albert was nearly drowned in that pond. There's a big flag over the guttering that runs into this pond, one stream coming down Crofts Hill and the other one there. Well on this big flag that covers a guttering Don Wiles, who used to go down to play, and they used to have bits of stick and wood and stick a feather in it for a ship. And they used to get near the guttering and it would go underneath this flag into the pond. Whether they'd been arguing or whether Don said his was racing or what I don't know, but anyway he pushed Albert and he went in. There was a poor old man, I can't remember his name, coming down Crofts Hill in a pony and trap and he saw what had happened and he tried his best to get out of the trap quick because he'd seen him go down twice and he thought, 'I shall never get him'. Poor old

man, he hurt his leg, he ran as best he could and just grabbed him as he was going down for the last time. He was so upset he carried him across to the house, you know where Kingston's used to live, and Mother wondered what had happened so he said, "He just slipped in and I happened to be coming down Croft's Hill and I caught him". Well, Mother had to strip him all and put him all dry clothes on and that. He didn't want to play out, he stayed in and he laid on the settee. Well, at night time that poor old man came down, "I've just come to see how that poor bairn is". So Mother said, "Come in like", and he did and he talked to Albert and said, "You won't go near that pond again will you?" Poor old Albert. At one end there was a big flag over the ditch that ran into the pond and it was on this flag that Albert was standing. It was deep enough to drown anybody, as it goes further back it was deeper still.

Frank Woodhouse

Son of a joiner, Frank was born into a very large family and worked on farms his whole life. He is a very keen gardener and still dresses heavy horses for competition.

Frank   We lived in Back Street Hill. As far as I know we were born there. Mi father was born at back-a-church, at Sunnyside Cottage down there. There was ten or twelve of us in the first house. Lizzie was oldest, I was next, then Dick, he's at Kirbymoorside, then Arnold, Arthur and Sam; then Doris, Marion, Barbara, oh, and Dennis. Dennis is youngest lad. And we only had two bedrooms upstairs, but they med the front room a bedroom. The bedrooms were very low and we had to bend down in them as we got taller. And of course when we were fourteen we had ti get under somebody else's table, fost three or four of us. You know we couldn't all stop at home as we were all getting bigger. They kept having young children and I went up to "Ocean View" when I was fourteen.

Wilkinson's had "Ocean View". I had twelve pounds a year. Your relation was up there then, Mr Kingston. His nickname was Dass – Dass Kingston. He was bullocky. There was five of us living in. I don't know how many hours a week, but five or six hours Saturday and Sundays. The horsemen were very lucky, but I was with Mr Kingston among cows. They were lucky, they could knock off Saturday dinnertime and turn their horses out in summertime, but we had ti go back ti milk like Saturday afternoons and Sundays. It was a stable lamp job and if you didn't follow down with waggoner, Henry Carter, you were left

~ 304 ~

in dark. You only had one stable lamp and you all had ti get up together and get out tigither and we used ti go inti breakfast at twenty to seven.

I went to "Ocean View", and we had to be in by nine o'clock every night, up at six o'clock in a morning, ten to twelve hours a day, and there was no dinner hour. You got your dinner and then you had to be up on top throwing down straw for night. That was five days a week. Then you had to go back Saturday afternoons and Sundays to milk. As I said, the horsemen were lucky. It was John Longden, Henry Carter and Tommy Loft in those days among horses, and Arthur Taylor, he was shepherd – he was alright in summertime as well.

Rita	How many horses did they have? 'Cos I remember going to play at the farm, and we stood in the middle of the road to stop the traffic as the horses came down the farm road and across the main road and into the paddock at the other side.

Frank   We had about ten. We always had a young one or two. Henry Carter and John Longden had six at one side, and Tommy Loft had four at the other side of stable. I had a year up there and then I went down to Glaves Foster's. Beacon Hill Farm. I had £14 a year there.

Mr Foster weren't married then – we had a housekeeper from Driffield, Betsy. Do you remember Joe Sterricker? He used to walk frae Brid every morning and he got there for breakfast. Bob Drake was there, me and Bob an' Joe, 'cos it was Martimuss in those days, you had ti wait, 23rd November. You had to wait for your money once a year.

Margaret   You only got it once a year? How did you manage all year then?

Frank   Why mi mother used ti give us sixpence or a shilling a week. That's all you had, like, and you used ti pay for your clothes at Martimuss. You had a fortnight off at what you called Martimuss Hirings – of course you didn't get paid for it. But I stayed on for another year. And Mr Foster got married and we came home 'cos Mrs Foster didn't want us in 'cos housekeeper left. And we came home ti live till Martimuss again. He got married in the June. Then I left, as Mr Foster was packing up by then, and I went ti Buckton Hall for £18 a year. That was like in fourth year. There was seven of us in there and we had £18 a year, but I was among horses up there, and you packed up Saturday dinnertimes and you had Saturday afternoons off. And of course it was the same, only one stable lamp there. And it was concrete steps to go up to bed there and concrete floors. There was no wood floors and no carpets.

Rita   Was that in the main house? Was it at the back?

Frank   Yes, down road and round to back facing west. Big kitchen, and we sat on forms.

Rita   And who was the farmer?

Frank   Mr Marr was there then. Tractors came out in that year and overtime came out 10d *[ten old pence]* an hour. So they packed up with horses and started with tractors. And we all very near left at Martimass 'cos there was only two or three horses for turnips. They were very good there, we could stay in at night. But on some farms you had to get out as soon as you'd had your tea. If you had been ploughing all day and your coat was wet through and you'd nowhere to dry it, we used to throw them over backs of horses that had been in all day and not working, to air them. You couldn't tek 'em inti house, in some cases like. Then I went to Marton and I got a good rise, £28! That was with Horace Waines 'cos I did bigger jobs; I was further on, carrying corn, 18 stones, all day long.

Margaret You were at Horace's when I was at Flamborough Station.

Frank   Yes, we had our fields up there and I used to wait for trains coming. I had only one lamp and if you were late you had to manage in dark, and, of course, there was always pranks going on like, not in badness like.

Margaret Such as?

Frank   Why, Herbert Good – can you remember him? He was wi' me frae Flamborough. When they kem in at night, if they had any money like, one lad was frae Filey, they would throw your socks under somebody else's bed and next morning you couldn't find your socks, and of course waggoner had gone down wi' stable lamp and you were scratching. You couldn't find your socks and when you got downstairs he'd gone out, and you were in the dark again as there was no electric. Same as when you went ti stable, carrying stable lamp ti go across foldyard.

Then it was starting ti fade out so we kem home and I went down ti Rex Stiles', then I went back ti Horace's. Then I kept swapping. I went ti Hunmanby when I left Buckton Hall. Then I went ti Horace's. Then I went back ti Burrell's and then I went back ti Horace's. I went back three times in ten years. Always with horses.

But that year I was at Hunmanby, 1939 winter, very bad winter, woss than we've ever had, woss 'n '47. There were some horses we never had out for twelve weeks. You couldn't see some roads or hedges or anything. When we lived in at Hunmanby we couldn't come down drive, you couldn't get up Hunmanby Road. You just had ti mek for Hunmanby Station. That's how it was for weeks, and we used ti go with a horse apiece on horse back wi' shopping bag each and go across. It carried you like you nivver saw hedge nor anything, and that's how we used ti get food inti house like. Those were what they called the "good old days".

Margaret	Now, what were you saying about when you lived up there, you were head to tail and you used to come down here for a bag of coal?
Frank	Yes, when we were all at home I never knew mi father have more than three pounds a week and he was head joiner at Wauds. Rent was only 1s10d *[one shilling and ten pence]* and a bag of coal was only 1s10d so of course when mi mother had 1s10d we used ti come knocking at door here. "Can you bring us a bag of coal?" Sometimes one of us would tek trolley or an old pram, so we hadn't ti bother 'em, like, and we used to tek it in turns.

That winter, 1940, mi dad was in hospital at Scarborough – he had cararacts at back off his eyes, you know. And we used to tek it in turns ti go wi'' mi mother, ti go and see him. It was United buses to Scarborough and we used ti go ti Brid and change ti get on United buses ti go ti Scarborough. Snow was piled up as high as double-decker buses on sides of road. Them that was out of work cut all snow then. Sometimes Johnnie Traves used ti tek us *[taxi]*. He used ti charge mi mother 2s6d to Scarborough Hospital – you had ti go right through Scarborough. Aye, it was a bad winter. They were cutting snow from Christmas and it was still there in June in some places. We used ti go on top of double-decker. They were new fangled and you couldn't see over snow at sides of road on bottom deck. They had to start cutting from a board on ground then cut solid steps ti throw snow up from one ti t'other. We had ti get home when we could, sometimes once a fortnight, it was all you could do.

Margaret	Was that the winter Laurie said the truck couldn't get up and down here *[Greenside]* for weeks on end.

Frank	I should say so – '39 to '40. 1947 was bad but '39 was worse.
Margaret	When there was so many of you at home how on earth did your mother manage to feed you all?
Frank	We had a big garden which went through to the High Street, and when we left school we had to go to somebody else's table. As soon as Dick left he went ti Kelk, and Arnold went ti Dick Hood's, and Arthur went ti Harold Waines' at Bempton. First we went out and others stopped at home. We used to have our dinners at twelve o'clock, soup and whatever, and potatoes.
Margaret	Was it sheep's head broth? Laurie used to say he thought every sheep had two heads in those days.
Frank	We used ti live on a lot of old hens in those days and we used ti sit outside back door plucking 'em before we went ti school. I got so stalled of 'em that I don't eat chicken today. We used ti keep about fifty old hens and we had at least one a week. Mrs Major next door always used to send us some pudding. She always did more than they needed, rice pudding, spotted dick and custard. They had their pudding before their savoury, so we could have what was left.
Joyce	There were some good neighbours in those days.
Frank	Oh aye, and Ada and Edie, the Major girls, used ti come in on a Saturday night to help mi mother bath the small uns. Anne was youngest, but some of them were hired out. Dick was out but Herbert and George were at home. There was about ten or eleven of them *[Majors family]*.
Margaret	Was Albert Major one of them?
Rita	No, he was one of Matt Majors.
Frank	There was a lot of them, wasn't there?
Rita	There was at least seven of them because there were seven in the band. There was George, Dorothy, Christie, Bessie, Albert, Robert...
Joyce	Their Dad was in the band as well.
Frank	They had an old charabanc and they all used to get in at the back. We hadn't owt to go to Brid with. We handed all our money to mi mother up till we were twenty-one – she gev us some back. We nivver answered our parents back, you daren't; nivver talked at table and we never had a drink of tea till we'd finished, nor mi sisters or brothers. Mi mother would nivver have got owt ti eat, she'd have been pouring tea all the time.

Margaret	Did your mother bake bread and that?
Frank	Aye, and then Doris and Marion used ti help and you had ti eat everything that was on table or you were up "wooden hill" and "you'll eat it tomorrow", there was no picking and choosing. As I say, we had a big garden at home and then we got another garden for a few years. We all helped mi dad.
Margaret	Did you have to do much before you went to school in a morning?
Frank	Yes, plucking chickens and that. We used ti help mi mother wash up, do potatoes and things. We used ti tek it in turns. Sam got butchering and he used ti do a bit and we all mucked in, you had to. When we were at home we used to go down to North Landing and help fishermen to pull cobles up and they'd give you a codling or two, and then we used ti walk ti Bempton on a night and sell a bit of fish, 2d or 3d, ti help. We all used ti go in turn and folks we knew we used ti ave a cup of tea with before we came back. Then we used ti sell postcards. We used ti get 'em from Redheads. I think they were ½d and we sold 'em for a penny or something like that. And fost three of us, one used ti go ti North Landing, one ti South Landing and the other ti Lighthouse. We used ti spell it like – him that had been ti Lighthouse went South or North. And then we had mi Uncle Bill lived with us for a long time. Well, he looked after us, Crutch; do you remember him?
Rita	Yes, I do.
Frank	He was mi mother's brother. He had nowt in winter and he used to do a bit for Bayes tekking fish, he sat on rulley going ti Brid,7.30 at night. He allus had two pockets. He always cut our hair, straight off and round with shears. We used to have a bit left in front, everybody had it like that, to keep it free of lice. If you didn't keep still, he'd give you a good old clout.
Rita	I used to be terrified of him when I was small, because he couldn't half land out with that crutch.
Frank	He broke his legs three times, once in two places at once and the other once. I know there was twice it was accidents, but once he'd had ower much to drink. Times were hard in those days, weren't they, for everybody but especially fishermen. There was no radio to tell you where ti go for fish and that, or compasses like there is today. I nivver had a car till I was 37 or 38. We had ti mek do with a bike, couldn't afford a car.

Margaret	Did you learn to drive tractors?
Frank	Oh yes, when horses went out. I was at Stiles' when horses went, I was foreman. We had one or two horses still. I nivver drove at Marton, only odd times 'cos they kept horses. But they nearly all got rid of horses when tractors kem in. It was when overtime kem out you see; insurance stamps and overtime, tenpence halfpenny an hour it was.
Joyce	Did you ever take horses to Show? They were a beautiful sight.
Frank	Yes oh yes, we got first one year and there was seventeen decorated horses in that year. It used to be at Knight's, Sands House. You used to think more about horse than you did about yourselves really, and when you got up at 5.30 in morning you were straight inti stable.
Joyce	Did you do grooming the night before?
Frank	Yes, we did, a few nights. You nivver gave a big feed 'cos you'd stall 'em. You'd give 'em a feed then tek 'em out to water 'em, then muck out and then give 'em another feed. Then foreman would blow a whistle or shout and you had to be ready to go out to field at seven o'clock. And then when you'd had your tea you had to do 'em again.
Margaret	You had to rub them down again?
Frank –	Oh aye, you were at it till maybe 6.30pm. Why, there was nowhere else ti go and we used ti sit in stable till bedtime.
Margaret	That's where you learnt to play cards, was it?
Frank	Aye, that's it. They used ti fetch coal frae Flamborough Station for 18 shillings a ton, weren't it? I used to lead it for foreman house and Mr Waines for eighteen shillings a ton, one and tenpence a hundred weight. You had ti 'ave some good horses 'cos there were shunting trains going all day long at Flamborough Station. You had ti tek 'em best way you could, you had ti tie 'em best way you could, you had ti get straight alongside a railway truck and then a train would come. There was always a Waines fetching coal, and a few other horses and carts there them days. And then all those waggons of Dixons coming in fetching shoddy for farmers for land.
Margaret	Do you mean the old woollens?
Frank	No, it was the old drains and that, owt from those towns, you know. They used to lead it frae Flamborough Station to put on the land – "manishment" *[fertiliser];* go round with a cart

	and empty the "deadman's buckets" *[toilets]*. Hartleys from Bempton, he used to do it and Bob Chapman.
Joyce	Everybody had outside toilets in those days and if you were on a farm you had to do it yourself and bury it in a field.
Frank	Aye, I think there's one or two septic tanks down South Landing Road still.
	One Friday afternoon we were cleaning chickens out at Marton and there was a Jerry plane came down low and bombed near Flamborough Station, then followed train up line and bombed it near Speeton. We cleaned 'em out with 'oss and cart and Ned Chandler was helping me and heard this plane and thought it sounded as though it had summat wrong with its engine, and we turned round and saw black crosses on it and realised it was German, and we dived inti hen hut. A few minutes later we heard a big bang and it knocked train off line – about Speeton.
Joyce	Do you remember when a German plane machine-gunned a field up North Landing Road – one of the fields behind Dick Bayes'?
Frank	One night we were harvesting about nine o'clock. White buses were on the go, I was just turning horses out. They reckoned he was going for White Bus but he got Council Houses instead. Can you remember they got those three houses? Mi Uncle Pete got a direct hit in middle house and they found his head in Stile Field. He was stood by door wi' little dog.
Joyce	Aye, didn't Pockleys get it as well?
Frank	Yes, there was a block of three but the others got two halves, if I remember right.
Rita	Janey Major was injured; that's why she's walked with a limp ever since.
Frank	That was one September time; it was nine o'clock, I was just turning 'osses out and I heard the bang and they said it was Council Houses so I biked home.
	I had a year at Thompson's when they first came, Grange Farm. Thompsons and Shipleys swapped over farms. Norman Shipley went up to Barn, and Thompsons left there and came to Grange.
	We used to play *[whist]* at Village Hall, thirty or forty tables in those days – whist till about nine o'clock, then a dance later on. And we used to go to Bempton playing as well. Then when Humberside kem in, it knocked it on head 'cos they put rent up

	– £7 an hour. You get three or four hours and you couldn't afford to mek owt on it.
Joyce	Do you remember my dad coming round threshing? He was with Barkers of Hunmanby; my granddad was foreman there.
Frank	Then Millers took it over didn't they? Everybody had stacks in them days. There used to be sixteen farms had cows in Flamborough.
	Walter *[Taylor]*, Dick Hoods had cows; Tom Waines had cows; Wold Farm had cows; Buttericks had cows; Byass had cows; John Robert *[Hall]* had cows; Fosters had cows; Tom Woodcocks had cows; "Ocean View" had cows; Burtons had cows. There was about sixteen farms had milk then. There would be ten or twelve had sheep then in those days, now – nobody.
Margaret	Would they all have horses then?
Frank	Oh yes, they all had horses.
Margaret	Then they would be growing the crops to feed them?
Frank	Yes, that's right.
Joyce	When they had too much milk, they made butter. Nicholson Hall used to go down to market with butter.
Rita	Yes, 'cos Jennis used to buy their butter from some farmer, and it was lovely butter.
Frank	There'd be seventy or a hundred horses around here in them days.
Joyce	There was two milk rounds, or was there more? Edith Waind, John Robert Hall's.
Rita	Taylor's.
Frank	I used to go from "Ocean View" up to Lighthouse with eggs and butter. I used to go with two two-gallon cans on mi bike – ha'penny a half and penny a pint.
Margaret	Did you used to go dancing?
Frank	No, I never was a dancer, I used to go and watch 'em. I've been football and cricket and darts and horses – that's been main.
Margaret	I've heard Laurie say he used to have a dartboard in here. Did you ever come in here?
Frank	Aye, I used to come in some nights.
Margaret	George Warcup used to come in some nights.

Frank	He did; a good player was George. He was Pish, the other was Twit. [*Nicknames to distinguish the two George Warcups*]
Joyce	There was three brothers and one got married. Where did the other two live?
Margaret	In the end cottage, and the married brother lived the other side of the passage. When we got married and the van brought the furniture, Frances Warcup polished her doorknob so she could see what we had bought.
Frank	When they had a pony tethered on Green they didn't want anybody else using that part of the Green. All the fishermen had donkeys, galloways, or there were one or two mules; but there were about a hundred donkeys – a lot of 'em tethered on the Green. We had ganders – and Majors – and they had ti cum through the house ti get inti back garden – and ducks. We used ti send 'em through passage and onti Green, and then they came back on their own at night to be fed. If they were old, we put a piece of wood to help them up the step.
Margaret	You would feed them on kitchen scraps, did you?
Frank	Aye, that's right. We used ti keep about fifty chickens 'cos it was eggs for us all – they were only about one and sixpence or one and tenpence for old hens; we used ti bring our own on.
Margaret	Father used to keep some and somebody gave him some bantams. And they were let out on the Green and some kept vanishing. He found out in the end where they went. Someone else was shepherding them across the Green with his own hens. So father kept his hens in the run after that. Were you ever in the band? [*the Village Band*]
Frank	No, mi father was – he used ti play cornet in band. Why, you see, we were on farms and you never gor home in winter time. I hadn't a bike at fost. I'll tell you who gev me mi fost bike, Vera Johnson. Do you remember her? When you got ti farm, that was it till weekend. And sometimes you didn't get down at weekend – you just got change of clothes, either on Saturday or Sunday. When you couldn't get home because of weather, Missus on farm used to do your washing for you. You had ti walk from Hunmanby, you couldn't afford train.
Margaret	How long did it tek you?
Frank	A good hour. We sometimes used to pick up a lad or two at Bempton, and then we used to get a ride on sometimes. When

we were on farm we used to help one another. When I was at Buckton Hall we biked ti Arram or Cansdale for sixpence, carrying corn. Then you had your 'osses ti do. You only got sixpence extra for half a day, a shilling for a full day. When I was at Marton, Horace's, we used ti do Harold's and Frank Bailey's. We used ti help them as well but it wasn't si far ti go and by then Horace had a car, and we went by car. When we were at Bempton we had ti do 'osses fost, then breakfast and on ti Arram or Cansdale *[near Wold Newton]*, be there for seven on a bike. Arram is between Bridlington and Grindale, and we used ti go ti Mrs Young at Reighton – that was Mrs Marr's sister. She married a Young. We used ti help them as well – only for a tanner and a half a day – carrying corn, eighteen stones across a stackyard and up steps into granary. It used to average eighty a day, a hundred and sixty with two of you. You got back ti end of machine weighing up and tying up bags, across stackyard and up steps again, you were tired by night.

Rita   When you were younger did you practice with smaller amounts?

Frank   No, you had ti start with that amount. You were tumbling about till you got knack of it like. No, if you were at corn end, you had ti start with that amount. You had a bit of a job at start like. Barley was sixteen stone, oats was twelve stone but I'd rather have barley because they used ti come down twice as sharp and you were running wi" bags, backwards and forwards wi" a bag on your back, 'cos you daren't drop a corn.

Joyce   Did different men have different jobs, such as on top of the stack.

Frank   Yes, that's older men. Good men for throwing sheaves and that, and another good man for stacking straw, or else it would fall over. There used to be about twelve men threshing. We used ti run about sixteen or twenty days a year at Marton. Then there was Harold, then there was Frank Bailey. You were out maybe thirty or forty days a year.

Margaret   Making a stack was an art, wasn't it?

Frank   Oh yes, yan ya way and yan ya way. We started by carrying caff *[chaff]* and it was a mucky job, especially if somebody put a fork full down your neck. Sometimes fooling around they'd put a brick or two in your carrying sheet. Then them that brought their dinners would fill their dinner tins with mice and then

	when they got home opened their dinner bags for their wives or foreman's wife, blooming mice would jump out and run about!
Joyce	My Uncle George would go and spend a bit of time with mi dad when he was about twelve, and he used to be catching mice and popping them in his pockets. My grandma used to make him empty his pockets outside before she'd let him inside, because she knew he'd have brought some home.
Frank	I used to like carrying corn when you got knack of it. It was hard work. You were tired at night and you didn't want any overtime or running about. You were pleased to lie down in the stable straw till nine o'clock and you went ti bed. You had horses to do after tea. They had to be fed and turned out for a drink, brush 'em and bed 'em. A hundred hours a week in them days for twelve or fourteen pounds a year – it was five shillings a week for over eighteens. Foreman, or hind as he was called, was allowed coal and electric as well 'cos we used to fetch the coal. There was some good "meat" houses and some bad uns.
Joyce	Plenty of fat bacon?
Frank	Aye, plenty of fat bacon. I didn't mind that but we used ti get beef three times a week – seven and sixpence a stone – blood following knife *[under cooked!]*.
Joyce	What was gravy like?
Frank	Oh, it wasn'y si bad thru and thru. But you got beef breakfast, dinner and tea, and a big plateful and half a slice of bread about two inches thick – you were about full. That's all you got, you didn't get supper. On Sunday night in Summer you might get a slice of curd cheesecake and a cup of cold water, or odd times a slice of apple pie, one piece each. In one or two houses you sat with the hind and his wife and had supper with them, different altogether.
Rita	When you were at "Ocean View" could you sit in the kitchen?
Frank	Yes, we played cards in there. There was a long table – Tommy Lofts, Henry Carter, Art Taylor, John Longden and me.
Rita	At Grange Farm, they had to go out.
Frank	Aye to Slum – wi" a stove in but it was draughty and rats ran about. We used ti walk down ti village, but those from away stayed in. It was a good stove and you could dry your clothes there.

Margaret	Did you go to the Club *[Victoria Institute]* then, 'cos they used to play all sorts there, like billiards?
Frank	No, I didn't join till about twenty years ago. I've never been a billiards man, but I like to watch 'em play. Why, you see, we didn't have the money then to join. Go home, or in summertime go to Post Office Corner. Or when we'd had our dinners, Saturdays and Sundays, we used to lay on bank in paddock; go for walks up fields looking at crops – inspecting whose ploughing was straightest or at other farms' horses. They don't bother now. There was always an art in drilling corn and everything. It was like railway lines when you were drilling corn.
	And then there was a nice few shows we used to go to. We used to share a waggon with Fosters. It was only about three pounds a day. That's where my interest is – horses. Can you remember when eight pairs in waggons set off again Chapel and went up to Flaneburg, turned round in there and down street ending up in Cricket Field? Tom Fenby was judge and John Robert Hall's got first and Wold Farm got second. We were about third. Tom Waines had a pair in – Byass, Almond's, Thompsons. It was in 1944. I was at Thompsons. We had some WAAFs billeted at Grange and they made me fourteen white roses. Dick Hood's had a pair – North Moor.
Margaret	Were the flowers paper?
Frank	Crepe paper. Mrs Jefferson used to mek 'em for us – you know Jeffersons, seed merchant. And I used to go and help her when we were decorating horses. But Christine *[Waind]* buys 'em now – plastic; and she decorates and we clean gear. There's three or four of us.
Margaret	How long does it take?
Frank	Three or four days. We have infra red lamp on all time or it goes mouldy.
Joyce	What about plaiting up, who does that?
Frank	Christine does that. William did a bit but he had a bad foot last year. He didn't go with us to many shows. You know years ago, when I was at Marton and I showed horses, we had a chap called Les Matthews. He was foreman then and I lived with them. For years he had a bad back had Les and he used to say, "I'll plait top if you'll do tail and wash their feet". So he used to sit astride horse and plait their manes and I used ti do bottom end, so I nivver

have learnt ti do it. I still plait tails and do their feet. There's three of us do it now. The horse pageant at Sewerby is first show, following week Cottingham. Then we go to Newport, Eastrington near Goole and then Malton, Syke House near Doncaster, we go there, Kirby Moorside, Thornton Le Dale, Egton, Burniston and Howden. We do about twelve. We have a waggon of our own. We can get four in for transportation. We've been doing two today, washing their feet and that. Camishes at Newbold, near Walkington, have a good show, ten or twelve horses and rare old breeds and old implements and that. It's a good day out. Camish judges Shires. He has some good ones himself – he knows his horse.

Margaret	Did Fosters have horses before the war?
Frank	Oh yes, they still had two till just recently.

Albert Major (and wife, Mona)

Albert worked as a joiner and, as the youngest child of a musical family, his involvement in their band contributed enormously to the social life of the village.

Albert   I used to have to ask George Emmerson if he was going *[to a dance]*, then he went ti bed and threw his clothes out of the bedroom winder and I used ti tek 'em down ti oor 'oose and he used ti cum and get changed, and same procedure when he came back. *[George's mother didn't believe in spending money on what she called gallivanting]* By gor, he was a rum un. Mrs Emmerson wanted me to go and live there when mi mother died. Dick Tuz *[Major]* used to live next door to them.

Margaret   She told me that I wouldn't be Flamborian till I'd lived here thirty years.

Albert   Why, she wasn't Flamborian; didn't she come from Pickering or somewhere?

Rita   She came to Grange Farm, 'cos she could lug twenty stone corn bags like men. She always helped at threshing.

Margaret   Laurie would say when five pound notes were changed officially a lot of old ones came to the fore out of old stocking hoards!

Albert   I think they do it to mek 'em bring their money out. I was once working for an awd man and he came out to me with his face all black as thunder and I asked him what was the matter. He says ti me, "Deean't tell anybody lad but I used ti stuff mi money, that I didn't want Missus ti know about, up chimney, and she's gone and lit fire. We nivver had a fire in there before and I can't tell her or she'll know I've been deceiving her".

Margaret	So were you an upstreeter or a downstreeter?
Albert	We were more or less in the middle so we could join which we liked – who was winning! There used to be seasons for whips and tops and boolers and skipping.
	Mi grandma lived to be ninety-three. I think she died 'cos she was tired out,;there didn't seem to be much wrong with her at all. Mi Mother died when she was fifty-two. Mi Dad was a tailor before he went into grocery. I didn't know till he told me that, but he could sew like anything.
Margaret	There was a tailor's shop in the village, wasn't there? At the fish shop?
Albert	Jack Major's.
Rita	No, at the other fish shop.
Albert	We used to climb up onti roof of the little fish shop and purr a bag ower chimney, and over Green to Custard's and Claxton's, and they used ti cum oot of 'oose covered in soot. Then on Tarry Row [Victoria Terrace], we used ti tie all doors tigither and then knock on front door. Then light a fire under drain pipe.
Rita	We used to do that to Matt Bailey when we were bored, and we used to irritate Harold Stork round near Snowden's because he could run quick, so it was good fun.
Albert	I used to be mates with Ron Coates and I used to go with him with Sid Coates' horse and cart to tek meat out before Sid Coates got his motor bike and side-car. Do you remember Don Sunley? He used to kill at Sid Coates' and I used to help him. You know they used to get bullocks into the fasting shed and they tied a rope round a pulley in floor and the awd bullock used to be hauled down by his nose to floor. Sometimes it got free and you all had ti scatter 'cos naturally they were mad. When they got 'em tied down to ring, they were killed with humane killer. It was awful really.
Rita	It was a great occasion when they killed. We used to line up against the gates trying to see through cracks and knot holes what was going on, very ghoulish!
Albert	Mi Mother used ti mek pickled onions and store them under stairs cupboard. One day I was missing and they heard a clink and found me sitting with a jar between mi legs. I'd got halfway down the coffee sized jar. Apparently I stank for days.

We used to go and play in the Dykes and all over the option and never a thought about anybody molesting you or anything. I'd be five years old or just ovver when I brok mi leg at school and they tuk mi inti hospital. I remember Broadbent was doctor then and he kem to our house. They strapped mi leg up wi' two orange boxes, and we went down ti hospital and last thing I remember they laid me on a bed with a red blanket. Apparently it was chloroform, and off I went to sleep. I had hair right down to here, and they didn't know whether I was a boy or girl.

Margaret	Where you born at the shop then?
Albert	Oh aye. And we used to keep pigs in backway – we always had three or four. There used to be a big barrel in corner of yard near gate and all fruit that went bad used to go in. And all bacon that was produced was lovely 'cos it was all good stuff they were fed with. Jinnie and Mary, cousins living next door, used to be brokken hearted when the pigs went to be killed for market. Lots of folk kept pigs in their backways.
Rita	Look at fisherman keeping their donkeys in those ellums. They all had donkeys or asses.
Albert	I'se think I started playing drums when I was about seven; they sent us down ti Miss Blackburn, at Manor Cottage. It used ti be sixpence for your lesson and me and our Bessie used to be racing down there to see who could get away soonest. You had ti tell 'em when you gor 'ome how you'd gor on and you always told 'em "alright". But they used to see awd Miss Blackburn and ask how we'd done. "Well, last week they did alright but this week not so good". Ooh, how I hated it. I hated music at that time, playing piano, 'cos when we cum home, mi Dad was a stickler for practising, you know. We used ti etty practise every night. My main piece was "Won't you buy my pretty flowers?" I'd have bought the bloody basketful to get out of it!! They used ti sit there – "That's wrong". And then awd Mr. Bee up there, do you remember him? He was teaching 'em all music. Monday night was practice night in front room against shop. In summertime I've seen visitors outside dancing in Redheads Square. Aye, it was lovely. Our George could play any instrument, and, after Mr Bee, finished he was leader.

They used to have all dances in old school and a row of desks used to be in front of band. I've seen 'em lined up in front to half way down school. They used to make fun of Mr. Bee 'cos he always used to say "TAKE YOUR PARTNERS FOR A WALTZ". George played saxophone mainly; Bessie was on piano and I was on drums; Robert was on violin; Dorothy was on guitar; Christine was on cello and George Leng Major was on trumpet. During war, I used ti play with Bob Langton, just me and him used ti play at Village Hall. Before Village Hall was built we used ti play at dances ti raise funds for a Village Hall. In them days it was five bob a night, but I only got half a crown. That was from eight o'clock ti one o'clock in morning, but mi Dad always used ti bring me home about eleven o'clock 'cos I warn't supposed to stop any longer than that. George Leng Major used ti play drums. When I went I used ti have ti sit on a cushion ti reach. Great were them days.

Margaret	Did you have to work in the shop?
Albert	Oh yes, and make ice-cream, you know. Mi mother used ti put copper on and we had a metal container that fitted in. It was filled with milk and boiled and mixed with Bird's Custard Powder or something. Then they used ti put it in drums that were wooden containers packed with ice and we had to turn 'em, and it took ages for it to go off. When it was stiff, our Bessie and me were always keen to clean the dashers *[the paddles]:* we'd go dashing across shouting "it's my turn". We had a shop at Lighthouse and one at North Landing. Part of the front of the present café is our newer shop which the company, building bungalows, built in brick. The original old shop was a wooden one. Dorothy and Christine used to work up at Lighthouse and North Landing. Bessie used to go in if they wanted time off, and ivvery Sunday I had ti tek their dinners to 'em on my bike. Mi Mother used ti put it in them earthenware containers and I used ti bike up there. Up at North Landing, old Tom was down on beach, and Reg and her used to be up top. Dick Bayes had that café there before 'Caravel' was built, didn't he? Mi Dad's café was at the end of Bayes' café. Burgin's was at the other side, and amusements as well.

We had a van, and George used to tek that and in the summertime, when we were off school, we used to go with him – our Bessie and me. When we got ti Kilham we had ti run behind 'cos our weight was too much on our back wheels. They used to go to Kilham, Wold Newton, Hunmanby, Beeford and all that area. It was an awd Post Office van, a model T Ford, and they only had two gears, top and bottom, and that was it. And I remember mi

Dad telling us that it stopped outside shop and it wouldn't go, so he got Billy Sayers. Billy said, "Start her up, Matt". They went a little way and then stopped, and he said, "She'll go now". And Dad realised as Billy laid on bonnet he was touching plug with screwdriver!! He was a rum fella was awd Billy.

You missed yer youth with war on, didn't you? Mi Grandma *[who lived with them]* used to sit in room and knit socks and underwear. She was fondest of George *[the eldest son]* and when he got married, he played for Ceres Harper.

A gang of 'em used to go for a walk on Sundays. Laurie Smith used to call for our George and get a quarter of toffee, and then they used to collect Albert Duke, Alf Leng and George Nordass. All had navy blue suits and trilbies except George Nordass. They used to walk to North Landing or Lighthouse.

Margaret	Did you used to sell fruit and ice cream at North Landing and Lighthouse? When you think they didn't have the means to keep ice cream like they do now....
Albert	It all had to be sold or it had gone. There was a bit of competition up at North Landing, 'cos you see Bayes were up there as well and they used to mek their own ice-cream; and then there was Burgins as well. When we were young, all lads used to go to North Landing and into Burgins on a Sunday afternoon, for a cup of tea and talk all afternoon. I bet they were as sick as muck of us; we hadn't much money to spend 'cos we didn't get pocket money.
	We went ti Scarborough once a year wi' Church. Village used to be empty. Some regarded it as going out of England altigither!!
Margaret	I have a photograph of Laurie taken on sea front at Scarborough before the war, still with his navy blue suit.
Albert	Oh aye, and white silk scarf! We used to go out into country for dances. We used to go in van 'cos it was a big one. It was lovely when you got there, there was always loads of food and it used to set you up for evening. I remember when war started they were all waiting for their call up papers and our George went on his round down South Landing Lane. The lady in the last house said she didn't want to buy food off him as he must be a conscientious objector. Our George was upset and the next day his calling up papers came.
	I started work for five bob a week at Spinks, as an apprentice, and if you worked any overtime you got sixpence an hour. Only

Bessie went out to work; she went to Halliwells, bakers. Chrissie and Dorothy worked in shop. Then mi Mother died whilst I was working London on bomb damage – it would be 1944. I remember we got down to King's Cross; they had buses laid on but they'd made 'em into ambulances to take bomb casualties to hospitals. But that was all they had to take us to Harringay Arena and folks were waving to us and giving us Victory sign 'cos they thought we'd been hurt and on our way to hospital! Awd Doodle Bugs you know, they'd come over and if the motor cut out they kem straight down. I was walking down road and I saw this thing as it came over and suddenly motor cut out. I dived and ended up behind a roll of felt. It's amazing what you can find to hide behind – and it blew up in the next street. We went to pictures one night and sirens went and you could hear it coming 'cos they used to go like a blow lamp, you know, and awd organist was playing softer and softer and we heard it cut out and down it came and missed cinema and hit next street. But awd Rockets, you nivver heard 'em until they blew up. One landed on a school. Fortunately the caretaker was the only one there, but he landed on the top of a pile of rubble that had been the school. They had to get a ladder to get him down. Blast had blown him there. Then we kem home and started 'Major and Davies' but that didn't last long.

Rita	When you took your apprenticeship did you work the full seven years?
Albert	Yes, until I was twenty-one. I think it took that long to ger it inti me. I got five shillings at start and it went up gradually. I think I was getting ten bob by the time I'd served my time. Everybody biked to work; it had to be very bad or snowed up before anybody thought of going on a bus.
Rita	And did you have to buy your own tools?
Albert	Aye, and you used ti leave 'em on display, hoping gaffer would see 'em and say, "Book 'em on your timesheet lad!"
Margaret	What kind of tricks did you get up to when you went to school?
Albert	I think old Chris Hartley was a sadist 'cos he used to bray you with a piece of hosepipe, didn't he? He used to be good at putting on pageants and things. Do you remember that trap door in the roof? He used to fasten maypole to it. One day he was fixing it and ladder slipped and he was left hanging on to the trap door and nobody would put ladder back up. Dick Chadwick was at

	school then and often felt Mr Hartley's pipe and one day he told Hartley he was going home to tell his father. The next thing was Sam, Dick's father came to school and set about Hartley good and proper. All the kids were delighted!!
Margaret	How many other green-grocers were there in the village beside yours?
Albert	There was Jim Cross's, Hilda Gibbon's, Clara Longden's, Jennis's, Jack-a-Bailey's and Co-Op. We didn't keep to our own trade particularly, but us and Jim Cross stuck mainly to green grocery.
	Do you remember old Bill Sunley, joiner at end house *[Ogle Cottages]*? There was a big old chalk stone at the end and old men used to sit and stand there and talk. Bill had that big workshop Keith Sunley has now, and on a weekend we used to sweep all the sawdust to make it tidy. Then on Monday morning he used to scatter it all over again to make folk think he was busy! He was a rum old lad. Peters was vicar and he'd asked Bill to mek him a wheelbarrow, and he was making it when the vicar came to see how he was getting on. Bill turned to the vicar and said, "Now bugger off, it'll be ready when I say so". "Now, now, Mr Sunley", the vicar replied.
Rita	There was Jarvis's, they used to sell all sorts of electrical goods and Tom Hindle's, and there was Bradey's cake shop.
Albert	We used to go for paraffin and fireworks at Hindle's. Bradey's was round in Chapel Street. He used to ride awd motor-bike side saddle, didn't he? He never sat astride it 'cos there was a box on side of it.
Rita	He always used to wear his tall white hat and his white apron when he came round, and I can remember him coming round on his pushbike with tray on the front, delivering our hot-cross buns early on Good Friday morning.
Albert	Mi dad was band master for a long time, and then Tom Cowling took it on after mi dad. They practiced in Drill Shed and there was quite a few in it. George Nordass was, and Nought, Alf Nicholson, and Billy Collins used to have the big drum.
Mona	We used to go *billeting to Lighthouse didn't we? *[*Coarse fish associated with Flamborough; season extends from August to October.]*

Albert	Aye, you caught dozens in the evening when they 'came in'. First sile, then billets and mackerel. Once we saw a chap laid on his stomach scooping sile out of sea with his hand. They were just coming in like sheets.
	When we were lads we used to go down cliff after eggs, especially on Saddles. We had a rope hidden in a hedge bottom. Dick Hood used to be chasing you off cliff top.

George Pockley

Born into a fishing family, George went all over the world on deep sea fishing trawlers returning to Flamborough to help his father and brothers when needed.

Mr. Pockley told us that, before 1865, Danes Dyke was the place used by the fishermen to reach the beach not South Landing. The Cottrell-Dormers were tired of being woken up by about eighty fishermen and donkeys passing near the house on their way down to the beach. The fishermen were told they could dig out a road down to the beach at South Landing and this road has been used ever since.

Margaret	How many were there in your family?
George	Four of us: me, Bob, Jack and Doreen and mi Dad and Mother.
Margaret	Whereabouts did you live?
George	We lived at bottom of Boxhill. *[There was a row of cottages up the hill at the end of the Green. They were pulled down when the council houses were built.]* There were seven cottages up hill to top. Jack Stevenson and Annie lived up there – about half way up. He had a three wheeler cart and he used to sell sweets and chocolates.
Rita	Yes, I remember Jack Stevenson. He used to sell ice-cream down at South Landing as well as sweets.
George	Bob Chapman, he lived up there as well. He was scavenger. We never locked our doors in those days, there was no need.

The school was built in 1845: there were 5 rooms. When I was there, Mrs. Kind, Fanny Grimes, Mr. Veeter, Miss Saranne Chadwick and Miss Sally Bayes were teachers. One day, when I was in Miss Bayes' class, she asked me if I knew when the school was built. I said I didn't know. She sent me round to the front of the school to look at the stone plaque. It was built in 1845 and I have never forgotten that date.

The Mere was deep and you could go out of sight. Where WI is now was a big high dyke you had to climb to get round or you got wet through in winter. This dyke was called Gough Dyke.

Margaret   Did water come that far up?

George   Aye, it did – 'osses used to go right through it.

Margaret   Did you all go into fishing then?

George   We all went into fishing with mi father: you'll see mi grandfather's photograph. It was at South Landing with big cobles, so we go back a long way. There's Pockleys in church records for three hundred and fifty years. I'll show you where cobles were kept. There's an inlet called Coal Hole and there was an old machine up in cliff and it pulled 'em right up there.

Rita   Are these herring cobles at South Landing 'cos they look bigger?

George   Oh, aye, they are a lot bigger and a bit of a cuddy on forard. They used to go to Dogger Bank. There used to be twenty to twenty-five cobles at North Landing.

I was last man to be taken on Matthew Middlewood – the last sailing lifeboat – before it was sold to Jo Lister. He kem from Rotherham or somewhere. He allus had one sock on and one sock off; I remember he never tied his shoe laces because he didn't want to die with his shoes on. The real old fishermen rowed the lifeboat round to Brid harbour and he (Lister) bought it for £25 for Sea Scouts.

In those days, you could get two bob or three bob [shillings] for a call out on a launch of the lifeboat. Old Jack Stephenson was coxswain and there was about eighty fishermen all wanting to draw out of the bag as it was a lot of money in those days. I know where Friendly Forrester [North Landing lifeboat] is now. She's in Isle of Wight museum. When I saw her, it brought a lot of memories back. I served in her both when Albert Duke was coxswain and mi brother was coxswain and we saved three lives. I remember when she fost kem, it was a bad day. George

Leng was fost coxswain in her. He took her round ti Thornwick and took this chap out of cliff and knocked a big hole on her lee side.

Before the war, crabs were two or three shillings a basket and about four stones in a basket: ten stones of fish in a basket. How those poor donkeys got up there I don't know. *[The slope from the beach to the top of North Landing is very steep.]* When our Pat *[an elderly relative]* was at North Landing in a bad storm, it was so cold his beard froze. The fish were all set out on the beach to sell and a big sea came and washed the lot out to sea.

I've sailed all over the world, in the fifty-two years I've been at sea: Spitzbergen, Greenland, Iceland, Faroe Islands, White Sea out on Russian coast – in trawlers out of Hull.

Rita	Which trawling company did you go with?
George	Kingston Steam Trawling Company. I went each winter and kem back to Flamborough each summer, to help with crabbing. Fishing trade wasn't good and I've often thought I wouldn't have gone fishing if I had my time over again.
Margaret	Someone was telling us that for Christmas dinner they had baked fish as they couldn't afford any poultry.
George	One time when we were off Russian coast and we'd run short of food, skipper told us to go into the hold and get a halibut for our dinner. By gor, it was good. We had a very good cook. We would come down on a morning and get little chat haddocks, chop tails off and by, they were good as well. They were big haddocks that were caught off here, till they started trawling out of Brid. There used to be plenty of lobsters and crabs as well, before they trawled, but they crushed a lot of stuff as the trawl dragged on the bottom.
Margaret	How much was fish before the war?
George	About two bob a stone, things were bad, especially if weather was bad. In 1942, it was a bad winter with a lot of snow. We went to Lighthouse, after bait for lines, and we had to walk in fields 'cos telephone wires was stuck into snow it was so deep on footpaths.

Do you remember Old Chesterman? He lived up North Marine Road. He had a slate outside and a lantern, and if the candle blew out, he wrote on the slate that it was bad weather and the fishermen could go back to bed because it was too rough to go to sea!!!

Doreen Shepherd and Betty Morris

An only child, Doreen is remembered fondly as a Guide leader and still lives in the village.

Daughter of a railway worker at Flamborough Station, Betty worked in the village and still lives in the same house.

Doreen	I was going down Allison Lane when I was quite little, going to shop, and this man says, "Will you bring us some matches", and I said yes, I would. I went for these matches and he wasn't there when I came back so I stand at door shouting, "Mr Sparrow Checks, Mr Sparrow Checks". Well, was I in trouble! I didn't know any different, but I think his name was Mainprize, to me he was Mr Sparrow Checks, and I was in terrible trouble about it.
	Do you remember at school we had that hole in Miss Chadwick's classroom?
Rita	Oh yes, we put her cane down it. Everything went down, the cricket wicket things went down, sweets, chewing gum everything but she had some more canes in her cupboard.
Doreen	But they had us so disciplined in those days they didn't have to speak to us; she pointed at you, beckoned, pointed at the hole and whatever it was, went straight down. When they were pulling it down we went to see if we could find the hole but they wouldn't let us, they said it was dangerous.
Betty	Joe Langton, she was for ever after him and she used to get him by his lug, run him up one aisle, run him back down, run him up

again and then he would say, "That didn't ott". Run him up and down again she'd go, and we'd sit and laugh at her, up and down this aisle and every time he said, "That didn't ott". So we called him, 'Joe plug with a leather lug', and it stuck with him you know. He was allus in trouble. When he got into the bigger class, sixth class was Mr Hartley, course then we used ti mek them airplane shooters and Joe started to do them with pen nibs and they stuck in somebody's bottom or summat like that. Anyway, Chris Hartley had a bit of cane only so long. By, didn't it ott when he leathered you right across your hand. Anyway, he threatened Joe about it so when he come back after dinner he'd a plate in his trousers. He'd rubbed his hands wi' onions and when he hit him it slithered off. "That didn't ott, that didn't ott", said Joe. Anyway, then he rapped, "Bend over", and when Joe bent over, plate dropped out of his trouser leg onto floor. Well, everybody was in uproar in class. Eh, he was a character, he got everybody inti trouble what was with him.

Doreen	They once clouted him in every classroom, I've forgotten what he'd done, but they took him round every classroom and he got caned in every one once, didn't they?
Betty	Yes! They did, if there was a bit of mischief he could find it and he allus had somebody with him, but he allus got it! He hadn't to do anything, he'd just sit sometime but he'd start fiddling with summat and all of a sudden something would shoot across at somebody and, "You out", and cane.
Doreen	Do you remember the Zeppelin going over when we were at Flamborough School, or was it before you went?
Rita	It would be before I went. Now, did you live in Dog and Duck Square first? I can always remember being there.
Doreen	Yes, we were there when you were there. I had a blow-up swan and mi mother used to have Rita across to play – they were right mates her and mi mum. Rita was a right bonny little bairn, all curls, and she'd got my swan one day and punctured it, and I've never forgotten about mi swan.
Rita	I can always remember your mum letting us play with the rabbits in the house and then when you went over the Green, your mum had a pet pig and it used to go upstairs with her to make the beds.
Doreen	She had one called Peggy, it used to play hide and seek with me. You'd run and hide and shout "Peggy" and she'd come and find

you. Oh yes, she lived in the house just like a dog, she was ever so clean, she was a lovely pig.

Betty	I had ducks, a couple of ducks. They lived in back yard and one got ti following me all o'er the house whenever I went over front door. But they got so fed up of that duck coming and doing its do-dahs in the house and mi mother had ti clean it up. Anyway, they didn't say anything and all of a sudden one day we had duck for dinner. I didn't want no duck; that was my duck. I didn't want any – no way. I was ages before they got me to touch duck again.

We used ti go on Mere, sink paths in and try ti go across ti island. We often got ti middle of island and got stuck there when bell was going and we had ti get back again. We got right in front of class for that as well.

Doreen	We spent a lot of time down Stylefield; that was a proper stream down there in those days not just a mucky gutter, a right stream.
Betty	Tadpoles and things, wasn't there, and we were allowed in there on a Friday afternoon to play rounders and things like that. If you didn't like it, we used ti sneak off into whin bushes across there ti play. And that was another thing, bell always went before we left whin bushes and we had ti gallop like mad.
Doreen	They let us all out of school as well for a mirage that was at South Landing once. We went down ti Roger Sellarslates to see this mirage, you know. Well, it was a wonder it was there by time we landed down but it was a beauty wasn't it? The whole length of the water, it was ever so beautiful.
Margaret	What do you mean a mirage?
Betty	Well, it's the reflection of another town across at other side, and it shows on the water. It's like a village in shadow. There were Church spires and things.
Doreen	It's only supposed ti last a few minutes, but it must have lasted longer because they marched us from school right a way down ti South Landing. I remember standing on Roger Sellarslates ti watch it, then when we were coming back up we wondered what we'd gone ti see, 'cos I didn't know and they never explained what a mirage was ti me and I thought 'what have I gone ti see?' Mind it was a lovely afternoon.

I can't remember how old we were when Zeppelin went over, I just remember everybody in school being out in't playground and everything was si quiet. Nobody moved and this great big silver grey thing just moved silently across sky, you know, but it was the size about it, it was really spooky in a way.

Betty   I've got a postcard of the R100 over Hull. That was round about First World War time, warn't it? I should say this would be another one. We should be about seven or eight.

Doreen   I came to Flamborough when I was about five. About 1928 onwards somewhere that way and there was an earthquake. Do you remember the earthquake? We were still in Dog and Duck Square then.

Betty   Yes, because Mr and Mrs Airie used ti live at end house, they call it Windridge then. Mi mother used ti go, there was only old man and old lady, and she was dying. She says ti mi mother she wants me ti go and see her. I were only a toddler, about three or four, and she insisted I went upstairs to see old lady and I wasn't very keen 'cos somebody dying; I didn't know what to expect, she took hold of mi hand and took me upstairs. They had lino floors. Any rate, old lady was saying sommat ti me and all of a sudden there was the biggest jumping and row going on and I flew down them stairs. She had one of them tall tin jugs underneath bed and it started dancing round bedroom floor. Ohh! I shot, I don't know what step I hit but I got ti bottom and I wouldn't go in no more before she died.

Before that, I often used ti go in't house. She had the biggest aspidistra plant in middle of room table. I would polish the leaves for her but I'd ti get on mi knees on't table ti do it but they wouldn't move it off table. They were a grand couple really and they kept chickens. I used ti chase these old chickens round and round yard. Everybody kept chickens or a pig, and rabbits as well. If you got a wild rabbit it was alright, you lived off them really, everybody had their gardens. It was tough here at times.

Doreen   Folks would help you more then. I mean if fishermen had a spare fish or catch, you know, "We've got so many fish or we've got so many crabs". Likewise, you would get a rabbit from somebody else or a few potatoes – or – "we've got a row of cabbages, do you want one?" that sort of thing. We used to go coaling on the beach.

Betty   We used ti go down South Landing when they were landing fish and they used ti gut the fish and we used ti get roes, didn't we? You'd soak 'em in salt water and boil 'em and then when they

	went cold, slice 'em in a sandwich, salt and vinegar. Oh, they were beautiful, weren't they! Now I can't see sight of 'em, I can't eat any thing fishy. I'll tell you what we used ti eat, but I can't eat now, periwinkles.
Rita	I still love roes, I like them fried as well. I didn't like smelts, just smears.
Betty	We used to go up Sand-Pit Road across that first field – it used ti be boggy – and come out of that gate on top of South Landing. We were allowed ti go ti South Landing on our own, our lads and me, but we couldn't go nowhere else, so we used ti nearly live at South Landing. Apart from Mabel Gilbank – when she come to Gutter's in summer holidays and then she took us ti Danes Dyke, every day for all day long, collect all kids fra bottom end.
Betty	If ever we walked down road ti South Landing and met Merry James – do you remember, Pete James's brother? He scared the daylights out of us, we were walking towards him and they kept pushing me ti this end nearest ti him, kept going round each other ti get away, he wouldn't say a word, he'd get right ti you and then, "Where's mi knife?" God, we used ti go. I once lost a shoe in bog going across field and I never did go back for it, I says, "No way". He really did scare us and all he said was, "Where's mi knife?" And he'd go for his pocket you know.
Doreen	Were you in that pageant we had at Danes Dyke? It was for the Coronation in 1936 or somat like that, but every kid in the school took part, it really was spectacular especially in Danes Dyke grounds, it looked real good.
Rita	Yes, I was a nurse with Betty Bancroft and Betty Kemp. I was the little one, only 'cos I had a nurse's uniform 'cos I'd been in a fancy dress. Jean Waines was an Indian or an African or something and they cocoa'd her face, and I went near Jean and got this on my cap. I did get into a row.
Betty	Me and Muriel Hall went as Chinese women. We had tight skirts and we couldn't walk down steps. Nancy Hudson was Britannia. Our John represented Canada, he had ti have a box with a label on saying Canadian products – you represented every country, didn't you? He drove mi mother and us up the pole because he had ti learn so many lines and he kept going over and over these lines and I says, "You're driving us crackers, shut up".
Doreen	If you go up to Danes Dyke on car park and you look onto grass part there's still the willow tree where they put the throne

	underneath where Britannia was sat. All the countries and all the different forces – you marched up to her said whatever you had to say then everyone grouped round and made a historical sort of scene.
Betty	We hadn't nothing ti say at all. I remember walking up wi' Muriel Hall when we were all dressed up for it saying, "I can't blooming well walk up them steps" – all smartened up and moon faced. Well, you had ti go on a gravel path out of that glass place then down these steps – there isn't si many now as there was, now that it 's a car park 'cos they took so many off the top – I couldn't climb down there!
Doreen	You know we had such a lot of shops when we were young?
Rita	When we were talking to Robert Leng we went through what he could remember and what I could remember but in this book that I have of 1901 there were eighteen shops because there were some in Tower Street as well – a bakery and something else.
Betty	Jack Chadwick had a shop in his house when we were kids. We used ti get five goodies for a penny ti go ti Chapel on a Sunday morning, we allus had ti pick biggest uns out of a jar.
Doreen	A bit like Miss Sunley with her goodies and the kids wasn't it? She must have stood there waiting hours because she never hurried you: you could spend your penny and that was divided into goodness knows how much – she just stood there waiting for you. She had a stool for little ones.
Betty	She used ti want ti know which lasted longest for our penny – gob-stoppers or what. Aniseed balls, lasted quite a long time. I used ti get those kaylie things. When they were nearly finished, you used to fill 'em with water and chucked it agin near Chapel there.
Doreen	What did they call that old man that used ti frighten life out of us in Chapel, he used to sit at back.
Betty	Tant Fell.
Doreen	He'd bawl out at top of his voice, every thing would be quiet and he'd bawl out, "Alleluia, Praise the Lord, Alleluia". You were sat there all of a tremble waiting for it. You'd been told to sit and be quiet in Chapel, and all of a sudden he'd shriek out, "Alleluia".
Betty	That was at Primitives, the other was the Wesleyans. I tried Wesleyans but it used ti be Dick Hood what used ti be one of teachers there and I said summat. He didn't say nowt and he had

	his walking stick round back o'my neck and pulled me out. That was it, I wasn't going no more to that Chapel, he used ti hurt your neck an' all.
Rita	That was one of his tricks wasn't it? I mean he would do it in the street if he thought you were doing something wrong. You always sort of walked round him, if you saw him anywhere near, you were at t'other side of street or gone down another alley out of way.
Doreen	I used to think Mrs. Longden was a witch, 'cos I mean it was a real dark shop painted dark brown wasn't it, and she used to come out of back place into front shop. I used to be, "Don't send me there, Mam". I was petrified of that woman.
Rita	I used to hate it when mi Grandma Cross used to send me there. It was even worse than going to Miss Stevenson's and Lord knows that was bad enough. They used to sell butter and fish and that, where they've made that house into two, next to Robert Leng's. I didn't mind going to Miss Hope's for bread and buns.
Betty	Stevenson's used ti stand back a bit, didn't it? And there was the big window and her shop front was all white tiles sloping in and she used ti put all her fish on there. I remember it well. Dolly Suddaby married Stevenson didn't she? What did they call him what she married? Was it 'Snow White' [nickname!]- Wilf – and they took fish round country after that for years. There was a lot went round with carts when we went ti school wasn't there? Jim Gardham used ti come round with a pony and trap with butcher's stuff on, braun and all that,and he allus come ti our house and we allus had ti have a penny duck. Oh, they were beautiful. He worked for a shop somewhere in Brid and we allus waited for him, and he sold 'em off this pony and trap. Then used ti be Means from Brid come round with fruit, great Victoria plums, beautiful.
Doreen	Oh baskets of fruit, – you didn't buy it in pounds you bought by the basket then. I wonder why they did come round so much, because we had practically everything we wanted in't village, hadn't we? There was such a lot of shops anyway.
Betty	We had hawkers. Then we had Pashley's paraffin he had a motorised one – a yellow one with side blinds and he carried everything but kitchen sink. You could get paraffin frae back and all ropes, scrubbing brushes and everything off this thing he brought. I allus remember that because we ran out once. Goods

lived across road, down from our place. There weren't any cars then and he was coming across ti our house and he knocked mi brother down. Luckily he was just setting off. By, mi brother did get twanked but I don't think it 'ot *[hurt]* him, because he'd no business ti come across on his own anyway. Do you remember fish cart coming round, because they used ti sell them rolled herrings? I remember mi mother getting herrings off 'em.

Doreen   There was Hindle's sold buckets and tins and things like that and paraffin. Your grandad was a cobbler wasn't he Rita? There were three cobblers on go at same time and about three butchers shops. Screeton's sold dresses and jumpers and wool and Readhead's sold wool and cottons and things as well as newspapers.

Rita   I suppose it was that not many people went shopping in Brid 'cos the butchers in the village delivered as well. And there was bakers and fruit shops.

Betty   There wasn't a lot of cars and things on road was there? I remember playing across road with whip and tops, and hopscotch.

Rita   I can remember when I was very young if we heard a car we used to go out to have a look at it. You could always hear them 'cos the streets were cobbled then, weren't they? Mr.Hartley, the head teacher, had one, hadn't he?

Doreen   Yes, that's right, the cars were noisier then. It was a great thing to see a car in Flamborough. And Major's fruit shop, they were about first shop to get one.

Betty   That was village band was Major's you see. They used ti be at Drill Hall, your place where the flats are now. It was Brass band. Then in war time up above it used ti be First Aid post, Miss Becket used ti go.

Doreen   William's was First Aid, wasn't it, and district nurse?

Betty   No, that was district nurse, Nurse Edmunson.

Margaret   It was St John's up above during the war because it's painted in that memorial in Church – St John's Ambulance and something else. *[Fire fighters]* I've heard Dad say when they were up there, there was so many hanging oil lamps but they took them all.

Betty   Parish rooms used to be above Vicarage garage. Guides and Brownies were there, weren't they? I know Miss Becket belonged ti St John's. Miss Becket had 'the Haven'. *[Cameron's Court B&B]* I went upstairs ti bed and I knew nothing till seven o'clock next morning and she woke me up ti tell me they'd bombed

	village when they bombed council houses. I knew nowt about it. I'd slept all night through it. She'd been out all night and left me on me own. I could sleep clock round then when I was sixteen.
Margaret	Were you a maid there?
Betty	Yes. I started when I was fourteen. When the war broke out we had a French girl there, she'd come over ti learn English ti go back ti teach English. Anyway she'd been a couple of months or summat like that, oh me and her used ti fall out like cats and dogs 'cos she'd say when I got summat it wasn't right. Any rate she had ti go back and she was taken a prisoner somewhere in wartime and we never heard ought more about her and that was end of it. We had a load of foreigners used ti keep coming, a Hungarian and all sorts. We had her two nephews frae Canada who was over in England in forces with their leaves and that. We had an Australian boy that got burned, fetched down in a plane, he come on leave here. We'd quite a few of them – she used ti translate letters for soldiers in wartime you know.
	I'd been there about a year and then I went to Mrs Stork's that lived across road at 'Katomba'. 'I did mornings at Miss Becket's and afternoon's at Mrs Stork's. She'd been a nurse, then they moved up ti North Landing, that bungalow bottom of David Lane. Then when Mrs Stork died and Jack remarried I went across ti Thompson's. Jack Stork was a fish buyer for Bogg's. I went across there and I had seven years at Thompson's. It were interesting and we had some fun but it was hard work.
Doreen	I was in the land army mostly, that was good.
Betty	I went ti Thompson's in house and Doreen was left, but she was outside before that weren't you – on land?
Doreen	Some of those poor lasses that come from towns, they'd never even seen a back garden let alone a farm. I mean a friend of mine, we're still friends, and she came onto a threshing machine. They'd no idea, it must have been absolutely soul breaking to 'em you know to come out inti country, most of 'em they hadn't a clue.
Margaret	What did they do, live in the farmhouse and work outside?
Doreen	Mostly, yes, but these two that came onti threshing machine they were at Mrs May's down at bottom end and they went out different places daily. But all the dirty horrible jobs to do. Those weeks that we had though were good in wartime, you know

'Battleship weeks' and 'Air weeks' and that; they put a whole week on. In those days they could put entertainment on for a week.

Betty   There was allus some event on in Village Hall every night and I allus remember going ti sixpenny hops on a Saturday – it used to be full didn't it?

Rita   Well there used to be a lot going on even before the war wasn't there? There was the 'Bright Young Things'.

Doreen   And the stage things they used to put on and even the Methodist Chapel used to put on plays and sing-songs and things. There was a Mrs.Warcup, Lilian's mother, she used to do dialect poems, and Connie Cross used to do a lot – they were wonderful.

Betty   I remember when Village Hall was finished and it was opening day. We all had ti go in road and we all had sailor suits on, a little short pleated skirt, and lads had similar, and we were stood doing sailor's hornpipe dancing.

Doreen   And we bought a brick, didn't we, every school kid had to pay for a brick.

Betty   The thing was when we bought the bricks they were building up the front of it and a gale got up. We were all on our way ti school and it fell down and everybody run from school, and bell was ringing like mad and we went down ti see all this. Oh, it was awful. It had all come in and we wondered where all our bricks had gone. Then we had ti stand out in a line, hadn't we, when we got back because we were late for school. We didn't half get some standing out in road and lines and that because we were late.

And there was school gardens there, wasn't there? When we used ti go ti school gardens we used ti pinch carrots, ti eat on our way back. Then we used ti get in a gang on a night, lads, we'd go ti Landing and that.

Doreen   Oh they were down-enders, bottom-enders that lot.

Betty   'Course I was among hands and we used ti rope Joe Plug into it, collect him on way an' all. We were allus inti mischief, putting a bit of paper at bottom of a drainpipe and lighting it till it hummed. Or we played the pin and button, or we tied every door handle down road tigether. Anyway, this particular night, I remember Mill Garth up here where Joe Row's cottage was. And Merry James and Pete lived there. There was a concrete footpath they went over and then was like a muck bank, where they went across to their toilets, and they were like tin sheds. One night we laid waiting for whoever was going across ti toilets. Merry James went across and we waited and waited and we thought he'd got sat on seat and Joe Plug got the biggest boulder and we dared him ti chuck it on top o'this tin shed and he did. 'Course we were half way down slope by time he'd got it sent. He come out trousers half up and half down, shirt hanging out and, "You buggers lets hev hodden you". We didn't half go. I don't think we stopped till we got ti bottom end. Oh, we used ti get up ti mischief up Mill Garth and across Highland. One night – you know donkeys used ti walk up and down round village – and we collared one and took it ti bottom of village. Mi Uncle George lived at 'Waverley', the end house, and there used ti be a long passage. Room door went off there and then there was a kitchen door there next ti it. We oppened front door – we hadn't half a job ti get this donkey up this step – and pushed it inti passage and shut door. Anyway, of course, when he oppened door it walked inti kitchen and round table. We ran when we saw him trying ti push this donkey out of front door. When he saw us next day, "You were one o'culprits I know who was among you".

Rita I can remember when there was a lot of donkeys on the Village Green. We used to go and sort of herd 'em till you got to top of High Street and then set 'em off. And there was a lot of geese on Green.

Betty The thing was though when they used ti go ti North Landing and that, all field gates were open and they just let them go on their own. They'd turn in any field gate would donkey on way down you know. Anyway, in wartime when it come ti lights out, I was coming down North Landing road on bike and I ran into back of one and I didn't know. I hit something you see – I had no light on, but I felt something swish mi face like that. "Oh it's a donkey". It's a wonder it hadn't kicked. They wandered all over road, didn't they? I did get a shock.

We were luckier than a lot of 'em because mi dad had a regular job, it was only about three pounds a week mind you, but it was a regular wage every week. Then mi mam used ti go out and char you know. She used ti work at Wilkinson's one day and she finished off working for Sam Leeson. But they didn't pay, they exchanged, giving blocks of lard, blocks of butter or summat like that you know.

Doreen	My father did any sort of odd job on a farm, or at brickworks when brickworks was on. He didn't work long, just long enough to get onto dole again then he'd knock off you know, so we had a hard time. But mi Mam never made it out that way – she was always an easy going person. I never suffered on account of it. It's only since I've grown up that I realised mi dad didn't work. She had a job on, she must have had, but she was a very good manager and she could do all sorts.
Betty	They always managed didn't they, well they had to do hadn't they. I mean to say, they used ti go and gather brambles frae fields and I remember we used ti go gleaning for chicken corn after they'd finished threshing, and crab apples for jelly, and sticking, didn't you?
Rita	It was a great occasion when you went sticking, we all had carts and if it was snow you took a sledge.
Doreen	Oh yes, to ride there on an old pram or a cart or something and then ride back on top of sticks. You didn't seem to fall off, did you? Anything that had old wheels on you used to go to Danes Dyke. Now a sledge used to come down Crofts Hill like the clappers – it used to come on its own.
Margaret-	Talking of Crofts Hill, someone has a photo of Crofts Hill and she was saying the road didn't come where it does now, it used to go round somewhere 'cos it looks a lot flatter. Where did it go?
Rita	Coming from Brid mi mother used to say – you know that gate almost at the bottom of Dykes on your left, the last farm gate, before you get to Dykes – it used to go through there and round and up somewhere and come out much further along than it does now.
Betty	I remember there used ti be a cart road at bottom of Danes Dyke, well that used to be the old road I think, as far as I've heard. That side's the Dene isn't it, as though you were going to Bempton Dykes. I remember going through there.
Doreen	That tunnel that we used to run through at Danes Dyke bottom was pretty recent when they built that road. I don't remember it but I know it was fairly modern. We used to dare each other to run through, or we used ti walk through it. Like that one at bottom of Brig Hill on the road to Lighthouse, but you used to have to bend double to get through there.
Betty	I've walked so far in that tunnel at North Landing at bottom of beach, but I never dare go right back 'cos I didn't know if I'd

	drop inti summat, it seemed ti go on and on under ground. I don't know where it ended up, whether there is an opening at back of it – I never did find out, I dassen't go ti look right ti end of it But there must be – the way water comes down.
Margaret	Did you go on the beach a lot or up North Landing and that sort of thing?
Doreen	Only with your parents or with somebody else, you weren't allowed to run around on your own – it was mostly Stilefield for us top ended kids and Maitlands for bottom enders.
Betty	I did it once 'cos we went ti South Landing, mind it was through our lads. Fishermen would say, "Come and help us ti do this, lads", carry these feertentrees or mebbe summat down for 'em when they were going off. "Come on, I'll giv you a ride roond ti North Landing". Oh no I weren't going on watter, no way, "I'll shall tell mi Mam when we get home. You'll get i'trouble – you'll get clouted". "Come on with you, get in", and I can remember them lifting me in ti this fishing boat. Oh it stood o'er end at Lighthouse, I nearly had a fit. It took us hours and we knew we should get i'trouble 'cos we had, 'Home by twelve o'clock dead'. One o'clock we were still at North Landing coming round and we'd all that way ti come down home. Didn't we cop it! Mi mother nearly had a fit because we tried not ti tell her we'd been on watter – she was frightened ti death of watter and I am. "Oh", she said, "Never ni more. You're not going ni more on your own and you don't go again or you're in trouble". I daren't, no more.
Rita	I can remember we were allowed to go to South Landing with Herbert Sayers and Herbert Gibbon after I was about eight. And we were allowed to go in swimming if they promised to look after us. But I can remember Herbert Gibbon once, he let me get in then stuck my head under – that was the favourite game. I've never ever been able to put my head under since then.
Doreen	I could go as you say, later on with Violet Mainprize and her gang and such like. They had a big car tyre and they sat me in the middle of it but I fell outside of it and being fat course I got stuck and, as you say, I was under water. And that has done it, you can't help it and even when you're shampooing your hair you get that feeling don't you? Not many kids did swim, especially fishermen – they didn't swim.
Betty	We were only allowed ti go ti South Landing, it was because our lads were looking after us with being four years older than me,

	but we only paddled, we never did manage ti swim. I don't know why, but we loved ti be in the water.
Rita	Mi mother taught us to swim. She used to swim out with us on her back and then tip us off – you soon learnt to swim! We always had to promise we would never climb cliffs.
Betty	Our lads once got into 'Kyhole'. There and up that bank side used ti be all sand and they'd dug a buried thing out of it and they were going in and it collapsed. That learnt 'em though it frightened them ti death, they never did it again. We used to all seem ti keep ti bottom of village though – it seemed ti be divided did village.
Doreen	Oh very much, us top-enders didn't play with bottom enders.
Betty	I never kem up ti top end of this village until I was about fourteen and I started work for Miss Becket and I got on to know Janet Duke and Norah Brown. Then I come up but afore that I knew nothing about fishermen, all farming. Oh, I got into any amount of trouble with Will Cross – walking over his lines. I wandered over his lines when I brought dog up.
Doreen	And yet they describe them as fishermen's cottages, don't they, down bottom end? They were farm workers cottages. It was very divided.
Betty	On a Sunday afternoon, we went for a walk. They only kept us going for a walk on a Sunday 'cos, when we reached Maitlands farm, we used ti go in for a tupenny glass of milk. It was in an old building with brick floor, spotless, with this long table, and there was the cooling thing on the wall.
Rita	Or ginger beer. That ginger beer was lovely, little half bottles with marbles in, or lemonade. Sarsaparilla, dandelion and burdock used ti be beautiful out of barrels. We used to go to Taylor's when we lived in the cottage with our glass, for a penny glass of milk.
Betty	Why, I think I went with a pint jug across Church yard ti John Robert Hall's. Mi mother said, "I think you'd better tek two". Any rate I used ti tek one and I'd half of it drank before I landed back. I know one day, we were going on and I was swinging it and coming up and I landed with handle in mi hand and chucking it at Churchyard wall. Well, I've been in some trouble sometimes....!!
Margaret	You'd go on Sunday School trips to Scarborough then did you?

Betty	I did but we always went by rail because mi dad had tickets you see with being on railway so we always used rail. We used ti wave at them at cuttings when the gates were closed and passed the buses.
Doreen	It seemed to be miles didn't it? Oh, it was a long, long way to Scarborough in those days.
Betty	When you went ti Chapel you all got tigether in Chapel Rooms. As a rule, with Primitives, you went ti a Chapel didn't you? I can remember it now – in a big schoolroom – big trestle tables, I couldn't tell you where it was, but I remember going in this big hall.
Doreen	Yes, big tables and you had a meal. Off Aberdeen Walk somewhere, I think.
Rita	We used to go to Boyes – all Church children had to go to Boyes.
Betty	And Peasholm Park were out of this world, warn't it? You'd got to heaven if you got to Peasholm.
Rita	That water chute, if you hadn't enough money to go on at least you could sit and watch the boats.
Betty	I never did go on it, Rita. No, I didn't like water. I do remember though going on the little boats. I got bribed into having a go. And, funny, that year we did go, Dennis Hunter fell over board and they had ti go and get him some more trousers. He was a big fattish lad, warn't he? He had this mop o'ginger hair hadn't he? He went in the Navy, didn't he, but I don't know what happened to him.
	Do you remember auld Sterriker what used ti live our way? He used ti sell bacca and that out of house, and goodies. We were never allowed ti go for goodies 'cos they weren't clean enough. Then there used ti be Jane Sunley next door and Ernest Sunley worked with mi dad on't railway. They had the two sons Ernest and Don, didn't they? And next door there was Ginny Mainprize and David and then there was an old man – that's where Willie Woodhouse, when he left Post Office, had that bungalow built – and there was three cottages and a barn there. The Drakes lived across the road from us, Beattie, she was marvellous, she could sing hymns like I don't know what, without a book; she'd stand at doorstep and soon she'd start singing – and she could sing.

Doreen	You'll be just that bit too young and won't remember wreck of Rosa, Rita, when we all went cindering. Cinders! It was black with cinders was North Landing. Mothers used to go down during day and then all us kids used to have to go down after school and then when dads came home they used to go and with any means whatever they used to go and collect all the bags full of cinders.
Rita	No, I don't remember that. There's a lot of folks in Flamborough have bits off Rosa.
Betty	I've a big mirror over my living place, the top's been damaged – it kem off Rosa. Our cart had big mangle wheels on and it didn't half rattle and crunch things. We were like hosses in front ti pull – I always had ti be fost, our lads used ti let me 'cos I was youngest you know. They'd say, "Pull, you aren't pulling", and they'd pile these bags up. Oh, the times we went up and down, any way i'finish I ended up riding up and riding down on top of them, all these great big cinders and oh, they were warm. By, they did burn. Whether it was salt water being in them, I don't know.
	Now me and Doreen goes down and we generally get a little bag full of coal. We did last week when we went down, we put it on fire in bag as it is at night, and oh there's some heat from it, only tiny, little bits like that but it was alright.
Doreen	Do you remember they used to give us one 'dolly mixture'? I mean, one 'dolly mixture', it was marvellous. Do you remember Mary Cross used to get Daily Express and read us "Rupert" at school? Every day, she'd read us what happened to Rupert. I used to hate mental arithmetic, but I loved school days, there was discipline.
Rita	Miss Chadwick used to read us something out of Teacher's World, Enid Blyton used to write in it.
Betty	Do you remember that big broad thing they used ti have right round classroom when you were ti learn the alphabet – 'A' and then a great big apple and 'B' and a banana painted – all for you ti learn and you had ti pick out which letter she said. Oh yes, she was ever so patient was Mary Cross. All the times tables on those boards as well, she really had patience, she was made for it somehow, wasn't she?
	We got ABC's and little times tables before we even went ti school, didn't you? When you look at it, they were long days but

	we didn't go like they do today, did we? I mean you solidly sat in desks all time – from nine till lunchbreak, then morning we had our milk or whatever and then we had it till twelve, back again at one till half past three.
Doreen	But Mr Ralph, it's a wonder somebody hadn't complained because he used to wear spongy soled shoes you know, and if you were talking he'd come up behind you (you were in double desks) get you both by the collars and bunch your heads together. And he could wallop, couldn't he?
Betty	Jimmy Mainprize was flaked out, he went clean out when he hit him.
Doreen	He did. Miss Bayes – when we were sewing, I've often thought I've had my brains and headaches since, -'cos she used to put a steel thimble on and give you a thump on top of your head. I could not sew, I was hopeless at sewing, I got this thimble every sewing lesson – those horrible pillow cases, and then it was nighties.
Rita	Oh, I can remember them. I was a very good seamer and feller and we did that in Miss Chadwick's. And they used to do orders for people, didn't they? Miss Bayes had an order for about a dozen pillow cases. She fetched me out of Miss Chadwick's to go to do these pillow cases and I put the needle through my finger and it bled and I put blood on these pillow cases. I got more than the thimble treatment, believe you me!
Doreen	Do you remember school dentist? He was barbaric; he was really a violent dentist. I mean they held her down in a chair.
Betty	Oh, it finished me off did school dentist. Now if I go ti dentist me knees are going. I was under a private dentist at the time an' all. I'd been down to Walkinston's in Manor Street, in them big houses, and I'd a big abscess on one of mi back teeth and he painted it and said come back when it comes down and we'll have it out. I thought, "That's what you think. If it doesn't ott, I won't come back". Meantime school dentist come and I was in Ralph's class and got this card with I don't know how many he was going ti tek out of mi teeth. I went in ti Miss Bayes' class and there was this great big chair. Mr Ralph stood there and they got me in that chair and he had ti hold me down and they pulled mi tooth out. Well, they had ti plug it and they had ti tek me home in car. Oh, I was sick. What a mess. I said, "Never no more, I'm having no more teeth out". Oh, it was terrible. He used to come every year or every couple of years.

Rita	Doctor Moffat – do you remember her – with her black velvet hat on? And that cloak thing she came in? But this black velvet hat had a very wide brim and then it sort of turned in gathered onto the top – it was the weirdest thing. I can remember I wasn't at school or I was just going in the afternoons like you could in Mrs Cross's, I wasn't five but you could go to be examined if you had an older brother.
Doreen	It's a wonder she didn't frighten the life out of a baby that age. Oh she did pull your hair, I used to think she's pulling it out in lumps.
Rita	I remember mi mother took me and she *[the doctor]* took one look at Les and said there was every thing wrong with him under the sun. And then, pointing at me, she said, "You know that child is the most healthy child I've seen today". Next morning I was laid unconscious with pneumonia.
Betty	Oh yes, you had to go if you had nits in your hair – I used ti call her 'Nit nurse'. Oh, she nearly rove hair out of you by time she finished, if you had any. By, didn't she go; you had a sore head next day hadn't you. I had long plaits, I could sit on 'em right way down bottom. Mi head was sore with mi mother going through with toothcomb and tying it si tight without her going through. Oh I said, "Glory be I'm not going back ti her ni more". She was an old tartar.
Doreen	I remember that one Rita's on about though. She used to stick a spatula down your throat and she poked it that so far back I said, "I'm going to be sick on you". "YOU ARE NOT", she said, but she was rough.
Rita	But do you know she must have been quite a good doctor because when I got to the High School she was there. I thought, "Oh Lord". The first year at the High School, when you were medically examined, it was her. I never liked school, it always seemed a waste of time to me, I'd much rather have been down at South Landing. I used to sit near the window when I was at High School so I could look out.
Betty	I didn't like school. I went like, and I can't remember even staying off, why I had a week off with tonsillitis and I think I had a couple or three days off when I had mumps and that's only time I ever had off school. I loved sewing classes. The year before I left school, when I was thirteen, I worked mi summer holidays at 'Butlers', what was 'Primrose Cottage', for Hoyles – he was

Church verger. Oh, the times mi mother drummed inti me, "You'll regret it, you'll want ti go back ti school when you leave". "I shan't". "You will you know". "I shan't", and do you know I never did. I think I've learnt more since I left school than when I was in school.

Doreen   You went till you were fourteen, you could finish on your birthday and you didn't have to finish all term out. I was fourteen in the October and I stayed on until New Year. I liked school. I'd nothing to do waiting for a job to come up so I went back. No, I think for a village school we were taught reasonably well.

Margaret Laurie always said there was never really a lot turned out that couldn't read and write,.

Betty   Has anybody said about the plane that come down in wartime up Lighthouse Road?

Rita   No, we haven't had anyone mention that. It was a Whitley bomber and it went through the hedge but it was very boggy. We used to go pester the guard's life out to let us go on to it. I can remember, I think it was a Magister came with the spare parts and it crashed, you know one of these little mono-planes, they had a right performance and then they had to bring another plane. But it did eventually get off under its own steam.

Betty   Dorothy Major's husband was one of crew, that's how Dorothy met him, his name was Lloyd Davis. When the war were over, he went inti electric business with Robert Major, Albert Major's brother, 'cos they put electric in our cottage. It dropped in the field – that's how it happened. With us being little, anyway, it looked such a monstrous thing – when you went near it on the ground.

Doreen   But they used Flamborough Lighthouse as a marker did planes, didn't they, for going out and coming back in again. You could hear 'em all going out and then back in again.

          Your Laurie used to go around a lot with Fred Chapman when they were lads, didn't he? Oh I remember you could hear 'em coming miles away – they'd be on back of coal cart singing and bawling and shouting at top of their voices, one seemed to out-shout the other one you know.

Margaret I know they got a coal cart in 1926, the first truck they had, 'cos I've got a photo of that. I've heard Laurie say when he was younger in his teens, a gang of them always went walking in their navy blue suits; they always had their best on, on a Sunday. They had gone up to North Landing but he wasn't supposed to go on cliffs and he'd gone with somebody down where they could walk down between North Landing and Lighthouse. Was it Newgum? Anyway, he'd gone down and he'd got mucky this time with his best suit on and he got played hell with 'cos he wasn't supposed to go on the cliffs.

Rita Fishermen did go for walks on Sundays 'cos I can remember they would pick a bunch of primroses for their mother – even before they got girl friends they did.

Betty You weren't allowed on cliffs were you? There was primroses all over; Bempton Dyke, North Landing, Lighthouse, Danes Dyke. You had six weeks of lovely summer holidays, you never had a cardigan on. When Mabel Gilbank, a teacher in Leeds, used to come to Gudsun's across road for her summer holidays, she'd collect all us kids up at bottom end for nine o'clock every morning. I remember we took sandwiches. We used ti get that lemonade powder stuff and mixed it up in a bottle and we used ti go for the full day ti Danes Dyke. She'd bring us back about five o'clock – trailing home, we were all struggling coming home and we never knew what it was ti have a cardigan or a coat on.

Doreen Well it started at Easter with your new summer dresses and a pair of sandals for best and sandals for school. And you got new things for Anniversary. Mi grandmother used to insist on these straw hats every Easter. They poked into your ears didn't they, your poor ears and elastic band used to gag you, oh they were agony.

Betty Sunday Anniversary – they got me onti stage once, I would never go but I went on once. I put mi head down and I sang, "I'm a little girl, I never spoke before, but if I live another year I'll tell you something more". I never went ni more so I didn't tell 'em ni more. I remember mi mother getting a velvet red dress made for me out of maybe a jumble sale dress. They used ti have jumble sales in George Thompson's garage, and somebody who lived next ti Miss Ruston used ti do dressmaking. She made me this red velvet dress specially for Sunday Anniversary and she put such a big hem on so it could go down when I grew, which I nivver hardly did. I remember Mam getting a silk green dress, long sleeves, and she allus had one of them little fronts with lace on. We all went 'cos I was saying this little piece at Anniversary.

And they'd varnished the seats and she stuck to the seat. Well,, of course, she thought it was ripping to pieces when she stood up. I bust out laughing and she clouted me across mi lughole. You'd have sworn it was but it was a bit tacky with her sitting on it. I nivver forget it, she nivver wore that dress ni more. She once made me a pink coat with fur top and fur round edge and I sat down and she'd left a big darning needle in bottom and I sat on it, by, didn't it 'ott!!

Mi mother used ti go umpteen times and she got coats and skirts, loads, armfuls from George Thompson's, tek 'em home and we used ti have a big imitation drawer but it was press bed with shelves in. And she used ti cut 'em all for clips and get 'em all done and we made clipped rugs. I've the frame yet, mi uncle used ti 'ave it from the table ti settee top and if you wanted ti be passed, you had ti go underneath, as they put 'em in I used ti pull 'em out.

Doreen   Clips used to be my punishment when I was a kid. Mi mother didn't smack me; according to mi crimes that was how many clips I had to put in ti mat at night. Mi mother used to make stair carpets as well, wool ones, lots of mats she made but they were strands of wool. You can't vacuum them, or clips pop out.

Violet Mainprize's mother lived next door to us and I used to like going into her house, sitting down on her mat, and she would tell me stories, "That was a bit from so-and-so's coat. Oh, I remember that skirt I got it from so-and-so", and she had a story for each little clip she had in her hand.

Betty   A plate i'middle or a diamond shape, and when you got inti middle you did one colour then you used to maybe do pieces across corners, various patterns. I haven't patience. I wouldn't mind doing one but I couldn't stand cutting all them clips – you used to get calluses on your thumbs with the scissors. I remember sitting on the clipped mat in front of fire when we used to have Primitive school. We had ti learn forty two verses out of the Psalms for a bible, you used ti go every Sunday and you had so many little verses ti do, maybe five or summat like that, off by heart, I've still got mi bible. When you went ti Sunday School you used ti get texts, do you remember them? Little cardboard ones with a pretty picture on.

Doreen   Surgery used to be at Wesleyan Chapel, the big one at the top, didn't it?

Betty	There used ti be one where Margaret Chadwick lived, that little cottage with low ceilings *[Hope Cottage]* in High Street – Doctor Watson was there before he moved to Billy Collins. I used ti knock about with Margaret Chadwick.
Rita	Doctor Broadbent, I remember when I was a kid, he was good. They had those big Windsor arm chairs to sit on, but they had little ones for kids to sit on. And if Susan, Doctor Broadbent's daughter, was out with her nanny and you were very, very good you were allowed to go and play in the garden on Susan's toys. But you had to be good!
Betty	I know when I had tonsillitis he brought me the biggest orange you ever saw 'cos I couldn't hardly drink or eat.
Rita	I can remember when I had pneumonia, I mean you were really ill in those days, I can remember Marjory Bayes was at home and she came and sat at night. But one night – I suppose it was the crisis you had in those days – he stayed all night. He was very thorough
Betty	When we were kids you ate all sorts and you was alright; a bit of hedgerow, sour docks, those white nettle flowers – they were gorgeous, they were like honey, lovely and sweet. When the hedges came out in the springtime we used to call it bread and cheese didn't we? But they never did you no harm, did they?
Rita	After I got better from pneumonia, we paid off the bill at half a crown a time and we had to walk to Bridlington because we couldn't afford the bus fare and pay the bill as well.
Betty	You're thinking of Blue and White buses, but the White buses were a shilling when they fost come in. Gilbert Readhead used ti drive White buses, and have it in Ronga' yard, and if we cleaned it out on a night and we found ought we could keep it. Tickets we used ti keep and we often found a ha'penny or a penny dropped i'bus. In Queen Street was bus station with fish shop above, and every Saturday night Gilbert'd go up to there and get us our fish and chips and bring 'em home on bus. It was only on a Saturday night we had a bath and we could wait up for our fish and chips. We only got chips like, but he fetched fish and chips on bus.
Rita	I used to go up and play with Ruth Wilkinson at the farm. I used to have a penny to come back on the bus – walked up but I came back on the bus – and if there wasn't anybody on the bus Gilbert would bring me for nothing.

| | A lot of folks had tin baths. Some were little round ones and we had a long one. I can remember Herbert Gibbon and Herbert Sayer used to come on a Friday night and we put the copper on to have our baths. Herbert Gibbon always used to rag me and say, "I've been bathed with you, don't forget!" |

Betty   Yes Saturday night was bath night; you'd have the tin bath in front of fire. Our lads used ti get bathed and I used ti get next lot of water, but lads used ti go one after the other. Then we sat like clems in our neet things waiting for this White bus coming with our chips for our supper! Oh it was marvellous and Gilbert used ti stop bus and, "Come on I've got your chips for you".

It was superstition with fishermen that water weakened you, when they went ti sea they used ti come back wet through I reckon they'd had their bath before they landed.

Rita   Well I mean they used to sew kids into their vests at beginning of winter didn't they? Do you remember one lad he used to reek by springtime, they used to put goose grease on first and then stitch 'em into their vests.

Betty   We used ti wear a camphor block in a little bag round our neck and that kept you from chest infections and colds and things. Mind'st you we never did catch a lot of things. When diphtheria was going round, when we were at school, a load at school were off with it. They didn't give you injections or owt like that, yet we never picked it up. There was only me had mumps and our lads used ti say, "Keep away from me, you've got bumps". And apart from that and having tonsillitis, I don't think our lads had owt. I don't remember them being off school. There was a lot of children died with diphtheria and scarlet fever as well. They used to cart 'em off to fever hospital, didn't they?

Doreen   I think kids were healthier then. Well you played out; as soon as you had your tea, you were out – you had very little time inside house, only for sleeping.

Betty   We were allowed out where there used ti be a street light between our cottages. We had ti play under there – till we got on their nerves playing 'tinny'. We had 'walking tins' clonking about wi' tins on your feet, do you remember? Treacle tins with string on 'em and you holed 'em and you walked on 'em, clonk, clonk, clonk till we got on their nerves and then, "You, IN, we've had enough of you lot". I remember when I was about ten or eleven we had one street lamp outside on the road. I'm not so sure if there in't a mark where it's put on wall.

Doreen	Do you remember how they used to gather outside Jack Major's fish shop every night, where the chemist shop was? It was a gathering place, wasn't it?
Betty	Yes. And Bailey, the grocer, every time he saw me, "Any raspberries, any raspberries", because when I was about thirteen I used ti work down at Jack Hoyles' and they always let him have raspberries ti sell at shop. Honestly, he drove me up pole wi' that, every time I came past shop he was stood there, this great big fella wi' white apron on, spotless and clean. "Any raspberries, any raspberries?"
Doreen	Your Grandad used to frighten me when I was a kid, Rita. I had to go to his place with shoes 'cos he was a cobbler and he had his mouth full of tacks you know. I used think, mi mam allus said, "Don't speak with your mouth full". If I say anything to him and he answers me, he'll swallow them and die before I can get out of shop. I was petrified for fear he said anything.
Betty	We allus used ti run into Matt Bailey's shoe shop in Dog and Duck Square, in back there and, "Have you come for a talk honey", he used ti say. And we used ti stop and have a game and, "I think it's time you were going home", and, "What for", and he allus had an answer. We liked watching them spinning on the last thing, shoes and boots and cutting them off. You know it was a craftsman job.
Doreen	Aye, there was another cobblers, he used to have a whole row of the things. You know they always had a fire because they had to melt their wax; it was always warm and smelt of leather.
Betty	Yes, it always smelt nice. Down Allison Lane the doors allus use ti be open with the old ladies knitting away, fishermen's jumpers. There used ti be an old woman, half way down, and she used ti tek in sewing – what did they call her? Do you remember she had that big aspidistra plant in middle of table? Same place there was a fireplace and in the corner it was piled up wi' clothes. She clouted me an' all for saying, "That woman's got loads of mucky washing piled up, don't she wesh?" It wasn't – it was the washing she'd tekken in ti repair. And I know we used ti allus go 'cos mi mother used ti get new neckbands put on, they used ti tek so much off the lap to mek neckbands. She was a marvellous sewer, I can see mi mother tekking these flannelette shets for mi dad ti be mended there, but I can't think what they called her.

Doreen	Mrs.Thurlow lived down Tarry Row, midwife, because I went and asked her if we could have a baby at our house because everybody else was getting 'em – why didn't we get any? So I went to see her and asked, and it did tek a lot of going there to her house, knocking on door, and saying "Would she please put her white pinny on and come to our house, 'cos I wanted a brother or a sister" 'cos every time she put her white pinny on somebody got a baby. It didn't work!
Betty	A nurse must have lived in the Square sometime 'cos I used ti come wi' mi mother and when she had our Chuck she had a prolapse and she had ti wear a ring and she would come up ti Mrs.Tunnicliffe to have this ring put in. She used ti allus tek me and I had ti sit in living place but never told me what she'd come for and I never did find out till I was a lot older.
Betty	Do you remember Nurse Edmonson being up at top of Co-Op? There used ti be a door at side -you went up some steps to top room.
Rita	I can remember Nurse Butterworth better than any of the others because she used to come to our house – that was where I got my nurse's uniform.
Betty	Do you remember at side where Billy Chadwick had 'Patisserie Belge' there was a window – there was a bedroom or storeroom that used ti be a nurses's place. It used ti be Nurse Morgan.
Doreen	Mrs Twigg took over that because in wartime she made me a jacket out of an Army blanket. She did sewing.
Rita	And then there was one at next door to Matt Major's in Auntie Annie Major's house, now she would be there during the war and she was an old tartar.
Betty	Oh I went with a great big bump on mi arm like half an egg. It must 'ave been a bite 'cos all she did was got a blue bag and 'clap' and, "That's it you can go home now, love". I was scared stiff about going, I thought what in the world I've been frightened of.
Rita	I scratched myself on a rose and it went septic. I used to have to go every night when I got back from school and she used to boil up the kettle, put it in a basin and stick my finger straight in and hold it in. Do you know I never did any work at school because I was always thinking about it and I had it wrapped up a whole term I remember, she kept the blooming thing wrapped up and to this day that bit of finger is thinner than the rest of 'em.

Betty   Didn't that Nurse Morgan, when she moved from that place, didn't she go ti that bungalow in School Lane ti live?

Rita   Yes, she did. Well, I should think was it after that, Nursing Association packed up. It could have been 1944 when health service started.

Glossary

With help from:

"East Riding Dialect Dictionary" – Norman Stockton

"The Yorkshire Dictionary" – Arnold Kellett

A

afoor	before
ageean	again
allak	hurry
app	to wrap
allus	always

B

back end	autumn
bonn	burn
booler	hoop and stick
bunn	bound to/ obliged

C

caff	chaff
cannle	candle
cattawd/kettled	drunk
cattaws	Hawthorn berries
cawd	cold
chiskeeak	cheesecake
chotch	church

cleeas	clothes
click od	catch hold of
climmer	climber
clobber	a) strike
	b) an article of clothing
cop	catch
corse appron	apron made out of sacking
crud	curd

D

darn't	dare not
dee	die
deea	to do
deear	door
dick	hair louse
diz	does
dizn't	does not
dopper	smock or waterproof

dossn't	dare not	**K**	
dowly	dull weather	keeak	cake
		keelpot	iron stewpot which hung on hooks over the fire
E			
eead	head		
eeardwark	headache	kelter	rubbish
ellum	outhouse	kep	catch
ezn't	has not	kessmass	Christmas
fawdyard	foldyard	kessnin	christening
fearten trees	skids (for sliding boats across the beach)	kest	to cast (as in "do not cast about till May is out")
flooar	floor	ket	bad meat, fish etc.
foggy/fost	first		
foorman	foreman	kinnlin	wood to start a fire
fother	further		
fotnith	fortnight		
fower	four	**L**	
frev/fre	from	laggy	last
funn	found	lahtle	little
		laid oot	arranged (after death) or fish arranged in size on the beach ready for fish buyers
G			
gallawa	Galloway pony		
gammy	lame; injured		
gan	go		
gannin	going		
gawp	stare		
getten	got	lake	to play
give ower	stop	lang sin	long since
		lark	play
I		larn	learn
ing	hang	lee/lig	lie
isha	is she	leeakin	looking
issen	himself	leet	light
istha	are you	let on	tell
iv	in	lick	beat at a game; cursory wash
ivvery	every		
		lig	lie
J		lillilow	flame
jawm	door post	lingy	agile
jiggered	exhausted	lip	impudence
jumm'lment	mess		

look on	mess	oppen	open
lop	flea/cut off	oss	horse
lowance	food and drink supplied to farm workers when in the fields or threshing	ott	hurt
		ower	over
		owt	anything
		owt like	fairly good weather
lowse it	let go		
lucks thu	look you	**P**	
lug	ear; carry	pankin	large pot with lid
		to keep	bread in etc.
M		peff	cough
mackin on	make the most of opportunity	peggy stick & tub	implements for washing clothes
mafted	too hot	ploo	plough
mair	more	posst	post
mak oot	make out	privvy	earth closet
Mar	the Mere		
maungy	in a bad temper	**R**	
maunt	must not	rahve	pull, tear
middlin	moderate	ranter	Primitive Methodist
mun	must	rawk	sea fog
		reead yat	red hot
N		rist	to rest
nab	to catch	rollak	telling off
nap- or – nawp	to strike	roor	to cry
narked	annoyed	rully	horse drawn farm cart
neean	none		
neet	night		
nithered	very cold	**S**	
nivver	never	saan't	shall not
nobbut	nothing but	sad	heavy – (cake , pudding)
noo	now		
nowt	nothing	same	lard
		sarten	certain
O		scrat	to scratch; to work very hard
od	hold		
odard	to pause		
okkad	awkward	seer	so much
onny	any	seet	sight
oor	our	selled	sold

sen	since	trod	footpath
set-teea	fight	tummel	fall
shav	sheaf		
shet	shirt	**U**	
shogg	to rock – (a baby to sleep)	ug	carry
shoot	shout	**W**	
sike	such	weean't	will not
sile	rain heavily	wemmle	topple, sway
sitha	look, see	wesh	wash
skeeal	school	wheea	who
sket	skirt	wicks	couch grass
slape	slippery	winnder	window
slop	police man	wiv	with
smeeak	smoke	wop	to hit; to cane
smitten	infected	worrk	work
sneck	latch		
spew	vomit	**Y**	
staggarth	stack yard	yal	ale
starn	stern	yam	home
starved	cold	yan	one
strang	strong	yance	once
summat	something	yat	hot
		yawp	shout
T		yet	still
tak	take		
taws	marbles		
tent	look after		
tewy	game played on ice		
thimmle	thimble		
think on	remember		
thodd	third		
thrang	busy		
thu	you		
ti tak ig	to take offence		
tiv	to		
tonn	turn		
tonnup	turnip		
trammel	stamp on		